Bay of
Bengal

Mullaitivu

AND
ORTH

Vavuniya

Nilaveli

Trincomalee

CULTURAL
ANGLE

Polonnaruwa

Passekudah

Dambulla

Batticaloa

THE EAST

Kandy

Mahiyangana

NDY AND
HE HILL
OUNTRY

Badulla

Nuwara
Eliya

Wellawaya

Arugam
Bay

Belihul
Oya

Kataragama

THE SOUTH

Yala

Hambantota

Tangalle

Matara

D0530600

EYEWITNESS TRAVEL

SRI LANKA

DK

LONDON, NEW YORK,
MELBOURNE, MUNICH AND DELHI
www.dk.com

Managing Editor MadhuMadhavi Singh

Senior Editorial Manager Savitha Kumar

Editorial Manager Sheeba Bhatnagar

Senior Manager Design and Cartography Priyanka Thakur

Project Editor Shreya Sarkar

Editor Vatsala Srivastava

Project Designer Namrata Adhwaryu

Cartography Manager Suresh Kumar

Senior Cartographer Subhashree Bharti

Senior DTP Designer Azeem Siddiqui

Senior Picture Research Manager Taiyaba Khatoon

Assistant Picture Researcher Ashwin Adimari

Photographer

Idris Ahmed

Illustrators

Chingtham Chinglemba, Sanjeev Kumar, Arun Pottirayil

Printed and bound by Leo Paper Products Ltd, China

First published in Great Britain in 2014

by Dorling Kindersley Limited

80 Strand, London WC2R 0RL, UK

14 15 16 17 10 9 8 7 6 5 4 3 2 1

MIX
Paper from
responsible sources
FSC™ C018179
www.fsc.org

**The information in this
DK Eyewitness Travel Guide is checked regularly.**

Every effort has been made to ensure that this book is as up-to-date as possible
at the time of going to press. Some details, however, such as telephone numbers,
opening hours, prices, gallery hanging arrangements and travel information are
liable to change. The publishers cannot accept responsibility for any consequences
arising from the use of this book, nor for any material on third party websites, and
cannot guarantee that any website address in this book will be a suitable source of
travel information. We value the views and suggestions of our readers very highly.
Please write to: Publisher, DK Eyewitness Travel Guides, Dorling Kindersley,
80 Strand, London, WC2R 0RL, UK, or email: travelguides@dk.com.

Front cover main image: Expansive tea plantations in Nuwara Eliya, the Hill Country

◀ Brightly painted fishing boats on a beach near Ambalangoda

Picturesque view of the palm-fringed Mirissa Beach

Contents

How to Use this Guide 6

Introducing
Sri Lanka

Elephants bathing in the Ma Oya river,
Pinnawela Elephant Orphanage

Seated Buddha images around the *dagoba* in Cave II, Dambulla Cave Temples

Dancers performing in the procession during Esala Perahera, Kandy

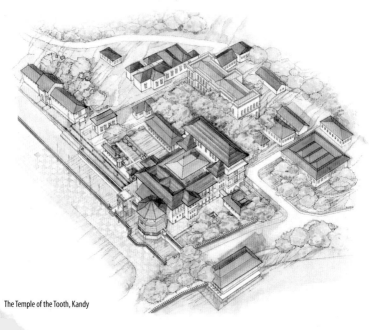

The Temple of the Tooth, Kandy

HOW TO USE THIS GUIDE

This Dorling Kindersley Travel Guide helps you get the most from your visit to Sri Lanka. It provides detailed practical information and expert recommendations. *Introducing Sri Lanka* maps the country and its areas, sets them in their historical and cultural context and describes events through the year. *Sri Lanka Area by Area* is the main sightseeing section, which covers all the important sights, with photographs, maps and illustrations. Information on hotels, restaurants, shops, entertainment and sports is found in *Travellers' Needs*. The *Survival Guide* has advice on everything from travel to medical services, banks and communications.

Sri Lanka Area by Area

The country has been divided into seven main sightseeing areas. These seven sections form separate chapters, each of which begins with an introduction and a map. The best places to visit have been numbered on a *Regional Map* at the beginning of each chapter. The key to the map symbols is on the back flap.

Each area can be quickly identified by its colour coding. A complete list of colour codes is shown on the inside front cover.

1 Introduction
The history, landscape and character of each area is described here, showing how the area has developed over the centuries and what it has to offer the visitor today.

2 Regional Map
This map shows the road network and gives an illustrated overview of the region. All the sights are numbered here and there are also useful tips on getting around.

Sights at a Glance lists the chapter's sights.

3 Street-by-Street Map
This gives a bird's-eye view of a key area covered in the chapter.

A suggested route for a walk is shown with a dotted red line.

A feature deals with a topic related to that region or place.
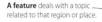

4 Detailed information
All the important places to visit are listed in order, following the numbering on the *Regional Map*. Each sight is described individually. Within each entry, there is detailed information on major buildings and other sights.

Story boxes explore specific subjects further.

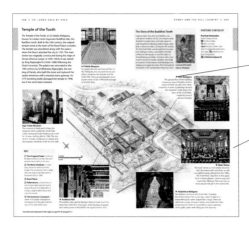

Stars indicate the features or sights that no visitor should miss.

5 Sri Lanka's Top Sights
These are given two or more full pages. Historic buildings have an illustrated artwork showing the layout of the site; and archaeological sites as well as national parks have maps showing facilities and trails.

The visitors' checklist provides all the practical information needed to plan your visit.

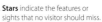

6 Town Map
Important towns and cities are described in detail, and numerous sights recommended. A handy map locates the main sights and transport hubs in town.

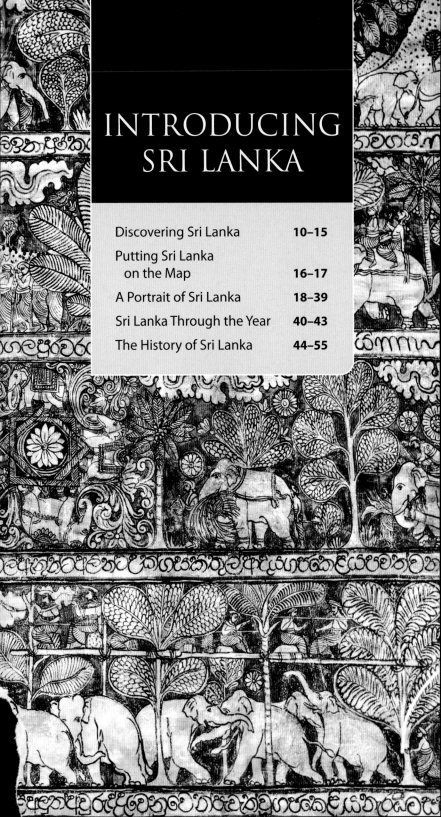

INTRODUCING
SRI LANKA

DISCOVERING SRI LANKA

The following tours have been designed to take in as many of the country's highlights as possible, while keeping travelling time to a minimum. The first itineraries outlined here are two 2-day tours of Colombo and Kandy. Extra suggestions are included in case visitors wish to spend more time in the capital city. Next is a week-long tour of the Cultural Triangle and the Hill Country, which can be extended to two weeks by incorporating the additional recommendations. Finally, the two-week itinerary caters to those who have more time and want to see a little bit of everything. However, don't feel constrained by these set itineraries; they are merely starting points to help when planning the trip. Pick, combine and follow your favourite tours, or simply dip in and out and be inspired.

Galle Ramparts Walk
A walk along the well-preserved Fort ramparts is an excellent way to explore Galle. The ramparts are especially lively in the evenings, when the townspeople gather here to fly kites, play games and relax.

Two weeks in Sri Lanka

- Sample a variety of cuisines in the fantastic restaurants of **Colombo** – a real gourmet's paradise.

- Visit the ruined city of **Anuradhapura** and imagine what life in the ancient capital was like when it was at the height of its power.

- Marvel at the beauty of the frescoes at **Sigiriya Rock**.

- Explore the Temple of the Tooth in **Kandy**.

- Hop in a jeep and go on safari through **Uda Walawe National Park** – noted for its elephant population.

- Spend time exploring the labyrinthine streets and ramparts of **Galle Fort**.

- Sip a sundowner on the terrace of the Colonial hotel in **Mount Lavinia**.

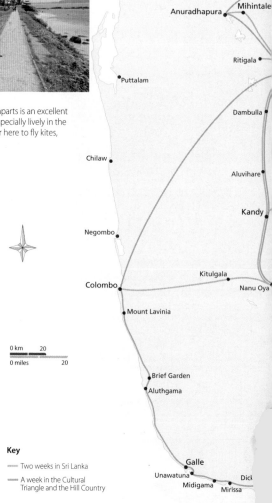

0 km   20
0 miles   20

Key

— Two weeks in Sri Lanka

— A week in the Cultural Triangle and the Hill Country

World's End
This sheer precipice drops down 880 m (2,887 ft) to the valley below and affords marvellous views of the surrounding hills.

A week in the Cultural Triangle and the Hill Country

- Observe pilgrims at the Sri Maha Bodhi Tree in **Anuradhapura**, said to have grown from a cutting of the bo tree under which the Buddha attained enlightenment.

- Enjoy stunning views of the countryside from the summit of **Sigiriya Rock**.

- Explore the ruins of the ancient kingdom of **Polonnaruwa**.

- Admire the frescoes that cover the walls and ceilings of the **Dambulla Cave Temples**.

- Attend the evening *puja* at the **Temple of the Tooth** and catch a glimpse of the casket containing the sacred Tooth Relic.

- Watch tea pluckers in action on the numerous tea plantations in the **Hill Country**.

- Look out over the hills at World's End in **Horton Plains National Park** to the distant South Coast or follow the Loop Trail to explore the green, misty highlands.

Kandy
The Temple of the Tooth, or Sri Dalada Maligawa in Sinhala, is one of the most sacred places of worship for the island's Buddhist population.

Uda Walawe National Park
Known for its large population of elephants, Uda Walawe is one of Sri Lanka's best-known national parks. Pachyderms roam the wilderness in herds and are easily spotted on a safari.

Murals adorning the interior walls of Sambodhi Chaitya, Colombo

Two days in Colombo

Sri Lanka's capital city can feel somewhat over-whelming at first. However, its quirks and charms grow on visitors as they come to understand it.

- **Arriving** Bandaranaike International Airport is located about 30 km (18 miles) north of Colombo. Buses and taxis take about 20 minutes to reach the city.

Day 1

Morning Begin at the historic **Fort** district (see pp64–5), where a number of Colonial-era buildings are juxtaposed with modern hotels – it is an ideal area to explore on foot. To the north, along the oceanfront, lies **Sambodhi Chaitya** (see p66), a unique *dagoba* balanced on stilts. Climb up to enjoy the amazing view of the harbour. If the mid-morning heat becomes too much, take refuge inside the cool **St Peter's Church** (see p66). For lunch, try the **Old Dutch Hospital** (see p67), home to a number of excellent restaurants and cafés.
Afternoon Take a three-wheeler to get to the **Colombo National Museum** (see pp78–9) and spend a couple of hours learning about Sri Lanka's ancient kingdoms. Next, indulge in some retail therapy in Colombo's boutiques, before heading to **Mount Lavinia** (see p81) for a sundowner on the terrace of the Mount Lavinia Hotel.

Day 2

Morning Rise early and visit the **Pettah** (see p68) before it gets too hot and crowded. Explore its narrow streets and soak up the atmosphere. The **Dutch Period Museum** (see p68) is located here, as well as the striking Jami-ul-Alfar Mosque (see p68) and some Hindu *kovils*. Afterwards, take a three-wheeler to Beira Lake and spend time at the serene **Seema Malaka** (see pp72–3). From here, it is a short walk to the **Gangaramaya Temple** (see p73). Take a taxi to **Galle Road** (see p80) and stop at one of the restaurants for a spot of lunch.
Afternoon Take a pre-arranged, guided tour of **No. 11, 33rd Lane** (see p76), Geoffrey Bawa's stunning town house. Later, explore Barefoot on Galle Road, famous for its bright fabrics and souvenirs.

> **To extend your trip…**
> Visit the **Kelaniya Raja Maha Vihara** (see p81) located 12 km (6 miles) northeast of Colombo.

Two days in Kandy

Visitors rub shoulders with pilgrims in this bustling town where modern life and the remains of an ancient kingdom coexist.

- **Arriving** Trains and buses run from Colombo to Kandy. The journey takes approxi-mately 3 hours by car.

Day 1

Morning Start off with a leisurely wander around the Kandy Lake before visiting the **Kandy National Museum** (see p134), home to traditional costumes and ancient *ola*-leaf manuscripts. A side road leads to the **British Garrison Cemetery** (see p138), where the headstone of the last-known European to have been killed by a wild elephant in Sri Lanka can be found.
Afternoon Enjoy a late lunch in one of Kandy's restaurants and then visit the colossal **Temple of the Tooth** (see pp136–7). The main attractions include the Raja Tusker Museum and the Sri Dalada Museum. Be sure to arrive in the audience hall in time for the evening *puja*. Afterwards, explore the *devales* that sit right in front of the Temple of the Tooth.

Day 2

Morning Arrive at the **Pinnawela Elephant Orphanage** (see p143) around mid-morning to watch the elephants making their way to the river to bathe. Alternatively, consider walking the **Three-Temples Loop** (see pp142–3) or visit the temples by car or three-wheeler. Note that undertaking the journey on foot will require an entire day.
Afternoon Spend the afternoon in the **Peradeniya Botanical Gardens** (see p142) and relax in the shade of the giant Javan fig tree. In the evening, watch a Kandyan dance performance at the Kandyan Art Association (see p236).

The Temple of the Tooth complex on the banks of the Kandy Lake

A week in the Cultural Triangle and the Hill Country

- **Airports** Arrive at and depart from Bandaranaike International Airport near Colombo.

- **Transport** A car and driver is essential for this trip. It takes about 5 hours to get to Anuradhapura from Colombo and it is a 3-hour drive back to Colombo from Nuwara Eliya.

Day 1: Anuradhapura

The perfect start to this itinerary, **Anuradhapura** *(see pp178–81)* is an ancient city that lies in ruins, a testament to thousands of years of Sri Lankan history. Be sure to visit the Sri Maha Bodhi Tree here, as well as the clusters of former monasteries, *dagobas* and reservoirs. The archaeological site is vast, and can be explored by bicycle.

> **To extend your trip…**
> Spend another day exploring the magnificent ruins of Anuradhapura.

Day 2: Mihintale and Habarana

Visit **Mihintale** *(see pp182–3)* early morning before it gets too hot, as there are 1,840 steps to climb to reach the summit. Do not miss the view from Aradhana Gala. Afterwards, head to the town of **Habarana** *(see p174)* – a good base for visiting the surrounding attractions. Embark on an afternoon safari to watch the elephants in one of the nearby national parks, such as **Minneriya** *(see p175)* or **Hurulu Eco Park** *(see p175)*.

Day 3: Sigiriya Rock and Polonnaruwa

Try to arrive at **Sigiriya Rock** *(see pp166–9)* before the sun is overhead. Devote the morning to exploring the Royal Gardens and admiring the frescoes on the western rock face. There are great views over the countryside from the summit. In the afternoon, head to the ruined capital of **Polonnaruwa** *(see pp170–74)* and hire a bicycle to get around. Make sure to visit Gal Vihara, where a magnificent Buddha statue lies in repose.

> **To extend your trip…**
> Stop by the **Ritigala** *(see p176)* forest monastery in the afternoon and spend the following day exploring Polonnaruwa's ruins.

Day 4 and 5: Kandy

Travel to **Kandy** *(see pp134–8)*, stopping en route at the **Dambulla Cave Temples** *(see pp162–3)* to admire the murals that decorate the interiors. Also spend time at **Aluvihare** *(see p158)*, which is situated on the main road. Once in Kandy, visit the **Temple of the Tooth** *(see pp136–7)* for the evening *puja*, or visit early the next day. Wander through the town and explore the many *kovils* at leisure.

> **To extend your trip…**
> Base yourself in Kandy and spend one night and two days trekking in the **Knuckles Range** *(see p144)*.

Day 6: Nuwara Eliya

Take the train from Kandy to Nanu Oya and enjoy the stunning vistas the journey offers. Arrange to be met by a car and driver for the short distance to **Nuwara Eliya** *(see pp144–5)*. In the afternoon, visit the charming **Mackwoods Labookellie Tea Estate** *(see p145)* and enjoy chocolate cake and a cup of tea in the café.

Day 7: Horton Plains National Park

Get up early to reach **Horton Plains National Park** *(see pp146–7)*, and experience World's End before the clouds roll in and enjoy the marvellous views from this vantage point. Spend the afternoon exploring Nuwara Eliya or trekking in the nearby hills.

> **To extend your trip…**
> Make a short stopover at **Kitulgala** *(see p148)* on the way back to Colombo for some whitewater rafting.

Buddha mural decorating the walls of Dambulla Cave Temples

View of Aradhana Gala, or Meditation Rock, in Mihintale

Two weeks in Sri Lanka

- **Arriving** Arrive at and depart from Bandaranaike International Airport near Colombo.
- **Transport** A car and driver is essential for this trip.

Day 1 and 2: Colombo
See the Colombo itinerary on p12.

Day 3: Habarana
Drive to **Habarana** *(see p174)* – a good base for visiting the Cultural Triangle. Go on a late-afternoon safari in **Minneriya National Park** *(see p175)* to see wild elephants, or take advantage of the Ayurvedic spas offering personalized treatments, ranging from massages to herbal baths, in the hotels here.

Day 4: Anuradhapura
Explore the sprawling ruins of **Anuradhapura** *(see pp178–81)*, an hour away from Habarana. Among the many attractions here are Ruwanwelisisya Dagoba, with its wall decorated with a frieze of elephants, and Jetavanarama Dagoba, which would have originally stood over 100 m (328 ft) high. A visit to the Sri Maha Bodhi Tree is a must.

To extend your trip…
Travel up the East Coast to the lovely beaches of **Nilaveli** and **Uppuveli** *(see p190)*.

Magnificent ruins of the Vatadage, Polonnaruwa

Day 5: Sigiriya Rock and Polonnaruwa
Get up early to beat the crowds at the breathtaking **Sigiriya Rock** *(see pp166–9)* – a short drive from Habarana. Although the colossal rock, with its frescoes, Mirror Wall and Lion Platform, is the main attraction, there are also lovely grounds to wander around in. Save plenty of time for the Sigiriya Museum, which has archaeological finds and other artifacts on display. In the afternoon, head to **Polonnaruwa** *(see pp170–74)*. Do not miss the Vatadage – possibly the most beautiful ruined building in all of Sri Lanka.

Day 5: Dambulla Cave Temples
Stop at the **Dambulla Cave Temples** *(see pp162–3)* en route to Kandy. Admire the frescoes adorning the rock-carved temples as well as the multiple seated and standing Buddha statues.

Day 6 and 7: Kandy
See the Kandy itinerary on p12.

To extend your trip…
Drive to Dalhousie to climb **Adam's Peak** *(see pp148–9)* and then travel on to the picturesque hill town of Nuwara Eliya.

Day 8: Nuwara Eliya
Catch the train from Kandy to Nanu Oya and then drive to **Nuwara Eliya** *(see pp144–5)*. Take a guided tour of one of the numerous tea factories here and try some fine single-estate tea.

Day 9: Horton Plains National Park
It would be a shame to visit Nuwara Eliya and not see the spectacular view from World's End at **Horton Plains National Park** *(see pp146–7)*. Horton Plains can easily be explored on foot and offers good birdwatching. In the afternoon, wander around Nuwara Eliya and visit the well-manicured Victoria Park, or play a round of golf at the Golf Club.

To extend your trip…
Visit **Ella** *(see p149)* and trek through the surrounding hills, before travelling to **Yala West National Park** *(see pp126–7)* for a safari. Alternatively, travel to the East Coast to **Arugam Bay** *(see p196)* and surf the superb waves.

Lush tea plantations stretching for miles, Nuwara Eliya

For practical information on travelling around Sri Lanka, see pp266–7

Day 10: Uda Walawe National Park

Drive from Nuwara Eliya to **Uda Walawe National Park** *(see pp122–3)*, and visit **Hakgala Botanical Gardens** *(see p145)* on the way. The gardens are particularly famous for their roses, which are at their best between April and August. On arrival in the national park, set out on a safari to see the elephant herds. Afterwards, make sure to drop by the Elephant Transit Home, located west of the park entrance. Arrive during feeding times and observe the elephants from a viewing platform.

Spectacular view of the cloud forest from World's End, Horton Plains National Park

Day 11: South Coast

There are a number of towns that can act as a good base to explore the South Coast. The beaches around **Tangalla** *(see p121)* have some lovely places to stay as well as excellent turtle-watching. **Mirissa** *(see p118)* is a good starting point to embark on whale-watching trips, while laid-back **Unawatuna** *(see p116)* is known for its party atmosphere, sheltered bay for swimming as well as diving and snorkelling opportunities.

To extend your trip…
Spend another day at **Unawatuna** *(see p116)*. Explore the surrounding Rumassala hillside, or simply lounge on the beach.

Day 12: A day on the coast

Spend time relaxing on the sand, or go on a whale-watching expedition. Later, travel inland from the coast to explore sights such as the **Martin Wickramasinghe Museum** *(see pp116–17)*, just east of Unawatuna. Continue eastwards to **Dickwella** *(see p120)*, a great starting point to explore the surrounding attractions including Wewurukannala Vihara, Hoo-maniya Blowhole and Mulgirigala. While returning to Unawatuna, be sure not to miss the fishermen perched on their stilts near Midigama.

Day 13: Galle

Travel along the coast to **Galle** *(see pp108–13)* and head to the atmospheric Galle Fort. Explore the labyrinthine streets and visit the fascinating Maritime Archaeology Museum. Next, take a long, guided tour of the ramparts. The Fort boasts some wonderful accommodation options and restaurants for those who wish to spend more time in the town.

Day 14: Galle to Colombo

Take the highway back to Colombo or choose the slower route to meander inland from the coast. Stop at the enchanting **Brief Garden** *(see p98)* near Aluthgama, the former house and garden of Bevis Bawa. Continue on the coastal road and spend the night in **Mount Lavinia** *(see p81)*, preferably at the Mount Lavinia Hotel, one of the best examples of Colonial grandeur in Sri Lanka.

The tranquil Goyambokka Beach, Tangalla

Putting Sri Lanka on the Map

Set in the Indian Ocean, Sri Lanka is separated from India by the 48-km (30-mile) wide Palk Strait and sits just north of the equator. The country covers a total area of 65,610 sq km (25,332 sq miles) and has a population of about 21.5 million. Colombo is the largest city and Sri Jayawardenepura Kotte is the administrative capital. The island is mostly made up low-lying areas and forest, with densely inhabited coastal regions. The South, however, has some mountainous areas and is home to Pidurutalagala, the island's highest peak at 2,524 m (8,280 ft), and the sacred Sri Pada or Adam's Peak at 2,243 m (7,360 ft).

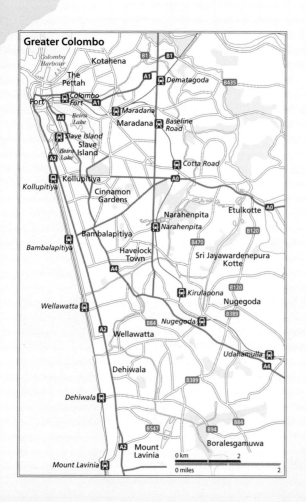

Greater Colombo

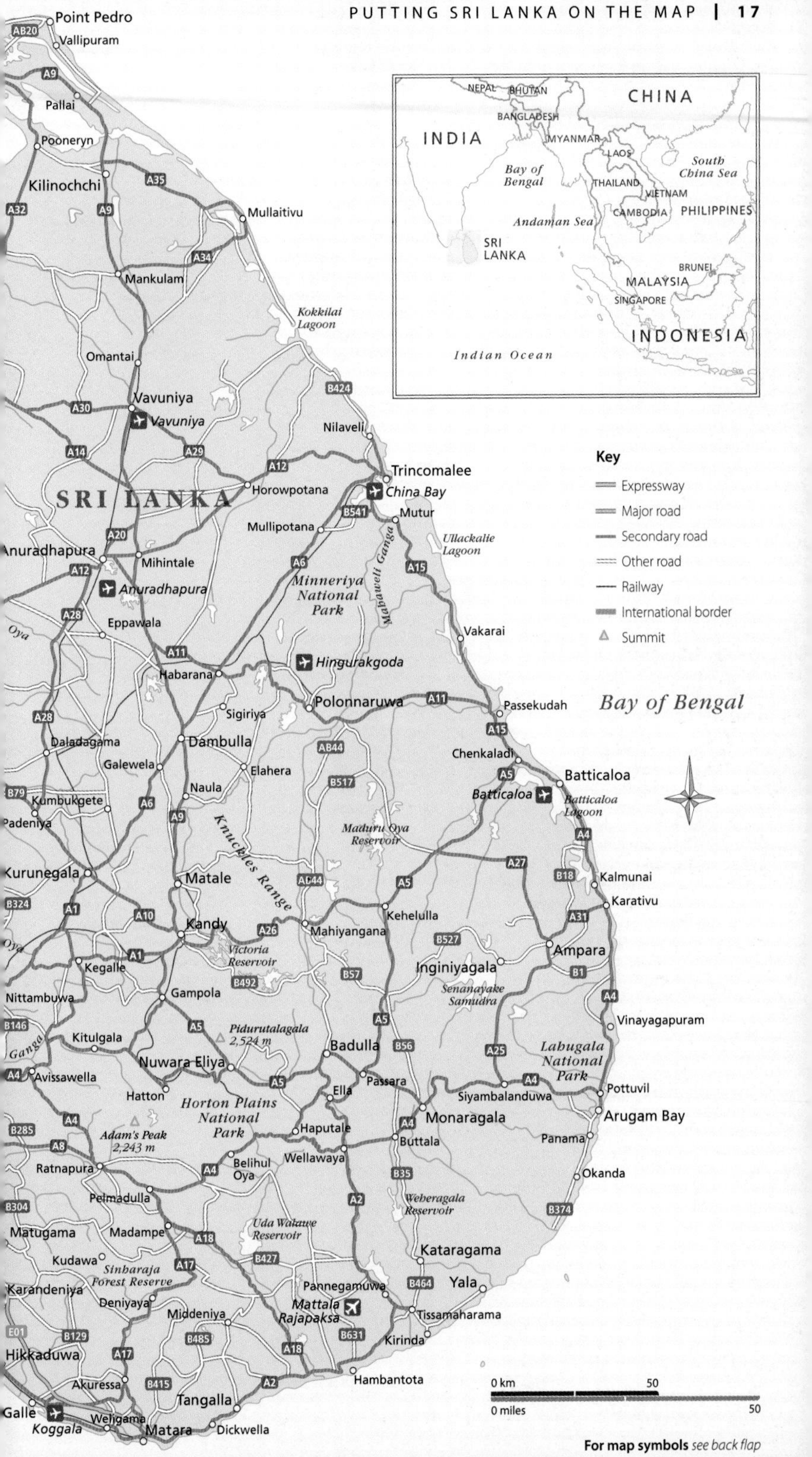

Point Pedro
AB20
Vallipuram
A9
Pallai
Pooneryn
Kilinochchi
A32
A9
A35
Mullaitivu
A34
Mankulam
Kokkilai Lagoon
Omantai
A30
Vavuniya
Vavuniya
Nilaveli
A14
A29
B424
A12
Trincomalee
SRI LANKA
Horowpotana
China Bay
B541
Mutur
A20
Mullipotana
Ullackalie Lagoon
Anuradhapura
A6
Mihintale
A12
Minneriya National Park
A28
Eppawala
Oya
A11
Vakarai
Habarana
Hingurakgoda
Sigiriya
Polonnaruwa
A11
Passekudah
A15
A28
Dambulla
AB44
Chenkaladi
Daladagama
Elahera
A5
Galewela
B517
Batticaloa
Batticaloa
B79
Naula
Maduru Oya Reservoir
Batticaloa Lagoon
Kumbukgete
A6
A9
Padeniya
AC44
A5
A4
Kurunegala
Matale
A27
Kalmunai
B324
A1
A10
A26
Mahiyangana
Kehelulla
B18
Karativu
Oya
Kandy
A31
Kegalle
A1
Victoria Reservoir
B527
Ampara
Nittambuwa
Gampola
B492
B57
Inginiyagala
B1
B146
Kitulgala
A5
Senanayake Samudra
A4
Ganga
Pidurutalagala 2,524 m
Badulla
A4
Vinayagapuram
Avissawella
Nuwara Eliya
A5
Ella
B56
Labugala National Park
Hatton
Passara
A25
Pottuvil
B285
A4
Horton Plains National Park
Siyambalanduwa
A4
Adam's Peak 2,243 m
Haputale
Monaragala
Panama
Arugam Bay
Ratnapura
A4
Wellawaya
Buttala
B304
Pelmadulla
Belihul Oya
A4
Okanda
Matugama
Madampe
A2
B35
Kudawa
A18
Uda Walawe Reservoir
Weheragala Reservoir
Karandeniya
A17
Sinharaja Forest Reserve
B427
Kataragama
B374
E01
B129
Deniyaya
Middeniya
Pannegamuwe
B464
Yala
Hikkaduwa
A17
B485
Mattala Rajapaksa
B631
Tissamaharama
Akuressa
B415
A18
A2
Kirinda
Galle
Tangalla
Hambantota
Koggala
Weligama
Matara
Dickwella

Bay of Bengal

Indian Ocean

Inset map:
NEPAL
BHUTAN
CHINA
BANGLADESH
INDIA
MYANMAR
LAOS
Bay of Bengal
THAILAND
VIETNAM
South China Sea
CAMBODIA
PHILIPPINES
Andaman Sea
SRI LANKA
BRUNEI
MALAYSIA
SINGAPORE
INDONESIA

Key
Expressway
Major road
Secondary road
Other road
Railway
International border
△ Summit

0 km   50
0 miles   50

For map symbols *see back flap*

A PORTRAIT OF SRI LANKA

Once known as Ceylon, this picturesque island has been attracting visitors for centuries with its diverse wildlife, lush tea plantations and miles of beaches. The country boasts great ethnic and religious diversity, and is home to several ancient Buddhist sites, splendid Hindu temples and impressive Colonial-era buildings. With almost 30 years of Civil War and the tragedy of the 2004 tsunami behind it, Sri Lanka is steadily moving towards peace and prosperity.

Shaped like a teardrop, the island country of Sri Lanka sits in the Indian Ocean, just off the southern tip of India. The country's geographical position on the Indian Ocean trade route means that its culture has been influenced by the numerous visitors, traders and invaders who arrived here by sea.

The island's earliest settlers came from north India in the 5th century BC, followed by Tamil invaders from south India in the 3rd century BC and then Arab traders from the Middle East in the 7th century AD. The Portuguese, Dutch and British colonialists arrived around 900 years later and left their mark on the country's cultural and architectural heritage. The island continues to retain cultural ties with India, particularly in the North where the Tamil population is more concentrated and where Hinduism has a strong presence.

Sri Lanka was declared independent of Britain in 1948. The early post-independence years were peaceful, but from 1983 until 2009 the island was in the grip of a bitter Civil War between government forces and the LTTE or Tamil Tigers. Today, with the conflict over, most Sri Lankans are looking to the future with cautious optimism.

Despite its small land mass, Sri Lanka boasts a wide range of landscapes, from dense rainforests to hills covered with tea plantations. The country is home to a wealth of wildlife, notably elephants and leopards, and is also a paradise for bird-watchers. While the remains of the early Buddhist civilizations are some of the most popular sights – including Anuradhapura and Sigiriya – the island's dazzling beaches are always a draw. The country also offers many adventure activities such as surfing, white-water rafting and hot-air ballooning.

Palm trees fringing the shores of a beautiful beach in Mirissa

◀ A woman lighting a lamp at the Temple of the Tooth, one of the most important Buddhist temples in Sri Lanka

Picnicking and flying kites at Galle Face Green, one of Colombo's biggest communal spaces

Peoples of Sri Lanka

Sri Lanka has a population of approximately 21.5 million, which is made up of four main ethnic groups: the Sinhalese (75 per cent), the Tamils (15 per cent), the Moors (9 per cent) and the Burghers (0.2 per cent). In addition, a small percentage of the population consists of minorities such as the Veddahs *(see p199)* and the Parsis, as well as modern-day European settlers.

The Sinhalese are descendants of Indo-Aryan migrants from north India who first arrived on the island in the 5th century BC. They make up the largest proportion of the island's population, and speak an Indo-Aryan language called Sinhala. The Sinhalese are mainly Theravada Buddhists.

The Tamils of the island are subdivided into two communities: Sri Lankan Tamils (11 per cent) and Indian Tamils (4 per cent). Most Sri Lankan Tamils live in the northern and eastern parts of the country. They trace their ancestry to those who crossed over to the island from south India as invading forces in the 2nd and 3rd centuries BC. The Indian Tamils are descendants of the workers brought over from India by the British in the 19th century to work on the tea plantations in the central highlands. Both groups are predominantly Hindu and speak the Tamil language.

The Moors go back to the Arab traders who settled on the island in the 7th century. They are Muslims and have a distinct cultural identity shaped by their religion, which distinguishes them from the other dominant ethnic groups on the island. There are also some Malay Muslims on the island, whose ancestors were brought from Java to Sri Lanka by the Dutch.

The Burghers are a small ethnic group who mostly live in Colombo, Trincomalee and Batticaloa. They trace their origin back to the Portuguese and Dutch colonialists, many of whom settled on the island and married local women. Their offspring came to be known as Burghers, which comes from the Dutch word *burger* (citizen). Burghers usually speak English as their first language and are predominantly Christian.

The original inhabitants of Sri Lanka are the Veddahs or *Wanniyala-Aetto* (forest people). They are thought to have descended from the island's aboriginal community that dates back to around 16,000 BC. Many have been absorbed into Sinhalese and Tamil cultures, but there are others who are trying to retain elements of their traditional, ancient culture. As hunter-gatherers and forest dwellers, their homes and livelihoods are constantly threatened by the encroachment of modern life.

Politics and Government

The Democratic Socialist Republic of Sri Lanka is run by an elected president who is the head of state, the head of government and the Commander-in-Chief of the armed forces. The parliament of Sri Lanka is made up of 225 seats, and members are elected for a six-year term. There are also regional councils in seven of the nine provinces, which can take decisions on issues such as education and health. The island is dominated by two political parties: the socialist Sri Lanka Freedom Party (SLFP) and the conservative United National Party (UNP). The SLFP is the main constituent of the currently ruling United People's Freedom Alliance (UPFA), headed by President Mahinda Rajapaksa.

Formerly the prime minister of Sri Lanka, Mahinda Rajapaksa was elected president of the country in 2005 for a six-year term. After the end of the bloody Civil War with the LTTE (Liberation Tigers of Tamil Eelam), Rajapaksa called for early presidential elections in 2010. A landslide victory in these elections secured him a second term in office, and the same year his ruling coalition won an overwhelming majority in the parliamentary elections. Later that year, members of parliament passed a

President Mahinda Rajapaksa in Colombo

constitutional amendment allowing the president to stand for an unlimited term in office. The amendment was met with considerable dissent, with some accusing Rajapaksa of running a dictatorship. However, the president maintained that he was providing Sri Lanka with much-needed stability after the Civil War.

Human rights remain a pressing issue in Sri Lanka. There have been reports of disappearances, restrictions on freedom of expression and freedom of the press, and unsolved crimes such as the assassination of Lasantha Wickrematunge, the former editor of the weekly newspaper *Sunday Leader*, in 2009. Many people continue to be held in detention without trial. Sri Lanka refused to undertake an independent investigation into war crimes that took place during the Civil War, and the credibility of Rajapaksa's Lessons Learnt and Reconciliation Commission (LLRC), which was set up in 2010 to look into the causes of the conflict, has been challenged by international bodies such as the UN and Amnesty International. In 2012, UN member states backed a resolution urging the Sri Lankan government to prosecute commanders guilty of misconduct during the Civil War, but whether anything will come of this resolution remains to be seen.

Inauguration of the Sri Lankan Parliament in Colombo on 22 April 2010

The two towers of the World Trade Center in Colombo

Economy

Despite the adversities of the Civil War and the 2004 tsunami, Sri Lanka's fortunes have changed dramatically in recent years and it is now considered to be a credit-worthy, middle-income country by the World Bank. The island's economy continued to grow at the rate of 8 per cent in 2011, but slowed down to an estimated 6.5 per cent in 2013.

The service sector, which includes revenues from tourism, accounts for nearly 60 per cent of the country's GDP and is the dominant sector in the national economy. Sri Lanka exports a wide range of goods, including textiles and clothing, tea, rubber-based products, coconut products, as well as gems such as blue sapphires, garnets and zircons. It also relies on remittances from migrant workers, many of whom work in the Middle East.

Most Sri Lankans enjoy a long life expectancy of 75 years and an advanced healthcare system. The country has a literacy rate of 91 per cent. The number of people living below the poverty line has also fallen from 15 per cent to 9 per cent in the last few years. Despite these advancements, there is great disparity in the Sri Lankan society. There is growing discontent about rising living costs, particularly the prices of fuel and electricity, which had increased by over 40 per cent in 2012. The island's economy remains in a state of flux, with a widening trade deficit and decreased inflow of foreign investment.

Religion

Sri Lanka is a multi-religious country. While the majority of Sri Lankans are Buddhist (71 per cent), there are also sizeable Hindu (13 per cent), Muslim (9 per cent) and Christian (7 per cent) communities on the island.

Buddhism is the belief system of the Sinhalese and has a huge influence on the country's art, architecture and literature. It was introduced to Sri Lanka by Mahinda, the son of the Indian king Asoka, in the 3rd century BC. Hinduism is the dominant religion of the Tamils. It was brought to the island by Tamil kings and their followers from south India. Hindus in Sri Lanka mostly worship the deities Vishnu, Shiva and Skanda. The country is also home to significant numbers of Muslims and Christians. While Islam arrived in Sri Lanka with the Arab traders, Christianity and its various denominations were brought by the European colonialists.

Most of these religions are represented all over the island, but there are some areas where the communities are more concentrated, such as the Catholics on the West Coast. Sri Lanka's many religious groups often mix freely, at times sharing the same pilgrimage sites such as Adam's Peak *(see pp148–9)* and Kataragama *(see p128)*.

Images of both Hindu and Buddhist deities in Maha Devale, Kataragama

A leopard lounging on the branch of a tree, Yala West National Park

However, in recent years, sectarianism has emerged as a major threat to the island's stability. In April 2012, hardline Buddhists firebombed a mosque in Dambulla, and in August 2013 they attacked a mosque in Colombo.

Conservation

For many visitors, one of the greatest draws of Sri Lanka is the wealth of flora and fauna that can be seen on the island. The country is recognized as a biodiversity hotspot for its staggering number of endemic animal and plant species. Protected areas cover around 12 per cent of the island and are variously classified as strict nature reserves (not open to the public), national parks, nature reserves and sanctuaries. Set in a wide variety of breathtaking terrains, the areas are run under the supervision of the Department of Wildlife Conservation. The country's most well-known parks are Yala West (see pp126–7), Uda Walawe (see pp122–3) and Horton Plains (see pp146–7).

Sri Lanka has often had to contend with poaching, illegal farming and gem-mining in its national parks. More recently, a lack of legislation and an increasing number of visitors and jeeps have begun to pose a huge threat to the wildlife in these parks. Loss of habitat is also a serious problem and the drive to increase tourism and build more resorts and roads has been concerning environmentalists. Fortunately, a number of organizations across the country are involved in conservation projects to preserve the biodiversity. It is hoped that more can be done to protect the island's treasures and at the same time allow tourists to delight in them.

Sport

The de jure national sport of Sri Lanka is volleyball, but cricket is by far the most popular on the island. In 2011, Sri Lanka co-hosted the Cricket World Cup with India and Bangladesh, and in 2012 it was the venue for the ICC World Twenty20. The country last won the Cricket World Cup in 1996. In 2011, the team reached the finals, only to be beaten by India by six wickets.

Cricketers enjoy widespread popularity across Sri Lanka. Many of them own restaurants and guesthouses and also endorse products on TV. During the 2011 World Cup, a feature film on cricket called Sinhawalokanaya was released, which featured the famous Sri Lankan cricketer, Tillakaratne Dilshan.

Sri Lankans play a number of other sports, notable among which is the traditional game of elle, which is still considered the de facto national sport. The game is similar to baseball but the ball is smaller, the field bigger and the bat is replaced by a long bamboo stick. There is a national elle championship every year and it is also played in schools and as part of festivities.

Young boys playing a game of cricket in a park, Vavuniya

Landscape and Wildlife

Sri Lanka packs an impressive variety of flora and fauna into its small land area. The country features a range of landscapes, from fairly dry plains in the north, east and southeast to verdant rainforests in the southwest. The heart of the island is dominated by the hills and mountains of the Hill Country. Covered with tea plantations, these hills occasionally rise to rugged summits, notable among which is the majestic Adam's Peak. Sandy beaches fringe the island's coastline, where salt pans and mangroves are also found. The abundant wildlife in the country includes mammals such as elephants and leopards as well as many reptile, bird and amphibian species.

The endemic Sri Lankan junglefowl, the national bird of Sri Lanka

Lowland Rainforests

Found below an elevation of 1,000 m (3,281 ft), these forests lie in the southwestern part of Sri Lanka, known as the wet zone. Home to numerous endemic trees and epiphytes as well as birds and amphibians, the rainforests are vital to the conservation of the country's rich biodiversity.

Cloud Forests

With much of the lower montane forests having been cleared for agriculture, these forests make up less than 1 per cent of the Sri Lankan landmass. The Horton Plains National Park contains patches of dense cloud forest, where many epiphytic plants such as orchids and ferns can be seen.

The tawny rajah butterfly can be spotted on a walk through the Sinharaja Forest Reserve. It is among the 250 butterfly species that have been recorded across Sri Lanka.

The black-lipped lizard, an indigenous species, is usually found in montane forests at an altitude of over 1,000 m (3,281 ft). They can often be spotted on the way to World's End in the Horton Plains.

The Ceylon rufous babbler, or the orange-billed babbler, has an orange bill and reddish-brown plumage. An endemic species, it can usually be seen in Kitulgala and the Sinharaja Forest Reserve.

The Ceylon whistling thrush is blue-black in colour with a rich blue wing patch that is visible in flight. An endangered endemic, it can sometimes be seen near forest streams.

The green pit viper is a venomous snake that lives mostly on trees, perfectly camouflaged by its green and black colouring. The snake's diet includes birds, lizards and frogs.

Daffodil orchid is a rare kind, with bright yellow flowers. It is hard to find due to over collection and loss of habitat.

Mangroves of Sri Lanka

The majority of Sri Lanka's mangroves are clustered around Puttalam, Jaffna and Trincomalee. Mangroves harbour a unique biodiversity, which includes a range of marine and terrestrial organisms. Owing to their dense root systems, they also protect coastal areas from soil erosion and act as a barrier against extreme weather conditions such as floods. In addition to being a prime nesting and migratory site for hundreds of bird species, they play a significant role in replenishing the coastal and lagoon fish populations. However, mangroves in Sri Lanka are currently under threat from water pollution, human habitation, prawn farms and hotel development, and many voluntary organizations are working towards their restoration. Besides setting up mangrove nurseries, these groups also run educational workshops for locals to improve their understanding of the importance of this ecosystem.

Mangroves in Pottuvil Lagoon

Mud lobster in a mangrove swamp

Dry Lowland Forest

Covering more than two-thirds of the country, these forests are found in the dry zone and feature deciduous and riparian vegetation. They comprise many of the island's best-known national parks such as the Yala West, Minneriya and Wilpattu.

Wood apple fruit, also known as elephant apple, is a round, greyish fruit that is believed to have medicinal properties.

Asian elephants can be seen throughout the year in Sri Lanka. Uda Walawe is a particularly good spot for elephant-watching.

Palu trees, or Ceylon ironwood trees, are mostly found in Yala West National Park. These slow-growing evergreens can reach a height of up to 20 m (66 ft).

Coast

Sri Lanka is ringed with beautiful beaches, many of which provide nesting grounds for marine turtles. While the waters around Kalpitiya Peninsula attract pods of dolphins year-round, migrating whales can be spotted off Mirissa between December and April.

Marine turtles are endangered in Sri Lanka. Five different species of sea turtles – green, leatherback, olive ridley, loggerhead and hawksbill – come to the island's beaches to nest.

Spinner dolphins, so named for their acrobatic displays, are abundant in the waters around the Kalpitiya Peninsula and areas of the South Coast.

Sea urchins have spherical bodies covered with sharp quills. Sri Lanka is home to 28 species of these marine animals, which are commonly seen while diving or when wandering along the beach.

Elephants in Sri Lanka

The elephant is an integral part of the history, culture and religions of Sri Lanka. Of enormous spiritual significance to the island's Buddhist and Hindu populations, elephants are commonly depicted in temple architecture. In fact, most Buddhist temples keep a resident elephant within their premises. These captive elephants play an important role in the country's religious festivities; the most revered of them is the Maligawa Tusker that carries the sacred Tooth Relic of the Buddha during Esala Perahera. Over recent years, however, deforestation due to a rise in the human population has dwindled elephant numbers considerably. Owing to the human-elephant conflict, elephants are being relocated to protected areas. Uda Walawe, Yala West and Minneriya national parks are some of the best places in Sri Lanka to see these pachyderms.

Elephant carvings adorning the wall of a Buddhist temple in Sri Lanka

Elephants during the British Rule
During the reign of the Sinhalese kings, no elephant could be captured, killed or maimed without the ruler's permission. But when the British acceded to power, this protection was withdrawn. The British saw them as agricultural pests and paid a bounty for each elephant killed, leading to the slaughter of thousands of elephants in the 19th century.

Human-Elephant Conflict

Human-elephant conflict has become a pressing conservation issue in Sri Lanka. Increased human habitation, agricultural expansion and infrastructure development have led to the elephant's loss of habitat and disruption of movement. Nearly 150 elephants are killed every year when they stray in search of food into areas inhabited by humans. With their enormous bodies and huge appetites, they end up destroying property, trampling crops and occasionally taking lives. Preventive measures that have been taken include the development of national parks and elephant corridors, relocation of frequent offenders and erection of electric fences. However, the problem still persists and it has been suggested that the protected areas are too small in size. There evidently is a real need to encourage compatible land use that would enable peaceful coexistence to reign in this conflict.

A herd of elephants confined by an electric fence in Uda Walawe National Park

Sacred Elephants

Buddhists and Hindus associate elephants with strength and courage. It is also widely believed that keeping an elephant in the temple brings good luck and prosperity. Often richly caparisoned, these elephants are the prominent feature of annual religious processions in the country. Animal welfare groups are, however, opposed to the practice of keeping elephants in captivity.

The trunk is not just used to drink, but also to grasp things using the finger-like extension at its tip.

The Sri Lankan Elephant

The Sri Lankan elephant is a subspecies of the Asian elephant. Distinct from the African elephant, the Asian elephant has smaller ears, a relatively flat back and a one-fingered trunk. Additionally, only a small percentage of male elephants have tusks compared to their African counterparts. Wild elephants usually live in a close-knit group of around 15 and eat about 150 kg (331 lb) of food every day.

Female elephants are usually smaller and lighter than the males.

The ears are capable of detecting sounds as low as 14 hertz to 16 hertz. Not only does this enable elephants to communicate with each other over long distances, but it also warns them of impending danger.

The skin colour of the Sri Lankan elephant is the darkest of all subspecies of the Asian elephant. Areas of depigmentation can be particularly seen on the ears, trunk and belly.

Working Elephants

During the time of the Sinhalese kings, elephants were used for transportation at times of war, aiding in construction work and even used to execute prisoners in the 17th century. In the Colonial era, elephants were trained to tow barges, move heavy artillery and clear land for tea plantations. Today, they continue to work in the timber industry and, more commonly, in the tourism sector.

Religions of Sri Lanka

Religion plays a very important role in the day-to-day life of Sri Lankans. Although the island is predominantly Buddhist, other religions such as Hinduism, Islam and Christianity also have a marked presence here. The country is an important pilgrimage destination for Buddhists from around the world, as it is said that the Buddha visited the island three times between 528 and 520 BC. Animism, albeit with a Buddhist or Hindu influence, is still practised among the Veddahs, the original inhabitants of the island. Sri Lanka has many sacred sites of significance to the island's various religious groups, including Kataragama, which is a holy site for Buddhists, Hindus and Muslims.

Pilgrims leading a religious procession during the Kataragama Festival

Buddhism

Theravada Buddhism is the most widely practised form of the religion on the island. The sect is older than the Mahayana school of Buddhism and preserves the orthodox teachings of the Buddha. It is based on the Pali Canon, which is believed to be the oldest record of the Buddha's teachings. All Buddhist temples in Sri Lanka comprise an image house, where the images and statues of the Buddha as well as of other gods are kept, a *dagoba* (a dome-shaped memorial) and a bo tree. Symbolic of enlightenment, lotus flowers are often used in the decoration of these temples.

The offering of coconut oil lamps is an important Buddhist ritual. It is followed by a wish or prayer to the Buddha, who is regarded as the "light of the three worlds" and the dispeller of darkness and ignorance. Besides oil lamps, worshippers also offer incense, flowers and food.

Mihintale is where the Buddhist monk Mahinda, son of the Indian king Asoka, is said to have converted King Devanampiya Tissa of Anuradhapura to Buddhism. This event marked the introduction of the religion to Sri Lanka.

Buddhist monks can be easily recognized by their yellow or orange robes. Admitted to the Buddhist Order as novices, they go through intensive religious training before becoming a member of the *sangha* (a monastic community of ordained Buddhist monks or nuns).

Stalls selling religious offerings are often found near the temples. The wide variety of offerings at these kiosks ranges from lotus flowers and images of the Buddha to food and drink and even plastic toys.

Hinduism

Hindu communities are concentrated in the northern and eastern provinces of the country. The Hindu belief system is based on the tenets of *samsara* (successive cycles of birth, death and rebirth), *karma* (the law of cause and effect) and *dharma* (righteousness). The three most important figures of the Hindu pantheon are Brahma, the creator of the world; Vishnu, who protects the world and preserves order; and Shiva, the god of destruction and regeneration.

Gopurams, or ceremonial gateways, mark the entrance to Hindu temples in Sri Lanka. These structures are often covered with brightly painted sculptures of Hindu deities. The inner sanctum of the temple is only opened during *puja* ceremonies so that worshippers can make their offerings.

Temple *pujas* are religious ceremonies performed as a tribute to the deities. They are usually atmospheric occasions, with incense burning, drums beating and recitations from the *Vedas* (the oldest scriptures of Hinduism).

Fruits and flowers offered to a deity during *puja* ceremonies are termed as *prasada*. It is believed that the deity partakes of the offering and then returns it. The consecrated offering is then distributed and eaten by the devotees.

Islam

Islam was brought to Sri Lanka by Arab traders in the 7th century. Mostly concentrated along the coast, the Muslim community comprises less than 10 per cent of the population. All Muslims adhere to the Five Pillars of Islam: *shahadah* (professing faith), *salat* (praying five times a day), *zakat* (giving to charity), *sawm* (fasting during Ramadan) and undertaking the Hajj pilgrimage to Mecca.

The rounded white cap worn by Muslim men and boys is known as a *taqiyah* or *topi*.

The *thobe*, a loose ankle-length white robe, is the uniform for boys attending *madrasas* (Koranic schools).

Christianity

Christians are known to have settled on the Sri Lankan coast in the early centuries AD. However, the religion, specifically Roman Catholicism, gained prominence only with the arrival of the Portuguese in the 16th century. Protestantism and other Christian denominations were introduced during the Dutch and the British eras. Since the end of Colonial rule, the number of Sri Lankan Christians has declined to about 7 per cent of the population.

The Catholic St Mary's Church in Negombo is one of the many reminders of Portuguese missionary activity in Sri Lanka.

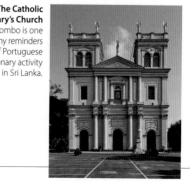

Traditional Dance

Sri Lanka has a rich heritage of traditional dance that is said to date back to the 4th century BC. The three main styles of classical dance are Kandyan dance, low country dance and Sabaragamuwa dance. Besides these classical styles, the country also has a variety of folk dances based on traditional beliefs and festivities. The costumes worn by the performers are often spectacular, such as the elaborate ornaments worn by Kandyan dancers and the striking masks used in devil dance. All forms of dancing in Sri Lanka combine graceful and vigorous movements, performed to the rhythm of drum beats. However, the gestures used in the dances differ, as do the costumes and the shape and size of the drums.

Mayura Vannam dancers mimicking the movements of a peacock

Kandyan Dance

The national dance of Sri Lanka is Kandyan dance. There are five types of Kandyan dance – Ves, Vannam, Udekki, Pantheru and Naiyandi. All of these are associated with Kohomba Kankariya, a ritual to appease Kandyan deities. Traditionally, the dance was performed solely by men, but since the 1950s women have also been trained in it. The typical costume of a male dancer comprises a white loincloth, a beaded breastplate, silver bangles on the arms and ankles, a headdress and large ear ornaments.

Ves

The most popular and sacred of the dance forms, Ves is said to have originated from an ancient purification ritual.

The dance was originally performed only by men within the temple precincts. Today, however, it can be seen at various religious ceremonies and processions. There are several rituals associated with the preparations for the dance – a special ceremony is held during which the sacred headdress is placed on the performer's head. The Ves headdress is of great significance as it is said to be a replica of the one worn by Kohomba, a Kandyan deity.

Vannam

A combination of poetry and dance, Vannam is inspired by nature, legend and Buddhist stories. There are 18 classical forms of Vannam, and another three new forms were developed in the 20th century. The dances often portray the movements of elephants (Gajaga Vannam), peacocks (Mayura Vannam), snakes (Uraga Vannam) and other creatures. Female dancers usually take centre stage for these dances, and there is greater freedom to either perform in the traditional manner or to add modern touches.

Udekki

This dance is named after *udekki*, a small hourglass-shaped drum that accompanies the performance. Legend states that the construction of the drum was ordered by Lord Sakra, the king of all gods. The Hindu god Shiva is often depicted holding this drum. The costume for Udekki resembles that for Pantheru, except that dancers wear elaborate beaded jackets and have frills around their waist.

Pantheru

This dance is said to have been performed originally to celebrate victory in war. The *pantheru* is an instrument that resembles a tambourine (without the skin), and has small cymbals attached around its rim. Pantheru dancers twirl the instrument and pass it from hand to hand during the performance. The costume for this dance is simpler than many of the other dance forms, featuring a white turban and a white handkerchief tied at the waist.

Elaborately costumed dancers performing Ves during Esala Perahera, Kandy

Naiyandi

The Naiyandi dance is traditionally performed during the lighting of the lamps for Kohomba Kankariya celebrations, but it can also be seen at the Vishnu and Kataragama *devales (see p134)* in Kandy on ceremonial occasions. Naiyandi dancers wear a white loincloth and turban, a beaded breastplate, a waistband as well as anklets.

Low Country Dance

Also known as Ruhunu dance, this form of dance can be seen in the coastal belt of Sri Lanka. The dances are often very ritualistic and are sometimes performed to propitiate demons causing sickness.

Devil Dance

A ritualistic healing ceremony, devil dance was traditionally performed to free a person from bad luck or illness. One of the many types of devil dance, Sanni Yakku is performed to rid a victim of the disease demon. During the night-long exorcism ritual, the demon making the person ill is summoned, offerings are made, and then the spirit is

A devil dance performer

forced to leave. There are 18 Sanni demons, each for a different disease and representing a distinct dance, mask and drum beat.

Kolam

Perhaps the most popular of all low country dance forms, Kolam comprises a series of dances loosely based on a Buddhist *Jataka* tale. A combination of dance and drama, a typical performance starts with a description of Kolam's origins by the narrator or master of ceremonies. According to legend, the mythical queen Menikpala craved to see a mask dance during her pregnancy. Vishwakarma, the god of artists and craftsmen, is believed to have fulfilled her craving by giving her husband, King Mahasammatha, the lyrics and the Kolam masks for the dance. A variety of masks are used in the performance, some caricatures and some grotesque.

Sabaragamuwa Dance

This style of dance can be called a mid-country dance, as it is particularly popular in

A collection of Kolam masks carved out of wood

the Ratnapura area. Although Sabaragamuwa is a fusion of low country and Kandyan dance forms, it has its own unique style. Its traditions include the ancient tribal dances performed by the Veddahs *(see p199)*.

Folk Dance

In contrast to the classical forms, folk dances are lighter and less ritualistic. Among the best known folk dances of Sri Lanka are Leekeli (stick dance), performed by men and women who hold two sticks aloft and strike them together to complement the drum beats; Kulu (harvest dance), in which women depict the reaping and separating of chaff; and Kalagedi (water ceremony dance), during which female dancers portray the fetching of water from rivers while dancing with clay pots.

Drums in Sri Lankan Dance

Drums provide the rhythmic sound patterns for all Sri Lankan dance forms. They are crafted out of various types of wood and are covered with animal skins on the sides. Different drums are used for each of the dance forms. The drum used in Kandyan dance is known as the *geta bera*, a double-ended drum, which tapers at the ends, with one end traditionally made of cow hide and the other monkey hide. The *yak bera* drum usually accompanies the mask dances of the low country and is played with both hands. The *dowla* drum in Sabaragamuwa dancing is played with a *kadippu* (stick) on the right side and with the hand on the left. The smallest drum is the *udekkiya*, which is played with one hand while the other hand applies pressure on the strings to control the sound.

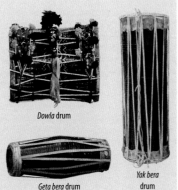

Dowla drum

Geta bera drum

Yak bera drum

Buddhist Art and Architecture

A range of architectural styles can be seen in Sri Lanka, however, the influence of Buddhism is particularly noteworthy. The temples, *dagobas* and Buddha statues demonstrate the skills of Sri Lankan builders as well as sculptors, and underline the island's unique interpretation of Buddhist iconography. While the influence of Mahayana Buddhism can be seen in the size of the standing Buddhas and the inclusion of *bodhisattvas* (enlightened beings who forgo *nirvana* to help others), Hindu Tamil rulers and south Indian builders also left their mark on Buddhist architecture. By the 13th century, Hindu and Buddhist architectural elements were being mixed freely. Today, it is not uncommon to see Hindu deities depicted in Buddhist temples or a Buddhist shrine in a Hindu temple.

Intricately carved guardstone at the entrance to Vatadage, Polonnaruwa

The grand Ruwanwelisiya Dagoba, Anuradhapura

Dagobas

Originating from ancient Indian burial mounds, *dagobas*, or stupas, enshrine the relics of the Buddha. The *dagoba* is also thought to represent Mount Meru, the sacred mythical mountain at the centre of the Buddhist universe, and the five elements of the cosmos. Sri Lankan *dagobas* are usually simple structures with little or no exterior decoration. The best-known examples can be seen in Anuradhapura *(see pp178–81)* and Polonnaruwa *(see pp170–74)*.

The bell, lotus and bubble are the most popular shapes of Sri Lanka's *dagobas*. Typically, these classic structures comprise an *anda* (brick mound), which stands on a square terrace and is topped by the *harmika* (squared-off platform) from which rise the tiers of the *chattravali* (discs).

Buddha Images

The Buddha is depicted in a variety of poses and with differing *mudras* (hand gestures). Sri Lankan artists were renowned for their ability to capture the serenity of the Buddha in their carvings, and it is said that the simplicity of the images parallels the simplicity of the *dagobas*. Mahayana Buddhism, which required images much beyond human dimensions, had a big impact on Sri Lankan art and resulted in the construction of giant Buddha statues. The best of these gigantic statues can be seen at Gal Vihara *(see p171)* in Polonnaruwa, although these are significantly smaller than the enormous Buddha statues that were built in Bamiyan in Afghanistan and Kanheri in India.

The ushnisha, the protuberance on top of the Buddha's head, is symbolic of his superior mental powers. Some Buddha statues also depict the *siraspata* (flame of wisdom) rising from it.

Buddhist Temples

While *dagobas* are simple and unadorned, temples have decorative details such as guardstones and carvings of elephants and dwarves. Semi-circular stones called moonstones are placed at the foot of steps leading to many different shrines and temples. To the usual group of temple buildings, Sri Lanka added the *bodhigara* – a shrine dedicated to the sacred bo tree. The Buddha is believed to have attained enlightenment under a bo tree in India.

The image house, found in all Buddhist temples, is where the Buddha's images are kept. There are often statues of other gods or attendants as well as paintings on the walls and ceiling, depicting events from the life of the Buddha.

A bodhigara is a shrine designed to house the bo tree. Railings are erected around the sacred tree, leaving it open to the sky, with seated images of the Buddha all around. The Sri Maha Bodhi at Anuradhapura is the most significant bo tree on the island.

Geese, said to represent purity and wisdom, are often depicted carrying lotus buds in their mouths.

Flames, often seen on the outer ring, purify those who step across them.

Lotus petals on the inner circle are turned inwards and symbolize nirvana.

Moonstones are made up of a series of concentric semi-circular rings. There is still debate about the symbolism of the imagery, but the rings are said to represent the spiritual journey to reach enlightenment. The moonstones at Anuradhapura depict elephants, horses, lions and bulls which symbolize birth, old age, illness and death respectively.

Mudras, or the various hand gestures of the Buddha statues, have symbolic significance. The *dhyana* and *bhumisparsha mudras* (see p177) are some of the mostly commonly seen in Sri Lanka.

Colossal Buddha statues made by Sri Lankan sculptors include the 12-m (40-ft) granite Buddha at Aukana (see p176) and the outstanding statues in different postures found at Polonnaruwa. These huge representations are still popular today, with modern versions being erected island-wide.

Arts and Crafts

Sri Lanka's rich heritage of arts and crafts has been shaped by the island's long history and strong Buddhist tradition. Most of its classical art has been influenced by religious beliefs, and traditional crafts such as wood-carving have been passed down through generations. Other craft forms, such as batik and lacework, which were brought to the country by colonialists, have also been adapted beautifully by artisans. Today, the country has a vibrant contemporary art scene, with sculpture and painting complemented by digital, installation and performance art.

Contemporary Sculpture
Most modern sculptors usually retain a link with the traditional art form by using classic materials such as stone and metal. However, artists are increasingly using recycled materials and experimenting with new techniques to create sculpture.

Traditional Sculpture
Sri Lanka has a rich tradition in sculpture, which is mainly religious in origin. From the huge Buddha statues at Anuradhapura and Aukana to the bronze sculptures of Hindu deities at Polonnaruwa, the skills of the early craftsmen are evident.

Art in Sri Lanka Today

The Green Path, also known as Nelum Pokuna Mawatha, opposite the Colombo National Museum, is where upcoming artists and students display their paintings at weekends. Works here range from traditional pieces to colourful abstracts. Nearby, Viharamahadevi Park hosts the annual Kala Pola art fair in January. Organized by the George Keyt Foundation, the event provides budding artists and sculptors the opportunity to showcase their works.

Crafts

Many of Sri Lanka's crafts are made using traditional techniques. The villages around Kandy specialize in specific artistic skills – Gadaladeniya is noted for brassware and Dumbara for mat-weaving. More recent crafts include batik and lacemaking, and these are mostly practised in towns on the South Coast. All crafts have evolved over the years to meet modern tastes, with new-age artists introducing contemporary designs. Among the island's most famous modern designers is Ena De Silva who founded the Aluvihare Heritage Centre (see p160) in 1982 where she trains villagers in carpentry, batik and needlework.

Palmyra leaves are used in the northern part of the country to make handicrafts such as baskets, trays, hats, rugs and wall hangings. While some of these objects retain the natural colouring, others are dyed in a variety of colours to create vibrant patterns.

Traditional Painting
Similar to sculpture, the best-known traditional paintings are centred on the Buddha, his life and his teachings; some of the finest examples can be seen in the Dambulla Cave Temples. Folk art gained popularity during the Kandyan period, with artists painting narratives in brilliant colours to illustrate religious themes. The temples around Kandy house the most impressive of these murals.

Contemporary Painting
The Modernist art movement began in 1943 with the formation of the 43 Group, whose members remain the island's most acclaimed artists. Among the leading contemporary artists are Laki Senanayake, Jagath Weerasinghe and Druvinka whose works deal with themes of politics, environment and spirituality.

Contemporary Artists in Sri Lanka

The famous 43 Group was made up of illustrious names such as George Keyt, Ivan Peries and Richard Gabriel. These artists produced works that went on to sell in top auction houses around the world. Today's artists are finding their own signature styles and embracing other art forms in addition to traditional painting and sculpture. Their works can be seen in established galleries in Colombo and abroad.

Laki Senanayake, one of Sri Lanka's best-known artists

Batik, originally an Indonesian art form, was brought to Sri Lanka by Dutch colonialists. Batik wall hangings and sarongs are popular among tourists, with patterns ranging from *perahera* scenes to abstract motifs.

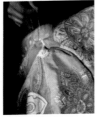

Needlework pieces are often produced by village women who have been introduced to the art as a means of earning a living.

Lacemaking was introduced by the Portuguese and was further developed by the Dutch. Galle and Weligama are famous for lace work.

Tea in Sri Lanka

Sri Lanka is one of the largest exporters of tea in the world. The country produces a wide range of varieties, including grades of the traditional black tea, flavoured teas, organic teas and green tea. The first tea plants, brought from China, were grown in Peradeniya Botanical Gardens in 1824, but it wasn't until 1867 that the first commercial tea plantation was established near Kandy. Before the cultivation of tea began on the island, coffee was the principal plantation crop. However, when the coffee trees were decimated by disease in the 1870s, tea became a profitable alternative. Today, the tea industry is of great importance to Sri Lanka's economy. The country's tea estates attract visitors from around the world and offer tours of tea factories, stays in plantation bungalows and picturesque views of rows of tea bushes.

Tourists on a special guided tour of a tea factory in Kandy

Tea Plantation

About 4 per cent of Sri Lanka's land area is covered with tea plantations. These are mainly found in the Hill Country, which offers the ideal terrain and climate for the plants to flourish. Tea bushes are carefully manicured and kept at waist height for ease of plucking. Tea cuttings are kept in a nursery for about a year before being planted in the fields.

The British and Tea
In 1852, a Scottish planter named James Taylor arrived in Sri Lanka to work for a coffee grower. He was put in charge of the Loolecondera estate near Kandy. In 1867, Taylor grew the first tea plants for commercial use in a section of the estate. The plantation's success eventually led to the expansion of the global tea industry in the late 19th century, with several large British companies buying the smaller estates.

The tea bush (*Camellia sinensis*) is an evergreen tree, which grows to a height of around 10 m (33 ft) in the wild.

Tea Pluckers
Most of the tea pluckers in Sri Lanka are women and the majority are descendants of the Tamil labourers who were brought from south India to work in the plantations by the British in the 1870s. The tea workers are required to pick at least 20 kg (44 lb) of leaves every day. Their wages are low and the living conditions are poor; they often live in barrack-style buildings comprising only one or two rooms.

From Bush to Cup in 24 Hours

Tea production in Sri Lanka is a labour-intensive industry. Tea leaves are still plucked by hand, and it is the youngest two leaves as well as the bud that are taken every six to 10 days. After the leaves have been collected, they are delivered to the factory where they are processed using either the traditional or the CTC (crush, tear and curl) method. The end product is then ready to be sent for auction to make its way onto shop shelves. Tea factories offer tours to explain the tea-making process and many of them continue to use machines that have changed little since the 19th century.

Traditional Method
The plucked leaves are dried in huge trays or "withering troughs" while hot air is blown over them to reduce moisture content. They are subsequently crushed, which causes enzymes to be released and the fermentation process to begin. Leaves are left to ferment for a short period after which they are fired in an oven. They are then left to cool before being sorted and graded.

Shade trees, such as the Australian silver oak, filter the sunlight and help retain moisture in the soil.

CTC Method
This method is much faster than the traditional method. Fresh leaves are passed through a series of cylindrical rollers that crush, tear and curl the tea. The ground-up leaves are then rolled into little pellets and oxidized. Tea manufactured by this process is mostly used in tea bags.

Tea Distribution
The majority of tea produced from both traditional and CTC methods is packed into sacks and sent for sale in Colombo, where a variety of grades are auctioned for export and blending purposes.

Grades of Tea

Sri Lankan tea is divided into various grades. While high-grown thrives above 1,200 m (3,937 ft) and is said to have the best colour, aroma and flavour, low-grown is found below 600 m (1,968 ft) and is less flavourful. Medium-grown is cultivated between these two altitudes. Teas are also graded by size and by quality. The finest among leaf teas is Orange Pekoe (OP), which is made with unbroken leaves, and the slightly lesser Broken Orange Pekoe (BOP). Fannings as well as dust are graded much lower and end up in tea bags.

Ayurveda

Sri Lanka's traditional form of medicine, Ayurveda uses plants, herbs and oils in its treatments. Translated as the "science of life", it works on the premise that the body is ruled by three *doshas* (humours): *vata* (air), *pitta* (bile or fire) and *kapha* (phlegm or earth). In medical terms, these refer to the nervous, digestive and immune systems respectively. Toxins, poor diet, bad digestion, lack of sleep and excess stress cause an imbalance of the *doshas* and lead to poor health. Ayurvedic treatments aim to balance the *doshas* and, thus, restore health. Ayurvedic physicians prescribe customized treatment plans that include a special diet, while Ayurvedic centres in mid- and top-range hotels offer practices aimed at relaxation, such as massages and skin treatments.

Panchabhutas, according to Hindu philosophy, are the five basic elements that make up the universe and all individuals. These are *prithvi* (earth), *jal* (water), *teja* (fire), *vayu* (air) and *akash* (ether).

Ayurveda in Sri Lanka Today

Originating in neighbouring India, the ancient science of Ayurveda continues to play an important role in the Sri Lankan healthcare system. Ayurvedic practitioners are trained in government-approved institutions and are registered under the Sri Lankan Ayurveda Medical Council. Besides local physicians, several resorts are dedicated to Ayurveda and many hotels also offer treatments.

Ayurvedic centres can be found across the island. Some cater mainly to tourists and offer relaxing treatments. Ayurvedic resorts, however, are for those in need of intensive curative treatments that are supervised by physicians. Several resorts also offer a wellness combination of Ayurveda, yoga and meditation.

Ayurvedic products are ubiquitous in Sri Lanka. These vary from medicines to beauty treatments and soaps. Ayurvedic medicines, made from herbs and spices, can be found in the form of capsules, oils, balms or teas. For a glimpse of a traditional Ayurvedic environment, head to one of the specialized pharmacies. These are typically stocked with packets and bottles of tablets, oils and teas as well as dried ingredients such as powdered herbs and whole roots.

Ayurvedic Treatments

Ayurveda aims to eliminate the body's toxins and balance its energy. Herbs, plants and oils are used to achieve this through treatments such as oil massages and steam baths. Ayurvedic therapies are believed to be beneficial for a range of medical conditions, including diabetes, high blood pressure, arthritis and skin ailments. They are also said to improve digestion and eyesight as well as slow the ageing process. Facial or head massages, steam baths and body wraps are ideal for reducing stress and detoxing. One of the best-known treatments is *shirodhara*, which offers relief from stress and insomnia.

A massage with medicinal, herbal oils is one of the oldest Ayurvedic treatments and is tailored for different ailments. It is believed a massage returns balance to the body's three *doshas*. De-stressing massages are a great way to relax the muscles after a day of sightseeing. Head, foot and full-body massages are particularly popular.

The oil "fountain" is a metal pot or bottle with a slow-flowing spout.

Shirodhara is a popular treatment where warm oil is poured steadily onto the centre of the forehead or "third eye".

Ayurvedic baths are considered highly therapeutic. Herbal and steam baths are believed to open the pores and rid the body of toxins. Flower baths, on the other hand, close the pores and are often taken at the end of a treatment.

Marmapuncture, or Ayurvedic acupuncture, is an ancient art in which needles are inserted into the skin at *marmas* (points) that correspond with the 14 *nadis* (main energy channels). This aims to restore balance to the body by unblocking the *nadis*, as it is believed that an imbalance of energy leads to illness. It is often used in conjunction with other treatments.

SRI LANKA THROUGH THE YEAR

There always seems to be some festivity or celebration taking place in Sri Lanka at any given time. With Buddhists, Hindus, Muslims and Christians making up the country's population, most events are religious in nature. Many of the Buddhist and Hindu festivities feature elaborate processions with dancers, drummers and even elephants, and attract pilgrims from around the island. Buddhist, Hindu and Muslim festivals follow the lunar calendar and their dates vary from year to year. All full moon or *poya* days in Sri Lanka are public holidays and are associated with an event in the life of the Buddha or the history of Buddhism. On *poya* days, Buddhists visit nearby temples with offerings, and places of entertainment are often closed. In addition to religious events, several other holidays such as National Day, celebrating Sri Lanka's independence, are also observed.

Devotees lighting coconut oil lamps at a Buddhist temple in Colombo during Vesak

Southwest Monsoon

Sri Lanka is affected by two monsoons, each hitting a side of the island at different times. The southwest monsoon arrives in the South, West and the Hill Country from April or May until September, when days can get very humid with short, heavy rainstorms. Many Colombo residents head to Nuwara Eliya (*see pp144–5*) over the New Year period to escape the heat of the lowlands. These monsoon months are the best time to visit the northern and eastern parts of the island. Some of Sri Lanka's biggest and best festivals take place during this period, including the Sinhala and the Tamil New Year.

April
Sinhala and Tamil New Year (*mid-Apr*), nationwide. This two-day celebration of the New Year is typically a family holiday. Houses are cleaned, traditional treats are prepared, new clothes are worn and gifts exchanged. On an auspicious day after the celebrations, a senior male member of the family anoints the others with a special oil to bring them luck for the following year.

May
May Day (*1 May*), nationwide. Originally, street demonstrations and marches were organized by workers and their unions on this day to promote workers' rights. Today, rallies and demonstrations still take place on the island, with the largest ones in Colombo and the main cities, but many are politically motivated to promote messages of political parties.
Vesak (*May*), nationwide. This is the most important *poya* day in the Buddhist calendar as it celebrates the Buddha's birth, enlightenment and death. Devotees dressed in white can be seen heading to the temple early in the morning. During this two-day festival, paper lanterns are hung outside homes, oil lamps are lit and *pandols* (large platforms) display scenes from the life of the Buddha. It is also considered propitious to distribute food and drink during this time, and *dansals* (roadside stalls) offering free refreshments to passers-by are set up across the island.

June
Poson (*Jun*), nationwide. Poson *poya* day celebrates the introduction of Buddhism to Sri Lanka. Devotees flock to Anuradhapura (*see pp178–81*) to see the festivities at the temples or climb the steps to the *dagoba* on the summit at Mihintale (*see pp182–3*), where Mahinda converted King Devanampiya Tissa and his courtiers.

July
Esala Perahera (*Jul/early Aug*), Kandy. The most famous event on the island, Esala Perahera

Drummers in a Poson *poya* day procession in Mirissa

Traditional dancers performing in the procession during the Esala festival, Kandy

celebrates the arrival of the Tooth Relic *(see p139)* in Sri Lanka. The festival lasts for 10 days, featuring a grand procession of elephants, dancers and drummers that parades through the streets of Kandy, growing larger and longer every night. Accommodation over this period should be booked well in advance. Dondra and Colombo also celebrate the Esala full moon on the tenth day.

Kataragama Festival *(Jul/ early Aug)*, Kataragama. This festival is also held at the time of the Esala full moon. Pilgrims descend on Kataragama town for the celebrations, which are perhaps best known for self-purification rituals that involve self-mutilation and fire walking. The festival marks the end of the two-month long Pada Yatra pilgrimage from Jaffna to Kataragama.

Vel *(Jul/Aug)*, nationwide. This Hindu festival is dedicated to Skanda or Murugan (Kataragama), the god of war. Ornate chariots bearing a statue of the god or his *vel* (spear) are paraded through the streets or around the temple grounds, accompanied by pilgrims. The deities are brought in a procession from the Sammangodu Sri Kathirvelayutha Swami Temple in Pettah to the Sri Manickavinayagar Temple in Bambalapitiya and separately,

from the Kathiresan Kovil in Pettah to the New Kathiresan Hall in Bambalapitiya.

Nallur Chariot Festival *(Jul/ Aug)*, Jaffna. This is Jaffna's main festival and it has steadily grown in popularity since the end of the Civil War. The festival is dedicated to Skanda and lasts for 25 days. Every day throughout the festival, a chariot procession takes place within the temple premises in the morning and outside the temple in the evening. Devotees, drummers and dancers also participate in the procession.

August
Elephant Gathering
(Aug–Oct), Minneriya National Park. Elephants gather at the Minneriya tank during the height of the dry season.

September
Dussehra *(Sep/Oct)*, nationwide. Also known as Durga Puja, this Hindu festival honours the goddess Durga, who defeated the demon Mahishasura, and also celebrates the Hindu god Rama's victory over Rawana (king of Lankapura).

Muslim Holidays

Like Hindu and Buddhist festivals, Muslim festivals are also dictated by the lunar calendar. The Buddhist and Hindu lunar calendars are kept in line with the solar calendars by the insertion of days or a month. However, the Islamic calendar is around 11 days shorter than that of the Western calendar, and Muslim festivals tend to fall earlier each year, depending on the sightings of the crescent moon.

Important Muslim holidays celebrated in Sri Lanka are Milad un-Nabi, celebrating the Prophet's birthday; Ramadan, the start of the month of fasting when most Muslims abstain from food and drink during daylight hours; Eid ul-Fitr, the three-day festival marking the end of Ramadan; and Eid ul-Adha, a four-day festival marking the beginning of the Hajj, the pilgrimage to Mecca. These festivals are celebrated by offering special prayers at the mosque.

Muslims praying at a mosque

A Tamil devotee lighting oil lamps at the Ponnambalam Vanesar during Deepavali, Colombo

Northeast Monsoon

The northeast monsoon is the weaker of the two and affects the North and East of the island from October until February or March, although other parts of the island can also experience rain during this time. The best time to visit Sri Lanka is between December and April, although this is when it is busiest, with prices rising significantly over Christmas and New Year.

October
Deepavali (late Oct/early Nov), nationwide. The Festival of Lights, symbolic of good triumphing over evil, is celebrated by all Hindus. It also commemorates Rama's return with the rescued Sita after 14 years in exile. Lamps are lit in Tamil households and in places of worship.

December
Unduvap (Dec), nationwide. This poya day, also known as Sanghamitta Day, marks the arrival of the sacred bo tree sapling from India, which was planted in Anuradhapura. It is said to be a cutting from the bo tree under which the Buddha gained enlightenment and was carried to Sri Lanka by Sanghamitta, King Asoka's daughter. The pilgrimage season to Adam's Peak begins on this day and continues until Bak poya day in April.

Christmas (25 Dec), nationwide. Celebrated by the Christian population, this festival, rejoicing the birth of Jesus, is a public holiday. Festive decorations and trees can be seen in shopping centres throughout the country and at roadside stalls.

January
Duruthu (Jan), Kelaniya. The poya day commemorates the first of the Buddha's three visits to Sri Lanka. A perahera (parade) is held at the Raja Maha Vihara in Kelaniya, north of Colombo.
Tamil Thai Pongol (mid-Jan), nationwide. This Hindu harvest festival, lasting two days, honours the sun god Surya and

A fire dancer performing in the Duruthu perahera at the Raja Maha Vihara, Kelaniya

Climate of Sri Lanka

Sri Lanka's climate varies depending on the altitude and the time of the year. While temperatures remain fairly constant year-round, the rainfall pattern is affected by two monsoons: the southwest and the northeast. Humidity is almost always high all over the island, rising to 90 per cent in the southwest and between 60 and 80 per cent across the rest of the country. Although it never gets too cold because of the island's proximity to the equator, the Hill Country is much cooler than other parts of Sri Lanka throughout the year.

Colombo enjoys fairly constant temperatures year round and rarely gets colder than 20°C (68°F). The southwest monsoon brings high humidity, but rainfall can occur throughout the year.

COLOMBO

°C/°F			
32/90	30/86	30/86	31/88
25/77	25/77	24/75	22/22

8 hrs	6 hrs	6 hrs	8 hrs
253 mm	125 mm	369 mm	62 mm
Apr	Jul	Oct	Jan

month

Costumed dancers participating in a National Day parade, Trincomalee

the cattle that have ploughed the fields over the last year. There are fireworks and festivities, and *pongol*, a sweet rice dish, is prepared in homes.

Galle Literary Festival *(Jan/Feb/Mar)*, Galle. This annual five-day literary festival based in and around Galle Fort attracts international and domestic authors. Several talks and workshops are organized.

February
Navam Perahera *(Feb)*, Colombo. The Navam *poya* day commemorates two significant incidents: the First Buddhist Council and the appointment of two chief disciples of Gautama Buddha. It is celebrated by a large *perahera*, in which a procession of elephants and dancers begins at the Gangaramaya Temple and

winds its way around the Vihara Mahadevi Park and Beira Lake in Colombo.
National Day *(4 Feb)*, nationwide. This event marks Sri Lanka's independence from British rule in 1948. The day is celebrated with parades and merrymaking.
Maha Shivarathri *(late Feb/ early Mar)*, nationwide. This Hindu festival is dedicated to the god Shiva. Devotees fast and all-night *pujas* are held in temples.

March
Good Friday *(Mar/Apr)*, nationwide. Passion plays are performed on the island of Duwa near Negombo, Jaffna and other coastal areas with Catholic populations. On the following Sunday, Easter is celebrated with re-enactments of Christ's crucifixion and large processions.

Public Holidays

Duruthu Poya Day (Jan)
Tamil Thai Pongal (mid-Jan)
Milad un-Nabi (The Prophet's Birthday) (Jan)
Navam Poya Day (Feb)
Maha Shivarathri (late Feb/early Mar)
Medin Poya Day (Mar)
Good Friday (Mar/Apr)
Bak Poya Day (Apr)
Day prior to Sinhala and Tamil New Year (Apr)
Sinhala and Tamil New Year (Apr)
May Day (1 May)
Vesak Poya Day (May)
Day following Vesak Poya Day (May)
Poson Poya Day (Jun)
Esala Poya Day (Jul)
Nikini Poya Day (Aug)
Eid ul-Fitr (Jul/Aug)
Binara Poya Day (Sep)
Eid ul-Adha (Oct)
Vap Poya Day (Oct)
Deepavali (late Oct/early Nov)
Il Poya Day (Nov)
Unduvap Poya Day (Dec)
Christmas (25 Dec)

Jaffna can get extremely hot and humid, with temperatures reaching above 30ºC (86ºF) on many days. Rainfall in the area is low, and most of it is brought by the northeast monsoon.

Nuwara Eliya, at an elevation of 1,889 m (6,199 ft) above sea level, enjoys a cool climate. The average daily temperature is around 16ºC (61ºF). The area receives high rainfall from the southwest monsoon.

Trincomalee has a tropical climate and temperatures rarely drop below 20ºC (68ºF). During the dry season, between May and September, it can get as hot as 35ºC (94ºF). Rain comes with the northeast monsoon.

JAFFNA

°C/°F			
33/91	33/91	31/88	28/82
27/81	25/77	25/77	23/73

8 hrs	6 hrs	6 hrs	8 hrs
44 mm	17 mm	248 mm	52 mm

| month | Apr | Jul | Oct | Jan |

NUWARA ELIYA

°C/°F			
23/73	19/66	20/68	20/68
20/52	13/55	12/54	9/48

7 hrs	7 hrs	6 hrs	6 hrs
151 mm	174 mm	228 mm	107 mm

| month | Apr | Jul | Oct | Jan |

TRINCOMALEE

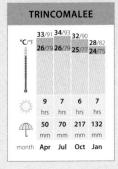

°C/°F			
33/91	34/93	32/90	28/82
26/79	26/79	25/77	24/75

9 hrs	7 hrs	6 hrs	7 hrs
50 mm	70 mm	217 mm	132 mm

| month | Apr | Jul | Oct | Jan |

THE HISTORY OF SRI LANKA

Sri Lanka boasts a remarkably rich history, shaped by trade, migration, wars and invasions. The island's early history is shrouded in legend – the first written accounts relate mythical tales of the origins of the Sinhalese. Sri Lanka was carved into small kingdoms by different ethnic groups and then subjected to centuries of Colonial rule until it attained independence in 1948, only to be devastated by decades of Civil War. Today, the country is in the midst of a revival and is back on the tourist map.

Archaeologists have found remnants of prehistoric human settlements dating from 125,000 BC in Sri Lanka. Excavations have confirmed the presence of a Mesolithic civilization on the island known as the Balangoda culture. Named after modern-day Balangoda, around which the remains of these early *Homo sapiens* were discovered, this culture seems to have spread widely across the country. In June 2012, Sri Lankan archaeologists unearthed a complete human skeleton from Fa Hien Cave in the Kalutara district, which is said to date back 37,000 years. Other Pleistocene-era remains, such as stone tools, bead ornaments and weapons made of bone, were found here during digs in the 1960s and 1980s. The closest living relatives to the Balangoda Man are the Veddahs *(see p199)*, who have inhabited the island since 16,000 BC.

There is not much evidence of the transition from the Mesolithic to Iron Age in Sri Lanka. However, evidence suggests that at the end of the Stone Age, there was a gradual shift from hunting and gathering to the cultivation of crops. Excavations in Horton Plains indicate the existence of agriculture

from around 8,000 BC. It is also known that cattle farming, rice paddy cultivation and pottery were present at this time.

The First Sinhalese Arrive

From the 5th century BC, Indo-Aryan migrants began to arrive in Sri Lanka. The present-day Sinhalese are the descendants of these immigrants. However, according to the *Mahavamsa (see p120)*, the father of the Sinhalese race is Prince Vijaya who was exiled from northern India. He is said to have arrived on the island in the 5th century BC with 700 companions on the same day that the Buddha attained enlightenment.

At first the migrants stayed in the lowlands and cultivated rice, but later they moved to the dry northern plains, implementing irrigation systems and building tanks to provide water for crops. These settlers probably assimilated the original inhabitants into their community or drove them out into more remote regions of the island. As these people gradually established themselves, they founded the kingdom of Anuradhapura in the northern plains in the 4th century BC.

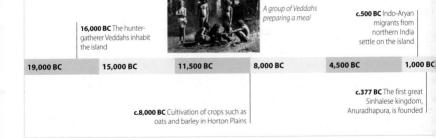

A group of Veddahs preparing a meal

16,000 BC The hunter-gatherer Veddahs inhabit the island

c.500 BC Indo-Aryan migrants from northern India settle on the island

19,000 BC	15,000 BC	11,500 BC	8,000 BC	4,500 BC	1,000 BC

c.8,000 BC Cultivation of crops such as oats and barley in Horton Plains

c.377 BC The first great Sinhalese kingdom, Anuradhapura, is founded

◀ A painting depicting the Indian princess, Hemamala, and her husband, Prince Dhantha, bringing the Tooth Relic to Sri Lanka in AD 313

Anuradhapura

The city of Anuradhapura was the capital of Sri Lanka for over a thousand years, during which it saw periods of stability, and also periods of chaos, dynastic struggle, civil war and invasion. It became the capital city under King Pandukabhaya in the 4th century BC, but rose to new heights under Devanampiya Tissa a century later, who, after his conversion to Buddhism, developed Anuradhapura into a major centre of Buddhist learning. The city was, however, subject to many invasions from south India and threats from Tamil mercenaries who fought for the Sinhalese kings. It fell under Tamil rule several times until the final invasion of the Cholas in the 10th century, who razed it to the ground. Anuradhapura was abandoned in the 10th century when the capital was moved to Polonnaruwa.

Pilgrims at the revered Sri Maha Bodhi Tree

Ruwanwelisiya Dagoba
The construction of this *dagoba* began during the reign of King Dutugemunu, but he died before it could be completed. It is said his brother, Suddha Tissa, created a false dome so that the *dagoba* appeared finished to the king as he lay on his deathbed.

Sanghamitta, Mahinda's sister and a Buddhist nun, is believed to have brought a cutting from the bo tree in India to Sri Lanka in the 3rd century BC.

King Dutugemunu
After defeating the Tamil general Elara in 161 BC, King Dutugemunu brought the whole island under Sinhalese rule for the first time. It was during his reign that the Mirisavatiya Dagoba and the Brazen Palace were built in this city.

Faxian
A Chinese Buddhist monk, Faxian, travelled to India in the 5th century AD and stayed there for a decade. He then sailed to Sri Lanka where he spent two years in the Abhayagiri Monastery in Anuradhapura, translating Buddhist texts. His writings provide important information on early Buddhism.

250–210 BC Reign of Devanampiya Tissa

247 BC Mahinda converts King Tissa to Buddhism

AD 67–111 Reign of Vasabha

AD 274–301 Reign of Mahasena

250 BC   **125 BC**   **AD 1**   **125**   **250**

244 BC Cutting from the bo tree arrives in Sri Lanka

144 BC Construction of the Ruwanwelisiya Dagoba begins

161–137 BC Reign of Dutugemunu

The Jetavanarama Dagoba, built during the reign of Mahasena

Rice Trough at Mahapali Refectory
This 3-m (10-ft) long trough bears three inscriptions on its eastern end dating from the 10th century. The trough was filled with rice for the monks, and is said to have fed as many as 4,000.

King Rajaraja I
Rajaraja I (r.985–1014) was one of the greatest kings of the Chola dynasty of south India. He conquered the northern areas of Sri Lanka, including Anuradhapura, after defeating the rival Pandyans of south India and forcing the Sinhalese king, Mihindu V, to flee to Ruhunu in AD 993.

Coins Found at Anuradhapura
The earliest-known usage of coins in Sri Lanka dates back to the 3rd century BC. The Roman coins discovered at the site indicates the city enjoyed international trade links during its heyday.

Sri Maha Bodhi Tree

Painted by renowned Sri Lankan artist Solias Mendis, this mural depicts the legend of Anuradhapura's Sri Maha Bodhi Tree. The tree is believed to have originated from a cutting of the bo tree in Bodh Gaya, India, beneath which the Buddha attained enlightenment. The original tree in India was destroyed, but its Sri Lankan descendant survived down the centuries. One of the island's most sacred sights, it attracts many Buddhist pilgrims year-round. It stands in an enclosure protected by gold railings.

The Cholas

The Tamil Chola Dynasty ruled much of southern India from the 9th to the 13th centuries AD. Over the course of the 9th and the 10th centuries, the Cholas launched brief incursions on Sri Lanka which ultimately led to the annexation of the island. It was under the rule of Rajaraja I that the Cholas occupied the northern half of the country. His son, Rajendra I (r.1014–1044), completed the Chola conquest of the island and captured King Mihindu V. After sacking the city of Anuradhapura, the Cholas moved the capital to Polonnaruwa, from where they ruled for over 75 years. They were eventually driven out of the country in the 11th century by the Sinhalese king Vijayabahu I.

Ruins of a monastery in Anuradhapura

AD 455–473 Reign of Dhatusena

AD 684–718 Reign of Manavamma

AD 846–866 The Pandyans plunder Anuradhapura

| 75 | 500 | 625 | 750 | 875 | 1000 |

AD 413 Faxian visits Anuradhapura

A portrait of the Buddhist monk, Faxian

AD 993 Chola invaders destroy Anuradhapura

The Arrival of Buddhism

The 6th-century *Mahavamsa* states that King Devanampiya Tissa converted to Buddhism in the 3rd century BC after meeting Mahinda, son of the Indian king Asoka. However, some sources claim that Buddhism had probably arrived on the island much earlier. Tissa's conversion to Buddhism ensured its positive reception among the people and by the 1st century BC the religion had become a prominent faith in the country. The religion became even more established with the arrival of the bo tree cutting (*see p47*) and then the Tooth Relic in AD 313. Buddhism also unified the island's Sinhalese and gave them a sense of common identity. A close link was forged between the state and Buddhism during Tissa's reign; he founded the monastery of Mahavihara in Anuradhapura, which became the stronghold of Theravada Buddhism in Sri Lanka.

Remains of a monastic structure in the Mahavihara

The Kingdom of Polonnaruwa

The Cholas from south India sacked and destroyed Anuradhapura, establishing themselves in the city of Polonnaruwa in the 10th century. They ruled over the island for the next 75 years until King Vijayabahu I (r.1055–1110) drove them out of the country in 1077.

With Anuradhapura in ruins, Vijayabahu I moved the capital to Polonnaruwa, which was further from India and easier to defend. Vijayabahu I re-established Sinhalese control over the island and ushered in a phase of recovery in the wake of the Chola rule. Upon his death, however, there was a long period of civil war until King Parakramabahu I (r.1153–86) emerged as leader. Under his rule Polonnaruwa experienced its golden age, until ambitious building projects and the wars he fought overseas took their toll on the country and probably contributed to the eventual fall of the kingdom.

After Parakramabahu I, the throne was inherited by his brother-in-law, Nissankamalla (r.1187–96). Like Parakramabahu I, Nissankamalla spent large sums on construction projects, which almost brought the state to bankruptcy. His death without a designated successor led to a period of unrest and political dissent. This instability caught the attention of Tamil invaders – the Cholas and the Pandyans – who saw the opportunity to invade and pillage.

The Gal Pota, or Stone Book, praising the achievements of Nissankamalla, Polonnaruwa

1153–86 Reign of Parakramabahu I, during which the Gal Vihara sculptures at Polonnaruwa are built

1236 Parakramabahu II defeats Magha

Buddha statue at Gal Vihara, Polonnaruwa

1070	1115	1160	1205	1250

1077 Vijayabahu I drives Cholas out of the country

King Nissankamalla

1187–96 Reign of Nissankamalla

1215 Magha seizes control over the island; rise of the Tamil kingdom in the north

After the Pandyans invaded Sri Lanka in 1212, Magha (r.1215–55), a prince from the Indian kingdom of Kalinga, launched a devastating attack on the island and seized power. His period of rule heralded a time of violence and suffering – the irrigation systems fell into disrepair, disease spread and the people started migrating southwards.

Frescoes at a temple in Dambadeniya, the capital of Sri Lanka in the mid-13th century

Independent Kingdoms in the North and the South

Magha's rule did not just bring disorder, but also caused two centres of power to emerge in the north and the south. The Sinhalese nobility began to move southwest of Polonnaruwa to Dambadeniya, where they founded a new capital under the rule of Vijayabahu III (r.1232–36). His heir, Parakramabahu II (r.1236–70), finally defeated Magha, who then moved to the Jaffna region. However, political tension followed and the Sinhalese capital moved several times. By 1340, the Sinhalese kingdom had fragmented into two rival principalities at Gampola and Dedigama.

The absence of Sinhalese authority in the northern part of the country had left a power vacuum. While the Sinhalese drifted further south to the safety of the Hill Country, the Tamils established control over the Jaffna Peninsula and the area north of Anuradhapura, and an independent Tamil kingdom was established in Jaffna in the 13th century. An ever-widening gap, also encompassing religion and language, appeared between these two kingdoms.

The Jaffna kingdom gradually expanded southwards and even began to tax the Sinhalese regions. However, the strength of the kingdom was short-lived. A fort was established at Kotte, southeast of Colombo, to impede Tamil invasions from the north on the West Coast. This was followed by the emergence of King Parakramabahu VI (r.1411–66), from the Gampola nobility in Kotte, who went on to become the last Sinhalese ruler to unite the island.

In 1450, Parakramabahu VI took possession of the Tamil kingdom and the independent kingdom at Dedigama, hence bringing the whole island under Sinhalese rule. When he died, however, it did not take long for the smaller kingdoms of Jaffna and the Hill Country to reassert their independence. By this time, there were three established kingdoms on the island: the Tamil kingdom of Jaffna in the north, the Sinhalese Kandyan kingdom in the Hill Country and the Sinhalese kingdom at Kotte.

1293 The capital of Polonnaruwa is finally abandoned after a period of decline under the rule of Magha

c.1350 Rise of the Sinhalese kingdom at Kotte

1450 Parakramabahu VI takes possession of the Jaffna kingdom and unites the island under Sinhalese rule

1295	1340	1385	1430	1475

1340 Emergence of two Sinhalese kingdoms at Gampola and Dedigama

Crumbling ruins of the ancient city of Polonnaruwa

1412 Parakramabahu VI founds the Kotte kingdom

1479 Jaffna re-establishes itself as an independent kingdom

Painting depicting the arrival of the Portuguese fleet on the shores of Sri Lanka in 1505

The Portuguese and the Dutch Arrive

Trade was becoming increasingly important to the Sinhalese. Colombo and Galle soon grew into major port cities attracting crowds of foreign merchants. These included the Arab traders who settled along the island's coast between the 7th and the 15th centuries, and were instrumental in spreading Islam across the country.

In 1505, a Portuguese fleet landed on the island and concluded a trading agreement with the king of Kotte. Their initial interest in Sri Lanka's cinnamon stocks rapidly grew into a desire to extend their control all over the country. In 1518, they built a fort in Colombo and gradually established authority over the island's coastal areas as far as Jaffna, except for the well-protected kingdom of Kandy. The Portuguese rule also marked the arrival of Roman Catholic missionaries and the resulting conversions to Christianity. Buddhists were subject to religious persecution, and as a result many sought refuge in the Hill Country.

Meanwhile resistance to the Portuguese persisted on the island, and Kandy continued to prevail as an independent kingdom. The kingdom successfully crushed a number of Portuguese attacks between 1594 and 1638 and began to look for a means to rid the island of the Portuguese.

The Kandyan king Rajasinghe II (r.1634–86) formed an alliance with the Dutch in 1638 in order to drive the Portuguese out of the coastal areas. The resulting agreement granted the Dutch a monopoly on the spice trade, with the Kandyans pledging to compensate the costs incurred in the ousting of the Portuguese.

In 1639, the Dutch captured the towns of Trincomalee and Batticaloa on the East Coast and handed them back to the Kandyans. However, when Galle and Negombo on the West Coast fell under their control, the Dutch held them as payment for their efforts – the two towns were of strategic importance for the spice trade. In May 1656, the Portuguese surrendered the Colombo fort and in 1658 the last Portuguese stronghold of Jaffna was seized, hence bringing an end to their rule.

Rajasinghe II considered the Dutch to be his hired mercenaries and expected them to return home once they had achieved their

View of the Negombo Canal, an important trade route used by the Dutch to transport spices

1505 A Portuguese fleet arrives in Sri Lanka

1594 The coastal areas are captured by the Portuguese

1619 Portuguese take possession of Jaffna

1658 The Dutch force the Portuguese out of the island

1500   1543   1586   1629   1672

1518 Portuguese build a fort in Colombo

Painting of Kandyan king Rajasinghe II

1638 King Rajasinghe II of Kandy forms an alliance with the Dutch to oust the Portuguese

aims. However, over time, the Dutch went on to rule over the entire coastline as well as control substantial cinnamon resources.

Surrounded by a foreign power, the Kandyans often organized destructive raids on the Dutch territories. There were also many uprisings in the Dutch-held lowland areas during the 1720s and the 1730s. Despite their many attempts, the Dutch never managed to capture the kingdom of Kandy during their 140-year rule on the island.

A portrait of the Kandyan king, Sri Wickrama Rajasinghe (r.1798–1815)

The British Take Over

In 1794, the French Revolution in Europe saw the Netherlands fall to the French. The Dutch invited the English East India Company to the island in 1796 to protect it against the French. However, the British realized the country's strategic value and gained control of it from the Dutch. In 1802, Sri Lanka was officially handed to the British under the Treaty of Amiens with France. But it wasn't until 1815 that the British managed to achieve what many others had sought to do – they deposed the Kandyan king Sri Wickrama Rajasinghe (r.1798–1815) and captured the kingdom of Kandy, bringing the entire island under unified rule.

During the British Colonial period, the transport network was improved, railways were built and a plantation economy was born. Coconut, rubber and coffee plantations were set up, although coffee was later replaced by tea. This period also saw the arrival of Tamil workers from south India, who were brought by the British to work on the plantations.

The Rise of Nationalism

By the end of the 19th century, there was a revival of Buddhist and Hindu movements and a rejection of efforts by missionaries to convert people to Christianity. These movements gradually gained a political motive and there was a demand for greater Sri Lankan participation in government. In 1910, a minor concession was granted, which allowed a small number of the Sri Lankan English-educated elite to elect one member to the Legislative Council.

During World War I, there was an upsurge of Buddhist nationalist sentiment, culminating in the 1915 riots of the Sinhalese and the Muslims. The British mistook these riots for a conspiracy against them and reacted harshly, which resulted in further opposition. This led to the formation of the Ceylon National Congress in 1919 with the objective of self-governance. In 1931, the Donoughmore Report recommended a semi-responsible government and the island's leaders were finally allowed to take part in the political process. Universal suffrage was also introduced, making Sri Lanka the first Asian colony to achieve this.

1720 Uprisings in Dutch-held areas

1796 The Dutch invite the English East India Company to Sri Lanka

1815 The British conquer the kingdom of Kandy

British officials depose the king of Kandy

1919 Ceylon National Congress is formed

| 5 | 1758 | 1801 | 1844 | 1887 | 1930 |

Anti-Dutch uprisings in occupied territories

1802 Sri Lanka is handed over to the British under the Treaty of Amiens

1840 The British begin to bring Tamils over from south India to work on the plantations

1931 Universal suffrage is introduced

Sirimavo Bandaranaike (1916–2000), who served as the prime minister of Sri Lanka for over 20 years

Independence and Beyond

Sri Lanka peacefully gained independence from the British on 4 February 1948. The first government was formed by the conservative United National Party (UNP) with Don Stephen (DS) Senanayake as prime minister. In the initial years of independence, the government was stable and the economy thrived. But in the 1950s, the economy suffered from falling rubber and tea prices in the world markets, rising costs of food imports and a rapidly increasing population. The ruling UNP began to fragment after DS Senanayake died in 1952. He was briefly succeeded by his son Dudley Senanayake.

In 1956, the UNP lost the general election to the socialist-nationalist Sri Lanka Freedom Party (SLFP) led by Solomon West Ridgeway Dias (SWRD) Bandaranaike. The new government passed the Sinhala Only Act, which made Sinhala the country's sole official language, consequently alienating the island's Tamil population. This led to widespread Tamil resentment and ethnic tensions. Bandaranaike opened dialogue with Tamil leaders to address the growing problem, but was assassinated by a Buddhist monk in 1959.

Bandaranaike was succeeded by his widow Sirimavo Bandaranaike – popularly known as Mrs Bandaranaike – who became the world's first woman prime minister. She continued to nationalize key industries, curtail Tamil political activity and deport Tamils working on the plantations to India. UNP returned to power in 1965, under the leadership of Dudley Senanayake, but the state of the economy failed to improve and Mrs Bandaranaike took back the reins in 1970 as the head of the United Front (UF) party. The country's economy continued to decline, and by 1977 unemployment had risen to about 15 per cent. The early 1970s saw the rise of Janatha Vimukthi Peramuna (JVP), a left wing, anti-Tamil movement mostly made up of young people. In 1971, they tried to overthrow the Bandaranaike government but were soon violently suppressed by the military.

The Rise of the LTTE

A new constitution was adopted in 1972 that declared Buddhism the foremost religion on the island. This, coupled with the recognition of Sinhala as the state language, was regarded by Tamils as blatant discrimination. As tensions escalated in the north and east, numerous Tamil militant groups emerged, calling for an independent Tamil state named Eelam (Precious Land). In 1976, the Liberation Tigers of Tamil Eelam (LTTE), or the Tamil Tigers, was formed under the leadership of Velupillai Prabhakaran.

LTTE leader Velupillai Prabhakaran (1954–2009)

SWRD Bandaranaike, leader of the SLFP

1959 SWRD Bandaranaike is assassinated by a Buddhist monk

1965 UNP returns to power under the leadership of Dudley Senanayake

1972 Ceylon changes its name to the Democratic Socialist Republic of Sri Lanka

1940

1950

1960

1970

1948 Ceylon is granted independence

1956 Sinhala is declared the official language

1970 Rise of the Sinhalese nationalist JVP

The UNP, headed by Junius Richard (JR) Jayewardene, defeated the UF at the 1977 elections. In 1978, a new constitution gave the country's president executive powers. The same year Jayewardene resigned as prime minister and was elected as president. Under UNP rule, Tamil and Sinhala were each made national languages, but Sinhala remained the only official language. Plantation Tamils, who had been disenfranchised in 1949, were also given the right to vote. Despite these reforms, violence continued to intensify with Tamil guerrilla groups gaining a foothold in the north.

The main turning point was "Black July" in 1983. After the LTTE ambushed an army patrol near Jaffna, Sinhalese mobs rampaged through Colombo, Jaffna and several other cities, destroying Tamil areas and killing hundreds in retaliation. As a result, many Tamils left the island and sought refuge overseas.

The Civil War

The conflict between the LTTE and the army continued between 1983 and 1987, despite a belated offer of limited self-government for Tamils in 1985. In 1987, government forces pushed the LTTE back to Jaffna. In an attempt to resolve the conflic, Indian Prime Minister Rajiv Gandhi and the Sinhalese President JR Jayewardene signed the Indo-Lanka Peace Accord. This outlined an agreement that provided for an Indian Peace Keeping Force (IPKF) to be sent to disarm the Tamil rebels. The presence of the Indian troops on Sri Lankan soil, however, led to violent anti-government protests and the regeneration of the JVP.

Charred remains of a Sri Lankan Airlines aircraft on the tarmac of Bandaranaike International Airport, 24 July 2001

Between 1987 and 1988, the JVP began a campaign of assassinations, sabotage and strikes. President Jayawardene retired in 1988 and was replaced by Ranasinghe Premadasa, who pledged to end the conflict with the LTTE and the violence advocated by JVP. The LTTE agreed to a ceasefire and the IPKF left Sri Lanka in 1990. However, hostilities resumed a few months later. In 1993, the Tamil Tigers were suspected of the bombing that killed President Premadasa. The SLFP-led People's Alliance (PA) won the presidential elections in 1994 under the leadership of Chandrika Kumaratunga, who promised to end the Civil War. Negotiations with the LTTE broke down in 1995.

The Civil War continued to rage through the second half of the 1990s. In December 1999, there was an assassination attempt against Kumaratunga. She survived the bombing but lost sight in one eye. By late 1999, the army had been forced back to Vavuniya and in April 2000 the LTTE captured the strategically important Elephant Pass. In July 2001, LTTE suicide bombers launched a raid on Bandaranaike International Airport destroying commercial and military aircraft.

1976 The LTTE is formed

1990 The IPKF withdraws from Sri Lanka; violence continues to escalate between government forces and the LTTE

1998 The Temple of the Tooth in Kandy is bombed by the LTTE

2000 LTTE forces take over the strategic Elephant Pass

1980

1990

2000

1983 "Black July", when Sinhalese mobs go on a rampage razing Tamil areas and killing hundreds of Tamils

1987 The IPKF arrives in Sri Lanka

1995 LTTE rebels sink two naval craft off the coast of Trincomalee

IPKF troops leaving Sri Lanka

Leader of the opposition Ranil Wickramasinghe greets Norwegian peace envoy, Deputy Foreign Minister Vidar Helgesen in 2004

The Ceasefire

In December 2001, the UNP won elections and Ranil Wickramasinghe was elected as prime minister. He called for peace talks with the LTTE and brought in a Norwegian peace mission for this purpose. By February 2002, an official ceasefire had been signed between the government and the LTTE. The road linking the Jaffna Peninsula to the rest of Sri Lanka opened after nearly a decade, flights to Jaffna resumed and weapons were decommissioned.

However, political problems soon began to crop up as Wickramasinghe and Kumaratunga belonged to different parties. Kumaratunga criticized the peace process for ceding too much to the Tamils and in 2003 the talks stalled and the LTTE pulled out. The ceasefire, however, continued. The same year Kumaratunga dissolved the parliament while Wickramasinghe was out of the country and held elections in April 2004.

Kumaratunga's party, the Freedom Alliance (FA), established an unlikely coalition with the JVP and formed a government with Sinhalese nationalist Mahinda Rajapaksa as prime minister. Violence resumed and the first suicide bomb since 2001 was set off at a Colombo police station.

On 26 December 2004, a massive undersea earthquake off the coast of Sumatra in Indonesia triggered a devastating tsunami that struck the east and southeast coasts of Sri Lanka. It killed thousands, displaced millions and destroyed business and transport infrastructure. It was hoped that the catastrophe would bring the country together, but instead there were arguments over aid and reconstruction. An aid package of nearly three billion dollars was to be shared between the Sinhalese, Tamil and Muslim communities. But the fact that the agreement would have allowed the

Mahinda Rajapaksa greets supporters after victory

LTTE to distribute aid in the north and east was condemned and caused the JVP to walk out of the coalition government. The party then pressured the Supreme Court into suspending the agreement, fearing that it would establish the LTTE as the de facto government in the north.

The End of the Civil War

The presidential elections of 2005 were won by the then prime minister Mahinda Rajapaksa, who rejected the idea of Tamil autonomy and refused to share the tsunami aid with the LTTE. Rajapaksa invited the Norwegians back to broker peace talks in 2006; however, the lull in violence lasted

2002 A ceasefire is secured by the Norwegian peace mission in February

LTTE fighters at a jungle warfare tactics training

2003 LTTE withdraws from peace talks on 21 April

2006 Intense fighting between the LTTE and the Sri Lankan Army; the worst clashes take place in the northeast

2001	2003	2005	2007

2001 War rages on; the LTTE attacks the Bandaranaike International Airport on 24 July

2004 The 26 December tsunami devastates large coastal areas

Destruction caused by the 2004 tsunami

2005 Mahinda Rajapaksa is elected president in November

2008 The government officially p out of the ceasefire agreemer January and begins a mas offensive against the L

President Rajapaksa inspects weapons captured from Liberation Tigers of Tamil Eelam (LTTE) forces in Kilinochchi

only a few weeks. The second half of 2006 saw some of the worst clashes and it was apparent that the ceasefire was over in all but name. In 2007, the police forced many Tamils to leave Colombo citing security concerns as the reason. Finally, in January 2008 the government officially withdrew from the 2002 ceasefire agreement and launched a massive offensive against the LTTE.

During the course of 2008, the army made its way northwards, recapturing LTTE strongholds and ignoring their call for a unilateral ceasefire. On 2 January 2009, the army captured the LTTE's administrative capital of Kilinochchi, and within a week Elephant Pass was also under their control. The LTTE found themselves hemmed in on a narrow strip of land on the northeast of the island. Thousands are thought to have died in the final months of fighting.

The last LTTE-controlled area fell in May 2009 when the Tamil Tigers surrendered, and several senior LTTE figures were reported killed, including the LTTE leader Vellupillai Prabhakaran. Rajapaksa declared victory and interned thousands of Tamil refugees in camps. He called for early presidential elections in 2010 in which he achieved a landslide victory. The opposition candidate, General Sarath Fonseka, challenged the poll results but was arrested and court-martialled on a number of charges.

Sri Lanka Today

There have long been calls for the Sri Lankan government to account for what happened at the end of the Civil War. In March 2009, the UN High Commissioner for Human Rights, Navi Pillay, accused both sides of violating humanitarian law. However, the issue has never really been addressed. In May 2010, the government established the LLRC (see p21), an internal panel of inquiry to investigate war crimes. The report published by the committee in December 2011 included some constructive recommendations such as a right to information bill and disarmament of those with illegal weapons, but did not focus on the issues of accountability. In November 2013, Sri Lanka hosted the Commonwealth Summit, which led to increased scrutiny of its human rights record. David Cameron, the UK's prime minster, attended the meeting and gave the country a four-month deadline to investigate war crimes. However, the country firmly denied the need to investigate further into the events that brought the war to a close.

Since the end of the Civil War, tourists and international investment have returned to Sri Lanka – Rajapaksa has forged close economic and diplomatic alliances with China and Iran. However, concerns remain about human rights, freedom of speech and the safety of journalists under Rajapaksa's rule.

2009 In January, the Sri Lankan Army captures Kilinochchi; President Rajapaksa calls for the LTTE to surrender	**2010** The constitution is amended in September so that Rajapaksa can stand for an unlimited term in office	*Navi Pillay, the UN High Commissioner for Human Rights, addresses Sri Lanka's youth parliament*		**2015** Presidential elections
2009		**2011**	**2013**	**2015**
2009 The LTTE surrender and the war ends in May; Prabhakaran is killed	**2010** Rajapaksa wins the early presidential elections in January	**2011** UN report on the Civil War is published in April, calling for an independent investigation into alleged war crimes	**2013** UN Human Rights Council adopts a resolution in March urging Sri Lanka to investigate alleged violations of human rights	

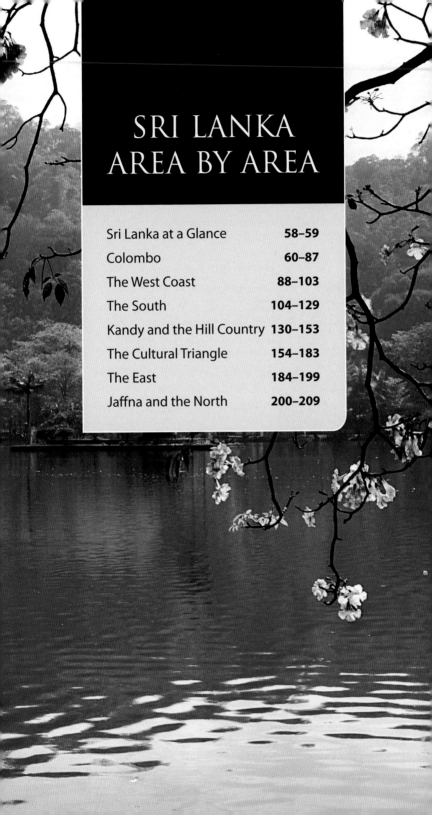

SRI LANKA
AREA BY AREA

Sri Lanka at a Glance

Spanning an area of just over 65,000 sq km (25,097 sq miles), the island nation of Sri Lanka offers much to see, owing to its long history and pristine natural beauty. While the remains of ancient cities, such as Anuradhapura and Polonnaruwa, attest to the country's cultural and religious heritage, the grand old hotels of Nuwara Eliya and the fascinating Galle Fort evince its Colonial legacy. The country is noted for a number of national parks and nature reserves, such as Yala West and Uda Walawe, which form secure habitats for a diverse variety of flora and fauna. The coastline is fringed with beautiful beaches that offer a wealth of activities for watersports enthusiasts, while the Hill Country rewards trekkers with trails meandering through manicured tea plantations peppered with waterfalls.

Jaffna Islands *(see pp208–209)* boast sparkling beaches and splendid Hindu temples. While Karaitivu offers superb swimming opportunities, Nainativu, further afield, is known for the striking Naga Pooshani Ambal Kovil, an ancient Hindu temple.

Po
Pe

Jaffna

Kilinoch

Mannar

Jaffna and the North
(see pp200–209)

Anuradhapur

Kalpitiya

Puttalam

0 km   50
0 miles   50

Anuradhapura *(see pp178–81),* the first capital of Sri Lanka, was founded in the 4th century BC. It is here that the sacred Sri Maha Bodhi tree can be found. The tree is said to have grown from a cutting of the bo tree in Bodh Gaya, in India, under which the Buddha attained enlightenment.

Chilaw
The West Coast
(see pp88–103)

Negombo

Colombo
(see pp60–87)

Kalutara   Ratnapu

Bentota

Hikkaduw

Galle Fort *(see pp108–113)* was originally built by the Portuguese in 1589. The best way to explore this UNESCO World Heritage Site is to wander the streets or clamber along the ramparts.

Galle

Weligar

◀ Breathtaking view of Kandy Lake in the heart of the city

Polonnaruwa *(see pp170–74)*, the country's capital from the 11th to the 13th centuries, is home to some of the finest ruins of temples and monasteries in the country. Among the highlights is the Gal Vihara rock temple, with a stunning reclining Buddha.

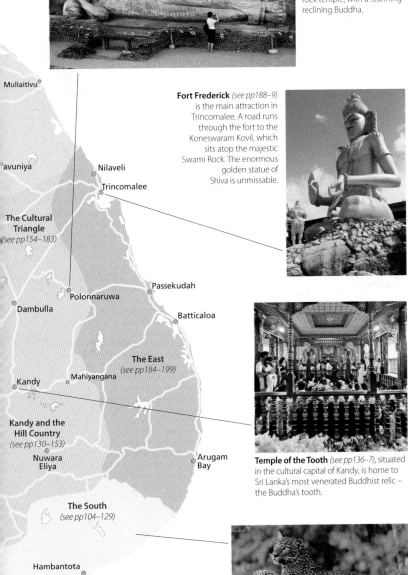

Fort Frederick *(see pp188–9)* is the main attraction in Trincomalee. A road runs through the fort to the Koneswaram Kovil, which sits atop the majestic Swami Rock. The enormous golden statue of Shiva is unmissable.

Mullaitivu

avuniya

Nilaveli

Trincomalee

The Cultural Triangle
(see pp154–183)

Passekudah

Polonnaruwa

Dambulla

Batticaloa

The East
(see pp184–199)

Kandy   Mahiyangana

Kandy and the Hill Country
(see pp130–153)

Nuwara Eliya

Arugam Bay

Temple of the Tooth *(see pp136–7)*, situated in the cultural capital of Kandy, is home to Sri Lanka's most venerated Buddhist relic – the Buddha's tooth.

The South
(see pp104–129)

Hambantota

Tangalle

Matara

Yala West National Park
(see pp126–7), famous for its large population of leopards, is popular with visitors who flock here every year.

COLOMBO

With its skyscrapers, chock-a-block traffic and frenetic pace of life, Sri Lanka's dynamic capital is markedly different from other Sri Lankan cities. For most visitors, Colombo is only a stopover on their way to the southern beaches, the Hill Country or the Cultural Triangle. However, this modern, overcrowded metropolis teems with energy and is one of the best places on the island to splurge in fashionable boutiques, sample a wide range of cuisines and enjoy a vibrant nightlife.

Colombo has long been a commercial centre owing to its natural harbour; Arab traders had established a trading outpost here as early as the 7th century. However, the city was still a relative back-water until the arrival of the Portuguese, who built a fort here in the 16th century. The Portuguese lost control of the area in 1656 to the Dutch, who then administered Colombo for almost 150 years before the British captured it in 1796. It was during the British era that the city's fortunes really changed.

Colombo was declared the capital of Sri Lanka in 1815; and by the 1860s, it was considered the country's major port, with road and rail links to the rest of the island. The city continued to prosper throughout the 19th century and has maintained its dominant status in post-independence Sri Lanka. However, Colombo has also had its share of tribulations. During the Civil War (1983–2009), the city was ravaged by suicide bombings orchestrated by the LTTE. The nation's capital took some time to recover from the war but it is now relaxing its security measures and welcoming large numbers of visitors once again.

The centrepiece of the city is undoubtedly Fort, where gleaming office blocks rub shoulders with Colonial-era buildings, while to its east lies the Pettah, a bustling bazaar district. The neighbourhood that attracts most visitors, however, is the well-heeled Cinnamon Gardens, home to superb museums and chic cafés. A plethora of upmarket hotels and swanky restaurants round off Colombo's charm.

The walkway leading to the inauguration hall, Seema Malaka temple

◀ View of the Slave Island neighbourhood, overlooking the glistening skyscrapers of Kollupitiya

Exploring Colombo

The vast urban sprawl of Colombo is divided into several neighbourhoods, each identified by a number similar to a postal code. To the northwest of the city, close to the harbour, lies the historic Fort (Colombo 1), punctuated by characterful Neo-Classical buildings dating from the British occupation. Fort is also the financial district with the best choice of high-end hotels. Located southeast of Fort, in the heart of Colombo, Slave Island (Colombo 2) is renowned for the glorious Gangaramaya Temple. The island is bounded on three sides by the Beira Lake, where the Seema Malaka shrine can be found. The southern suburb of Kollupitiya (Colombo 3) is Colombo's main shopping hub, while modish boutiques and cafés nestle in the shady avenues of Cinnamon Gardens (Colombo 7), which is also home to the superb Colombo National Museum. In addition, the city's neighbourhoods are dotted with *kovils*, mosques, churches and Buddhist landmarks.

Sights at a Glance

Historic Buildings
1 Grand Oriental Hotel
10 Old Town Hall
23 No. 11, 33rd Lane

Museums and Galleries
4 Maritime Museum
7 Dutch Period Museum
14 National Railway Museum
21 *Colombo National Museum pp78–9*
22 Natural History Museum and National Art Gallery

Religious Buildings
2 St Peter's Church
3 Sambodhi Chaitya
8 Mosques in Pettah and Kotahena
9 Hindu Temples in Pettah and Kotahena
11 Wolvendaal Church
12 St Anthony's Church
13 Santa Lucia Cathedral
17 Beira Lake and Seema Malaka
18 Gangaramaya Temple
28 Kelaniya Raja Maha Vihara

Parks, Zoos and Areas of Natural Beauty
15 Galle Face Green
20 Vihara Mahadevi Park
25 Talangama Wetlands
26 Dehiwala Zoo

Shops and Markets
5 Old Dutch Hospital
6 The Pettah

Streets and Neighbourhoods
16 Slave Island
19 Cinnamon Gardens
24 Galle Road
27 Mount Lavinia

Serene Seema Malaka shrine in the middle of Beira Lake

For hotels and restaurants in this region see p216 and pp226–8

Ninth-century bronze statue, National Museum

VISITORS' CHECKLIST

Practical information
Road map B5.
🚇 6,47,100 ✈ Bandaranaike
International Airport. ✈ 🚌
🚌 Ⓣ
ℹ️ Tourism Development
Authority: 80, Galle Road, Col 3.
Tel (011) 476 6330. **Closed** Sun.
🎭 Feb: Navam Perahera.

0 km		1
0 mile		1

Getting Around

Colombo is quite spread out and walking around can be pretty exhausting. Three-wheelers, which can be found on street corners all over the city, are the most popular form of transport among visitors. Many of these vehicles have metres installed – make sure that they are turned on before setting off. There is also the option of either hiring a metred taxi or travelling by local bus. Keep in mind that buses are often very crowded and are not ideal for travelling long distances. Some hotels and tour operators offer tours of the city in air-conditioned cars. The Sri Lanka Tourism Development Authority and Ebert Silva Holidays organize an open-top double-decker bus tour on weekends.

Greater Colombo

Key

🟦 Major sight
🟦 Sight
▬▬ Major road
═══ Minor road
═══ Railway

Key

🟦 Area of the main map

A Walk around Colombo Fort

Original site of Colombo's 16th-century Portuguese fortifications, the area known as Fort is the commercial hub of the city. Although the fortifications, which lent the area its name, have long since disappeared, and the district has extended far beyond the original fort's limits, Colonial influences are still apparent in the area's architecture. Today, Fort is home to government offices, banks, corporations and upmarket hotels, with the World Trade Center and the Hilton Colombo buildings dominating the skyline. The area is a High Security Zone, as the President's House is located here, and security checkpoints and barricades are commonplace. However, navigating Fort's streets is fairly easy and this walk is a great introduction to the city.

❹ Maritime Museum
Occupying a former Dutch prison, this museum is easily identified by the cannons that flank its entrance.

❸ Sambodhi Chaitya
This unusual yet imposing *dagoba* is perched on four stilts with the road running beneath it. Head up to the terrace for excellent views of the harbour.

Lighthouse
Constructed in 1952, this lighthouse was decreed out of bounds for the public during the Civil War. The tower, surrounded by four lion sculptures, still cannot be visited but there is a walkway around the base which offers good views. Below is a Colonial-era saltwater pool.

Tips for Walkers

Starting point: Old Parliament House
Length: About 3 km (2 miles).
Getting there: Colombo Fort is easily reached from the main hotels by three-wheeler or taxi.
Stopping off points: The Old Dutch Hospital has a number of restaurants and bars, and cafés are plentiful in the World Trade Center.
Word of warning: Visitors are advised to steer clear of touts and should politely but firmly refuse any offers they make.

❺ Old Dutch Hospital
This shopping and eating area is an exciting addition to Fort. The complex's ochre-coloured buildings are home to a fine selection of restaurants and stores.

Maritime Museum
Sambodhi Chaitya
Lighthouse
CHURCH STREET
CHAITYA ROAD
BUCK ROAD
GALLE
FLAGSTAFF STREET
GORDON GARDE
JANADHIPATHI MW
President's House
CHAITYA ROAD (MARINE DRIVE)
FLAGSTAFF STREET
JANADHIPATHI MAWATHA
Old Du Hosp
BANK

❷ St Peter's Church
This grey-blue Neo-Classical
building is a peaceful place to
escape the hubbub of Colombo.

❶ Grand Oriental Hotel
Advertised in the 19th
century as "the first
modern hotel known
in the East", the Grand
Oriental was once the
accommodation of choice
for visitors arriving in
Sri Lanka by sea.

Key

••• Walk route

Cargills
The red-and-white façade of the Colonial-era
Cargills department store is a Fort landmark.
Inside, the iconic heavy wood display cases
seem to date all the way back to the store's
opening in 1906.

0 metres	150
0 yards	150

Old Parliament House
Built by the British in the 1930s, this
impressive building served as Sri Lanka's
parliament until 1983. It is now the
Secretariat and can only be viewed
from the outside.

World Trade Center
Opened in 1997,
these modern twin
towers of glass and
concrete house
offices, cafés and
gem retail outlets.

For map symbols *see back flap*

Colonial façade of the Grand Oriental Hotel, Fort area

❶ Grand Oriental Hotel

2 York Street, Col 1. **City map** 1 B3.
Tel (011) 232 0320. Ⓣ **Open** daily.
📧 from Harbour Room restaurant.
♿ 🕸 **grandoriental.com**

Located opposite the Port of Colombo, this landmark was originally built in 1837 as an army barracks before being converted into the Grand Oriental Hotel in 1875. It was once one of the finest hotels in the city, and accommodated passengers who arrived in Sri Lanka by ocean liner. Anton Chekhov was a guest at the hotel in 1890. According to some sources, his short story *Gusev* was penned during his stay here.

Although no longer attracting film stars or royalty, and lacking most of its former Colonial elegance, the hotel retains its imposing façade. Don't miss the view of the port from the large windows of the fourth- floor Harbour Room restaurant.

❷ St Peter's Church

26 Church Street, Col 1. **City map** 1 B3.
Ⓣ **Open** 7am–5pm daily. ♿ 🕇
Communion: 12:30pm Wed, 10am Sun.

Tucked between the Grand Oriental Hotel building and the military checkpoint, St Peter's Church is easy to miss. Although the area east of the hotel is off limits to the public, the church can be accessed by ducking under the military barricade.

A Dutch governor's residence in the 17th century, the building was first used for worship in 1804 by the British as a garrison church before being officially consecrated on 22 May 1821. Despite the pleasing blue-grey exterior, the church's interior is quite bare except for some memorial stones adorning the walls. Cool and quiet, the church is an atmospheric place that is usually deserted unless a service is in progress, and provides welcome relief from the bustle of Colombo. Visitors who are interested in learning more about St Peter's can pick up a free leaflet near the door.

Murals adorning the circular wall inside the shrine, Sambodhi Chaitya

❸ Sambodhi Chaitya

Chaitya Road, Col 1. **City map** 1 A3.
Ⓣ **Open** daily. 📧

A modern Buddhist *dagoba*, Sambodhi Chaitya was built in 1956 to commemorate the 2,500th anniversary of the Buddha's death. Perched on stilts, 20 m (66 ft) above the ground, with the harbour road running underneath, it is a landmark for visitors arriving in Colombo by sea. The *dagoba* can also be seen from some rooms of the nearby Grand Oriental Hotel.

Inside, colourful murals depicting scenes from the life of the Buddha and important Buddhist events line the circular walls of the shrine. The elevated walkway inside the *dagoba* offers fantastic views of the busy harbour as well as Colombo's skyline.

There is usually a guardian on the grounds of the temple who takes visitors up in the lift and unlocks the door to the temple. There is also a staircase with some 260 shallow steps leading to the top. Visitors are expected to take off their shoes before entering the complex as a mark of respect. Note that the area around the temple, being in the vicinity of the President's House, is a High Security Zone (HSZ).

Simple interior and wooden altar, St Peter's Church

❹ Maritime Museum

Chaitya Road, Col 1. **City map** 1 A3.
ⓣ **Open** 10am–7pm Tue–Sat.
Closed Sun, Mon & public hols.
🎨 ♿ ♻

With old ships' cannons flanking the entrance, the Maritime Museum is housed in a former Dutch prison that was built in the late 1600s. It lies adjacent to the Sambodhi Chaitya temple grounds, and is maintained by the Sri Lanka Ports Authority.

Inside, an exhibition charts the history of maritime travel and trade in Sri Lanka, starting from the 5th century BC when Prince Vijaya from south India is believed to have landed on the island with his followers. Paintings depicting important maritime events adorn the wall and model exhibits of sailing ships are also showcased. In addition, the museum houses

Restaurant tables arranged along the corridor, Old Dutch Hospital

Old cannon situated at the entrance to the Maritime Museum

sculptures of prominent historical figures, notably Sri Lankan kings, artifacts relating to the workings of the port and various objects used by lighthouse keepers, pirates and sailors. The old, cumbersome diving suit on display will make visitors appreciate the sleek modern-day gear.

❺ Old Dutch Hospital

Bank of Ceylon Mawatha. **City map** 1 B4. ⓣ **Open** daily. ♿ ♻ 🖥 📷

Believed to date from the 17th century, the Old Dutch Hospital is one of the oldest structures in the Colombo Fort area. The hospital was originally built close to the harbour to treat officers and staff of the Dutch East India Company. The building has been restored and

is now an attractive shopping and eating precinct with outdoor seating.

With its low-slung, sloped-roof buildings arranged around two rectangular courtyards, the complex is a fine example of 17th-century Dutch Colonial architecture. The original 20-in (50-cm) thick walls block out the noise of the traffic and make this a popular after-hours meeting place for office workers, especially those from the World Trade Center, and tourists. Barefoot (see p236) and Odel (see p235) both have outlets here and there is also a good spa. The Colombo Fort Café, Ministry of Crab (see p228), the Hilton managed WIP (Work in Progress) (see p227) and The Brewery by O are some of the eating and drinking options; Heladiv Tea Club offers tea and cake as well as free Wi-Fi.

Stringent Security

On 31 January 1996, the Liberation Tigers of the Tamil Eelam (LTTE) drove a truck crammed with explosives into the Central Bank building on Janadhipathi Mawatha in Fort, and the resulting blast killed 120 people. This area – the commercial hub of Sri Lanka as well as home to the President's House – was already a designated High Security Zone, and following the attack, safety measures became even more stringent. Although security has been relaxed in recent years, visitors walking around the area will still see a number of military personnel as well as the occasional roadblock. Be aware that photography is still not permitted in certain parts of Fort.

Special Task Force commandos on patrol, Colombo

The well-manicured courtyard garden in the Dutch Period Museum

❻ The Pettah

City map 1 C4. 🚇 🚌 100, 101.
🚹 🅿

East of the Fort lies the Pettah, Colombo's chaotic and colourful commercial district. The name "Pettah" comes from the Tamil word *pettai*, meaning village. Compared with the rest of Colombo, this area has a particularly strong Muslim and Tamil influence. However, a range of different ethnicities and religions can also be found here. Hence, there are not only Hindu temples and mosques in the Pettah, but also churches and other places of worship.

Shops in the area are organized in a bazaar layout, with each street dedicated to a particular trade. While Front Street offers a huge variety of bags, suitcases and shoes, 2nd Cross Street is the place to come for textiles. Among the other famous streets is Gabo's Lane, where visitors can check out a variety of Ayurvedic ingredients (see pp38–9). Sacks filled with twigs,

Monks making their way through a busy street in the Pettah

bark, roots and leaves are a common sight outside the shops lining this street. North of Gabo's Lane lies Sea Street, known for its gold jewellery shops. In addition, the Pettah's open-air fresh markets are a delight for food lovers for the wealth of fresh produce and spices on offer.

Many visitors find exploring the Pettah hard work, as its streets are usually packed with traders, shoppers and vehicles. It is best to tour the area either early in the morning before the heat of the day takes hold, or during midday to avoid rush hour. Walk down one of the side roads such as Front Street, 2nd Cross Street or Bodhiraja Mawatha to reach the bustling heart of the area, which is best negotiated on foot.

The Pettah is also home to the Fort Railway Station and Colombo's bus stations. In front of the train station is a statue of Henry Steel Olcott, an American-born Buddhist who is honoured across Sri Lanka for championing the cause of Buddhism during Colonial times. He was also the co-founder and the first president of the Theosophical Society. Olcott Mawatha, the street named after him, is opposite the railway station.

❼ Dutch Period Museum

Prince Street, Col 11. **City Map** 1 C3. 🚹
Tel (011) 244 8466. **Open** 9am–5pm
Tue–Sat. **Closed** public hols. 📷

Formerly the residence of a Dutch governor, Count August Carl Van Ranzow, this 17th-century colonnaded town house served as a British military hospital in 1846 and as a post office in 1932. After undergoing renovation from 1977 to 1981, it reopened to the public in 1982 as the Dutch Period Museum, dedicated to the Dutch Colonial era in Sri Lanka.

Rooms downstairs contain a fairly decent collection of tombstones as well as old coins, military memorabilia and Kandyan artifacts. Upstairs, there are letters and documents as well as Dutch Colonial furniture such as beds and ebony writing tables. Although the displays here are only moderately interesting, the mansion and its charming courtyard garden are worth a visit for an insight into how the colonialists lived in the 18th century.

The exhibits are well labelled and the museum is fairly easy to navigate independently. However, be aware that it is common for staff members to guide visitors around the museum and expect a fee at the end.

❽ Mosques in Pettah and Kotahena

City map 1 C3 & E3. 🚹 Note: mosques remain closed to non-Muslims during prayer times and on Fri.

Islam was brought to Sri Lanka by Arab traders in the 7th century. These merchants, who dominated much of the trade on the Indian Ocean, gradually settled in its port cities. Of these, Colombo has a significant Muslim population, with many living in the Pettah and the neighbouring suburb of Kotahena to the northeast. Consequently, the area is dotted with mosques of all sizes.

Located north of Main Street, the main thoroughfare in Pettah, is the **Jami-ul-Alfar Mosque**. Built in 1909, the mosque has a striking, red-and-white brick exterior.

The impressive red-and-white exterior of the Jami-ul-Alfar Mosque

A short distance southeast from the Jami-ul-Alfar lies the more traditional **Hanafi Mosque**, which is the principal Memon mosque in Sri Lanka. Further east, Main Street leads to New Moor Street in Kotahena, where the large but relatively austere **Grand Mosque** stands. The most important mosque in Sri Lanka, this is where decisions affecting the island's Muslim population are made. This mosque was constructed in 1826, but further additions were made to the building in 1897.

C Jami-ul-Alfar Mosque
228, 2nd Cross Street, Col 11. **Tel** (011) 245 1975. **Open** 5am–8pm daily.

C Hanafi Mosque
3rd Cross Street, Col 11. **Open** 5am–8pm daily. ✉

C Grand Mosque
151 New Moor Street, Col 12. **Tel** (011) 243 2110. **Open** 5am–8pm daily. ✉

❾ Hindu temples in Pettah and Kotahena

City map 1 D1 & D2. 🚖 🎎 Jul/Aug: Aadi Vel Festival.

Hinduism was brought to Sri Lanka by the Tamil kings and their followers in the 3rd century. The religion's influence was particularly strong in Sri Lanka during the 5th century when it underwent a period of resurgence in south India. Today, *kovils* (Hindu temples) can be found all over Colombo. Many are situated in the Pettah and Kotahena, which retain a strong Tamil presence.

Located on Sea Street, the **New Kathiresan** and **Old Kathiresan** *kovils* are hard to miss, with intricately carved statuary of Hindu deities adorning their *gopuram* (gateway). The two temples are dedicated to Murugan or Skanda, the Hindu god of war and son of Lord Shiva. During the annual Aadi Vel Festival, these temples serve as the starting point for the colourful chariot procession.

Another *kovil* worth visiting is **Sri Ponnambalam Vanesar** in Kotahena. This temple was built in the mid-19th century from granite believed to have been imported from south India. It is simpler in appearance than the majority of Hindu temples; the grey-stone *gopuram* here stands in contrast to the richly painted ones seen elsewhere in Sri Lanka.

Shops selling garlands and temple offerings near the New Kathiresan Kovil

The *kovils* usually remain closed in the morning. The best time to visit is in the late afternoon or early evening when the temple priests perform the evening *puja*.

🏯 New Kathiresan Kovil
Sea Street. **Tel** (011) 243 1426. ✉ 🎎 Jul/Aug: Aadi Vel Festival.

🏯 Old Kathiresan Kovil
Sea Street. **Tel** (011) 259 9431. ✉ 🎎 Jul/Aug: Aadi Vel Festival.

🏯 Sri Ponnambalam Vanesar
Sri Ramanathan Road. **Tel** (011) 243 1252. **Open** 4:30pm onwards. 🚫 ✉

Gopuram of the Old Kathiresan Kovil with elaborate Hindu statuary

⑩ Old Town Hall

Kayman's Gate, Col 11. **City map** 1 D3.
ⓣ Note: the doors are usually open during the day.

Dominating the area known as Kayman's Gate is the Moorish-style Old Town Hall, which was built in 1873. The two-storey building served as the premises of the Colombo Municipal Council for 65 years, after which it fell into disrepair and was used as a public market. In 1984, the building was restored and reopened as a municipal museum that is now largely defunct. Today, it is possible to climb the stairs to the second floor to see a reconstruction of a council meeting, with wax figures seated around a table. The western side of the build-ing is lined by some picturesque fruit and vegetable stalls.

The adjoining wrought-iron market building houses indus-trial and municipal artifacts, including the first mobile library in Sri Lanka, a steamroller and old street signage.

⑪ Wolvendaal Church

Wolfendahl Lane, Col 13. **City map** 1 E2. ⓣ **Open** 9am–5pm Tue–Sun. 🈺 (donation). ⓣ 9:30am Sun (in English). 🔳 **wolvendaal.org**

The oldest Protestant church in Colombo, the Wolvendaal Dutch Reformed Church is considered to be one of the most interesting Dutch relics in

Wax figures portraying a council meeting from the Colonial era in the Old Town Hall

Sri Lanka. Started in 1749, the building was constructed over a period of eight years on the site of an earlier Portuguese church on Wolfendahl Hill.

Built in the shape of St Andrew's cross, this large sized church, with a red-and-white Neo-Classical façade, is easy to spot. It boasts an elegant interior, with a beautiful wooden pulpit, lectern and pews as well as an organ with patterned pipes. There are memorial tablets on the walls, and the floor is paved with tombstones. A number of 18th-century headstones of Dutch governors as well as those of other Dutch officials can be seen in the south transept. Some of the oldest tombstones can be found against the northeast wall of the church. Visitors are advised to use the rear entrance.

The old belfry that used to summon worshippers to the church in its early days now stands at Kayman's Gate in the Pettah.

⑫ St Anthony's Church

St Anthony's Mawatha, Col 13. **City map** 1 D1. ⓣ **Tel** (011) 232 9303. **Open** daily. 🈺 ⓣ 6am daily (in Tamil) and 12:15pm daily (in Sinhala). 🔳 **stanthonyshrine kochchikade.org**

Built in the 19th century, this Catholic church is dedicated to St Anthony of Padua, the patron saint of lost and stolen articles. St Anthony is believed to be a performer of miracles; it is said that a miracle by the saint compelled a Catholic priest to build a small mud chapel on this spot in the 18th century.

St Anthony is usually portrayed holding the infant Jesus in his arms, and a dozen such statues greet devotees both outside and inside the church. However, the most venerated statue of the saint can be seen on the side altar. Brought from Goa in India by a member of the church's congregation in 1822, the statue is thought to have miraculous properties.

The church is particularly busy on Tuesdays when people from all over the country, both Catholic and non-Catholic,

The red-and-white brick façade of the Wolvendaal Church

come to pray to St Anthony, who was buried on a Tuesday in 1263. The church is especially worth visiting on St Anthony's Feast Day (13 June), when it is decorated with brightly coloured lights reminiscent of Catholic celebrations around the world.

⓮ Santa Lucia Cathedral

St Lucia's Street, Col 13. **City map** 1 E1. **Tel** (011) 234 2850. Ⓣ **Open** 6am–7pm daily. **Closed** for lunch. 🕆 5:30am & 7am Mon–Sat, 6pm Sun (in English). 🎊 13 Dec: St Lucia's Day.

A Roman Catholic cathedral, Santa Lucia was built to resemble St Peter's Basilica in Rome. Pope John Paul II led a service here in January 1995.

Although the cathedral's origins can be traced back to the 18th century, work on the current structure only began in 1873. Crowned by a silver dome that can be seen from afar, the cathedral has an imposing façade, with a large clock installed in 1934, above the entrance. It is wound by hand every 48 hours. The four bells in the belfry were shipped from Marseille in France and date from 1903. The largest of these is known as Anthony Thomas and weighs over 1,950 kg (4,300 lbs).

One of the many old locomotives on display at the National Railway Museum

Large and airy with high ceilings, the cathedral can seat up to 6,000 people. In contrast to the impressive exterior, the interior is relatively simple. Among the highlights are the statues of various saints, including that of St Lucia to whom the cathedral is dedicated, on the main pillars. There are also confessionals carved in dark wood along the aisles.

On the altar is a huge statue of St Lucia holding her eyes in the palm of her hand. The patron saint of those afflicted by eye problems, she is often depicted holding her eyes on a plate. Legend has it that a nobleman wanted to marry her for the beauty of her eyes. Wanting to live only to serve God, she tore them out and gave them to him. Other stories claim her eyes were gouged out at the

time of her martyrdom. The day of St Lucia is marked here, as elsewhere in the world, with a large procession.

⓮ National Railway Museum

Olcott Mawatha, Col 10. **City map** 1 E5. **Tel** (011) 243 5845. Ⓣ **Open** 8am–4pm Mon–Fri. **Closed** public hols. 🅿 🇼 railwaymuseum.lk

Housed in the well-preserved building of the former Colombo Terminus station, this museum is somewhat difficult to find, but train enthusiasts will find it worth a visit. The main room displays station clocks, various signs and railway crockery. The station platform showcases a collection of old locomotives, of which the Class 040ST, a steam engine, is the star attraction.

Five of the seven statues adorning the elegant exterior of the Santa Lucia Cathedral

The promenade in front of Galle Face Green, crowded with hawkers and locals

⓰ Galle Face Green

City map 3 A1. 🚌 100, 101. Ⓣ

A large, grassy strip of lawn with a promenade facing the Indian Ocean and the busy Galle Face Centre Road running behind it, Galle Face Green is a Colombo landmark. The Green was laid out in 1859 by Sir Henry Ward, who was the governor of British Ceylon from 1855 to 1860. There is a plaque commemorating him along the promenade.

The lawn was formerly used by British colonials for horse racing. Nowadays, it is a communal space where locals gather when the heat of the sun has faded. Kite flying is a popular activity here during weekends and holidays.

The promenade makes for a pleasant stroll and many hawkers sell food, kites and children's toys along the seafront. However, scammers and con artists prey on tourists here, so it is advisable to always be on guard.

⓱ Slave Island

City map 3 A1. Ⓣ

To the east of Galle Face Green is the area known as Slave Island, bounded by Beira Lake on three sides. The name is thought to date back to the Dutch occupation, when slaves – brought from the eastern coast of Africa – were used to rebuild Colombo's fort. The slave numbers grew and in the 18th century they staged an insurrection. However, the rebellion was quashed and from then on they were kept on the island overnight. The Dutch packed the waters surrounding the island with crocodiles to thwart any attempts to escape. Slavery was eventually abolished in Sri Lanka in 1845 by the British but the name persists.

The Island is home to **Sri Siva Subramaniya Kovil**, one of Colombo's most impressive Hindu temples. Dedicated to Skanda or Murugan, the temple was constructed for Indian troops deployed here during

The *gopuram* of Sri Siva Subramaniya Kovil, decorated with colourful paper flags

Colonial times. Its defining feature is a large *gopuram* topped with the usual colourful and exquisite Hindu statuary.

Slave Island is still a slightly scruffy neighbourhood with a derelict charm. However, since the construction of the luxurious Cinnamon Lakeside hotel *(see p216)*, the area's fortunes are changing.

🔲 **Sri Siva Subramaniya Kovil**
Kew Street, Col 2. **Open** 8–9am & 5–6pm daily. ⊠

⓲ Beira Lake and Seema Malaka

Beira Lake, Col 2. **City map** 3 B2.
Ⓣ **Open** 6am–6pm daily.

Located in the heart of Colombo, the placid Beira Lake attracts a variety of water birds such as pelicans, egrets and cormorants.

Walkway and main inauguration hall, Seema Malaka

For hotels and restaurants in this region see p216 and pp226–8

Visitors can hire a swan-shaped pedal boat to take a trip around the lake.

On the southern side of Beira Lake sits Seema Malaka, a meditation temple used as an inauguration hall for monks from the nearby Gangaramaya Temple. It was financed by a Muslim businessman who, having been ostracized by his community, decided to invest money in a Buddhist venture.

The temple was built to a design by Geoffrey Bawa (see p77) and is made up of a series of three platforms that are connected to each other and to the shore by walkways.

The colossal Buddha statue in the main image house, Gangaramaya Temple

⑱ Gangaramaya Temple

Sri Jinaratna Road, Col 2. **City map** 3 C2. **Tel** (011) 243 5169. 🚹 **Open** 8am–6:30pm daily. 🏛️ 📷 Feb: Navam Perahera. 🌐 **gangaramaya.com**

A short walk southeast from Beira Lake lies the Gangaramaya Temple, one of Colombo's most important Buddhist shrines as well as the focus of the Navam Perahera festival. The temple was established during Sri Lanka's 19th-century Buddhist revival, and comprises an unusual mix of Minimalist and modern Indian architectural styles.

The temple complex is made up of a group of buildings clustered around the main courtyard with a *dagoba* at the centre and a bo tree growing out of a raised platform. This is also where the temple elephant can be seen. Located across the courtyard is the main image house – home to a large orange-robed Buddha in meditation pose, flanked by elephant tusks and surrounded by devotees. Although the statue is brightly coloured and overpowering, the effect is nonetheless impressive. It is also worth looking around to appreciate the carvings on the walls and along the base of the image house.

The wooden pavilion opposite the image house is the library, where piles of antique ola-leaf manuscripts are flanked by Buddha statues from abroad. The upper floor can be accessed via the bo tree terrace, and a walk along the adjacent balcony affords a good overview of the complex.

Just off the courtyard, the temple museum contains an extraordinary collection of gifts accumulated over the years – ranging from Buddha statues to cameras. The 1930s Mercedes Benz parked outside was also presented to the temple and is a popular photo opportunity.

Visitors must take their shoes off inside the temple. Note, however, that the floor here can get very hot from the sun, so it is advisable to bring a pair of socks.

⑲ Cinnamon Gardens

City map 4 D3. 🚹 🏨 🏛️

Named after the cinnamon trees that used to grow here during Colonial times, this wealthy Colombo suburb is characterized by large houses, wide leafy streets and government offices. This is also where a number of foreign embassies are located. When the bustle of Colombo gets too much, the peace and quiet here is a welcome change, as is the range of tempting chic cafés and shops nearby.

Navam Perahera

Organized by the Gangaramaya Temple, the Navam Perahera takes place on *poya* day in February. Dating back to 1979, the two-day event draws people from all over the country and abroad. A procession of elephants, dancers, acrobats and drummers makes its way from Perahera Mawatha to the temple complex in a riot of movement, colour and music. The temple elephant, adorned in brightly coloured finery, carries the Buddha relics on its back. In stark contrast are the *bhikkus* – newly ordained monks in their saffron robes who make their way sedately past the onlookers.

Drummers heralding the temple elephant during the Navam Perahera

Magnificent array of buddha statues and *dagobas*, Gangaramaya Temple ▶

Bawa's bedroom at 33rd Lane, with the bed framed by an enormous traditional batik

⑳ Vihara Mahadevi Park

Ananda Coomeraswamy Mawatha (Green Path), Col 7. **City map** 3 C2. Ⓣ **Open** 6am–6pm daily. ♿ 📷

A large green space in the centre of Colombo, Vihara Mahadevi Park is named after the mother of King Dutugemunu (r.161 BC–137 BC). It is a welcome shady spot with tropical trees as well as orchids and exotic plants. The park attracts a wide variety of birds and occasionally the odd elephant may be spotted here with its *mahout* (caretaker).

The railings to the south of the park, along Green Path, display works of upcoming artists during the week and students' works on Sundays. The white-domed Town Hall, dating back to 1927, overlooks the park to the northeast. Reminiscent of the US White House, it is hard to miss. Further north is De Soysa, or Lipton Circus, one of Colombo's major intersections, where the Odel store (see p235) is located. Across the road from Odel is the impressive looking Devatagaha Mosque.

Local art displayed along the south railing, Vihara Mahadevi Park

㉑ Colombo National Museum

See pp78–9.

㉒ Natural History Museum and National Art Gallery

Ananda Coomeraswamy Mawatha, Col 7. **City map** 3 C3 & D3. Ⓣ Natural History Museum: **Tel** (011) 269 4767. **Open** 9am–6pm daily. **Closed** public hols. 📷 (additional charge for photography). National Art Gallery: **Open** 9am–5pm daily. **Closed** public hols.

Part of the same complex as the Colombo National Museum, this museum is dated and dusty but those interested in the island's diverse flora and fauna may find it appealing. There are various specimens in jars, including a pickled two-headed goat by the entrance, and informative display panels.

Next door, the National Art Gallery comprises a large room displaying paintings by Sri Lankan artists in a range of styles. Notable among these are canvases by George Keyt (1901–93). Temporary exhibitions are held in the rooms at the back.

㉓ No. 11, 33rd Lane

Off Bagatelle Road, Col 3. **City map** 3 C4. **Tel** (011) 433 7335. Ⓣ 📷 ⬤ pre-arranged tours 9am–5pm (last tour 4pm). ♿ 🌐 geoffreybawa.com

In 1958, Geoffrey Bawa bought the third in a row of four bungalows on 33rd Lane and converted it into a small living unit. He persuaded the landlord to sell him the other bungalows as and when they became available, and over 40 years he created this glorious town house, part of which can be visited today.

It was here that Bawa developed his interest in bricolage; incorporated into the house are articles salvaged from old buildings in Sri Lanka and south India. Stone rubbings from the ancient towns of Anuradhapura and Polonnaruwa coexist with a contemporary batik by Ena de Silva, one of Bawa's earliest associates. Another feature is the set of doors painted by Donald Friend, an Australian artist. The house has a sense of infinite space, despite having been built on a small suburban plot. Lightwells and courtyards allow ample natural light and the white floors and staircase add to the tranquil air.

Visitors enter the house through what was originally the first bungalow and is now a four-storey Modernist structure with a car port where a 1950s Mercedes and a vintage Rolls Royce are displayed. Bawa's bedroom on the ground floor, with its huge stacks of books, can merely be peeked into. The first floor's main draw are the inlaid doors by Ismeth Rahim, a well-known Sri Lankan architect. A sun-drenched stairwell leads to the rooftop terrace from the first floor.

The guided tour of the house includes a documentary on Bawa's life and works.

Geoffrey Bawa

Geoffrey Bawa (1919–2003) is considered to be one of the most important Asian architects of the 20th century. Born to wealthy Burgher parents, Bawa read English at Cambridge University and followed in his father's footsteps to become a lawyer. He soon realized that a career in law was not for him and went travelling. However, it was only after returning to Sri Lanka and buying the estate at Lunuganga (see p100) that he decided to become an architect. Bawa enrolled at the Architectural Association in London in 1956 and returned a year later to Colombo, where he set up a practice with other budding artists and architects, including Ena de Silva. Bawa's earliest collaborator was the Danish architect Ulrik Plesner, and together they worked on projects in the Tropical Modernist style. Although they parted ways in 1966, Plesner had a marked impact on Bawa's development as an architect. Bawa sought to create practical structures that blended modernity with tradition and which fused the inside with the outside. During his 40-year career he completed over 200 projects, of which very few survive in their original form.

Buildings in Colombo

Bawa was interested in blurring the boundaries between the interior and exterior in his designs, and sought to integrate buildings with their surrounding landscape. The capital is home to some examples of Bawa's signature style.

No. 11, 33rd Lane was developed between 1960 and 1998. A constantly evolving project, the house was designed to create an illusion of space in the congested urban environment of Colombo.

New Sri Lanka Parliament, in Kotte, was built to a design by Bawa between 1979 and 1982. An artificial lake was created with an island at its centre, and from this rose the symmetrical parliament buildings. References to Sri Lankan and south Indian architecture are apparent.

Seema Malaka, a modern temple on Beira Lake, was built between 1976 and 1978. Its design is thought to have been inspired by the forest monasteries of Anuradhapura, which had raised platforms connected by bridges.

Interior of bungalow at the Lunuganga estate

Other Bawa-designed Buildings

Bawa's legacy of great architectural designs is not limited to Colombo. Lunuganga was an abandoned rubber estate when he purchased it; today the property demonstrates Bawa's fascination with landscape design. Kandalama hotel (see p220) is another of Bawa's creations. A jungle hideaway with views over the Kandalama tank to Sigiriya, the hotel seems to melt into its surroundings. The Lighthouse hotel (see p217) was one of Bawa's last designs. Its colonially inspired architecture may be muted but look for the dramatic spiral staircase designed by Laki Senanayake.

㉑ Colombo National Museum

Located in a Colonial-era building dating from 1877, the Colombo National Museum was founded by Sir William Henry Gregory, the British Governor of Ceylon. The museum houses a plethora of interesting collections that provide a good introduction to the island's temples and ancient cities. The most engaging galleries on the ground floor are 2 to 5, which feature exhibits from the Anuradhapura period through to the Kandyan era. The highlight here is the elaborate Kandyan throne, which was used by the last king of Kandy, Sri Wickrama Rajasinghe. Upstairs, there are several paintings, masks, coins, jewellery, puppets and a skeleton of a blue whale that washed ashore in 1984.

★ Kandyan Throne
The gold-and-red Kandyan throne dominates the room. A gift from the Dutch governor in 1693, it was used by generations of kings, including Sri Wickrama Rajasinghe until he was captured by the British in 1815 and subsequently exiled.

Ground floor

Sword of Bhuvanekabahu I
Decorated with precious stones and the head of a dragon, this silver sword is said to have belonged to King Bhuvanekabahu I (r.1273–1284) of Yapahuwa.

★ Hindu Images
Most artifacts in this collection date from the Polonnaruwan era. The representations of Nataraja, the dancing form of Shiva, are particularly striking.

★ Bodhisattva
This bronze *bodhisattva* statue, sitting in a combination of the *lalitasana* (the position of royal ease) and the *rajalila* (the king's posture), dates from around the 9th century.

VISITORS' CHECKLIST

Practical information
City map 3 C3.
854 Sir Marcus Fernando
Mawatha, Col 7.
Tel (011) 269 5366.
Open 9am–6pm (last ticket sold
at 5pm). Closed public hols.
Note: Room 14 closed for
renovation.
w museum.gov.lk

Transport

Puppets
Puppets from India, Russia and other countries
can be seen here – all in the shadow of the blue
whale skeleton (1984) hanging from the ceiling.

Arts and Crafts
The objects of ivory, wood,
brass and shell displayed
here are fine examples of
Sri Lankan craftsmanship.
Highlights include jew-
ellery, delicate combs,
household items and
musical instruments.

Arms and Armaments
All manner of weapons,
from ceremonial ones
to those used in war,
can be seen in this
room. Exhibits include
richly decorated
swords, Colonial-era
guns, Kandyan
cannons and shields.

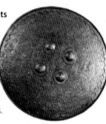

First floor

Gallery Guide

*The museum has two floors. Artifacts on the
ground floor are organized in chronological
order, while the first-floor collection is arranged
by theme.*

Entrance

Coins and Currency
Over 85,000 coins, from
the 4th century BC to
modern times, make
up the museum's
collection. Look
out for the ancient
punch-marked coins
as well as for the
Roman and Arabic
currency that is a
testament to the island's
trade history.

Key

- Pre and protohistoric periods
- Anuradhapura and Polonnaruwa periods
- Transitional period
- Kandy period
- Stone antiquities
- Paintings, textiles and ceramics
- Coins and currency and banners and standards
- Arts and crafts
- Arms and armaments
- Hon DS Senanayake Memorial Gallery
- Traditional agriculture
- Non-exhibition space

Visitors in front of the elephant enclosure, Dehiwala Zoo

㉔ Galle Road

City map 3 A2. 🚌 🚐 100, 101. 🚕

The backbone of southern Colombo, Galle Road connects the coastal suburbs to the city centre. The road splits into two one-way streets from Colombo Fort to Wellawatta, and runs a length of 8 km (5 miles). The further south the road advances, the less prosperous are the areas, but neighbourhoods such as Wellawatta make for an interesting wander for those keen to step off the tourist trail.

Immediately south of Galle Face Green (see p72) is the neighbourhood of **Kollupitiya**, where many of the hotels as well as the Tourism Development Authority are located. Also along this stretch of road are the US and Indian embassies and the heavily guarded prime minister's official residence, Temple Trees. As the road approaches central

Shoppers browsing through merchandise at Barefoot, Kollupitiya

Kollupitiya, visitors will find a number of popular cafés and shops, including the stylish Barefoot (see p236). Beware of scam artists who offer to take visitors to a gem show or an elephant festival, and persistent three-wheeler drivers looking for a fare.

Further south, Galle Road bisects the lively suburb of **Bambalapitiya**. This is one of the busiest areas of Colombo, with small roadside shops, large shopping malls, such as the Majestic City Mall, and a number of enticing restaurants.

A few kilometres south of Bambalapitiya, **Wellawatta**, also known as Little Jaffna, is an area with a large Tamil population. There are a number of kovils located here and many family-run businesses that offer a range of goods, including saris.

㉕ Talangama Wetlands

10 km (6 miles) SE of Colombo city centre. 🚕 **Open** 6am–6pm daily. 🚻

A short distance southeast of Colombo city centre are the Talangama Wetlands, made up of ponds, canals and paddy fields. Home to over 100 species of bird, this diverse area of wetland offers some exciting birding opportunities. Among the permanent residents are water birds such as the purple swamphen, egrets, herons, water jaçanas and kingfishers; and forest birds can also be seen year-round. During the migrant season from November to

April waders such as the common sandpiper, redshanks, greenshanks and plovers use this wetland as a stopover on their journey to the South Coast. Apart from birds, numerous species of butterflies and dragonflies can also be seen here, as well as some small mammals, such as the endemic purple-faced leaf monkey.

An urban oasis, the wetlands are bordered by motorable roads and are easily accessible.

㉖ Dehiwala Zoo

A Dharmapala Mawatha, 11 km (7 miles) S of Colombo city centre. **Tel** (011) 271 2751. 🚌 🚐 118. 🚕 **Open** 8:30am–6pm daily. 🚻 🚻 🚻
🅦 **colombozoo.gov.lk**

Spread over 11 ha (23 acres), Dehiwala Zoo is a popular attraction with locals. The animals housed here include elephants, jaguars, leopards, sloth bears, porcupines and monkeys. In addition, a rich diversity of birdlife can be seen in the attractive walk-in aviary. There is also a butterfly house brimming with 30 species. The afternoon display of elephant acrobatics is popular among locals, although many visitors will find this uncomfortable to watch.

Owing to the damage it suffered during the Civil War, the zoo has been undergoing extensive renovation. Although the enclosures for the big cats and bears are somewhat crammed, the zoo is better than a number of its Asian counterparts.

A pheasant-tailed jaçana perched on lily petals, Talangama Wetlands

Detailed Buddha mural at the image house, Kelaniya Raja Maha Vihara

㉗ Mount Lavinia

12 km (7 miles) S of Colombo city centre. 🚗 🚌 100, 101. 🚆 ⛵ 🚤

A beachside suburb of Colombo, Mount Lavinia is said to have been named after Sir Thomas Maitland's lover, a Portuguese-Sinhalese local dancer named Lovina. Maitland, who served as Governor General of Ceylon from 1805–11, established a residence in this area in 1806. Legend maintains that a tunnel connected the building to Lovina's house so the lovers could meet in secret. The building was lived in and expanded by successive governors until it was converted into the **Mount Lavinia Hotel** (see p216) in the late 19th century.

The imposing Colonial hotel, poised on a small promontory, towers over the beach and attracts many visitors, especially foreigners, to Mount Lavinia. The hotel has maintained its old-world charm despite modernization. There are excellent views across the sea from here, which can be enjoyed over an evening drink.

Mount Lavinia is a good, laid-back alternative to the bustle of Colombo. The beach is decent but can get particularly busy at weekends and holidays, when locals descend for the day. The sea is not great for swimming, but it is possible to watch the fishermen preparing to cast their nets. There are also a number of beachside bars and restaurants. Visitors are advised to exercise caution when walking back to their hotel after dark.

🏨 **Mount Lavinia Hotel**
100 Hotel Road. **Tel** (011) 271 1711.
Open daily. ✳️ 🏠
🌐 mountlaviniahotel.com

㉘ Kelaniya Raja Maha Vihara

12 km (7 miles) NE of Colombo city centre. 🚌 235. 🚆 **Open** 7am and 7pm daily (till 10:30pm on *poya* days). 🎭 Jan: Duruthu Perahera.

Located to the northeast of Colombo is the Kelaniya Raja Maha Vihara, a venerated Sri Lankan Buddhist shrine considered second only to the Temple of the Tooth (see pp136–7) in importance. Earlier shrines on this spot were destroyed by Indian invaders and later by the Portuguese colonialists; the present-day structure dates from around the 18th and 19th centuries.

A fairly plain *dagoba* marks the spot where the Buddha is said to have preached during one of his three visits to Sri Lanka, but this is upstaged by the elaborate image house. Made of yellow-orange coloured stone, the eye-catching exterior boasts detailed decoration with ornate door knockers and pillars; look out for the elephants flanking the entrance. The interior is covered with paintings, the most striking of which are the 20th-century murals by Solias Mendis, a renowned artist, depicting the Buddha's visits to Sri Lanka.

The tree-shaded temple grounds are home to a large bo tree, an impressive bell tower, two large statues and a small museum. Raja Maha Vihara is also the focus of the Duruthu Perahera festival (see p42).

The impressive Colonial façade of the Mount Lavinia Hotel

COLOMBO STREET FINDER

The map below shows the areas of Colombo covered by the Street Finder maps. The map references given for sights of interest in the Colombo section of the guide refer to these maps. Map references are also provided for Colombo hotels *(see p216)* and restaurants *(see pp226–8)* as well as for useful addresses in the *Travellers' Needs* and the *Survival Guide* sections at the back of the book. The first figure in the map reference indicates which Street Finder map to turn to, and the letter and number that follow refer to the map's grid. The symbols used to represent sights and useful information on these maps are listed below in the key. An index of street names can be found on the following page.

Key

- Major sight
- Sight
- Other building
- Train station
- Bus station
- *i* Visitor information
- Hospital
- Police
- Church
- Hindu temple
- Buddhist temple
- Mosque
- Railway line
- Pedestrian street

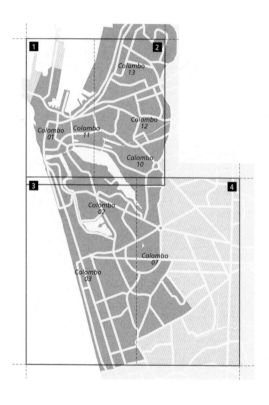

0 km   1
0 mile   1

Busy Sea street teeming with traffic, the Pettah

Scale of Map 1–2

0 metres   250
0 yards   250

Scale of Map 3–4

0 metres   500
0 yards   500

Street Finder Index

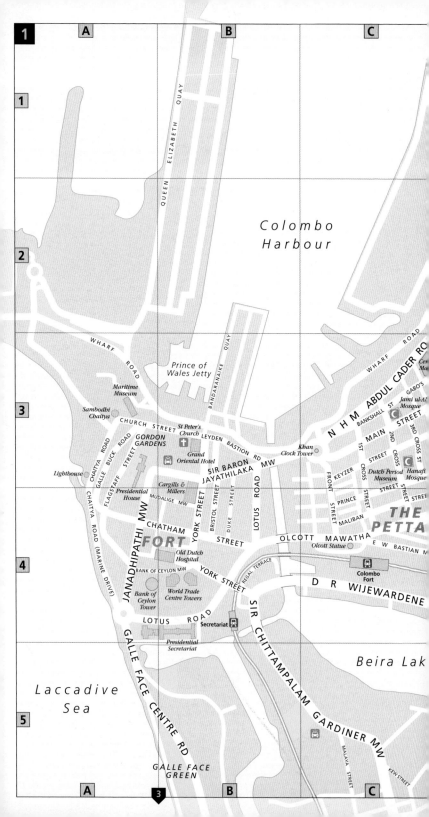

1

A   **B**   **C**

1

2

Colombo
Harbour

QUEEN ELIZABETH QUAY

BANDARANAIKE QUAY

Prince of
Wales Jetty

WHARF ROAD

WHARF ROAD

N H M ABDUL CADER RO

Cer
Ma

3

Maritime
Museum

Sambodhi
Chaitya

CHURCH STREET

St Peter's
Church

LEYDEN BASTION RD

GABO'S

BANKSHALL ST

Jami ul-Al
Mosque

C

MAIN STREET

3RD CROSS ST

GORDON
GARDENS

Grand
Oriental Hotel

Khan
Clock Tower

1ST CROSS

2ND CROSS

Lighthouse

CHAITYA ROAD

GALLE BUCK ROAD

FLAGSTAFF STREET

SIR BARON
JAYATHILAKA MW

KEYZER STREET

FRONT STREET

Dutch Period
Museum

Hanafi
Mosque

C

STREET

Presidential
House

MUDALIGE MW

Cargills &
Millers

YORK STREET

BRISTOL STREET

DUKE STREET

LOTUS ROAD MW

PRINCE STREET

MALIBAN

STREET

THE
PETTA

JANADHIPATHI MW

CHATHAM STREET

FORT

Old Dutch
Hospital

YORK STREET

STREET

OLCOTT MAWATHA

Olcott Statue

E W BASTIAN ST

4

CHAITYA ROAD (MARINE DRIVE)

Bank of
Ceylon
Tower

BANK OF CEYLON MW

World Trade
Centre Towers

YORK STREET

REGAL TERRACE

Colombo
Fort

D R WIJEWARDENE

LOTUS ROAD

Secretariat

SIR CHITTAMPALAM

Presidential
Secretariat

Beira Lak

GALLE FACE CENTRE RD

5

Laccadive
Sea

GARDINER MW

MALAYA STREET

KEW STREET

GALLE FACE
GREEN

A   ▼ **3**   **B**   **C**

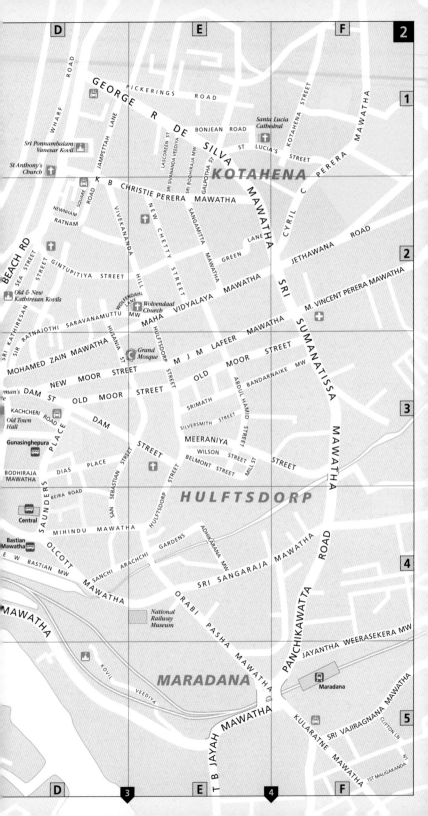

THE WEST COAST

Sri Lanka's West Coast was once a land of extremes, with the north a diverse yet isolated area barely visited by tourists during the Civil War, and the south offering beach resorts dedicated to mass tourism. Today, vacationers are beginning to choose the beachside resorts north of Negombo and making their way to the Kalpitiya Peninsula to enjoy the wildlife and beautiful beaches, while the famously attractive southern resorts continue to draw an ever-increasing influx of visitors.

Home to the capital city and principal coastal resorts, the West Coast is Sri Lanka's most developed region, and tourism is the main industry here. Stretching over 100 km (62 miles), the unbroken, palm-fringed coastline attracts many travellers to this part of the island every year. A diverse region, the West Coast offers attractions varying from busy commercial resorts, bucolic towns and pristine white-sand beaches.

For centuries, this region has served as a gateway into the country for foreigners; Arab traders as well as European colonialists were drawn to its strategic position along the major trade routes. Even today, the West Coast provides visitors their first taste of the country, as a major international airport is located here.

With numerous coastal resort towns, the northern seaboard is now firmly on the tourist trail. However, rural life carries on as usual in the region's provincial fishing villages. Further up the coast, the Kalpitiya Peninsula has much arable land and crops grow here abundantly. Yet it also has a few urban boutique resorts and is frequented by those who wish to escape the tourist rush.

In stark contrast, the picture-postcard southwestern beaches have always been popular with holidaymakers. There are watersports on offer as well as opportunities to observe diverse marine life. Premier resorts, such as Bentota, have a selection of high-end accommodation options as well as budget alternatives. The West Coast also attracts backpackers, who are drawn to the party atmosphere and surf in Hikkaduwa.

Sea turtle in the shallows near Hikkaduwa

◀ Palm trees leaning over the golden sands on a beach, Hikkaduwa

Exploring The West Coast

The seemingly endless West Coast is ideal for travellers seeking sun and sand. Towards the north of the province lies the largely untouched Kalpitiya Peninsula, carpeted by white-sand beaches and boasting exceptional resorts centred around Alankuda Beach. The peninsula offers great kitesurfing and whale- and dolphin-watching, and trips to Wilpattu National Park can be easily arranged from here. While travelling along the southwestern seaboard, many visitors choose to stay in the resort towns of Bentota and Beruwela, which are great bases to explore the surrounding area. Bentota is particularly well-known for its golden beach and characterful accommodation. In addition, visitors can undertake half-day excursions inland to the fantastic Brief Garden and the enigmatic Lunuganga estate. Surfers and diving enthusiasts are naturally drawn to Hikkaduwa, while Kosgoda lures wildlife lovers with its numerous turtle hatcheries.

Bungalow nestled amid vines and vegetation, Brief Garden

Sights at a Glance

1. Kalpitiya Peninsula
2. Wilpattu National Park
3. Munnesvaram Temple
4. Negombo
5. Muthurajawela Marsh
6. Henerathgoda Botanical Gardens
7. Kalutara
8. Beruwela
9. Aluthgama and Bentota
10. Brief Garden
11. Lunuganga
12. Induruwa and Kosgoda
13. Balapitiya
14. Ambalangoda
15. Hikkaduwa
16. Gangarama Maha Vihara and Seenigama Temple

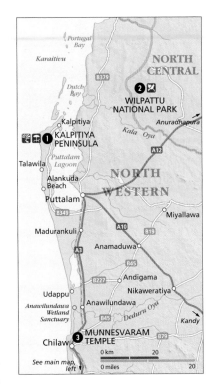

Getting Around

Many buses and trains operate in the West Coast. Some trains make frequent stops at stations, while some are express services to a particular destination. The main train stations are Negombo, Hikkaduwa and Bentota. However, the best way to travel around this region is by arranging a car and driver. In fact, visitors heading to the remote Kalpitiya Peninsula are limited to travelling by road. Many people choose to hire a bicycle when exploring Negombo and its surrounding areas. Outlying sights such as Brief Garden, Lunuganga and the temples located inland can be reached by car or three-wheeler.

Key

══ Expressway

═ ═ Expressway under construction

▬▬ Major road

∷∷∷ Minor road

⊶⊶ Railway

▬▬ Provincial border

Signs offering surf lessons on the beach in Hikkaduwa

For map symbols *see back flap*

❶ Kalpitiya Peninsula

Road map B3. 150 km (93 miles) N of Colombo. 🚌 🚊 🚲 at the fort in Kalpitiya. 🎐 Aug: St Anne's Church Feast Day, Talawila.

Located in the Puttalam district, between the Puttalam Lagoon and the Indian Ocean, Kalpitiya is no longer the isolated backwater it once was. The windswept peninsula and its outlying islands are now at the forefront of tourist development. However, the area, fringed with idyllic white-sand beaches, is largely unspoilt for the time being and makes for a superb getaway.

The peninsula has become a prime kitesurfing destination, and also offers dolphin- and whale-watching in season (see p119); spinner dolphins are abundant in the waters here. In addition, it is a good place to observe pelagic birds and waders, owing to the range of aquatic habitats that include mangroves and saltpans. Birding enthusiasts should take a boat trip on Puttalam Lagoon, and it is also possible to spot the Indo-Pacific Humpback dolphins – an elusive in-shore species – while out on the water early in the morning.

Many of the boutique resorts found along the coast facilitate other exciting activities such as fishing, snorkelling and windsurfing for guests. Among the most popular resorts are those at the alluring **Alankuda Beach**,

Colonial-era gravestones in the St Peter's Kirk complex, Kalpitiya

on the western side of the peninsula. About 10 km (6 miles) north from Alankuda is the village of **Talawila**, where the 19th-century St Anne's Church attracts thousands of pilgrims for the annual Feast Day in August. Some 20 km (12 miles) further north lies the small town of **Kalpitiya**. The Dutch constructed a fort here on the site of an older Portuguese fortification. It was built at the entrance of the lagoon to control King Rajasinghe's trade with India. The fort is currently occupied by the navy. Another reminder of the area's Colonial past is the rustic St Peter's Kirk, with gravestones dating from the Dutch occupation.

Windsurfing in Kalpitiya

The government's development plans for this beautiful and diverse area have been fraught with controversy. There have been accusations of land grabbing, as well as concerns for the local fishermen. There is also the added risk to the large coral reef off the coast of Kalpitiya, which is under threat from fishing, pollution and human interference. If the transformation of this area of rich biodiversity into a tourist centre is sensitively managed, it will help preserve the livelihoods of those who have lived here for generations.

❷ Wilpattu National Park

Road map B3. 86 km (53 miles) NE of Alankuda. 🚌 🚊 **Open** 6am–6pm daily. 🚲 🏛 Note: jeep and driver can be hired to explore the park at the entrance.

At 1,320 sq km (510 sq miles), Wilpattu is the largest national park in Sri Lanka comprising a wide range of habitats, including thick jungle, grassy plains, a section of coastline as well as a series of *villus* (natural lakes). Although most of the large mammals found in Sri Lanka, such as elephants, barking deer and water buffaloes, can be seen here,

Crocodile basking in the late-afternoon sun in one of the many *villus*, Wilpattu National Park

leopards are the biggest attraction. The park is also home to the elusive sloth bear.

Before the Civil War, Wilpattu was one of the island's most popular parks. However, it was shut down in 1985 following an attack on its wardens by LTTE cadres. The park reopened briefly between 2003 and 2006, but was closed again until it started welcoming tourists once more in 2010.

Wilpattu is a lot quieter than other Sri Lankan national parks. Wildlife suffered greatly at the hands of poachers during the Civil War and is still recovering; numbers here are significantly lower than in parks such as Yala (see pp126–7) and Uda Walawe (see pp122–3). Also, the vast expanse and thick undergrowth of the park keep animal sightings few and far between. Birders should have more luck than wildlife enthusiasts – Wilpattu is home to birds such as the crested serpent eagle, the brown fish owl and the brown-capped woodpecker. In addition, visitors may catch sight of crocodiles and water monitors in the *villus*.

For the last few years Wilpattu has been at the centre of a conflict between conservationists and the government. A Chinese-funded road, being built through the park to link Puttalam with Mannar, was considered "illegal" by conservationists because it passed

Devotees inside the richly decorated complex of the Munnesvaram Temple

through a recognized national park. Environmentalists highlighted the damage that the construction would cause to the park's ecology and wildlife. As a result, work on the road has been halted, but it is yet to be seen if the jungle will be left to reclaim the area.

❾ Munnesvaram Temple

Road map B4. 57 km (35 miles) S of Puttalam. 🚉 **Open** daily, evening *puja* at 5pm. 📷 🎦 Aug/Sep.

One of the few temples dedicated to Shiva on the island, Munnesvaram is an important place of pilgrimage. The main shrine houses a *lingam* (a phallic symbol representing Shiva) in its inner sanctum. The complex also has a number of other shrines dedicated to other Hindu gods as well as a Buddhist shrine.

The temple was destroyed by the Portuguese on a couple of occasions. It was later rebuilt before undergoing renovation in the 19th century and then again in the 20th century. Hence, certain sections of the temple look newer than others.

Munnesvaram is also the venue for a month-long local festival that takes place in August and September. Pilgrims come to make their offerings and chariots are paraded around the complex and through Chilaw town, located about 4 km (2 miles) to the west of the temple.

Those wanting to visit the temple must ensure they are modestly dressed, and remove their shoes before entering the complex.

Legends of the Munnesvaram Temple

Munnesvaram is thought to be one of the oldest Hindu temples on the island and there are many legends associated with its construction. According to folklore, the temple was established by Lord Rama after he achieved victory over Rawana, as recounted in the Hindu epic *Ramayana*. Following the battle, while returning to India in the *Puspaka* (flying chariot), Rama was suddenly seized by a sense of guilt at the blood spilled in the war. Seeing a temple on the ground below, he descended to pray. Consequently, Shiva and, his consort, Parvati, appeared and ordered him to establish *lingams* in three locations: at Konesvaram in Trincomalee, Thirukethesvaram in Mannar and at Munnesvaram. The modern-day temples are believed to be built over these very spots. Another version of the legend describes how Rama, passing over uninhabited land, saw a place to rest and decided to pray to Shiva. He sent Hanuman back to India to fetch a Shiva *lingam* but Hanuman, easily distracted, took a long time to return. Unwilling to defer, Rama fashioned a *lingam* out of sand to use in his worship. After his prayers were done – Hanuman had returned in the meantime – the group carried on to India but left the *lingam* in place, marking the spot where the temple foundations were subsequently laid.

Ornate *gopuram* with Hindu statuary, Munnesvaram Temple

❹ Negombo

Road map B4. 36 km (22 miles) N of Colombo. 🏘 1,21,933. 🚌 🚏 🛈

Many visitors choose Negombo rather than Colombo as their gateway to Sri Lanka due to its proximity to the Bandarnaike International Airport. It was one of the first territories occupied by the Portuguese and their missionaries converted many citizens to Catholicism in the 16th century. Portuguese surnames are common, and Easter is celebrated every year with the staging of the Passion Play in Duwa, a small island in the Negombo Lagoon.

The town has a smattering of roadside Catholic shrines and churches. Among them,

Fish spread out to dry under the sun at Negombo Beach

Painted ceiling depicting biblical scenes, St Mary's Church, Negombo Town

St Mary's Church, with its brightly painted ceiling and several alabaster statues of saints, occupies pride of place. There are also a few remnants of the Colonial period such as the Fort, built by the Dutch in 1672, which now serves as a prison. Additionally, there are some interesting temples, both Hindu and Buddhist, to explore.

Negombo offers a lively insight into life in coastal Sri Lanka. The economy relies heavily on fishing, and a visit to one of the fish markets can be a fascinating experience; but consider wearing closed shoes to avoid the inevitable slush.

Located a couple of miles north of the town, Negombo's beach is where most tourists decide to base themselves, as a wide range of accommodation options, as well as a number of restaurants and shops, line the sandy shore. While less hectic than the beach in Colombo, there are still many activities to choose from here, such as diving, kitesurfing and fishing. Swimming is not recommended since the sea can be rough, but many hotels have pools that are open to non-residents for a fee. Local boatmen also hang out on the beach, offering to take tourists out to sea or to the Negombo Lagoon in their *oruvas* (stylized canoes).

Visitors should note that Negombo Beach is not always very clean. Fishing boats and nets litter the sand at its southern end, and fish drying in the sun is a familiar sight. The northern part of the beach, however, is far more pleasant.

🛈 **St Mary's Church**
Grand Street. **Tel** (031) 222 2393.
Open early morning–mid-afternoon.
♿ ♁ Sunday mass.

Negombo's Canals

Negombo became a significant commercial centre during the Dutch occupation and its 15th-century waterways were expanded to help transport spices – particularly cinnamon, which grew abundantly in the area – from inland towns to the coast. These waterways, or canals, formed a sizeable network. Extending south to Colombo and north to Puttalam, they covered a distance of 120 km (75 miles), and once teemed with flat-bottomed *"padda"* boats. Today, it is possible to cycle or walk along the banks, or take a boat trip to observe bucolic life, while watching out for birds that frequent the area.

Settlements along the banks of the Negombo canal

❺ Muthurajawela Marsh

Road map B5. 15 km (9 miles) S of Negombo. 🚌 🚏 🛈 **Open** 7am–4pm daily. 📷 🛈 **Tel** (011) 483 0150, call in advance to arrange a boat trip.

Spread over 60 sq km (23 sq miles), this estuarine wetland, encompassing the Negombo Lagoon as well as mangroves and marshes, makes for a rewarding half-day excursion from Negombo. The marsh's varied aquatic habitats support the diverse coastal ecosystem that thrives here today.

The marsh is home to Eurasian crocodiles, macaque monkeys and water monitors as well as one of the world's largest snakes, the Indian python. Various species of birds such as kingfishers, egrets, herons, ducks and sandpipers can also be easily spotted throughout the year. However, a greater variety can be seen between September and April, when migrant birds arrive. Many species of butterflies and dragonflies have also been recorded here.

The visitor centre, located at the entrance to the marsh, provides information about the wetland. Boat trips can be arranged here or booked through hotels; a guided tour through the wetland is highly recommended. It is best to come very early in the morning or later in the afternoon, both to spot more wildlife as well as avoid the sun.

❻ Henerathgoda Botanical Gardens

Road map B4. 29 km (18 miles) SE of Negombo. **Tel** (033) 222 2316. 🚌 🚉
Open 8am–5pm daily. 🚫

These historic gardens were established in 1876 under the British. It was here that the first rubber tree, imported all the way from Brazil, is reputed to have been planted. Today, the gardens are home to an extensive range of palms, orchids and trees endemic

Serene golden Buddha statues surrounding the smaller *dagoba*, Gangatilaka Vihara

Taking a boat trip around the Muthurajawela Marsh

to Sri Lanka. Although not as impressive as Peradeniya (*see p142*), the gardens are still worth a visit and make for a pleasant wander.

❼ Kalutara

Road map B5. 42 km (26 miles) S of Colombo. 🚶 39,700. 🚌 🚉 🚉

Lively Kalutara is a large town situated next to the estuary of the Kalu Ganga river, from which it derives its name. Formerly a spice-trading outpost, today it is more famous as a scenic resort town.

South of the bridge across the Kalu Ganga is **Gangatilaka Vihara**, which was built in the 1960s. The temple complex houses a huge, white and entirely hollow *dagoba*. The cavernous interior shelters a smaller *dagoba* surrounded by four golden Buddha statues with a Buddhist flag suspended from the ceiling. The walls of the larger *dagoba* are decorated with murals depicting scenes from the *Jataka* (body of literature recounting the former incarnations of the Buddha). The windows below afford good views of the Kalu river and the town. On the opposite side of the road is a bo tree and some other temple buildings.

Kalutara offers Sri Lanka's finest mangosteens between May and September.

🏛 **Gangatilaka Vihara**
Open daily.

❽ Beruwala

Road map B5. 15 km (9 miles) S of Kalutara. 🚶 34,250. 🚉 🚌 🚉

The coastal town of Beruwala is popular with those seeking a quick dose of sun and sand. The beach here is broad, and lined with resort hotels and guesthouses. Beruwala fish harbour is especially popular among visitors who come to enjoy the lively atmosphere and watch different varieties of fish being unloaded from sizeable vessels; bargaining begins as early as 7am.

Historically, Beruwala is where the first Arab traders landed in Sri Lanka in the 7th century and established a Muslim settlement. **Kechimalai Mosque**, to the west of the harbour, is believed to mark the site of the landing.

🕌 **Kechimalai Mosque**
Open daily.

Colourful fishing vessels crowding the Beruwala harbour

Oruvas gracefully sailing in the sea just off Negombo's coast ▶

Donald Friend's installation at Brief Garden depicting scenes from daily Sri Lankan life – an outstanding example of mural design

❾ Aluthgama and Bentota

Road map B5. Aluthgama: 9 km (6 miles) S of Beruwela. 🚌 3,719. 🚍 🚉 Bentota: 9 km (6 miles) S of Aluthgama. 🚌 49,733. 🚍 🚉

The little coastal town of Aluthgama is a lively place with photogenic markets, as well as a selection of charming accommodation set back from the beach across the Bentota Ganga Lagoon. The town's main street is lined with shops; stretching along its west side is the vibrant fish market, where all varieties of seafood is piled on benches. The open-air produce market to the south of the road is also worth a visit. It is particularly busy on Mondays, when it is packed with vendors.

About 1 km (0.6 miles) inland, the serene **Kande Vihara** temple stands perched on a hilltop. It is home to a colossal white Buddha statue seated in the *bhumisparsha mudra* (see p177).

Sun-dried seafood for sale at the fish market, Aluthgama

Bentota is a favourite with tourists seeking package resorts. However, there is a wide range of accommodation available in town, including guesthouses and high-end hotels and villas. The beach is attractive, especially at its southern end, where dense groves of palm trees rise behind the wide stretch of sand.

The Bentota Ganga is a centre for a range of watersports. It is also possible to set off on a river cruise; visitors can spot many aquatic birds on these trips.

❿ Brief Garden

Road map B5. 8 km (5 miles) SE of Aluthgama. **Tel** (034) 227 04 62. 🚉 **Open** 8am–5pm daily. 🚫 📷 house.

Sprawling across 2 ha (5 acres), the paradisal Brief Garden is the former estate of Bevis Bawa (1909–1992), the older brother of Geoffrey Bawa (see p77). The estate was bought by Bevis's father in the 1920s and his mother lived here for many years. Bevis began work on the land around the house in 1929. It was still a rubber plantation then, but Bevis's painstaking labour gradually transformed it into the idyllic site it is today. He inherited the house from his mother in the 1940s.

The tranquil landscaped garden, with shady paths and stone steps, is a splendid space to wander and explore. A hilltop lookout, cement moonstone and the Japanese garden are only some of the many attractions. However, it is the low-slung bungalow that forms the centrepiece of the garden. Bevis Bawa was a writer and artist as well as sculptor, and the house is filled with artworks he created. The house also contains pieces of art designed by Bawa's friends, the most striking among which is the mural at the top of the stairs by Australian artist Donald Friend. Friend came for a visit to Brief Garden in 1957 and stayed almost six years; needless to say he left his mark on the decor. Apart from artworks, there are also photographs of Bawa himself, as well as his famous house guests, who included actors Lawrence Olivier and Vivien Leigh as well as British author Agatha Christie.

After a tour of the estate, visitors can enjoy a leisurely cup of tea under the shade of the trees.

Bungalow hidden behind the foliage, Brief Garden

For hotels and restaurants in this region see pp216–17 and pp228–9

Watersports in Bentota

The calm waters of the broad Bentota Ganga Lagoon are perfect for a gamut of thrilling activities year-round, making Bentota the de facto watersports capital of Sri Lanka. The area is popular among visitors, who come to enjoy windsurfing, kitesurfing, water-skiing and banana-boat rides on the river. In addition, angling enthusiasts can spend a rewarding day aboard a fishing boat as a variety of game fish including marlin, barracuda and tuna thrive in the waters. Diving and snorkelling are also popular activities along the coast and can be enjoyed from November through to April before the monsoon arrives. Canoe Rock is among the most notable dive sites in Bentota, accessible to divers of all levels. With extensive colonies of beautiful coral and schools of brightly coloured fish, this is a very large site that requires several dives to be explored fully. Equipment rental, lessons and package deals are all available at hotels, guesthouses and watersports centres in Bentota.

Water-skiing is among the most sought after activities on the Bentota Ganga, with both beginners as well as seasoned skiers guaranteed a great time.

Diving along the coast can make for a great experience. There are a number of dive schools that organize lessons for novices, and help them explore sites.

Banana boating on the lagoon is bound to elicit screams and shrieks of delight as the inflatable boat is towed at speed, with the driver navigating some sharp turns.

Deep-sea fishing boats spend around four hours out on the ocean casting for snapper and grouper fish. Anglers can take their catch back for dinner.

Windsurfing is popular in Bentota, with strong winds making for ideal conditions. Beginners are encouraged to practise within the lagoon whereas the more experienced surfers can take to the ocean.

⑪ Lunuganga

Road map B6. 6 km (4 miles) SE of Bentota. ☎ **Tel** (034) 428 7056. **Open** 9am–5pm daily. 🅿 🚫 of the garden by appointment (tour of the house only for visitors staying overnight). 🆆 lunuganga.com

Spacious suite in the main house, on the sprawling Lunuganga estate

The country retreat of Geoffrey Bawa (see p77), Lunuganga is one of the West Coast's most enchanting sights. Bawa bought the estate in 1947 at the suggestion of his brother, Bevis. The property was no more than an unremarkable bungalow amid acres of rubber trees at the time. The architect spent 50 years moulding it into what has been called a "civilized wilderness". In fact, it was Bawa's vision of Lunuganga that persuaded him to train as an architect in the first place. It was on this estate that Bawa often entertained his friends and where he worked on his ideas and honed his skills.

The gardens here appear so natural that it is easy to overlook the amount of work that went into transforming the land; earth has been moved, shrubs planted and tree branches been weighed down to give them a certain shape. The old rubber plantations have given way to a new landscape that often unveils stunning vistas at the most unexpected moment. Look out for the view over Cinnamon Hill, which is topped by a

dagoba and statuary of the Katakuliya temple. There are also many buildings around the estate, such as the elegant Hen House and the serene Cinnamon Hill House, which are typical examples of Bawa's brand of architecture.

Visitors who wish to spend more time exploring the estate can book accommodation in the main house or in one of the outlying properties.

⑫ Induruwa and Kosgoda

Road map B6. Induruwa: 6 km (4 miles) S of Bentota. 🚆 56,961. 🚉 🚌 ☎ **Road map** B6. Kosgoda: 11 km (7 miles) S of Bentota. 🚆 3,000. 🚉 🚌 ☎

Induruwa and its neighbour, Kosgoda, are Sri Lanka's prime turtle tourism destinations.

Several endangered species of turtles nest along the coastlines of these towns. In fact, the stretch of sand near Kosgoda is the most important site for turtle nesting on the West Coast. The Turtle Conservation Project (TCP) has set up a watch scheme to safeguard the eggs laid on the Kosgoda beach. There are also many turtle hatcheries on the coast near the town. These are frequented by tourists who come to watch the baby turtles being incubated.

Kosgoda also offers a decent beach and accommodation options, while Induruwa boasts a beautiful stretch of coast and the sea here is safe for swimming.

⑬ Balapitiya

Road map B6. 8 km (5 miles) S of Kosgoda. 🚆 67,207. 🚌 ☎

The tiny village of Balapitiya is the starting point for boat trips up the Madu Ganga river. These river safaris offer visitors the chance to see a range of birdlife as well as amphibians and reptiles. There are 64 islands along this stretch of river, some of which are inhabited. One island is home to a large Buddhist temple adorned with paintings and sculptures. On another, visitors can watch a demonstration of how cinnamon oil is extracted from the tree bark by residents. For many tourists, the highlight of the trip is passing through the dense mangrove forest or "mangrove caves". Note that the boat rides can be quite expensive.

Boat crossing the mangrove caves on the Madu Ganga, Balapitiya

Turtle Hatcheries and Conservation

Five of the world's seven species of turtles – the green turtle, the leatherback, the olive ridley, the loggerhead and the hawksbill – nest on the beaches of Sri Lanka, especially around the southwest coast. These nesting sites are protected by the Turtle Conservation Project (TCP), which was set up in 1993 to conserve the dwindling population of these marine creatures. The TCP has field offices in Kosgoda and Kalpitiya as well as in Rekawa on the South Coast, and arranges viewings of turtles nesting and hatching on the beaches. It also aims at devising and pursuing sustainable conservation strategies through education, research and community participation. Hatcheries, such as those around Induruwa and Kosgoda, have been around since the 1970s. Their job is to collect recently laid eggs from nearby rookeries or buy them from egg collectors, re-bury them in protected areas and release the hatchlings into the open sea.

Turtle species, such as the green turtle, remain endangered despite many programmes put in place around the world to try and safeguard their declining numbers.

Baby turtles hatch from eggs laid in nesting sites. Female turtles usually return to the same beach every time they nest, and can lay over 100 eggs at a time.

Hatcheries keep young turtles in tanks for three days, during which time they can be observed by visiting tourists. However, the TCP is working with some hatcheries to encourage them to release the young the day they hatch as they miss out on valuable swimming time.

Hatchlings are released into the sea under the cover of darkness. Unfortunately, many succumb to predators on their journey back to the water.

Crowded coastline – a peril to nesting habitats

Threats to Turtles

Eggs being pilfered from nesting sites for consumption or sale is perhaps the greatest threat to turtle conservation in Sri Lanka. Nesting habitats are also in peril because of coastal development that leads to pollution on beaches. Moreover, the brightly lit coastline at night can confuse hatchlings on their way to the sea. Despite heavy fines levied on the poaching of turtles, they are still being killed for their meat and shells, in addition to being accidentally caught in fishing nets or hooked on long lines.

⑭ Ambalangoda

Road map B6. 24 km (15 miles) S of
Bentota. 🚶 20,133. 🚌 🚐 🚕

The town of Ambalangoda
is an interesting stopover
en route to Hikkaduwa, since
it is a production centre for
traditional Sri Lankan masks.
Hand-carved and hand-painted,
these masks were originally
worn by performers in low-
country (southern) dances,
especially Kolam, an elaborate
dance-drama, and Sanni Yakku,
a form of devil dance.

The **Ariyapala & Sons Mask
Museum**, in the town centre,
comprises two well laid out
rooms that display a superb
collection of masks focusing on
low-country dances. In addition,
photos of performers donning
the masks are exhibited.
The shop upstairs has masks
for sale, and it is possible
to see them being
made in the work-
shop next door.

There are many
other shops scattered
around town that
attract visitors, as the
masks make for great
souvenirs. However, it is
advisable to assess the work-
manship before buying one.

It is very rare to see the
dance performances for which
these masks were carved, but
the Bandu Wijesuriya School of
Dance *(see p240)* sometimes
stages shows during the tourist
season. Contact the Ariyapala
Museum for the schedule.

The immense reclining Buddha at Galagoda Sailatharamaya Temple, Ambalangoda

🏛 **Ariyapala & Sons
Mask Museum**
426 Main Street. **Tel** (091) 225 8373.
Open 8:30am–5:30pm. 📷 📷
🌐 masksariyapalasl.com

Environs

Mask on display at
Ariyapala Museum

About 8 km (5 miles) inland
from Ambalangoda, in the
village of Karandeniya,
the **Galagoda
Sailatharamaya
Temple** houses one
of the longest reclining
Buddha statues in Sri
Lanka. The sculpture is
all the more striking for
its faded orange and
red paint, which contrasts
starkly with the newer statues
elsewhere in the complex.

Further south, near
Meetiyagoda, there are many
moonstone mines. Peer down
the mine shaft to see the dirt
being sieved and observe
the gemstones being cut
and polished outside.

🏔 **Galagoda
Sailatharamaya Temple**
Open daily. 📷 (donation).

⑮ Hikkaduwa

Road map B6. 12 km (6 miles)
S of Ambalangoda. 🚶 1,01,382
🚌 🚐 🚕

Back in the 1970s, Hikkaduwa
was Sri Lanka's bona fide hippie
hangout. Today the town is
firmly on the tourist trail – a
typical beach destination for
a budget holiday, which
comprises lazing on the
sand and soaking up the sun.
Hikkaduwa is also popular with
young, independent travellers
who are drawn to the nightlife
and surf. The area boasts four
popular surf breaks; conditions
for surfing are best from
November to April. There is also
a range of other activities that
can be enjoyed here, such as

Hundreds of fish swimming in the shallow, translucent waters at the Coral Sanctuary, Hikkaduwa

For hotels and restaurants in this region see pp216–17 and pp228–9

diving, snorkelling, visiting the nearby turtle hatchery or taking a boat trip on Hikkaduwa Lagoon, situated just east of the town.

The **Coral Sanctuary**, at the northern end of the beach, has been an attraction for generations, and was declared a national park in 2002. Unfortunately, it has been a victim of the elements as well as of its own success. The coral reef was badly affected by bleaching in 1998 and was damaged further by debris from the 2004 tsunami. Over the years, it has also been ravaged by pollution, dynamite fishing, harvesting of the coral for lime and by people walking on the reef. Although most of the coral is now dead, there are certain areas where it is beginning to recover. Visitors can observe the coral from a glass-bottomed boat; trips are offered everywhere in Hikkaduwa but these are largely unregulated and the boats can damage the coral if they bump against it. A better way to explore the reef is to go snorkelling. It is a delight to spot colourful tropical fish and the occasional turtle, but keep an eye out for the hordes of boats drifting on the water above.

To the north of Hikkaduwa, at Telwatta, there is an evocative **Tsunami Museum**. Photographs of the disaster and exhibits on the subsequent reconstruction efforts are on display here.

Although a lively town, Hikkaduwa bears signs of rife and unchecked development. An unbroken succession of shops, restaurants, hotels and guesthouses are sandwiched between the busy main road and the beach, which erosion has reduced to a narrow strip of sand. However, newer and relatively pristine tourist destinations, such as Wewala, Narigama, Thirangama, and Dodanduwa, have cropped up south of the town. Things are quieter and more spread out in these places, and it is possible to find restaurants and accommodation options to suit all budgets.

Vibrantly coloured parrotfish swimming near the coral, observed during a dive

Diving in Hikkaduwa

One of Sri Lanka's most popular dive destinations, Hikkaduwa has a good range of dive sites. Some, such as off Coral Gardens, offer swim-through caves and valleys that can be explored. Tropical fish abound, but the real reason go underwater is to see the red and orange coral. Diving the rock formations at Kirala Gala, about a mile offshore, can also be very rewarding, with its stunning coral and an abundance of fish such as wrasse, angelfish, parrotfish and trigger fish. It is, however, a deep dive at 40 m (131 ft) and is only open to experienced divers. There are also a number of shipwrecks that can be explored, such as *The Earl of Shaftesbury*, a 19th-century sailing ship, and SS *Conch*, an oil tanker that sank in 1903. Diving conditions are best from November to May and there are plenty of dive schools to choose from.

🏛 **Coral Sanctuary**
Open daily. 🖼

🏛 **Tsunami Museum**
Telwatta junction. **Tel** (091) 390 0884. **Open** 9am–6pm daily. 🖼 (donation).

⑯ Gangarama Maha Vihara and Seenigama Temple

Road map B6. Gangarama Maha Vihara: Baddegama Road. **Road map** B6. Seenigama Temple: 2 km (1 mile) N of Hikkaduwa.

Located about 500 m (547 yards) east of Hikkaduwa, **Gangarama Maha Vihara** is worth visiting for its informative murals depicting the life of the Buddha. There is a bo tree and various shrines in the complex, which is often busy with locals.

The **Seenigama Temple**, located offshore on a tiny island, is dedicated to Devol Deviyo, a deity invoked by those seeking to avenge a perceived wrong. The smell of spices pervades the air during puja; chillies are crushed as part of the revenge ritual. The temple sustained no damage in the 2004 tsunami, which was considered very auspicious and symbolic of the power of the deity. Local fishermen also pray at the temple for protection and a successful catch.

The towering white *dagoba* and serene complex of the Gangarama Maha Vihara

THE SOUTH

Sri Lanka's South Coast is primarily a rural region, made up of somnolent fishing villages and towns, where stilt fishermen can commonly be seen perched above the surf. The province was badly hit by the 2004 tsunami, although little evidence of the destruction remains. Rich in both history and culture, the South boasts attractions ranging from Colonial-era forts to atmospheric religious centres. Visitors can explore the wealth of national parks in the area or even undertake a whale- or turtle-watching expedition.

The South Coast was part of the ancient kingdom of Ruhunu, with Tissamaharama as its capital and principal settlement. The region flourished mainly from trade conducted through the ports in Galle and Matara. The Portuguese arrived in Sri Lanka in the 16th century and constructed a Fort in Galle, but they had to capitulate the area to the Dutch East India Company in 1640. When the British took over the country in 1802, Colombo became the main port and the south slipped into relative obscurity. Parts of the region still remain untouched by Sri Lanka's tourist industry.

However, the province is gradually changing. The Southern Expressway from Colombo to Galle has cut the journey time to one hour from three. The highway continues on to Matara, and combined with the new international airport near Hambantota, it is expected to bring many more visitors to the South coast.

The sheltered bay of Unawatuna, offering safe swimming and snorkelling, is a major draw for tourists, whereas surfers keen to escape the crowds can be found at the smaller beachfront settlements of Midigama and Weligama. Tissamaharama acts as a base for trips to the superb national parks nearby, as well as to the venerated town of Kataragama. However, much of the region's charm lies in simply travelling along the coast to experience local life in the villages. Fishermen and farmers continue to live and work as they have done for generations, even as large hotels spring up nearby.

A leopard sunning itself on a tree branch in Yala West National Park

◀ Stilt fishermen patiently awaiting their catch, Weligama

Exploring the South

The South Coast encapsulates all of Sri Lanka's characteristic features. It is home to some of the most beautiful beaches on the island, with snorkelling and diving on offer at Unawatuna and Tangalla. Whale-watching tours are frequently organized out of Mirissa, and Rekawa Beach offers some excellent turtle-watching. Wildlife-lovers can spend a rewarding day observing elephants at Uda Walawe National Park or tracking leopards at Yala National Park. Other important sights include the Colonial town of Galle, which boasts an atmospheric 18th-century fort, and Mulgirigala, a Buddhist site where the key to translating the *Mahavamsa* was discovered. However, Kataragama enjoys pride of place among the South Coast's diverse attractions. One of the most sacred places on the island, it is where pilgrims descend in droves during the annual Kataragama Festival.

Spoonbills wading in the lagoon at Bundala National Park, Tissamaharama

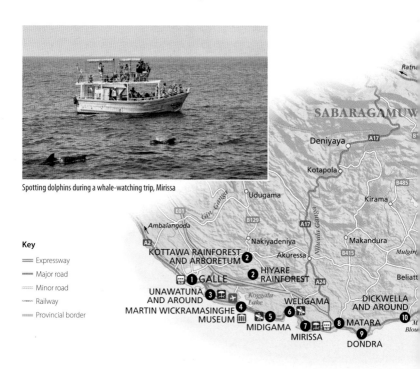

Spotting dolphins during a whale-watching trip, Mirissa

Key

▬▬▬ Expressway

▬▬▬ Major road

▭▭▭ Minor road

▬▪▬ Railway

▬▬▬ Provincial border

Sights at a Glance

Jet-ski and surfboats at the beach in Unawatuna

Well-preserved sculpture at the Mulgirigala temple

Getting Around

The best way to get around the South Coast is by car or bus, since distances between towns are often large and trains only run as far east as Matara. Bus services are plentiful along the coast, but having a car and driver makes it easy to stop at sights en route. Most visitors base themselves in Galle or Unawatuna to explore the surrounding area, and then travel on to Mirissa or Tangalla. Tissamaharama makes a good base to visit Bundala and Yala national parks. Three-wheelers are easily hired for journeys to outlying sights or between coastal settlements.

For additional map symbols *see back flap*

● Street-by-Street: Galle Fort

With excellent examples of Colonial architecture and well-preserved fortifications, Galle Fort is an atmospheric place to wander around. Located in the heart of the town, the fort encompasses the old Dutch quarter, and is far removed from the busy town just outside its walls. Galle's harbour had been attracting traders, sailors and explorers to its shores for centuries before the Portuguese built a fort on the promontory here in 1589. When the Dutch seized the port in 1640, they extended the fortifications, which survive to this day. Galle Fort's heyday was during the Dutch occupancy, when it housed a large number of families as well as administrative buildings and warehouses. In 1796, Galle was handed over to the British, who modified the fort, and over time its influence began to wane as Colombo became the focal point for commercial activity.

❶ Clock Tower
A Galle Fort landmark, the clock tower was constructed in 1882, on the spot where a Dutch belfry once stood.

0 metres	100
0 yards	100

❹ Dutch Reformed Church
An attractive Colonial building, this church was originally constructed in 1755 on the site of a Portuguese convent. It was restored in 2004.

Post office

❺ All Saints Church
Dating from the 19th century, this church was specifically built for the British community and remains primarily Anglican.

Clan House was a commercial building that once accommodated the offices of Lloyd's of London. The well-preserved Ships Arrivals Board can still be seen outside.

RAMPART STREET

LIGHTHOUSE STREET

MIDDLE STREET

CHURCH STREET

PEDLAR STREET

❷ Galle National Museum
This museum has archaeological and anthropological exhibits recovered from Sri Lanka's southern region. Exhibits include traditional masks and wood-carvings.

VISITORS' CHECKLIST

Practical information
Road map B6.
125 km (78 miles) S of Colombo.
🏠 90,270. 📅 Feb: Galle Literary Festival.

Transport
🚉 🚌

Main Gate

CHURCH STREET

❸ Amangalla Hotel
Originally built for the Dutch governor in 1684, this building was later converted into the New Oriental Hotel. It was one of Galle's most popular hotels and many ocean liner passengers stayed here in the 19th century. The hotel was renamed Amangalla in 2005.

Dutch bell tower

❻ National Maritime Archaeology Museum
Opened in 2009, this large museum is housed in a former Dutch warehouse, where ships' provisions and valuable cargo such as cinnamon, cloth and cowrie shells were stored.

QUEENS STREET

Dutch Government House

LEYN BAAN STREET

❼ Historical Mansion Museum
A private collection of antiques and miscellaneous objects belonging to Abdul Gaffar, a local gem merchant, is on display in this restored Dutch house.

Key
— Suggested route

For map symbols see back flap

Walking Tour of the Fort Ramparts

While constructing Galle Fort, the Portuguese concentrated on bolstering its landward side. When the Dutch expanded the fortifications they corralled the headland as well. The western ramparts, which are the most accessible, give the best idea of what the original Dutch fortifications would have looked like. The overall defences run for 3 km (1.8 miles) and the outer and inner walls are over 1-m (3-ft) thick. It is a testament to Dutch industry that Galle Fort has not only survived since the 17th century, but also withstood the force of the 2004 tsunami, suffering very little damage. The best way to appreciate these defences is to walk along the ramparts. Visitors may follow the suggested route or amend it, making forays into the fort and then clambering back up to the ramparts.

① **Main Gate**
The gate is part of the newer additions to the Fort, made by the British in the 19th century.

⑪ **Sudharmalaya Temple**
The temple complex houses a stark white *dagoba* dating from 1886. A bo tree can be seen on the opposite side of the road.

⑩ **Triton Bastion**
Cricket games are often underway around this area, which comes to life at dusk.

Tips for Walkers

Starting point: This walk starts from the Main Gate but the ramparts may be accessed from a number of points in the Fort.
Time taken: About 90 minutes.
Best time for walk: Go in the morning or during the evening to avoid the harsh midday sun. Triton Bastion is a lovely spot to hang out at dusk.
Stopping-off points: There are a number of excellent cafés and restaurants within the Fort, some with terraces overlooking the ramparts.
Guided tours: Themed walks around the Fort are organized by Sri Serendipity Publishing House (*see p249*).
Word of warning: Beware of touts.

0 metres   100
0 yards   100

⑨ **Flag Rock**
Located at the southernmost end of the Fort, Flag Rock is the point from where daring free-style divers fling themselves into the ocean.

THE SOUTH | 111

② Northern Bastions
This section of wall is the most heavily fortified as it faces the landward side. The Dutch enlarged the existing Portuguese fortifications, resulting in the impressive Sun, Moon and Star bastions.

④ Zwart Bastion
The Zwart (Black) Bastion is thought to be the oldest of the fortifications, and retains sections of the original Portuguese fortress.

③ Old Gate
This was the original entrance to the Fort. While the Fort side of the gate is inscribed with the Dutch East India Company's coat of arms, the port side is adorned with a British crest, which replaced the original Dutch crest.

Key

••• Walk route

⑥ Hospital Street
This street was where the Portuguese and Dutch hospitals were located.

⑤ Akersloot Bastion
Situated at the far corner of Court Square, this bastion is named after the birthplace of Commander Wilhelm Coster who captured Galle from the Portuguese in 1640.

⑧ Point Utrecht Bastion
This part of the Fort's defences is topped by a lighthouse dating from 1938. Behind the lighthouse are the ruins of a Dutch powder magazine.

⑦ Meeran Jumma Mosque
Rebuilt at the beginning of the 20th century on the site of the original mosque, this big white building closely resembles a church. Upon closer inspection the crescent and the Arab script reveal its true function.

Stark white façade of the Dutch Reformed Church

Exploring Galle

The most important town on the South Coast, Galle comprises the old Dutch quarter – enclosed within the Fort – and a sprawling New Town located outside the Fort's walls. The Fort forms the centrepiece of the town as most tourists come to Galle to explore the extensive Colonial-era fortifications – a UNESCO World Heritage Site – and other Dutch-period relics.

New Town has a few attractions for visitors. Unlike the Dutch quarter, which was largely protected by the sturdy walls of the Fort, the New Town was badly damaged by the 2004 tsunami. It has now been rebuilt, and an amble along its streets is a perfect way to enjoy the town's atmosphere. The bus and train stations are located here, and there are also a number of shops and other amenities befitting a big town. The Main Street, with its colourful pavement shops, is the perfect place for an evening stroll. Cricket enthusiasts might want to visit the Galle International Cricket Stadium, next to the Fort's Main Gate.

⬆ Dutch Reformed Church

Church Street. **Open** daily.
Ⓦ wolvendaal.org

The Dutch Reformed Church was built in the 18th century by Commander Casparus de Jong to commemorate the birth of his daughter. Cruciform in shape with a high, vaulted ceiling, the church is an imposing sight. Its pulpit is topped by a large, impressive canopy, and a balustraded staircase leads to the organ loft. However, the most striking feature of the church are the ornate tombstones laid into the floor and adorning the walls, which were moved here from Dutch cemeteries. The memorials underline just how hard life on the island was for the early colonialists. More tombstones can be seen in the church's grounds.

⏷ National Maritime Archaeology Museum

Church Street. **Open** 9am–5pm Tue–Sat. 📷

Housed in an old Dutch warehouse, this large museum showcases miscellaneous marine artifacts. The visit begins with a film screening that details the history of various shipwrecks, such as the HMS *Hermes* (*see p191*), off the East Coast of Sri Lanka. Items recovered from some of these sites are on display in the halls, and include maps, earthenware, beer mugs, smoking pipes and artillery guns. The beardman mug, excavated from the wreckage of the Dutch ship *Avondster*, is one such relic. In addition, the museum also covers other subjects related to the sea, such as the influence of shipping and foreign trade on Sri Lankan language, culture and history.

The museum's collection suffered extensive damage during the 2004 tsunami, and a number of artifacts were lost. In their place are some new exhibits that were found in the aftermath of the disaster, such as a wooden Buddha statue, believed to have been towed by the waves from an unknown location.

⏷ Galle National Museum

Church Street. **Open** 9am–5pm Tue–Sat. 📷 (extra for cameras and video cameras).

Located in a 17th-century building next to the Amangalla Hotel, the Galle National Museum exhibits traditional Sri Lankan dance masks, ancient wood carvings, ornamental objects and items dating to the Portuguese and Dutch periods. Some of the most interesting displays include weapons,

Detailed model of a ship on display at the Maritime Archaeology Museum

For hotels and restaurants in this region see pp217–19 and pp229–31

Artisan making lace using the bobbin technique, Historical Mansion Museum

furniture and porcelain, belonging to the Dutch East India Company and some exhibits relating to crafts such as lace-making. Note, however, that the museum is a bit dark and dingy and hasn't been renovated for many years.

Colonnaded exterior of Galle National Museum

🏛 Historical Mansion Museum
31–39 Leyn Baan Street. **Tel** (091) 223 4114. **Open** 9am–6pm Mon–Sat. **Closed** 12:30–2pm Fri

This restored Dutch mansion houses a private collection of antiques and bric-a-brac, belonging to Abdul Gaffar, a resident of Galle. Laid out in rooms around a small courtyard, the museum displays a number of interesting objects, such as a cabinet dedicated to vintage telephones and cameras, all of which have been accumulated by the owner over the last few decades. Lace-makers, gem-cutters and jewellery-makers can be seen at work in the building's courtyard and their wares are for sale, as are many of the displays in the museum.

Serpentine walking trail in the middle of the Kottawa Rainforest

❷ Kottawa Rainforest and Arboretum and Hiyare Rainforest

Road map C6. 17 km (11 miles) NE of Galle. **Open** 8am–5pm daily. 🚤 boat rides in Hiyare Rainforest.

Situated not far from Galle, the Kottawa Rainforest and Arboretum makes for an interesting day excursion. This isolated area, with a 1-km (half a mile) long walking trail, offers an easily accessible introduction to the Sri Lankan rainforest. The trail is shaded by towering dipterocarps, and visitors can meander around the undergrowth while admiring the epiphytes and keeping an eye out for reptiles, giant squirrels and purple-faced leaf monkeys. Leeches are rife here, especially in the wet season, so appropriate walking gear is a must.

Southeast of Kottawa, the second tract of rainforest centres around the serene Hiyare Reservoir, and offers excellent birdwatching opportunities. The rainforest is also home to hog deer and the rusty-spotted cat – the smallest member of the feline family. Wildlife-lovers can organize boat trips on the reservoir or visit the animal rescue centre, where injured animals are treated and then released into the wild.

Galle Literary Festival

Founded in 2007 by Geoffrey Dobbs, a prominent Australian hotelier, the Galle Literary Festival has become an eagerly awaited annual event. Over the years, many acclaimed international and Sri Lankan writers have attended the festival, including Germaine Greer, Tom Stoppard and Richard Dawkins. However, there was a call to boycott the festival in 2011 by literary giants such as Nobel laureate Orhan Pamuk, in the wake of the Sri Lankan government's alleged involvement in the persecution of writers and journalists. The boycott was not continued the following year but discontent carries on, with authorities being accused of organizing the festival in a "bubble of unreality". However, organizers claim that voices of dissent are welcome at the festival, and there are those who believe it is indeed a forum for open discussion.

Organizers at the pre-opening press conference

Baby elephants rummaging around the undergrowth, Uda Walawe National Park ▶

Kolam puppets on display at the Martin Wickramasinghe Museum, Koggala

❸ Unawatuna and around

Road map C6. 5 km (3 miles) SE of Galle. 3,800.

The village of Unawatuna is one of Sri Lanka's most popular resorts. There is a fine stretch of beach, although it has somewhat narrowed in places due to erosion and encroachment by local businesses. Numerous guesthouses dot the village, and restaurants, shops and tour operators abound. There are also street vendors trying to sell souvenirs or touts offering services such as taxis and guided tours.

Despite becoming increasingly commercialized, Unawatuna still attracts visitors with its laid-back charm and year-round swimming. A semi-circular belt of sand, the beach is set in an attractive bay protected at both ends by a headland. The water here is calm for most of the year and there are a number of watersports on offer, including snorkelling and wreck-diving. Other interesting activities include cookery lessons and yoga classes. Unawatuna also offers a vibrant nightlife, although it can sometimes get very noisy; music blaring from bars at all hours of the night during high season is commonplace.

At the western end of the beach is a *dagoba*, from where there are some good views over the surrounding area. Another attraction is **Rumassala**, a rocky outcrop behind the village. Legend states that it is a fragment of the Himalayas dropped by the Hindu monkey god Hanuman as he made his way back to Lord Rama, carrying the herb needed to save his wounded brother, Lakshmana. Another bit of the mountain is said to have fallen on Ritigala *(see p176)*. Higher up the Rumassala hillside is the modern, white Japanese **Peace Pagoda** from where visitors can enjoy great views of the Galle Fort. The hill is also known for the number of rare plants and medicinal herbs that grow on it.

On the other side of the hill is **Jungle Beach**. Often largely deserted, this is a good spot for snorkelling and can be a welcome relief from the busy main beach. Visitors can either hire a three-wheeler or walk the flatter, longer route around the hill to get to the beach.

❹ Martin Wickramasinghe Museum

Road map C6. 12 km (7 miles) E of Unawatuna. Open 9am–5pm daily. martinwickramasinghe.org

The excellent Martin Wickramasinghe Museum lies in the small town of Koggala. Although popular with the locals, the museum does not see many tourists. However, visitors will be rewarded with a glimpse of what life was like on the island up to a century ago.

The museum is inspired by, and devoted to, the life of Martin Wickramasinghe (1890–1976), a renowned Sri Lankan writer who, although fluent in English, chose to write in Sinhala. During his career, he penned a number of novels as well as non-fiction works, such as *Gamperaliya* (The Transformation of a Village, 1944), *Madol Doova* (Mangrove Island, 1947), *Yuganthaya* (The End of an Era, 1949) and *Kaliyugaya* (Age of Darkness, 1957), many of which have now been translated into a range of languages.

Spread around a huge garden, the museum complex comprises two sections: the **Folk Museum** and the writer's

Mask on display, Folk Museum

Turquoise waters and palm-backed beach, Unawatuna

Taprobane Island hidden under its cover of luxuriant trees at low tide, Weligama Bay

house. The Folk Museum displays a range of exhibits from traditional village life. The various objects of folk culture that the writer collected during his lifetime formed the basis of the collection when the museum opened in 1981. There are tools, cooking utensils, traditional games, a superb collection of masks and puppets as well as a re-created village kitchen. A number of exhibits are informatively labelled in both English and Sinhala. Behind the museum is a display of traditional modes of transport, including carts.

The house where Martin Wickramasinghe was born and spent his early life can be found towards the rear of the garden. Wandering through its rooms, visitors can see furniture such as the writer's desk as well as photographs, awards and books charting his life and career. Wickramasinghe's ashes are buried next to the house along with those of his wife.

❺ Midigama

Road map C6. 18 km (11 miles) SE of Unawatuna. 🏛 4,477. 🚉 🚌 ⓣ

Quieter than Hikkaduwa (see p102), the small village of Midigama is a surfer's paradise. It offers some of the most consistent conditions in Sri Lanka for surfers of intermediate and advanced levels. Popular spots include Lazy Left, a left break that is easily accessed from the beach, and Ram's Right, over a shallow reef in front of the famous Ram's Guesthouse.

❻ Weligama

Road map C6. 9 km (6 miles) N of Midigama. 🏛 21,783. 🚌 ⓣ

A sleepy fishing town, Weligama lies within the crescent-shaped Weligama Bay; visitors can check out the catch of the day at the roadside fish stalls. The town has also become a popular spot with surfers, especially beginners, as the waves here are fairly constant. A number of guesthouses strung out along the Matara Road offer board for hire and surf lessons.

Weligama is probably most famous for being home to Taprobane Island (see p219), which lies a short way offshore. The island was owned by the French Count de Maunay in the 1930s, who built an elegant mansion here. Covered in verdant trees, it now offers luxury accommodation complete with a private chef.

Stilt Fishermen

Stilt fishermen are synonymous with Sri Lanka. The poles, or stilts, are carved with notches to help the fishermen climb up to their crossbar, where they carefully balance themselves as they fish. The best place to catch sight of the fishermen is the coastline between Midigama and Koggala, particularly around Ahangama. They can usually be seen during the early morning hours or at dusk. Note that those out on the poles later in the day are primarily there for the tourists, and will usually charge a small fee for posing for photographs.

Fishermen balanced on their stilts, Weligama

❼ Mirissa

Road map C6. 7 km (4 miles) SE of Weligama. 🚏 7,163. 🚌 🚆

The languid village of Mirissa is worth a visit for its lovely beach and relaxing atmosphere, since it has mercifully escaped much of the development that has overrun the other beach towns on the South Coast. Busy resorts are conspicuous by their absence; instead tiny shacks and modest guesthouses line the stretch of sand, which is backed by a dense swath of palm trees. In the evening, restaurant tables spill out onto the beach and diners can enjoy their meals while looking out to sea. Giragala or Parrot Rock at the beach's eastern end boasts great views at sunset.

Mirissa's popularity has grown in recent years as it has become one of Sri Lanka's leading whale-watching destinations. In addition, both the western and the eastern ends of the beach are good for surfing as well as for other watersports such as snorkelling and sport fishing.

Inland, the town offers some pretty walks into the jungle; visitors can ask their hotel or guesthouse for directions. The Buddhist Kandavahari temple is located to the south of the beach and is accessed via a series of steep steps from the town's main road. Although the temple is rather ordinary and offers little to see, there are great views of the ocean from this vantage point.

The idyllic, palm-fringed beach at Mirissa, with a small cluster of shacks

❽ Matara

Road map C6. 45 km (28 miles) SE of Galle. 🚏 76,000. 🚉 🚌 🚆

A busy commercial town, Matara is a major transport hub with a railway terminal and a bus station. Not many tourists stop here and those who do usually stay in the nearby suburb of Polhena to the south. However, Matara has a rich history and there are some atmospheric sights to explore.

The Nilwala Ganga divides Matara into two parts, namely the Old Dutch Town and the New Town. The Old Town lies to the south of the river and is home to a fort built by the Dutch in the 18th century. Its eastern side is bound by ramparts that encompass a gateway dated 1780, and there is also a British clock tower, which was added later. The streets behind the ramparts hide dilapidated yet imposing Colonial buildings. There is a well-maintained **Dutch Reformed Church** here, with tombstones paving the floor. North of the river, the New Town boasts the hexagonal Star Fort. It was built by the Dutch in 1763, and is believed to have been erected to defend the main fort area after a Sinhalese rebellion in 1760. The structure has now been restored and houses a small museum.

Matara's seafront is pleasant despite the busy main road situated behind it. Additionally, the suburb of Polhena offers snorkelling as well as year-round swimming. Note that the area is often busy with locals at weekends and holidays.

❾ Dondra

Road map C6. 9 km (6 miles) SE of Matara. 🚏 477. 🚉 🚌 🚆

This tiny town was formerly an important religious centre. Known as Devi Nuwara (City of the Gods), it was home to a greatly revered temple dedicated to Vishnu, which was destroyed by the Portuguese in 1588. All that remains of the original structure is a small shrine thought to date from the 7th century. Today, the **Devi Nuwara Devale** is the town's main temple, with a huge statue of the Buddha within the temple complex.

A little way south of town, Dondra Head is where a 19th-century lighthouse marks the southernmost point of Sri Lanka.

🛕 **Devi Nuwara Devale**
Tangalla Road. **Open** 5am–7pm.
🎎 Jul/Aug: Devi Nuwara Perahera.

Peaceful spot on the Matara beach affording gorgeous views of the ocean

Whale- and Dolphin-watching in Sri Lanka

Over the last few years, whale- and dolphin-watching has really taken off in Sri Lanka. The country sits alongside one of the world's great cetacean migratory routes, and sightings are guaranteed for large parts of the year. Mirissa and Dondra Head on the South Coast are perfectly placed for some excellent whale-watching, with the former being the hub for expeditions and accommodation. While the migratory season lasts from December to April, the first and the last months are the best time to spot blue and sperm whales, as well as dolphins. Trincomalee *(see pp188–9)* on the East Coast has also been renowned for whale sightings since the 1980s and continues to attract large numbers of visitors. Blue whales can be seen here from February through August as they continue their migration around the island from the South Coast. Over on the West Coast, the Kalpitiya Peninsula *(see p92)* is best-known for its pods of spinner dolphins and sperm whales, spotted on a regular basis between November and March. As a result, Sri Lanka offers around 10 months of whale-watching every year at different destinations along the coast.

Spinner dolphins are regularly seen during whale-watching trips. One of the most commonly sighted marine mammals in Sri Lanka, these creatures enthrall their audience by leaping in the air and spinning a number of times before diving back into the ocean.

Blue whales can be seen off the Mirissa and Trincomalee coasts. A member of the baleen family of whales, they are thought to be the largest mammals ever to have lived on Earth and can reach up to 30 m (98 ft) in length. Also watch out for sperm whales, particularly around Kalpitiya.

Striped dolphins, spotted dolphins and bottlenose dolphins can all be seen in the waters off the island, while Risso's dolphins are less frequently spotted. They are a great tourist attraction but are increasingly being threatened by poaching.

Researchers from around the world visit Sri Lanka to study its aquatic mammals, in particular the blue whales. These can be seen just off the coast and some are thought to stay year-round instead of migrating.

View of the lush countryside from the third terrace, Mulgirigala

⑩ Dickwella and around

Road map C6. 15 km (9 miles) NE of Dondra. 🚏 54,370. 🚌 🚕

Located between Matara and Tangalla, Dickwella is a good base for exploring sights in its surrounding area. Although the town does not offer much to see, the long sandy beach here is worth a visit. The grilled cashew nuts sold at the roadside stalls are a must-try.

About 3 km (2 miles) north of Dickwella is the colourful temple of **Wewurukannala Vihara**, which is home to a 50-m (164-ft) high seated Buddha statue. Constructed in the late 1960s, it is the largest seated Buddha image on the island. A seven-storey building behind the statue allows visitors to climb up to the head from where there are good views of the temple complex. A large number of cartoon-strip depictions of scenes from the life of the Buddha can be seen along the steps leading to the top of the statue.

Dating from the late 19th century, the main image house in the temple complex contains numerous statues. However, the most unforgettable sight is a rather gruesome "chamber of horrors", which lies next to the main image house. The life-size models here portray various punishments inflicted on sinners; the narrow corridor past the models is lined with paintings of sins and the relevant punishments for such misdeeds.

The **Hoo-maniya Blowhole** can be found 7 km (4 miles) east of Dickwella. It is named after the sound it makes just before spouting water skywards. The blowhole is most impressive during the monsoon season, especially in June, when the waves are at their strongest and the water jets can be over 15 m (49 ft) high. At other times, it can be disappointing.

Located 22 km (14 miles) northeast of Dickwella, **Mulgirigala** is a monastic site comprising temples carved out of a huge rock outcrop. Rising dramatically from the surrounding forest, the 200-m (656-ft) high rock is reminiscent of Sigiriya (see pp166–7).

A gruelling climb leads to the summit, from where there are sweeping views of the countryside. There are four terraces en route where the small rock temples can be found. Housing reclining Buddhas and a variety of other figures as well as murals, the temples date back to the 2nd century BC, but were extensively renovated during the reign of Kandyan kings in the 18th century.

Translation of the Mahavamsa

The *Mahavamsa* (Great Chronicle) – a historical poem detailing the story of Sri Lanka – was written in the Pali language and was long considered untranslatable. In 1826, however, George Turnour (1799–1843), a Ceylon-born British civil servant and scholar, is said to have climbed the Mulgirigala rock with his Pali teacher, who was a learned monk. Here, at the Raja Vihara temple, he found among the *ola* leaf manuscripts a commentary on the *Mahavamsa* that proved to be the key to its translation. In 1836, he published 20 chapters of the chronicle with an English translation and more followed in 1837. Turnour did not live long enough to complete the whole chronicle, but his work paved the way for further translations from Pali.

The *Mahavamsa*, translated into English by George Turnour

The Buddha statue at Wewurukannala Vihara rising majestically behind a town building

The peaceful rocky shore of the Marakolliya Beach, Tangalla

As a result, the paintings here are similar in style to those found at the Dambulla Cave Temples *(see pp162–3)*. Of the four terraces, the third terrace is the largest and is home to the Raja Vihara temple where George Turnour found the key to translate the *Mahavamsa*. The summit has a small *dagoba*.

🧍 **Wewurukannala Vihara**
Open 6am–midnight. 📷

🌊 **Hoo-maniya Blowhole**
Open 8am–6pm daily, 📷

🧍 **Mulgirigala**
Open 6am–6pm daily, 📷 📷

⓫ Tangalla

Road map C6. 13 km (8 miles) NE of Dickwella. 🏘 10,500. 🚌 🛈

Visitors come to the town of Tangalla mainly because of the superb beaches that are located to the east and west. The town is also well-placed for day excursions to sights in the surrounding area and turtle-watching at Rekawa Beach.

Stretching to the east of Tangalla are the beaches of Medilla and Medaketiya. Dotted with guesthouses and restaurants, these beaches are the busiest and also the most developed. Around 4 km (3 miles) northeast of the town is Marakolliya, which offers more secluded stretches of sand backed by the Rekawa Lagoon.

Immediately southwest of the town are the tranquil Pallikaduwa and Goyambokka beaches with rocky coves and a series of bays.

⓬ Rekawa Beach

Road map C6. 10 km (6 miles) NE of Tangalla. 🛈 📷

Rekawa Beach is one of the most important sea turtle nesting sites in Sri Lanka. It can be reached from Tangalla via Tangalla Road. The beach is visited by five species of sea turtles *(see p25)* that come ashore at night to lay their eggs in the sand.

Although turtles lay eggs year-round at Rekawa, the best time to spot them is between March and September. Note that April and May are usually the busiest months for turtle nesting. The ideal time to turtle-watch is around the full moon, when they emerge out of the ocean onto the beach in large numbers and there is sufficient natural light to see them.

The Rekawa Beach turtle-watching enterprise is very low key, organized by Eco Team Pvt Ltd. Turtle watches are held at night, usually from 8pm onwards. It might take hours or only a few minutes to spot a turtle, so be prepared for a wait. Locals are spread out along the sand and will signal with a torch when a turtle has been spotted. Be aware that flash photography is not allowed as the light disturbs the turtles and confuses any hatchlings trying to make their way to the sea. There is a small hut at the top of the path where some information on turtles is exhibited.

⓭ Kalametiya Bird Sanctuary

Road map C6. 26 km (16 miles) NE of Tangalla. 🛈

An area of coastal wetland with saltwater lagoons, mangrove swamps and scrub jungle, the Kalametiya Bird Sanctuary is an excellent place for birdwatching. Among the birds that can be commonly sighted here are spot-billed pelicans, painted storks and crested fish eagles as well as egrets, lapwings and plovers.

A greater variety of birdlife can, however, be spotted during the winter months, from November to March, when the area is visited by a large number of migratory birds. The sanctuary also boasts a beautiful strip of beach.

Red-beak lapwing, Kalametiya

It is possible to arrange bird-watching tours at the village of Hungama that lies 6 km (4 miles) southwest of the sanctuary.

A green turtle laying eggs on the beach at night, Rekawa Beach

⑭ Uda Walawe National Park

One of Sri Lanka's most popular national parks, Uda Walawe was created in 1972 to protect the catchment area around the enormous Uda Walawe Reservoir. Spread over an expanse of 300 sq km (116 sq miles), the park lies in the dry zone and its landscape consists of scrub jungle, grasslands and an abandoned teak plantation. Although the park harbours a variety of wildlife, ranging from water buffalo and sambar deer to the rarely sighted leopard and sloth bear, it is best known for its large resident population of elephants. Home to about 600 of these pachyderms, Uda Walawe is a great place to observe elephants in their natural habitat. The park also supports a thriving population of water birds as well as birds of prey.

A safari jeep at the entrance to the Uda Walawe National Park

Water Birds
The Uda Walawe Reservoir attracts a large number of aquatic birds such as painted storks, spot-billed pelicans and cormorants. A greater variety of birds can be spotted from November to April, when migrants join the resident population.

Water Buffaloes
Large herds of water buffaloes can frequently be seen wallowing in the reservoir or near the numerous rivers meandering through the park.

Uda Walawe Reservoir

Elephant Transit Home

B427

Uda Wa Hydroel Power P

Uda Walawe Reservoir
This 308-sq km (119-sq mile) reservoir was built in the 1960s. Its waters are used to irrigate the agricultural areas nearby and also to generate electricity at a small hydroelectric power plant. The lesser adjutant, the largest bird in Sri Lanka, is often spotted near the reservoir.

Raptors

Birds of prey are plentiful in Uda Walawe. The park's open grasslands, peppered with light forest cover, form a suitable habitat for the raptor species. It is possible to catch sight of a white-bellied fish eagle near the reservoir, or a shikra flying low over the scrub jungle.

VISITORS' CHECKLIST

Practical information
Road map C5.
80 km (50 miles) NE of Tangalla.
Tel (047) 347 5892.
ℹ **Open** 6am–6pm dawn–dusk (last tickets are sold at 5pm).

Transport
🚌 Arranged Tour/Private Car.

Key

═══ Other road
═══ Minor road
▪▪ Trail
▬ ▬ Park boundary

Kauduli Ara

Mau Ara

ℹ

Mau Ara Reservoir

B427

B427

Entrance

Teak Trees from the abandoned plantation can be seen near the visitor centre. These trees were planted at the time the reservoir was constructed.

Elephant Sightings

Elephants are found throughout the park. They are usually seen in small groups, but it is possible to see herds of up to 50 or more. In the dry season, they mostly congregate near the Uda Walawe Reservoir or the rivers.

Elephant Transit Home

Supported by the Born Free Foundation, the Elephant Transit Home lies about 5 km (3 miles) west of the park entrance. Orphaned elephants are raised at the home until they are about 4 or 5 years old, when they are released back into the wild. Unlike at the Pinnawela Elephant Orphanage *(see p143)*, visitors here are kept at a distance from the elephants. There is a viewing platform, from where young elephants being fed in an enclosure can be seen. Feeding times are scheduled daily at 9am, noon, 3pm and 6pm. Be sure to arrive early before each feeding.

Feeding time at the Elephant Transit Home

Exploring the Park

A vehicle is required to enter and explore the park. It is possible to hire a 4WD at Kalu's Hideaway *(see p218)* or from outside the park gate. While elephants can be seen here year-round, birdwatching enthusiasts are recommended to visit the park between November and April. The best time to sight elephant herds is early in the morning or in the late afternoon.

⑮ Hambantota

Road map D6. 43 km (27 miles) NE of Tangalla. 55,249 🛫 🚌 🚍 🛈

Hambantota suffered a great deal of damage in the wake of the 2004 tsunami. However, both the town and the district have been at the centre of a concerted reconstruction effort. Being the home constituency of the president of the country has proved to be advantageous for the area. Construction of the Mahinda Rajapaksa Port, a largely Chinese-funded deep-sea harbour, began in January 2008. The port became operational in 2010; it is said that on full completion it will be the largest port in South Asia. In addition, an international airport, situated 28 km (17 miles) north of the town, commenced operations in 2013 and is expected to bolster trade and tourism in the area.

While Hambantota can be a good base for exploring the nearby Bundala National Park, the town itself doesn't offer many attractions to lure the casual visitor. It is pleasant enough to wander around though, and the viewing platform opposite the bus station is a good spot to observe the fish market or to look out over the old port. Three-wheeler drivers may offer to take visitors out to see the new port, the new convention centre, the airport site or the tsunami memorial on the beach. It is advisable to agree to a price before setting off.

Colourful fishing boats on the water, Hambantota

⑯ Bundala National Park

Road map D6. 15 km (9 miles) E of Hambantota. 🛈 **Open** 6am–6pm daily. 🚗 🛈 Note: jeep and driver required to explore the park can be hired in Hambantota.

A quieter alternative to nearby Yala National Park *(see pp126–7)*, Bundala offers ample bird-watching opportunities. The park extends along the coast for 20 km (12 miles) and is made up of scrub jungle and coastal dunes that are punctuated by brackish lagoons and salt pans. Among the birds that can be spotted here are brown-capped babblers, spot-billed pelicans, whiskered terns and painted storks. Bird numbers swell between September and March with the arrival of the migrants; many waders also visit during these months. Bundala is also known for its large flocks of visiting flamingoes, but

Water lily in Bundala

their numbers have dropped considerably in recent years. This decline has been attributed to changes in the salinity of the lagoons.

Along with birds, there are also many mammals here, including elephants, jackals and monkeys. Crocodiles can be seen around the lagoons, and the beaches are nesting sites for turtles.

⑰ Tissamaharama

Road map D6. 27 km (17 miles) NE of Hambantota. 63,367. 🚌 🛈

Founded in the 3rd century BC, "Tissa" was the capital of the southern province of Ruhunu. Today, it serves mainly as a base for Yala and Bundala national parks, though it does have a few attractions of its own.

A large tank called the **Tissa Wewa**, 1 km (0.6 miles) north of the town, dates from the 3rd century BC. It attracts a huge diversity of birdlife. To the west of the tank are other reminders of Tissa's rich history. Dating from the 2nd and 3rd century BC, **Menik Wehera** and **Yatala Wehera** are thought to be part of what was once a monastery complex. The latter is a white *dagoba* surrounded by a wall, which is decorated with sculpted elephant heads. Between the tank and the town lies the **Tissa Dagoba**. It is said to have been built by King Kavan Tissa, father of King Dutugemunu, and is thought to enshrine a forehead bone of the Buddha.

The large white dome of the Tissa Dagoba, a Buddhist shrine in Tissamaharama

Birds of Sri Lanka

Sri Lanka is a popular and rewarding birdwatching destination due to its diverse range of habitats, from the coastal wetlands to the rainforests and the Hill Country. Over 400 species of birds have been recorded in Sri Lanka, of which 33 species are believed to be endemic. Most of the resident species are found in the southwestern part of the country. Among these are the yellow-eared bulbul and the junglefowl, which is the national bird of Sri Lanka. Migrant birds arrive from Europe and other parts of Asia every year and add to the number of residents. A trip to a national park will usually yield some good sightings. Home to tanks, or reservoirs, the parks attract a large number of water birds and visitors are likely to see sandpipers, terns, egrets and storks. Other common species that are frequently sighted around forests and water bodies include parakeets, warblers, thrushes and brightly coloured kingfishers. The best time for birding in Sri Lanka is from November to March, but sightings can be had all year-round.

Lagoons, such as the one found in Bundala National Park *(see p124)*, offer fantastic opportunities to observe a wide variety of shore and seabirds.

The crested-serpent eagle is endemic to Sri Lanka and can be found amid thick forest cover. It has a dark body, with wings that have a bold black-and-white pattern.

The lesser adjutant is a large bird with a yellow bill and head, and thin grey down. It can be seen near water bodies or paddy fields in the low country dry zone and is listed as an endangered species.

The yellow-eared bulbul is named for its distinctive yellow ear tufts. This endemic bird is commonly seen in areas 1,300 m (4,265 ft) above sea level.

The male Indian peafowl has a distinctive train, or plumage. Found mainly in reserves in the low country, this bird can be spotted foraging in the undergrowth.

⓲ Yala West (Ruhuna) National Park

Situated in the southeastern part of Sri Lanka, the expansive Yala National Park is divided into five blocks, of which only Blocks I and II are open to visitors. Covering an area of 141 sq km (54 sq miles), Block I or Yala West (Ruhuna) is the more visited part of the park, largely due to its accessibility and leopard population. Punctuated by rocky outcrops, the park's sprawling landscape varies from thorny scrub forests and open grasslands to dense jungles and coastal lagoons. The park boasts a great variety of fauna, which includes elephants, spotted deer, civets and crocodiles. The birdlife here is also very diverse, with migrants swelling the ranks of the resident population in winter. Yala is also home to a number of cultural attractions, notable among which are the historic sites of Situlpahuwa and Magul Maha Vihara.

Area illustrated

Leopard Sightings
The Sri Lankan leopard is a subspecies endemic to the island. Home to around 35 leopards, Yala West is said to be one of the best places in the world to observe and photograph these felines. Although they can be sighted year-round, it is easier to spot them during the dry season (May–September).

Magul Maha Vihara
The evocative ruins of this temple date from the 1st century BC. Legend states that it was built on the spot where King Kavan Tissa (see p124) married Princess Vihara Mahadevi.

Exploring the Park

A 4WD vehicle is required to enter and explore the park, since walking is not permitted here. Jeeps can be easily arranged through one of the many tour operators in Tissa. All vehicles are assigned a guide, who accompanies visitors into the park. While it is possible to explore the place on a full- or half-day safari, most people choose the latter as a whole day can be exhausting. The ideal time to visit the park is either early in the morning or late afternoon. There are currently no limits on the number of vehicles entering the park, hence it can be very busy on weekends and public holidays. Visitors are advised to avoid making noise as it can frighten the animals and lower the chances of a sighting.

Situlpahuwa

Dating from the period of the Ruhuna Kingdom (around 200 BC), the monastic settlement of Situlpahuwa is an important pilgrimage site en route to Kataragama (*see p128*). A steep staircase leads to the bright white Situlpahuwa *dagoba*, which sits atop a 122-m (400-ft) high rock; the summit affords splendid views over the park.

VISITORS' CHECKLIST

Practical information
Road map D5.
20 km (12 miles) SE of Tissamaharama. 🛈 by the park entrance. **Tel** (047) 348 9297.
Open dawn–dusk.
Closed Sep–Oct (call ahead to check). 🐾 🎫 🏕

Transport
🚌

Tsunami Memorial

The park was badly affected when the tsunami hit the coast in 2004. This memorial was erected on Patangala Beach in memory of the tourists and park employees who lost their lives in the disaster. Next to the memorial stand the remains of a tourist bungalow.

Situlpahuwa

Menik Ganga

Akasachethiya

Yala

Gonagala
Wewa   Butawa
Wewa

KIRINDA – PALATUPANA – YALA ROAD

Tsunami
Memorial

INDIAN
OCEAN

Sloth Bears

The best time to spot sloth bears in the park is from June to July, when they can be seen perched among the branches of the Ceylon ironwood or palu trees, feasting on its fruit.

0 km   2
0 miles   2

Key

═══ Other road
═══ Minor road
▬ ▬ Trail
▬ ▬ Park boundary
-- -- Block boundary

Black-necked Storks

An endangered species, the black-necked stork can occasionally be spotted near the Butawa Wewa Lagoon on the coast.

For map symbols *see back flap*

⑲ Kataragama

Road map D6. 19 km (12 miles) NE of Tissamaharama. 🚶 18,000. 🚌 🚉 🎭 Jul/Aug: Kataragama Festival.

Sacred to Buddhists, Hindus and Muslims alike, Kataragama is one of the most revered places of pilgrimage in Sri Lanka. The town, named after the guardian deity of Sri Lanka, is busiest during the annual Kataragama Festival, but pilgrims come here year-round.

The sacred precinct, dotted with shrines and religious buildings, is located to the north of Kataragama. It is separated from the town by the Menik Ganga river, which is a place of ablution where pilgrims purify themselves before continuing on their way. The streets surrounding the precinct are lined with stalls selling fruit platters, lotus buds and garlands to take to the temples.

On entering, visitors will first come across the **ul-Khizr mosque**, which houses the tombs of Muslim saints. Adjacent to the mosque is a small *kovil* dedicated to Shiva. A series of other minor shrines line the avenue that leads to the **Maha Devale** – the main complex. Inside are three shrines, one of which is dedicated to the god Kataragama, also known as Skanda or Kartikeya. However, the god is not represented by an image but by his principal symbol,

Pilgrims ascending the steps of the Kiri Vihara

a *vel* (spear). The other adjacent shrines are dedicated to the Hindu deity Ganesha, and the Buddha.

The wall surrounding the main courtyard is decorated with impressive elephant heads and images of the peacock, Kataragama's *vahana* (vehicle). According to legend, the peacock sprang from the body of a demon who was defeated but spared by the god, after which the bird promised to serve the merciful Kataragama as his mount.

A typical fruit platter

The precinct comes alive during the evening *puja*, with queues of supplicants heading to the main shrine bearing fruit platters and other offerings.

Pilgrims also smash coconuts against stones in front of the shrine, sometimes setting them on fire first; it is considered unlucky if the coconut fails to break. Additionally, musicians playing trumpets and drums circulate around the complex. The ringing of temple bells, the music, the mass of people and frenetic activity make for a surreal experience.

An avenue behind Maha Devale leads to the **Kiri Vihara**, a *dagoba* that dates back to the 1st century BC. It is believed that the Buddha came here during his third visit to Sri Lanka and that the *dagoba* enshrines his hair relic. Surrounded by peaceful lawns, Kiri Vihara is far less busy than the Maha Devale.

Situated next to the Maha Devale is the **Kataragama Museum**, which houses religious objects, statuary as well as copies of the rock carvings at Buduruwagala (see p150).

Many visitors choose to visit Kataragama on a day trip from Tissamaharama, but it is also possible to stay overnight to observe the evening *puja* and soak up the spiritual atmosphere.

🛕 **Maha Devale**
Evening *puja* at 6:30pm.

🛕 **Kiri Vihara**
Pujas at 4:30am, 11am and 6:30pm.

🏛 **Kataragama Museum**
Open 8am–5pm daily. ♿

The Kataragama Museum in the sacred precinct

For hotels and restaurants in this region see pp217–19 and pp229–31

Kataragama Festival

The famous Kataragama Festival takes place at the time of the Esala full moon in July or August. During the festival, thousands of Hindus and Buddhists descend on the town to express devotion to the deity, to ask for forgiveness for their sins, to make vows and to request favours. However, the festival is best known for the various forms of physical mortification and self-mutilation that pilgrims undertake as a form of penance. Some of the most extreme measures include penitents rolling half-naked on burning hot sand, walking around the temple on spiked sandals and piercing their cheeks or tongues. Another unnerving spectacle is when a devotee is pierced with hooks and is then strung up on a pole and hangs face down. A couple of days before the end of the festival there is a fire-walking ceremony where devotees walk barefoot on red-hot coals. The festival ends with a symbolic water-cutting ceremony at the Menik Ganga.

The sacred relic, or *yantra*, is taken nightly from the Maha Devale atop an elephant and placed at the *kovil* dedicated to Valli. It is left there for 15 minutes and then returned to the Maha Devale, except on the last night of the *perahera* when it stays overnight.

Some devotees roll on burning hot sand near the temple to demonstrate their piety or to ask forgiveness for their sins. Others go to greater lengths and pierce their skin with hooks and other sharp objects.

During the fire-walking ceremony, worshippers, thought to be in a self-induced trance, walk barefoot across burning embers while chanting. Surprisingly, most emerge unscathed.

Coconuts topped with burning camphor are broken inside the temple to symbolize humility. This ritual is practised during *puja* as well as at the festival time.

The water-cutting ceremony at the Menik Ganga river marks the end of the festival. Once the priest has "cut" the water, pilgrims rush to the spot to absolve their sins by bathing in the river.

KANDY AND THE HILL COUNTRY

The third point of the Cultural Triangle that also comprises Anuradhapura and Polonnaruwa, Kandy is the cultural capital of Sri Lanka with a rich heritage of music, dance and architecture. Home of the sacred Tooth Relic, the city is on nearly every visitor's itinerary. It also serves as a gateway to the Hill Country, the mountainous core of the island, where the countryside is dotted with tea plantations and towns still preserve the remnants of the British Colonial legacy.

Set amid verdant hills in the heart of the island, Kandy was founded during the reign of Wickramabahu III of Gampola (r.1357–1374). The city became the capital of Sena Sammatha Wickramabahu's (r.1473–1511) kingdom in the 15th century, and its reputation was further cemented when the Tooth Relic arrived in 1592. Over the years, successive kings built, renovated and rebuilt sections of the city, as they staved off Colonial powers. The British, however, were determined to conquer the whole island, and finally, in 1815, succeeded in overthrowing this last bastion of independence, thanks to the unpopularity of the tyrannical Sri Wickrama Rajasinghe. Kandy soon became an important centre for trade,

with a railway line linking it to Colombo. Today, it is Sri Lanka's second city, renowned for the Temple of the Tooth and the spectacular Esala Perahera.

Beyond the bustle of Kandy, the pace of life slackens and the temperate climate provides a welcome relief. The southern Hill Country presents a range of contrasts – from wild and rugged landscapes with gushing waterfalls to carefully manicured tea plantations carpeting the hillsides. The Colonial-era railway creaks along at dizzying heights, past former British hill stations, such as Nuwara Eliya and Badulla, which are now modern towns. The area's other attractions include the hill towns of Ella and Haputale, which offer scenic views and lovely winding walks.

Splendidly caparisoned elephants parading down the street in Kandy during Esala Perahera

◀ Breathtaking view of the verdant valley from World's End in the Horton Plains National Park

Exploring Kandy and the Hill Country

Located in the heart of the island, Kandy is home to the famous Temple of the Tooth, which attracts visitors and pilgrims from across the world. The area surrounding the city offers a mix of historical and natural attractions, which include Kandyan-era temples, the picturesque Peradeniya Botanical Gardens and the Pinnawela Elephant Orphanage. Those keen to explore the countryside can head for the Knuckles Range, north of the city. The southern Hill Country provides tea aficionados the chance to visit factories and learn about tea production. Many visitors stop over at Nuwara Eliya to stay in one of its Colonial-era hotels or bungalows; the town also makes a good base for excursions to the Horton Plains National Park. Southwest of the town is Adam's Peak: climbing this mountain during the pilgrimage season is a moving experience. Walkers may also want to venture south to Sinharaja Forest Reserve to trek through the rainforest. The town of Ratnapura, famous for gem mining, can be visited on the way to or from Colombo.

View of the Temple of the Tooth on the banks of Kandy Lake

Sights at a Glance

1. Kandy pp134–8
2. Peradeniya Botanical Gardens
3. Three-Temples Loop
4. Ceylon Tea Museum
5. Pinnawela Elephant Orphanage
6. Millennium Elephant Foundation
7. Knuckles Range
8. Mahiyangana
9. Nuwara Eliya
10. Pedro Tea Estate
11. Mackwoods Labookellie Tea Estate
12. Hakgala Botanical Gardens
13. Horton Plains National Park and World's End pp146–7
14. Kitulgala
15. Adam's Peak
16. Badulla
17. Dunhinda Falls
18. Ella and around
19. Buduruwagala
20. Haputale
21. Adisham Monastery
22. Dambetenne Tea Factory
23. Diyaluma Falls
24. Belihul Oya
25. Ratnapura
26. Kudawa
27. Sinharaja Forest Reserve

For hotels and restaurants in this region see pp219–20 and pp231–2

Map labels

Kurunegala
Galketigedara
Dam[
Polgahawela
A6
PINNAWELA ELEPHANT ORPHANAGE
A10
MILLENNIUM ELEPHANT FOUNDATION 6
PERADENIYA BOTANICAL GARDENS
Ambepussa
Kegalle
A1
THREE-TEMPLES LOOP 3
A1
Dedigama
Bible Rock 798 m (2,618 ft)
Gampola
B457
A21
B132
B67
B445
Nawalapitiya
Karawanella
A7
KITULGALA 14
Kelani Ganga
A7
Kalu Ganga
Avissawella
Dim
A7
Colombo
Hatto
Eheliyagoda
Castlereagh Reservo[
A4
Dalhousie
Palabaddale
B222
Maha Saman Devale
ADAM'S PEAK 15
A8
Kalu Ganga
25 RATNAPURA
B[
A4
SABARAGAMUW
Kuda Ganga
B160
Pelmadulla
Kalawana
A
Madamp
Koswatta
KUDAWA 26
Weddagala
Gin Ganga
27
Go[
1.3
SINHARAJA FOREST RESERVE
(4.4
Deniyaya
SOUTHERN
A17
Ga[

Getting Around

Travelling by train is the best way to truly appreciate the scenery of the Hill Country. Trains and buses run regularly throughout the Hill Country, and with a base in one of the major towns visitors can organize three-wheelers to get to outlying sights. Those with a car and driver can catch the train from Kandy to Nanu Oya, the train station for Nuwara Eliya, and arrange for a pick up. The area is also great walking country and wandering around on foot is an excellent way to enjoy the views and see more of everyday life. However, in Kandy, the roads around the Temple of the Tooth are still closed to traffic, a security measure put in place after the 1998 LTTE bombing.

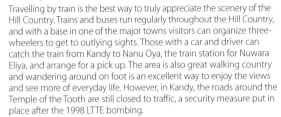

The lush, manicured tea plantation at the Mackwoods Labookellie Tea Estate

Feeding time at the Pinnawela Elephant Orphanage

Key

━━ Major road

┄┄┄ Minor road

⌇⌇⌇ Railway

▬▬▬ Provincial border

△ Summit

For additional map symbols *see back flap*

● Kandy

A charming, culturally vibrant city, Kandy is the capital of the Hill Country. It was the seat of government of the last Sinhalese kingdom, until it was taken over by the British in 1815. Today, it attracts tourists and pilgrims alike who come here to visit the Temple of the Tooth, the most sacred Buddhist shrine in Sri Lanka, and to experience the famous Esala Perahera. Easy to wander around, Kandy also has some interesting museums and markets to explore. There is a range of accommodation to choose from, with many of the town's hotels set in the surrounding hills. Kandy also makes a great base for exploring the Knuckles Range and the outlying temples.

Picturesque view of Kandy Lake

🦋 Kandy Lake
Located in the heart of the city, this lake was created by the last king of the Kandyan kingdom, Sri Wickrama Rajasinghe, in the 19th century. The island in the centre was used as the king's pleasure house before the British converted it into an ammunition store after they conquered Kandy in 1815. The building on the south shore, opposite the Temple of the Tooth complex, was formerly a monk's bathhouse; it is now a police station. Visitors can hire a boat on the western end of the lake for a tour across the water. Lone travellers are advised to avoid the eastern end after dark.

🏛 Temple of the Tooth
See pp136–7.

Devales
Open daily. 🖼 (donation).
🖼 Jul/Aug: Esala Perahera.
Kandy is popularly believed to be protected by four gods: Pattini, Natha, Vishnu and Kataragama. Each of these guardian deities

has a *devale* (temple) dedicated to them in the city. These *devales* demonstrate the intermingling and coexistence of Hindu and Buddhist beliefs in Kandy.

The **Natha Devale** is the oldest of the four and its shrine dates from the 14th century. Nearby stands the **Pattini Devale**, a simple shrine devoted to Pattini, the Buddhist goddess of chastity. The temple is said to enshrine the goddess's golden anklet. Opposite Natha Devale is the **Vishnu (or Maha) Devale**, which

is reached by a flight of carved stone steps. The temple complex features a *digge* (drummers' pavilion), beyond which lies the main shrine. A short distance to the west lies the **Kataragama Devale**, which can be hard to find among the shops. The main Kataragama shrine is surrounded by shrines dedicated to Hindu and Buddhist deities.

🏛 Archaeological Museum
Open 8am–5pm Wed–Mon.
Closed Tue.
Occupying the former palace of King Vimala Dharma Suriya I (r.1590–1604), this dusty museum contains a collection of sculptures, old wooden columns, pots and various other archaeological finds. It is possible to take a guided tour of the museum, for a small tip.

🏛 Kandy National Museum
Behind the Temple of the Tooth. **Open** 9am–4:30pm Tue–Sat. **Closed** Sun, Mon & public hols. 🖼
On a small hill east of the Temple of the Tooth stands the Kandy National Museum, housed in a white building that used to function as the Queen's Palace. The exhibits in this museum depict life in Kandy before the arrival of the Europeans. Among the displays are weapons such as bows and arrows, knives and daggers as well as jewellery and traditional costumes. In addition, items of day-to-day use such as jaggery moulds with elephant designs, and areca nut cutters shaped like people can be seen near a display of devil dance masks and wooden carvings. This museum is a good

Stone-carved steps leading to Vishnu Devale

A display of bows and arrows at the Kandy National Museum

VISITORS' CHECKLIST

Practical information
Road map C4.
134 km (83 miles) E of Colombo.
11,000. in the Kandy
City Centre shopping complex.
Jul/Aug: Esala Perahera.

Transport

place to take a closer look at *ola*-leaf manuscripts and to appreciate the skills of the craftsmen of the Kandyan kingdom.

Museum of World Buddhism

Behind the Audience Hall. **Open** 8am–7pm daily. Note: shoes must be removed before entering the museum.

Those interested in Buddhism will find a visit to this museum rewarding. Housed in a Neo-Classical building from the British era, the museum explores the history of Buddhism in Sri Lanka, and also has exhibits on Buddhism in other Asian countries. A large number of the sculptures on display here are replicas, while some of the other objects have been donated by

the relevant countries. Tourists who have visited Aukana and Sasseruwa *(see p176)* will find the photographs of the colossal Bamiyan Buddha statue in Afghanistan especially interesting. The replica of the fasting Buddha statue in the Pakistan pavilion is also striking. Rooms upstairs are filled with exhibits focusing on Buddhist beliefs in countries such as India, China, Korea, Vietnam and Japan.

Malwatte and Asigiriya Viharas

Open daily. (donation).

The senior monks of these two *viharas* (Buddhist monasteries) are the most important in Sri Lanka. Founded around the 16th century, the **Malwatte**

Vihara is home to over 300 Buddhist monks. The Ordination Room, with its magnificently painted ceiling, is worth a visit. The monastery also has a modest museum that contains Buddhist artifacts. Northwest of the city centre is **Asigiriya Vihara**, which houses a large reclining Buddha image and a collection of *ola*-leaf manuscripts.

Bahiravakanda Buddha

Sri Dharmarama Road. **Open** 6am–8pm daily.

Perched on a hill overlooking the town, this modern, white, seated Buddha statue is hard to miss. At the base of the huge statue is a temple, from where there are superb views over Kandy. It is possible to walk to the site or take a three-wheeler up to the temple by following the road that leads to the Topaz Hotel.

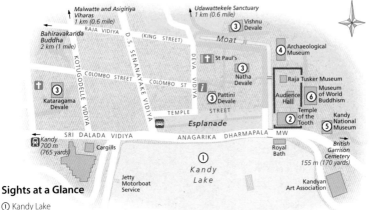

Sights at a Glance

1. Kandy Lake
2. Temple of the Tooth
3. Devales
4. Archaeological Museum
5. Kandy National Museum
6. Museum of World Buddhism

Key

Pedestrian street

0 metres 150
0 yards 150

Temple of the Tooth

The Temple of the Tooth, or Sri Dalada Maligawa, houses Sri Lanka's most important Buddhist relic, the Buddha's tooth. Built in the 16th century, the original temple stood at the heart of the Royal Palace complex. The temple was plundered along with the palace when the Dutch attacked the city in 1765. The main shrine was originally constructed during the reign of Vimala Dharma Suriya I (r.1590–1604); it was rebuilt by King Rajasinghe II (r.1634–1686) following the Dutch incursion. The palace was renovated in the 19th century by Sri Wickrama Rajasinghe, the last king of Kandy, who built the moat and replaced the earlier entrances with a massive stone gateway. An LTTE bombing badly damaged the temple in 1998, but it has since been restored.

Sri Dalada Museum
Occupying the first and second floor of Alut Maligawa, this museum showcases objects related to the temple and the Tooth Relic. There are photographs showing the extent of the 1998 bomb damage on the first floor.

Raja Tusker Museum
The museum is dedicated to Raja, the elephant which carried the Tooth Relic casket during the Esala Perahera (see p139) for 50 years until he died in 1988. The taxidermic remains of Raja are on display and photographs detailing his life line the walls.

KEY

① **The Octagonal Tower** is home to the library where a number of ancient *ola*-leaf manuscripts can be seen.

② **The Maha Vahalkada**, or Great Gate, marks the entrance to the temple. The moonstone here is visibly new; the original was destroyed in the bomb blast in 1998.

③ **Royal Palace**

④ **Pallemaluwa**, a shrine room, is said to have been built during the reign of King Kirti Sri Rajasinghe. It houses a large Buddha statue and colourful murals.

⑤ **The Drummers' Courtyard** is where most people congregate at the beginning of the *puja* to see the door to the main shrine open.

0 metres 30
0 yards 30

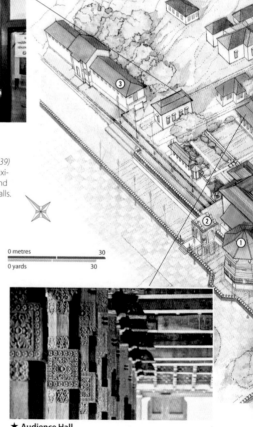

★ **Audience Hall**
This pavilion was used by Kandyan kings to hold court. The treaty that ended the sovereignty of the Kandyan kingdom and ceded power to the British was signed here in 1815.

The Story of the Buddha's Tooth

Legend states that after the Buddha was cremated in India in 543 BC, his remains were divided into eight parts and were given to eight kingdoms, following which stupas were built to house the relics. During the 4th century AD, the Tooth Relic was brought to Sri Lanka from Kalinga in India, concealed in the hair of Princess Hemamala. It was first taken to Anuradhapura and then, to keep it safe, it was moved around Sri Lanka; temples were built to house it in Polonnaruwa, Dambadeniya and Yapahuwa to name but a few. The Tooth arrived in Kandy in 1592 and has been here ever since.

A portrait of the Indian princess, Hemamala

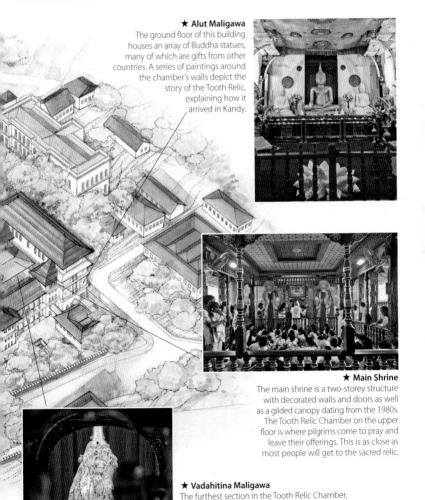

★ **Alut Maligawa**
The ground floor of this building houses an array of Buddha statues, many of which are gifts from other countries. A series of paintings around the chamber's walls depict the story of the Tooth Relic, explaining how it arrived in Kandy.

★ **Main Shrine**
The main shrine is a two-storey structure with decorated walls and doors as well as a gilded canopy dating from the 1980s. The Tooth Relic Chamber on the upper floor is where pilgrims come to pray and leave their offerings. This is as close as most people will get to the sacred relic.

★ **Vadahitina Maligawa**
The furthest section in the Tooth Relic Chamber, this shrine houses the sacred relic, which is kept in a bejewelled gold casket shaped like a stupa. There are said to be a series of seven caskets, one inside the other, protecting the Tooth. It is possible to catch a glimpse of the gold casket while filing past the doorway.

Well-manicured burial ground of the British Garrison Cemetery

British Garrison Cemetery

Garrison Cemetery Road. **Open**
8am–1pm & 2–6pm Mon–Sat.
Closed Sun. 🖼 (donation).

The British Garrison Cemetery
was founded in 1817 as the
final resting place for deceased
British colonialists. The cemetery
eventually fell into disrepair,
but was restored in the 1990s.
Today, it is a well-tended and
tranquil spot, despite the many
monkeys cavorting around the
place. There are around 163
graves of varying shapes and
sizes in the cemetery. The
headstones give an idea of
how hazardous life was in
the 19th century – cholera,
malaria, sunstroke, accidents
and infant mortality are all
given as common causes
of death.

If there is time, take a guided
tour of the grounds with the
cemetery caretaker who can
point out the most interesting
tombstones and help decipher
the weathered inscriptions.
Visitors are likely to come across
the grave of the last person
to be interred in the cemetery
in 1951 – burials officially
stopped taking place in the
1870s and special permission
had to be sought thereafter –
and of John Spottiswood
Robertson, the last-known
European to have been killed
by a wild elephant in Sri Lanka
in 1856. The caretaker's cabin
at the entrance has a register
that contains a record of all
the graves in the cemetery.

Udawattekele Sanctuary

Open 8am–5pm daily. 🖼

Stretching beyond the Temple
of the Tooth north of Kandy
Lake, this forest was once
reserved for the royal family.
After the fall of the Kandyan
kingdom in 1815, the British took
over the forest area and began
felling trees for their own use.
However, when the condition of
the forest began to deteriorate,
they declared it a protected area
in the mid-19th century.

Covering an area of 104 ha
(257 acres), Udawattekele is
home to a great variety of flora
and fauna. Endemic plants can
also be seen here, including a
number of orchid species and
other epiphytes such as ferns.
Birdwatchers should be able to
catch sight of golden-fronted
leafbirds, yellow-fronted barbets
and the yellow-browed bulbul
among other species. There are
also butterflies, squirrels,
monkeys and reptiles to keep
an eye out for.

It is possible to explore
Udawattekele by following one
of the numerous paths or trails,
most of which are named after
British governors' wives. The
5-km (3-mile) Lady Horton's
Drive, which begins from inside
the sanctuary, is one such path
that takes in a good portion of
the forest, including the pond
where royalty once bathed.
According to legend, gold
coins lie beneath the surface
of the pond, guarded by a
red-eyed serpent. Alternatively,
visitors can head for the hills
from here. The forest also has
rock-cut caves that are still
used by Buddhist monks for
meditation.

It is advisable to be cautious if
visiting the forest independently
and avoid a trip here after dark.

The entrance to Udawattekele Sanctuary

Esala Perahera

This 10-day festival, celebrated in honour of the Tooth Relic, attracts thousands of pilgrims and tourists to Kandy. The *perahera* took shape in the 18th century during the reign of King Kirti Sri Rajasinghe, when Buddhist monks visiting from Thailand expressed their disapproval at the Hindu nature of the festival, with parades in reverence of Natha, Pattini, Vishnu and Kataragama from the four *devales* in the city. The king, therefore, ordered that the Tooth Relic be carried at the head of the four processions, hence incorporating the Temple of the Tooth parade into that of the *devales*. Esala Perahera begins with the Kap Tree Planting Ceremony, followed by the Kumbal Perahera that marks the first five days of the festival. The last five days, known as Randoli Perahera, are when festivities become more spectacular. Every night there are processions, featuring dancers, drummers and acrobats as well as splendidly decorated elephants. The water-cutting ceremony, the concluding ritual of the festival, takes place before dawn on the last day of the *perahera*.

The Maligawa Tusker carries a replica of the Tooth Relic on its back, accompanied by the temple guardians in all their finery. However, during the Anuradhapuran times, the original relic used to be carried in a procession all over the city. Today, the relic is no longer taken out of the temple.

Dancers make up some of the thousands of performers in the *perahera*. From *ves* to *pantheru (see p30)*, a range of Kandyan dance forms can be seen at the parade.

Drummers dressed in traditional costume, comprising a sarong, a red cummerbund and a white turban, accompany the dancers in the procession. A variety of drums, such as *dowlas* and *geta beras*, are used in the *perahera*.

The *perahera* usually begins between 8 and 9pm. Be sure to arrive hours before the procession begins and find a spot on the pavement next to the route. It is also possible to reserve one of the special window or balcony seats made available during the *perahera*.

The enormous Javan fig tree in the Great Lawn, Peradeniya Botanical Gardens

❷ Peradeniya Botanical Gardens

Road map C4. 6 km (4 miles) SW of Kandy. 🚌 from Kandy. 🕐 **Open** 8am–5:30pm daily. 🅿️ ♿ 💻 🛍️

These grounds were originally laid out as pleasure gardens for the Kandyan royalty in 1371. But after the British dethroned the last Kandyan king Sri Wickrama Rajasinghe in 1815, the royal park was turned into botanical gardens in 1821.

A useful map at the entrance helps visitors explore some of the 60 ha (148 acres) of foreign and endemic plants and trees. The most notable among these are the giant bamboo, palmyra palms and tailpot palms. Near the entrance is the Orchid House, which displays over 300 varieties. Close by, the spice garden teems with a wealth of plants such as clove, cinnamon, vanilla and nutmeg. A short walk to the north lies the fernery.

Lined with exotic varieties of trees, the attractive avenues make for a pleasant stroll. West of the entrance is Cook's Pine Avenue, which is bordered by twisted Cook's pines. Running down the centre, Royal Palms Avenue is one of the most impressive. Another road of note is the Double Coconut Avenue near the entrance, which is fringed by stumpy coco de mer trees. West of the Royal Palm Avenue lies the Great Lawn, with a gargantuan Javan fig tree in the middle. The cool shade of the tree's sprawling branches are a draw for picnickers and casual visitors. Just north is the Grand Circle where memorial trees planted by various international figures can be seen.

❸ Three-Temples Loop

Road map C4. 11 km (7 miles) SW of Kandy. 🕐 Note: visitors can also hire a three-wheeler to explore the loop.

Among the many Kandyan-era temples that dot the area around Kandy, the **Gadaladeniya**, **Lankatilaka** and **Embekke Devale** temples are exceptional. These three temples date from the 14th century, when the Kandyan kingdom was in its early days.

Situated atop a rock, the Gadaladeniya Temple complex was built during the reign of King Bhuvanekabahu IV in 1344. The first building within the temple complex is the cruciform subsidiary shrine. Each wing of this shrine houses a Buddha image and is crowned by a small *dagoba*. The interior is adorned with attractive wall paintings.

Guarding the steps leading to the main stone temple are two small elephant sculptures. The carvings of dancers and drummers on the temple's exterior walls mark the influence of south Indian architecture in its construction. Inside, a serene golden Buddha sits under a *makara torana* (ceremonial arch) decorated with murals.

Located 2 km (1 mile) southwest of the Gadaladeniya Temple, the imposing, bright white Lankatilaka Temple is probably the most impressive of the three shrines. Visitors arriving by car enter from the western side of the complex, while those on foot reach the site by a steep flight of rock-cut steps on the eastern side. The west door leads to a series of Hindu shrines. However, the main attraction here is the Buddhist image house, the entrance to which lies on the eastern side. Flanking the doorway leading into the chamber are two guardian *gajasinghas* (elephant-lions). Inside, there is a seated Buddha statue under a *makara torana* surrounded by Kandyan-era paintings on the walls and ceiling. To the left of the building is a rock inscription detailing the construction of the temple, which was completed in 1344.

Dedicated to the guardian deity Kataragama, the Embekke Devale lies 2 km (1 mile) southeast of the Lankatilaka Temple. The shrine is famous for the richly carved wooden pillars of its

The splendid golden Buddha statue in Gadaladeniya Temple

Elephants bathing in the Ma Oya river, Pinnawela Elephant Orphanage

digge (drummers' pavilion). The intricate design on each of these pillars portrays flowers, dancers, soldiers and wrestlers among other themes. Just behind the *digge* is the main shrine, and to its right is a subsidiary shrine with a Buddha statue as well as a wooden statue of a peacock, the bird associated with Kataragama.

🏛 Gadaladeniya Temple
Gadaldeniya Road. **Open** 6am–7pm daily. 📷

🏛 Lankatilaka Temple
Lankathilaka Vihara Road.
Open 6am–7pm daily. 📷

🏛 Embekke Devale
Embekka Pilimatalawa Road.
Open 6am–7pm daily. 📷

❹ Ceylon Tea Museum

Road map C4. 5 km (3 miles) S of Kandy. **Tel** (081) 380 3204. 🅣 **Open** 8:30am–4:30pm Tue–Sat (last ticket: 3:30pm). **Closed** Mon, Sun & *poya* days. 📷 🎥 🆆 ceylonteamuseum.com

Located in the Hantane Estate, the Ceylon Tea Museum occupies a former four-storey tea factory dating from 1925. Exhibits on the ground floor include drying furnaces, grinders and sorters used in the 19th century. The highlights here, however, are the miniature working model of a tea factory and an 80-year-old tea bush.

The first floor contains displays on two of Sri Lanka's greatest tea pioneers: James Taylor and Thomas Lipton. There is a small collection of Taylor's personal articles, which includes his books and walking stick, as well as a display on the life of Lipton. The floor also houses other tea-related paraphernalia, including Sri Lanka's oldest surviving packet of tea in its original packaging, dating from 1944.

The third floor has small shops selling tea, and on the top floor is a restaurant, where visitors can enjoy a free cup of the beverage while admiring glorious views of the Knuckles Range *(see p144).*

❺ Pinnawela Elephant Orphanage

Road map C4. 40 km (25 miles) W of Kandy. **Tel** (081) 226 5804. 🚌 from Kandy to Rambukkana, then three-wheeler. 🎥 🅣 **Open** 8:30am–6pm daily. 📷 additional fee for video camera and feeding baby elephants. 💻

Spread over an area of 10 ha (25 acres) in Pinnawela village, this government-run elephant orphanage is one of Sri Lanka's most popular tourist attractions. Originally set up in 1975 to take care of five orphaned elephants, today it is home to the world's largest group of captive elephants.

Pinnawela is now home to over 80 elephants of all ages; these include orphaned and abandoned elephants as well as those found injured in the wild. In addition, there are some baby elephants that were born here in captivity. The younger elephants are herded into the feeding sheds three times a day – 9:15am, 1:15pm and 5pm – to be bottle-fed with huge quantities of milk. At 10am and again at 2pm, the elephants are taken across the road and down to the Ma Oya river, where they can be seen splashing around and playing for about an hour.

❻ Millennium Elephant Foundation

Road map C4. 41 km (25 miles) W of Kandy. **Tel** (081) 226 3377. 🅣 **Open** 9am–4pm daily. 📷 🆆 millennium elephantfoundation.com

Established in 1999 to look after old and disabled elephants, the foundation's centre has just eight elephants, one of which was born here while the other seven are retired working animals. The foundation also runs a mobile veterinary unit, which provides medical services to domesticated and wild elephants across the country.

The centre offers elephant rides – the fee depends on the duration of the ride. For an additional charge, it is also possible to bathe and feed the elephants as well as tour the pachyderm paper factory, which produces paper from elephant dung. A small museum on site has informative displays on the elephants.

Skeleton on display in the museum, Millennium Elephant Foundation

❼ Knuckles Range

Road map C4. 25 km (16 miles) NE of Kandy. 🚉 **Open** 6am–6pm daily. 🐾 🚗 book in advance. 🌐 **knuckles range.org**

Also known as Dumbara Hills, the Knuckles Range was so named by the British for its resemblance to the knuckles of a clenched fist. The range consists of five main peaks and several smaller ones, the highest of which is over 1,800 m (6,000 ft).

A UNESCO World Heritage Conservation Area and a biodiversity hotspot, the mountain range supports a wide range of flora and fauna. The vegetation varies from dry evergreen forests to wet grasslands. These ecosystems support numerous animal species, such as deer, wild boar, langurs and even slender loris; as well as a rich variety of birds.

The Knuckles Range is also a popular trekking destination. It is possible to wander unaccompanied, but for longer walks it is advisable to hire a guide. The walk begins through the lowlands, which are dotted with small villages, before winding through montane forest and past waterfalls. There are excellent vistas from the many viewpoints or from any of the peaks.

❽ Mahiyangana

Road map D4. 70 km (44 miles) E of Kandy. 🚌 🚉

The town of Mahiyangana is famous in Buddhist legend as the first of the three places in Sri Lanka that the Buddha visited

The charming post office building in Nuwara Eliya

after he gained enlightenment; the other two being Kelaniya and Nainativu (see p208).

About 1 km (0.6 mile) south of the town centre, the huge **Rajamaha Dagoba** marks the spot where the Buddha is believed to have preached during his first visit to the country. Said to enshrine a lock of the Buddha's hair, the *dagoba* was expanded by King Dutugemunu in the 2nd century BC, and further renovated during the reign of King Voharika Tissa in the 3rd century AD. The attractive complex, backed by picturesque hills, is reached by a long walkway.

Another temple of note here is the Sri Maha Bodhi Seya, which is located west of the centre. It was commissioned by President Premadasa in the early 1990s to look like the Mahabodhi Stupa at Bodh Gaya in India.

The town also serves as a good base for visiting the Maduru Oya National Park (see p199).

🏛 **Rajamaha Dagoba**
Off Maluwa Road. **Open** daily.

❾ Nuwara Eliya

Road map C5. 88 km (55 miles) SW of Mahiyangana. 🏔 30,000. 🚌 🚐 🚉 🎎 Apr: Sinhalese and Tamil New Year.

Established by the British in the 19th century, Nuwara Eliya is often referred to as Sri Lanka's "Little England". Set in a wooded valley beneath the 2,524-m (8,281-ft) Pidurutalagala or Mount Pedro, the tallest peak in the country, it is the highest town on the island. With a cool though unpredictable climate, the town provides a welcome relief from the hot and humid lowlands.

The popular town becomes particularly busy in April during the Sinhalese and Tamil New Year holidays, when Sri Lankans flock here in droves. A festive atmosphere prevails during this period – many horse- and motor-racing events are organized and stalls line the streets – and accommodation prices tend to be higher.

Walking around is a good way to see a number of sights. In the town centre is the well-maintained 18-hole **Golf Club**, which was founded in 1889. Behind the Club House are the remains of a **British Cemetery**, where the infamous elephant hunter Major Thomas William Rogers is buried. Also in the town centre is the pink Colonial-era post office with a conical clock tower. Nearby, the charming **Victoria Park** offers some excellent birdwatching; and also has a play area for children near the entrance. A little further on, there is an interesting covered market on

Tree-lined walkway leading to the striking Rajamaha Dagoba, Mahiyangana

New Bazaar Street, where vendors sell a wealth of fruit and vegetables as well as meat and fish.

Nuwara Eliya also retains some elegant Colonial-era hotels such as the Hill Club (see p220) and the half-timbered Grand Hotel, located further north along the Grand Hotel Road. Visitors can go in for a drink, or simply admire the period exterior and colourful flower gardens. To the east of the centre stands the Anglican Holy Trinity Church. Built in 1825, the church still holds regular services.

Further east lies **Lake Gregory**. The landscaped area around it is a pleasant spot for a stroll. An on-site boat house rents out pleasure boats or pedaloes for a ride across the lake. The racecourse is located south of the town.

Environs
The surrounding countryside offers some excellent walks. The shortest and easiest of these is a 2-km (1-mile) walk southwest to **Single Tree Hill**, from where there are panoramic vistas of Nuwara Eliya. For an extended, day-long hike, walk 4 km (2 miles) north from Single Tree Hill through tea plantations to the isolated settlement of **Shantipura**, the island's highest village. From here, continue southwest to the viewpoint at Uda Radella, for sweeping views south to Adam's Peak. It is advisable to hire a guide for this walk.

Victoria Park
Open 7am–6:30pm daily.

Well-manicured gardens in Victoria Park, Nuwara Eliya

Tea pluckers hard at work, Mackwoods Labookellie Tea Estate

⑩ Pedro Tea Estate

Road map C5. 3 km (2 miles) E of Nuwara Eliya. **Tel** (052) 222 2016. **Open** 8–11am & 2–4pm Mon–Fri.

This small, suburban tea estate is worth a visit for those interested in learning more about the local tea industry. Established in 1885, it offers guided tours of the garden and factory to show how tea is processed, right from picking to grading. The factory handles about 2,500 kg (5,511 lbs) of tea every day.

After the tour, a complimentary cup of tea can be enjoyed at the pleasant café overlooking the plantation. Note that tea is sold here only in packs of three or more.

⑪ Mackwoods Labookellie Tea Estate

Road map C5. 17 km (10 miles) N of Nuwara Eliya. **Tel** (052) 223 5106. **Open** daily. English, German, French & Italian. **W** mackwoodstea.com

This expansive, 415-ha (1,025-acre) tea estate is set in a lovely location, with tea plantations stretching into the distance. It is part of the Mackwoods group that was established in 1841.

In addition to a guided tour of the factory, housed in a huge iron building, it is possible to join the tea pluckers on the slopes and help pick the leaves. The tour ends with a free sampling of the estate's tea in the café.

⑫ Hakgala Botanical Gardens

Road map C5. 10 km (6 miles) SE of Nuwara Eliya. **Open** 7:30am–5pm daily. Note: parking is available, but there is an additional charge. **W** botanicgardens.gov.lk

These gardens were originally laid out in 1861 to cultivate cinchona, the bark of which is a source of the anti-malarial drug quinine. Today, Hakgala is famous for its roses that bloom from April to August. Spread over 27 ha (67 acres), the garden is divided into different sections, including a Japanese garden, a fernery and a rock garden. The beds here host a diverse range of flowers, from sunflowers and pansies to orchids. The plants and trees labelled in red are indigenous to Sri Lanka.

Environs
Located 2 km (1 mile) east of the gardens is the **Sita Amman Temple**. Dedicated to Sita, wife of Lord Rama, the shrine is thought to mark the spot where she was held prisoner by Rawana.

Ornate carvings of Hindu deities decorating the exterior of the Sita Amman Temple

⑬ Horton Plains National Park and World's End

Set in the central highlands of Sri Lanka, Horton Plains is unlike any other place in the country and is often compared to the Scottish highlands, for its windswept landscape and cool, wet climate. It is named after Sir Robert Wilmot-Horton, the British governor of Ceylon from 1831 to 1837. Formerly a wildlife sanctuary, the area was declared a national park in 1988. At an elevation of over 2,000 m (6,562 ft), the park is situated on the highest plateau in Sri Lanka, with its terrain characterized by undulating grasslands interspersed with dense cloud forests, rocky outcrops and waterfalls. Home to a wide variety of wildlife, Horton Plains also boasts a large number of bird species. However, the key attraction in the park is World's End, a sheer precipice affording panoramic views across the southern part of the island.

Loop Trail
This 9-km (6-mile) long trail begins at the visitor centre near the entrance and covers World's End and Baker's Falls before looping back to the visitor centre. The round-trip takes 3 to 4 hours.

Baker's Falls
This beautiful 20-m (66-ft) high waterfall was discovered by British explorer Samuel Baker in 1845. Reached by a steep forest path, the falls can be seen from a viewing platform. The waterfall is at its best after a spell of heavy rainfall.

Dayagama
9 km (6 miles)

Kelani Ganga ⑤

Kirigalpotha
2,389 m (7,839 ft)

Belihul Oya

Baker's Falls

World's End

KEY

① **Chimini Pool** is a man-made dam.

② **Nellu** shrubs take 8 to 10 years to grow from seed. During the flowering season in April, they cover the forest floor with purple blooms.

③ **Farr Inn**, a former hunting lodge dating from the Colonial era, houses the visitor centre. Leaflets and books about Horton Plains and Sri Lankan wildlife can be bought from here.

④ **Sambar**, the largest of the deer found in Sri Lanka, gather in large numbers in the park. Visitors can see a few tame sambar by the Farr Inn.

⑤ **The Mahaweli, Kelani and Walawe**, three of Sri Lanka's largest rivers, originate in the park.

World's End
A stunning escarpment plunging over 880 m (2,887 ft) into the lowlands below, World's End is the main draw at Horton Plains. On a clear day, it is possible to see as far as the island's southern coast from here. On other days, the view may be limited to the nearer Uda Walawe reservoir in Uda Walawe National Park *(see pp122–3)*.

Birdwatching
A popular birdwatching spot, Horton Plains is home to as many as 87 species of birds, including many migratory birds. Montane endemics such as the Sri Lanka whistling thrush and the yellow-eared bulbul can be sighted here.

Pattipola 6 km (4 miles)

Thotupola
2,357 m (7,733 ft)

Pattipola Gate

WORLD'S END ROAD

Mahaweli Ganga

Entrance

World's End
Trail Head

Walawae Ganga

Ohiya Gate

OHIYA ROAD

Ohiya
4 km
(2 miles)

ttle (Small)
orld's
nd !

Key

〓 Other road

▪▪ Trail

▪▪ Park boundary

0 km   1
0 mile   1

Little (Small) World's End
With a smaller vertical drop of 300 m (984 ft), this escarpment may not be as impressive as World's End, but it still offers excellent views of the surrounding landscape and the tea plantations below.

Cloud Forest
These montane cloud forests contain a diverse range of flora, including many medicinal plants and spices. The forest canopy is dominated by the umbrella-shaped keena trees. In April and July, the white blooms of the keena contrast with the red rhododendron bushes.

Exploring the Park

Unlike other national parks in Sri Lanka, Horton Plains can be explored on foot and without a guide, provided visitors stick to the marked trails. While there are several trails in the park, the majority of people follow the Loop Trail. It is possible to head in the direction of either World's End or Baker's Falls. Although most choose to go to World's End first, the last stretch of this trail between Baker's Falls and the entrance is an open grassland with no shade. It is advisable to wear good walking shoes as the paths are rocky and uneven. The best time to visit the park is early in the morning, around 7am, to allow plenty of time to reach World's End before 10am, when clouds roll in and the view is obscured from the escarpment. Avoid visiting the park on weekends and public holidays as it can be very busy and noisy. Although the park can be chilly in the morning, it warms up quickly, so bring a hat and sunscreen.

For map symbols see back flap

The majestic Adam's Peak towering over its verdant surroundings

⓮ Kitulgala

Road map C5. 73 km (60 miles) NW of Nuwara Eliya. 🚌 🛈

Surrounded by low wooded hills, the small village of Kitulgala is perhaps best known for being the location where David Lean filmed *Bridge on the River Kwai* (1957). A path signposted from the main road leads to the banks of the Kelaniya river, where the filming site can be seen. Those familiar with the Oscar-winning film will recognize some of the riverside scenery and the remains of the bridge's concrete foundations.

Kitulgala serves as a base for a range of adventure activities, such as whitewater rafting. Most hotels in the area can also arrange rock climbing, cycling, abseiling and overnight river trips. A boat trip across the river leads to the **Kitulgala Forest Reserve**, which offers good birdwatching and trekking in lowland rainforest. Among the many birds that

can be spotted here are the grey hornbill, the yellow-fronted barbet and various kingfishers.

🏞 **Kitulgala Forest Reserve**
⏱ Note: the reserve is reached by boat.

⓯ Adam's Peak

Road map C5. 52 km (32 miles) SE of Kitulgala. 🚆 to Hatton, then bus to Dalhousie. 🚌 🛈 🅿 🍴

Kingfisher, Kitulgala

The 2,243-m (7,359-ft) Adam's Peak is also known as Sri Pada, which means Sacred Footprint – referring to the rock formation at the summit. While Buddhists believe it to be an imprint of the Buddha's foot, Hindus associate it with Shiva, Muslims with Adam and Christians with St Thomas. The peak is, however, primarily a Buddhist site. Saman, one of the island's most important gods, is believed to be the guardian deity of the peak.

The easiest and shortest route up the mountain is from Dalhousie, where the majority

of visitors base themselves, but many pilgrims also climb from the Ratnapura *(see p152)* side. The 7-km (4-mile) ascent consists of around 5,500 steps. The climb is traditionally made at night – most people set off at 2am and take about 4 hours to reach the peak to watch the break of dawn. It is possible to climb during the day, but the peak is often shrouded in cloud then and the views are obscured.

The summit itself is covered in a jumble of buildings. The footprint lies sheltered under a pavilion, where people can be seen praying or ringing the two bells nearby to mark their ascent. As dawn breaks, the sun casts a unique triangular shadow of the peak that seems to hang in mid-air in front of the mountain.

The pilgrimage season begins in December and continues until May. During this period, the steps leading to the peak are illuminated, and there are little stalls along the route offering tea and snacks to pilgrims and tourists. However, it may be a good idea to bring a torch, as some spots near the starting point can be dark if the lights are not working. On *poya* days, long weekends and during the Sinhalese and Tamil New Year in April, the mountain paths can get very busy. Be sure to set aside enough time to reach the summit – it is common to get stuck in a slow-moving queue.

Although a guide is not needed in season, as there will be many others making the ascent, it is advisable to hire one during the off season when the way up can be lonely and dark. Solo travellers can organize a guide or team up with others; dinner at the

Whitewater Rafting

The stretch of Kelaniya river around Kitulgala is considered to be the best place for whitewater rafting in Sri Lanka. The main rafting stretch is about 4 km (3 miles) long and the rapids vary from Grade 3 to 5 depending on rainfall. The best time to embark on a trip is from April to November when the water level is higher. A typical trip covers a range of major and minor rapids, and usually includes a swimming stop. Experienced rafters can arrange for longer and more challenging trips as well. Rafting excursions can be organized on arrival in Kitulgala. Be sure to take to the water with a reputable operator and remember to check the quality of the gear.

Rafting on the Kelaniya river

Slightly Chilled Guest House *(see p219)* is a good opportunity to strike up conversation and find walking partners. Bringing warm clothing is recommended, since it can be cold at the summit. It is also advisable to wear sturdy shoes and carry water, a hat and sunscreen – once the sun is up, it can be scorching.

When making the descent, be sure to walk the right way down and not follow the path heading to Ratnapura – if there are few people on the path, it is probably not the right one.

⓰ Badulla

Road map D5. 125 km (78 miles) E of Kitulgala. ⚐ 42,000. 🚗🚌🚉 May: Vesak Perahera.

The capital of Uva Province, Badulla is thought to be one of the oldest towns in Sri Lanka. Today, it is an important transport hub and visitors are likely to pass through it while travelling between the Hill Country and the East Coast.

The highlight here is the **Kataragama Devale**, a Hindu temple that was built in the 18th century. The Kandyan-style main shrine houses an image of Kataragama, flanked by statues of Saman and Vishnu. The shrine's outer walls are painted with murals depicting a *perahera*. Some fine carvings of human figures, animals and floral motifs can be seen on the pillars and other areas of the temple.

Kataragama Devale
Entrance on Lower Street. **Open** 6am–6pm daily.

Interior of the 18th-century Kataragama Devale, Badulla

Breathtaking view of the roaring Dunhinda Falls

⓱ Dunhinda Falls

Road map D5. 6 km (4 miles) N of Badulla. 🚌 from Badulla. 🚉🚻

Fed by the Badulla Oya river, the 63-m (210-ft) high Dunhinda Falls are a picturesque sight, with an enormous volume of water gushing into the pool below in a cloud of spray.

The 1-km (0.6-mile) long path leading to the falls can be a bit of a scramble. It is narrow in places and slippery if there has been rainfall. Stalls selling drinks and snacks can be found along the way, but watch out for thieving monkeys when taking a break or enjoying the scenery.

On the way to the waterfall, the lower, wider Kuda Dunhinda falls can be seen. There is a concrete observation point at the end of the path. The falls can be visited year-round. However, the place is very popular with locals and can be busy at weekends and on public holidays.

⓲ Ella and around

Road map D5. 21 km (13 miles) S of Badulla. 🚗🚌🚉

The small town of Ella is a beautiful place to spend a few restful days. The town is largely made up of a long main street lined with restaurants, and paths leading off to attractive guesthouses where some excellent home cooking can be sampled. One of the prime attractions here is **Ella Gap**, a cleft in the hills where the land drops a dizzying 1,100 m (3,609 ft) into the plains below. The best

view of the Gap is from the garden of the Grand Ella Motel *(see p231)*.

Ella is walking country and guesthouses will be able to provide hand-drawn maps of scenic walks, such as the 4-hour long hike southeast of the town to **Ella Rock**, from where there are splendid views across the Hill Country. An easy, mostly flat 2-hour long walk winds through tea plantations southeast to **Little Adam's Peak**, which affords great views of the surrounding countryside. Visitors are advised to set off early to reach here before the clouds descend.

Environs
About 4 km (2 miles) south of Ella is the **Rawana Ella Cave**, where Sita is said to have been held captive by Rawana. A few kilometres south of the cave are the 90-m (295-ft) high **Rawana Falls**, which are especially photogenic after a bout of rain.

Steps leading to the entrance of Rawana Ella Cave, Ella

⓲ Buduruwagala

Road map D5. 37 km (23 miles) SE of Ella. ⓣ **Open** dawn–dusk daily. 🖼

Little visited by foreign tourists, Buduruwagala boasts seven colossal rock-cut figures that are said to date from the 10th century. Carved in low relief, the impressive sculptures belong to the Mahayana school of Buddhism, which enjoyed royal patronage between the 3rd and 10th centuries AD.

In the centre is a 16-m (52-ft) high standing Buddha in the *abhaya mudra (see p177)*, flanked on either side by a group of three sculptures. The central of the three figures to the Buddha's right is thought to represent Avalokitesvara, the *bodhisattva* of compassion in Mahayana Buddhism. He can be identified by the image of the meditating Buddha on the crown he wears. The figure still bears orange paint around the head and white stucco on the body; all the other sculptures may originally have been decorated in a similar fashion. The female figure to the right is thought to be the Mahayana goddess, Tara.

Among the group of figures to the left of the Buddha, the one in the centre is believed to be Maitreya, the fifth and future Buddha. The sculpture to his left depicts the Tibetan *bodhisattva* Vajrapani (or Sakra), holding a thunderbolt symbol, while the figure to his right is thought to be Vishnu.

The central Buddha image flanked by a group of three rock sculptures, Buduruwagala

⓳ Haputale

Road map C5. 47 km (29 miles) NW of Buduruwagala. 🚠 4,700. 🚉 🚌 ⓣ

Situated on the southern edge of the Hill Country, Haputale is a market town with a mainly Tamil population – many of whom still work in the tea plantations nearby. While the town does not have much in the way of sights, it boasts superb vistas. On a clear day, it is possible to see all the way to the South Coast. The views are obscured by clouds around midday, when it often rains.

North of the town centre is the Anglican **St Andrew's Church**, an attractive Neo-Gothic building reminiscent of the town's Colonial past. Memorial plaques and gravestones of 19th-century tea planters can still be seen in the churchyard.

Haputale serves as a good base for exploring sights around town or to embark on scenic walks in the surrounding hills. Visitors can take the 10-km (6-mile) route through beautiful tea estates to the Dambetenne Tea Factory.

⓴ Adisham Monastery

Road map C5. 3 km (2 miles) W of Haputale. **Tel** (057) 226 8030. ⓣ **Open** 9:30am–12:30pm, 1:30–4:30pm Sat, Sun & *poya* days. 🖼 📷 🌐 adisham.org

Set in tranquil surroundings, this stately mansion was built in the 1930s by Sir Thomas Villiers, a British tea planter. Villiers named the place after the village in Kent where he was born. In the 1960s, the house was bought by the Sylvestro-Benedictine monastic order, and has functioned as a monastery ever since.

Visitors are permitted to see only a section of the monastery, which comprises the well-preserved living room and the library. The property is surrounded by orchards and features a well-manicured rose garden. There is a small shop on site that sells jams, cordials and jellies made by the monks.

Exterior of the Adisham Monastery fronted by charming flower gardens

㉒ Dambetenne Tea Factory

Road map D5. 10 km (6 miles) E of Haputale. 🚌 ⓣ **Open** 8am–6pm Mon–Fri. 🎫 📷

The Dambetenne Tea Factory was built by famous tea tycoon Sir Thomas Lipton in 1890. Housed in a long white building, the tea factory still uses most of its original Colonial-era machinery to process tea. Guided tours of the factory provide an insight into the whole tea-making process, from drying and rolling through to grading.

Environs

Located 7 km (4 miles) east of the tea factory is the **Lipton's Seat** lookout, which is said to rival World's End (*see p146*). Perched on the edge of a cliff, the lookout affords sweeping views of the surrounding countryside. A 2-hour climb winding through lush tea plantations leads to the

View of the spectacular Bambarakanda Falls

viewpoint, but it is also possible to arrange for transport to reach the place. Be sure to reach the lookout early as mist rolls in by mid-morning. Consider taking a taxi up and walking back down.

㉓ Diyaluma Falls

Road map D5. 30 km (19 miles) SE of Haputale. 🚌 ⓣ

The attractive Diyaluma Falls are the second highest in Sri Lanka at 170 m (557 ft). A circuitous walk leads to the top of the falls, where it is possible to cool off in one of the large natural bathing pools.

The hike to the pools begins at the bottom of the falls from where it winds a few hundred metres east to the estate track that cuts through rubber plantations. Upon reaching the small rubber factory, bear left and head uphill on an indistinct and rough path. The climb takes

Well-manicured grounds of the Dambetenne Tea Factory

about an hour each way. The route can be tricky to follow, so confirm the way with locals or arrange for a guide in order to stay on the right track.

㉔ Belihul Oya

Road map C5. 35 km (22 miles) W of Haputale. 🚌 to Kalupahana, then a three-wheeler to the falls. ⓣ

A pretty town set amid tea estates on the banks of a river, Belihul Oya serves as a superb jumping-off point for visiting the breathtaking **Bambarakanda Falls**, which lie 11 km (7 miles) northeast of the town at the village of Kalupahana.

At around 240 m (787 ft), the waterfall is the highest on the island. The cascade is especially impressive after a spell of heavy rainfall; however, in the dry season it can be reduced to little more than a trickle.

Thomas Lipton

Sir Thomas Lipton was born in Glasgow in 1850. At the age of 15, he travelled to the US where he worked on a number of jobs before returning to Scotland a few years later. Lipton's story really began in 1871 when he opened a grocery shop in Glasgow. The shop's success led him to gradually establish a chain of around 400 shops across Great Britain as well as a few in South Africa and Australia. Lipton, by then, had become known for selling his wares at competitive prices and for advertising aggressively and innovatively. In 1889, he started buying tea at auctions in London and went on to sell 10 million pounds of tea within two years at a much lower rate than the then market price. His tea empire reached new heights in 1890 when he bought several tea estates in Ceylon en route to Australia. Upon returning to Scotland, he marketed Ceylon tea with his usual panache and eventually became synonymous with the beverage.

Sir Thomas Lipton, one of the great figures in the history of Ceylon tea

An assortment of gems on display at one of the many gem museums, Ratnapura

㉕ Ratnapura

Road map C5. 92 km (57 miles) SW of Haputale. 47,800.

Ratnapura is best known as Sri Lanka's gem capital – in fact the name, Ratnapura, translates to "City of Gems". The busy town is home to numerous gem museums, where visitors can see local precious stones as well as numerous exhibits related to gem mining. At the heart of the town lies the clock tower, the area around which is the best place to watch locals buying and selling gems. The huge variety of gemstones found here include sapphires, zircons, garnets, rubies and cat's eyes.

Ratnapura receives abundant rainfall and as a result the surrounding countryside is very green. Large tea and rubber plantations as well as paddy fields are a common sight in this area. The paddy fields are dotted with gem mines, which can be recognized by their wooden shacks. Mining here is still carried out in the traditional manner using hand tools such as chisels, shovels and hammers. The process begins with digging a pit in the ground, after which earth is removed, washed, sieved and gemstones (if any) are separated. Visitors cannot descend into the mine itself and can only see the workings from the top. Visits to an operational mine can be arranged by local travel agents as well as by guest-houses and hotels.

Environs

Located 4 km (2 miles) west of Ratnapura, the **Maha Saman Devale** is dedicated to Saman (see p148). There has been a temple on this site since the 13th century, although it was damaged by the Portuguese in the 16th century. The shrine was then restored during the Dutch era. A carving on the wall to the right of the entrance steps depicts a Portuguese invader killing a Sinhalese soldier.

An intricately carved doorway leads to the main shrine where *puja* is conducted twice a day. It is flanked by two attractively decorated subsidiary shrines devoted to the Buddha and Pattini, goddess of fertility

and health in Theravada Buddhism. The complex also contains accommodation for monks. A large *perahera* is held at the temple in July or August to coincide with Esala *poya* day.

🔲 **Maha Saman Devale**
Horana Road. **Open** 6am–9pm daily.
🎭 Jul/Aug: Esala Perahera.

㉖ Kudawa

Road map C5. 30 km (19 miles) SE of Ratnapura. from Ratnapura, then change at Kalawana to reach Kudawa. Sun: local market.

Most visitors to the Sinharaja Forest Reserve base themselves in the village of Kudawa where the northern entrance to the reserve is located. The drive from Ratnapura to Kudawa is a pleasant one; winding through villages and past rubber plantations, with an occasional glimpse of toddy tappers collecting the sap of palm trees to ferment into an alcoholic drink. If in the village on a Sunday, a visit to the local market is recommended. The roadside is lined with market stalls selling a variety of fresh produce as well as handicrafts.

Entrance to the main shrine dedicated to Saman, Maha Saman Devale

ⓗ Sinharaja Forest Reserve

Road map C6. 108 km (67 miles) SE of Ratnapura. 🚌 from Ratnapura, then change at Kalawana to reach Kudawa. 🕐 **Open** 6am–6pm daily. 🎫 📷 Note: it is possible to enter the reserve from the south coast, east of Deniyaya.

The Moulawella Trail meandering through the rainforest, Sinharaja Forest Reserve

Considered the largest undisturbed rainforest in Sri Lanka, this reserve stretches over an area of 89 sq km (34 sq miles) and is bounded by the Gin Ganga river to the south and the Kalu Ganga river to the north. Sinharaja, meaning "Lion King", is believed by some to be the home of the mythological Sri Lankan lion from whom the Sinhalese trace their descent. Others think it was once a royal reserve, when it covered an even larger expanse of the island's lowlands. The forest became property of the British Crown in 1840. The area suffered damage from logging in the early 1970s, until it was recognized as a reserve in 1977 and as a World Heritage Site by UNESCO in 1989. The surrounding villages are still allowed to access the forest reserve to collect wood and tap kitul palms for making jaggery and palm wine.

Sinharaja receives up to 599 cm (236 inches) of rainfall annually and the climate inside

Sign for Sinharaja Forest Reserve

the rainforest is hot and humid. The forest is a treasure trove of unique flora and fauna. Of the 211 trees found here, over 60 per cent are endemic. The reserve supports a thriving bird population, with as many as 21 endemic species. These include the crested goshawk, Sri Lankan spurfowl, yellow-fronted barbet and the Ceylon blue magpie. A wide variety of rare butterflies, amphibians and reptiles, such as the rough-nose horned lizard, can also be glimpsed in this forest. However, mammals such as the purple-faced leaf monkey or the giant squirrel may be harder to spot because of the thick foliage. Leopards can be rarely sighted.

The best time to visit Sinharaja is during the dry months, which extend from January to early April and August to September. It is compulsory for visitors to hire a guide to get around the forest. There are trails of varying lengths in the reserve, ranging from 5 km (3 miles) to 14 km (9 miles). Most tourists follow the 8-km (5-mile) Moulawella Trail, which begins at the Kudawa Conservation Centre and winds through the rainforest to the Moulawella Peak. There are a number of observation points along the trail, which offer great opportunities for wildlife-watching. Leeches abound because of the abundant rainfall so be sure to wear appropriate footwear.

Sri Lankan Rainforests

Known as the wet zone, the southwestern lowlands of Sri Lanka are home to the last remaining rainforests in the country. The largest tract of rainforest is Kanneliya-Dediyagala-Nakiyadeniya (KDN), but human activities such as logging have had a serious impact on it. As a result, Sinharaja, albeit smaller, is considered the primary remnant of rainforest on the island. There is a high degree of endemism in the Sri Lankan rainforest, particularly with regard to the flora. The forests are made up of three distinct layers – ground, sub-canopy and canopy – and each of these has unique environmental conditions and organisms. Most of the primary canopy trees are members of the Dipterocarps family, which have winged seeds and large, straight trunks, and can grow up to a height of 45 m (147 ft). Rainforest trees usually have shallow roots, which enable them to reach the nutrients found on the surface level. Epiphytic mosses, orchids and ferns grow on the forest floor and cling to the trunks of the trees; the insect-eating pitcher plants are also commonly found in these forests. The rainforests provide a diversity of habitats to a number of rare birds, insects and reptiles, in addition to endemic species of mammals and butterflies.

Ceylon blue magpie, often seen in the Sri Lankan rainforest

THE CULTURAL TRIANGLE

The Cultural Triangle has a wealth of attractions, including five UNESCO World Heritage sites. The ruins of Anuradhapura and Polonnaruwa, along with the town of Kandy *(see pp134–9)* form the triumvirate of unmissable sights that lend the region its name. Beyond these cultural hotspots lie other fascinating ruins and some superb national parks.

Located in Sri Lanka's northern plains, Anuradhapura and Polonnaruwa are bastions of Sinhalese traditions as well as architectural marvels. All that remains of these great cities today are captivating ruins that provide an insight into Sinhalese culture and inform visitors about the history of Buddhism. In fact, Mihintale, not far from Anuradhapura, is said to be where Mahinda introduced Buddhism *(see p48)* to Sri Lanka.

The Cultural Triangle has, however, much more to offer visitors who venture beyond these sights. The nymph frescoes at the spectacular Sigiriya Rock, and the murals in the Dambulla Cave Temples are excellent examples of Sri Lankan art, while tourists gape at the sheer size of the standing Buddha sculptures at Aukana

and Sasseruwa. There are also the tranquil, abandoned monastery ruins of Ritigala and Arankele for those who want to escape the crowds.

Aside from the cultural sights, this diverse region also boasts a wealth of natural attractions. Visitors can intersperse their sightseeing with trips to Minneriya and Kaudulla national parks, where "the Gathering" of elephants takes place each year during the dry season. The parks also have a wide variety of birdlife.

The Cultural Triangle is well established on the tourist trail and visitors are catered for with comfortable and atmospheric hotels, a host of transport options and tour operators offering a variety of interesting outdoor activities such as hot-air ballooning and cycling.

The awe-inspiring Sigiriya Rock rising above the dense forest

◀ The enormous seated Buddha statue in *dhyana mudra* at Gal Vihara, Polonnaruwa

Exploring the Cultural Triangle

The Cultural Triangle sees more visitors than most areas of Sri Lanka as it is home to numerous sights of historical interest, ranging from staggering ruins of great Sinhalese capitals and Buddhist monasteries to remarkable cave temples carved out of granite outcrops. Centrally located Habarana and Sigiriya are excellent tourist destinations in their own right, along with being good bases for day trips to Polonnaruwa and Anuradhapura. Smaller and less-visited attractions towards the south of the region, such as the temple at Aluvihare or the Nalanda Gedige, can also be comfortably accessed but trips will need to be planned in advance. The region's national parks are ideally positioned to break up an itinerary of historical sights.

Sights at a Glance

1. Matale
2. Aluvihare
3. Nalanda Gedige
4. Ridi Vihara
5. Arankele
6. Panduwas Nuwara
7. Dambulla
8. Popham Arboretum
9. Jathika Namal Uyana
10. *Sigiriya Rock pp166–9*
11. *Polonnaruwa pp170–74*
12. Habarana
13. Minneriya National Park
14. Kaudulla National Park
15. Hurulu Eco Park
16. Ritigala
17. Aukana
18. Sasseruwa
19. Yapahuwa
20. *Anuradhapura pp178–81*
21. Mihintale

Murals depicting the Buddha adorning the wall of a cave temple, Ridi Vihara

For hotels and restaurants in this region see pp220–21 and p232

Visitors making their way towards the giant Sigiriya Rock

The grand Thuparama Dagoba, Anuradhapura

0 km   15

0 miles   15

Getting Around

Visitors to the Cultural Triangle often hire a car and driver, which makes getting around easier and less time consuming. Trains run from Colombo to both Anuradhapura and Polonnaruwa and bus services in the region are regular and reliable. Habarana is a key point for changing buses. Bear in mind, however, that some of the north-bound buses can be extremely crowded and travelling in them can be difficult. Dambulla, Habarana and Sigiriya are ideal bases for day trips to surrounding areas. To visit towns and sights located further afield, tourists without a car often choose to arrange tours through guesthouses or hotels, or hire a three-wheeler. The ruins at Anuradhapura and Polonnaruwa are best explored on bicycle and these can be hired from nearby guesthouses. A jeep and driver are needed for park safaris, which can be arranged through hotels or at the entrance to the parks.

Key

━━━ Major road

═══ Minor road

┅┅┅ Railway

━━━ Provincial border

For map symbols *see back flap*

The *gopuram* of Sri Muthumariamman Thevasthanam, Matale

❶ Matale

Road map C4. 150 km (92 miles) NE of Colombo. 🚗 482,000. 🚌 🚍 🚉

Matale is a busy town that does not have many attractions of its own, but serves as an entry point to Sri Lanka's ancient cities. Tourists en route from Kandy *(see pp134–9)* to Dambulla *(see p160)* often make a stop over in Matale to visit the **Sri Muthumariamman Thevasthanam** – an attractive *kovil* located on the town's main road, and dedicated to the goddess Mariamman. The statuary on the *gopuras* is painted in muted colours, in stark contrast to the vivid colouring of other temples found on the island.

About 2 km (1 mile) north of Matale is the **Aluvihare Heritage Centre** set up by renowned Sri Lankan artist Ena de Silva. Visitors can walk around and explore the sprawling gardens and watch artisans producing intricate batik and fine embroidery in the centre's workshops. If arranged in advance, it is possible to have lunch at the centre's Aluvihare Kitchens, where a buffet offering various rice dishes and as many as 24 different curries is served to groups of four or more.

🏛 **Sri Muthumariamman Thevasthanam**
King's Street. **Open** 6am–6pm daily.
🚫 🚷

🏛 **Aluvihare Heritage Centre**
Tel (066) 222 2404. **Open** 9am–5pm Mon–Sat. 🚫 📷

❷ Aluvihare

Road map C4. 4 km (2 miles) N of Matale. 🚍 🚉 **Open** 6:30am–6:30pm daily. 🚫 🚷

Comprising a series of caves carved out of rock, the Aluvihare monastery complex is an atmospheric site. It marks the spot where the *Tripitakaya* – the Theravada Buddhist canon – was first penned in the 1st century BC. Prior to this, the Buddha's diverse teachings were passed orally from one generation to the next. The *ola-leaf* manuscripts, which were transcribed from the Pali language by 500 monks, remained safe here until the mid-19th century when they were destroyed by British troops during an attack on the temple.

The monastic caves are linked to each other by a flight of steps and small paths between the rocks and boulders; triangular

Mural depicting sinners being punished in the afterlife, Aluvihare

shapes have been carved into the stone to act as holders for lamps. The first cave temple has a 10-m (32-ft) long reclining Buddha and colourful lotus flower paintings adorning the ceiling. Some steps up, the second cave is also home to a reclining Buddha statue. However, the most striking aspect is the graphic murals on the walls of the cave depicting sinners being tortured in hell. Transgressors are shown being beheaded, their heads impaled, or their skulls being cut open.

The cave opposite this one depicts life-size plaster figures enduring these torments. A gap in the rock between the first two cave temples leads to a smaller cave with a brightly painted exterior. This cave is dedicated to the Indian Buddhist scholar, Buddhaghosa, known for his extensive work on the *Tripitakaya*. From here steps lead up to a bo tree, a *dagoba* and a terrace that offers lovely views of the surrounding hills.

To the left of the temple complex, up a flight of steps, is the **International Buddhist Library and Museum**. Inside are old photographs, Buddha statues and a display detailing how palmyra leaves become *ola-leaf* manuscripts.

❸ Nalanda Gedige

Road map C4. 20 km (12 miles) N of Matale. 🚍 🚉 **Open** 7am–5pm daily. 🚫 ♿

Named after the famous Buddhist university in northern India, Nalanda Gedige is a unique structure built in the south Indian architectural style. Despite looking like a Hindu temple, complete with a *mandapa* (pillared porch), the *gedige* (image house) bears no signs of any Hindu gods and it is thought to have only ever been used by Buddhists.

Constructed entirely of stone, the *gedige* is believed to have been built between the 7th and 11th centuries. However, it has only stood on its present location since the 1980s when the building was meticulously moved from its low-lying home amid paddy fields to make way for a man-made lake.

Much of the original structure has been reduced to ruins. The carvings on the exterior walls are aged and weather-beaten, but it is still possible to make out details such as faces, a carving of a god on the south side and a row of miniature buildings carved on the entrance archway. Careful inspection will also reveal a *tantric* carving on the southern side of the base plinth.

There is a newer brick *dagoba* next to the *gedige*, as well as a museum that displays photographs of some of the details from the building and also an inscription pillar recovered from the area.

Atmospheric ruins of the Nalanda Gedige

❹ Ridi Vihara

Road map C4. 36 km (22 miles) NW of Matale. 🚌 ⏲ **Open** 7am–10pm daily. 📷

The little-visited Ridi Vihara, or Silver Temple, was founded by King Dutugemunu on the spot where a vein of silver was discovered. The temple complex comprises rock-cut shrines, hermitages and *dagobas*; some of the best examples of traditional Kandyan frescoes can be seen here.

Upon entering the complex, the shrine on the left is the Varakha Valanda Vihara, or the Jackfruit Temple. Originally built as a Hindu temple in traditional south Indian style, it was converted into a Buddhist shrine during the Kandyan period. The main temple, Pahala Vihara,

lies further ahead. It houses a golden seated Buddha and a large reclining Buddha. A platform in front of the reclining statue is inset with blue and white Dutch (Delft) tiles, depicting biblical scenes. There is a beautifully carved door frame inlaid with ivory right next to the entrance.

The nearby Uda Vihara was built by King Kirti Sri Rajasinghe. A Kandyan-era moonstone, flanked by large elephants with intricate carvings under their trunks, can be seen by the entrance. The main chamber has a seated Buddha statue as well as some very beautiful 18th-century frescoes.

The complex is set amid attractive countryside and affords great views of the surrounding area.

❺ Arankele

Road map C4. 48 km (30 miles) W of Matale. ⏲ **Open** 6am–6pm daily.

Another little-visited site, Arankele is where the remains of a 6th-century monastery can

be found. Isolated and heavily forested, the hermitage is home to a community of monks, who have devoted themselves to an austere and meditative lifestyle.

Beyond the monastery buildings, lies the meditation walkway, a long paved path interspersed with small flights of steps. En route, visitors will see the ruins of meditation chambers, bathing ponds and the remains of the principal monk's residence. The path continues to a small shrine devoted to the Buddha.

❻ Panduwas Nuwara

Road map B4. 91 km (56 miles) NW of Matale. ⏲ **Open** 9am–5pm daily.

Dating back to the 12th century, Panduwas Nuwara was used by King Parakramabahu I as a temporary royal capital before he built his citadel at Polonnaruwa (*see pp170–74*). The remains of the city are scattered over a sprawling site stretching for several square kilometres. The main attraction is the royal palace, thought to have once been multi-storeyed, which is enclosed within the citadel; the area where the protective moat once was can still be seen. An inscription inside the palace building records a visit by King Nissankamalla. Beyond the royal complex is a renovated tooth temple, which is open to visitors. The site has not yet been entirely excavated, although in recent years a new initiative has been launched to uncover more of the ruins.

Reclining and seated Buddha statues inside the Pahala Vihara, Ridi Vihara

Impressive façade of the Golden Temple Buddhist Museum, Dambulla

the Veddahs, before moving through to the frescoes of Sigiriya, the 12th-century wall paintings at Polonnaruwa, and works from the prolific Kandyan period. The exhibition finishes with reproductions of early 20th-century paintings. In addition, the museum explains the new tradition of painting scenes depicting hell in Buddhist shrines.

🏛 **Golden Temple Buddhist Museum**
In the Dambulla Cave Temples complex. **Tel** (066) 228 3606 (ext 181/182). **Open** 7:30am–9pm daily. 🅦 **golden temple.lk**

🏛 **Dambulla Museum**
Main Road. **Tel** (066) 228 4760. **Open** 8am–4pm daily. 🏛

❼ Dambulla

Road map C3. 47 km (29 miles) N of Matale. 🏔 72,000. 🚌 🛈

A small town situated in the heart of the Cultural Triangle, Dambulla lies at a junction of the Kandy-to-Anuradhapura and Colombo-to-Trincomalee roads. There are several accommodation options in town and in the surrounding countryside, so Dambulla serves as a good base for exploring sights in the nearby area. While most visitors come here to see the famous Dambulla Cave Temples *(see pp162–3)*, there are also some museums to take in. South of the city centre is a vibrant wholesale fresh produce market, which makes for a fascinating visit.

The imposing golden Buddha statue at the foot of the steps leading up to the Dambulla Cave Temples is hard to miss. This 30-m (98-ft) high image portrays the Buddha in the *dharmachakra* (wheel-turning) pose. At the base of the statue lies the **Golden Temple Buddhist Museum**, the entrance to which is through the mouth of a kitsch-looking dragon. Exhibits on display include Buddha statues from Thailand, Myanmar, Korea and Japan, panels illustrating the story of the Buddha's life, *ola*-leaf manuscripts, many

paintings of *peraheras* and drummers as well as a number of artifacts.

A short distance south of the Golden Temple Buddhist Museum stands **Dambulla Museum** that traces the history of Sri Lankan art from cave paintings to the Colonial era. The museum exhibits excellent canvas reproductions of both well-known and lesser-known frescoes and murals from all over the island, enabling visitors to appreciate art that would otherwise remain inaccessible.

On the first floor is an excellent exhibition detailing the history of mural painting in Sri Lanka, The seven rooms are in chronological order and begin with the rock and wall paintings of

❽ Popham Arboretum

Road map C3. Kandalama Road, 3 km (2 miles) E of Dambulla. **Tel** (077) 726 7951. 🛈 **Open** 9am–5pm Thu–Tue (call ahead of visit). 🏛 book in advance. Note: donation is appreciated.

Founded in 1963 by British tea planter and dendrologist Sam Popham, this is the only dry-zone arboretum in Sri Lanka. When Popham bought this abandoned piece of land, it was covered with scrub. After clearing the scrub vegetation, he noticed that the indigenous trees, which were unable to grow previously due to the dense scrub cover, were starting to thrive. Following this

A painting from the pre-modern phase on display at the Dambulla Museum, Dambulla

The rustic-looking visitor centre in Popham Arboretum

observation, he developed the "Popham Method", an experiment in reforesting that involved selectively clearing a scrub jungle so that native trees could seed and grow.

Spread over an area of 14 ha (35 acres), the arboretum has around 200 species of trees and shrubs, including many endemic ones. Among the tropical trees here are satinwood, ebony, tamarind and ironwood, which in turn provide habitat for a variety of birds such as the endemic Sri Lankan jungle fowl, the grey hornbill and the blue-tailed bee eater, in addition to small mammals.

Sign for Popham Arboretum

Designed by Geoffrey Bawa, the visitor centre of the arboretum used to be Popham's home before he left Sri Lanka in the 1980s and headed back to the UK. An album containing photographs of what the arboretum looked like in its early years, and of the mud hut that was Popham's first home, is available on request.

There are three colour-coded trails that meander through the arboretum grounds. Visitors can explore these trails independently, or arrange for a guided walk; all trails begin from the visitor centre. It is also possible to come for an evening walk when there is a chance of sighting a slender loris, a spotted deer or a pangolin.

❾ Jathika Namal Uyana

Road map C3. 7 km (4 miles) NW of Dambulla. **Tel** (025) 325 3816.
🚌 from Dambulla. 🕐 **Open** 6am–6:30pm daily. ♿ 🌐 **jathikanamal uyana.com**

Seldom visited by tourists, Jathika Namal Uyana, in Ulpathgama, is worth a visit for those who enjoy walking and wildlife-watching. Covering an area of over 105 ha (260 acres), it is said to be the largest Na tree, or ironwood, forest in Asia. The forest is home to diverse flora as well as a wide range of birds, butterflies, lizards and mammals, such as monkeys and giant squirrels. It is believed that the forest was planted by King Devanampiya Tissa in the 3rd century BC. But another legend states that the forest was a sanctuary for Buddhist monks in the 8th century. These monks offered refuge to people in need, and all those who took shelter here had to plant a tree and tend to it, which eventually resulted in the large forest that can be seen today. The area is dotted with various monastic remains, and there are also the ruins of a stupa near the entrance.

Besides Na trees, Jathika Namal Uyana is also famous for a range of pink quartz hills, which are made up of seven peaks and are thought to date back more than 550 million years. A small, pink Buddha statue stands on the summit of the lowest hill, which can be reached by following a gently rising forest trail, crisscrossed with streams. There are great views of the surrounding countryside from the top.

Pink quartz hills in Jathika Namal Uyana

Dambulla Cave Temples

The beautifully painted cave temples of Dambulla were designated a UNESCO World Heritage Site in 1991. The cave temples date back to the 1st century BC, when King Valagambahu (r.103 BC and 89–77BC) sought refuge in the caves after being exiled from Anuradhapura. When the king regained his throne after 14 years, he converted the caves into rock temples in gratitude to the monks who had offered him sanctuary. Further improvements and embellishments were made to the temples by various kings down the centuries. The temple complex is made up of a series of five caves that are filled with statues of the Buddha in various sizes and *mudras*. The walls and ceilings of the caves are adorned with paintings depicting religious and secular themes. The murals date from between the 2nd century BC to 18th century AD.

Cave III (Maha Alut Viharaya)
King Kirti Sri Rajasinghe converted this cave from a storeroom in the 18th century. The reclining Buddha by the left wall is carved out of rock, as is the Buddha figure facing the entrance. The frescoes here are largely painted in the Kandyan style.

★ **Cave IV (Pascima Viharaya)**
Relatively small in size, this cave contains a *dagoba* in the middle that was broken into by thieves who thought it contained some of the jewels of Queen Somawathie, wife of King Valagambahu. The cave also contains a splendid seated Buddha under an elaborate *makara torana*, along with several larger seated Buddhas.

KEY

① Bo Tree
② Lotus Pond

Cave V (Devana Alut Viharaja)
This cave is the newest and smallest of the temples. Unlike the statues in the other caves, some of which are carved out of rock, the images here are built of brick and plaster. The cave features a 10-m (33-ft) reclining Buddha, and on the wall, behind his feet, are paintings depicting the Hindu deities, Vishnu and Kataragama.

VISITORS' CHECKLIST

Practical information
Off Kandy-Jaffna Highway.
Tel (066) 228 3605.
Open 7:30am–6pm daily.

🅦 goldentemple.lk

Transport
🚌 🚉

Temple Exterior

The five cave temples are carved out of a granite outcrop that towers 100 m (350 ft) above Dambulla town. There are excellent views over the surrounding countryside from the terrace; on a clear day, it is possible to see as far as Sigiriya *(see pp166–9)* in the distance.

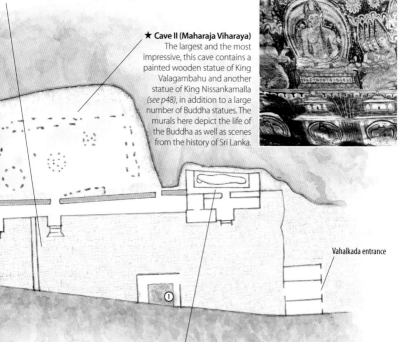

★ Cave II (Maharaja Viharaya)
The largest and the most impressive, this cave contains a painted wooden statue of King Valagambahu and another statue of King Nissankamalla *(see p48)*, in addition to a large number of Buddha statues. The murals here depict the life of the Buddha as well as scenes from the history of Sri Lanka.

Vahalkada entrance

★ Cave I (Devaraja Viharaya)
The highlight here is a 14-m (46-ft) long reclining Buddha, carved out of solid rock. A statue thought to be of Ananda, the Buddha's loyal disciple, stands at his feet. The paintings on the walls and ceiling of this cave are faded by smoke from incense.

Ruins of King Parakramabahu's magnificent palace in the ancient city of Polonnaruwa ▶

⑩ Sigiriya Rock

Declared a UNESCO World Heritage Site in 1982, the ancient citadel of Sigiriya (Lion Rock) sits atop a giant granite rock rising 200 m (656 ft) above the surrounding countryside. There are conflicting theories about the history of Sigiriya, but according to the *Mahavamsa* King Kassapa killed his father, King Dhatusena, in AD 477 to inherit the throne. Fearing retribution from his half-brother, Mogallana, Kassapa built an impregnable palace-fortress on the summit of the rock between AD 477 and 485. The site is thought to have been occupied for millennia, but much of what can be seen here today is attributed to the time of King Kassapa. The ruins were first discovered by British archaeologists in the early 20th century, and excavations have continued here ever since.

Aerial view of Sigiriya Rock

Western Entrance

①

The Royal Gardens
These landscaped gardens are divided into water, boulder and terrace gardens. The water gardens on the way to the rock form an avenue, with brick-lined pools and islands with ruined pavilions on either side. Beyond these lie the boulder and terrace gardens at the base of the rock.

Legend of Sigiriya

The history of Sigiriya is shrouded in many legends. It is popularly believed that Kassapa immured his father, King Dhatusena in a wall, in order to usurp the throne. He then moved the capital from Anuradhapura to Sigiriya Rock and, fearing attack from Mogallana, built a palace on the summit. There is, however, a different theory that has been put forward by Dr Raja de Silva, the former Archaeological Commissioner of Sri Lanka. He maintains that there was never a palace or fortress on the rock, but rather a Buddhist monastery. There is evidence to suggest that monks lived here before, during and after the time of Kassapa and that they were here until the site was abandoned in the 12th century. However, most people favour the theory of Kassapa's impenetrable rock palace and fortress.

Bust of King Kassapa in Hotel Sigiriya

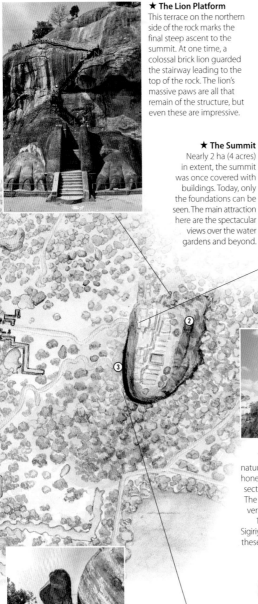

★ The Lion Platform
This terrace on the northern side of the rock marks the final steep ascent to the summit. At one time, a colossal brick lion guarded the stairway leading to the top of the rock. The lion's massive paws are all that remain of the structure, but even these are impressive.

★ The Summit
Nearly 2 ha (4 acres) in extent, the summit was once covered with buildings. Today, only the foundations can be seen. The main attraction here are the spectacular views over the water gardens and beyond.

VISITORS' CHECKLIST

Practical information
Road map C3.
28 km (17 miles) NE of Dambulla.
🛈 Open 7am–6pm daily
(last entry around 5pm). 🚻 📷
📷 Sigiriya Frescoes.

Transport
🚌 🚕

The Mirror Wall
This wall was originally coated with a natural concoction of lime, egg white and honey, which lent it a brilliant shine; some sections look highly polished even today. The wall is covered with graffiti – often in verses – by visitors between the 7th and 13th centuries on their impressions of Sigiriya and the frescoes here. Translations of these can be seen in the Sigiriya Museum.

Cobra Hood Cave
Named for its resemblance to a cobra hood, this cave has a drip ledge with an inscription in Brahmi script dating from the 2nd century BC. The cave's ceiling is adorned with floral patterns and paintings.

KEY

① **The Sigiriya Museum** details the history of the rock, from its formation to its use as a palace and a Buddhist monastery through the centuries. The museum also contains models, archaeological finds such as statues and ceramics as well as reproductions of the famous frescoes.

② **Sigiriya Frescoes** *see pp168–9*

③ **Cistern and Audience Hall rocks**

Sigiriya Frescoes

One of the highlights of a visit to Sigiriya Rock are the beautiful frescoes that can be seen in a sheltered gallery in the western rock face. Of the estimated original of 500 frescoes, only 21 remain today. Dating from around the 5th century, the paintings were initially thought to depict Kassapa's concubines but are now believed to be portraits of *apsaras* (celestial nymphs) with their attendants. However, a theory suggested by Dr Raja de Silva claims that these are actually depictions of the Mahayana goddess, Tara. Among the island's most iconic images, the frescoes have been likened in style to those in the Ajanta Caves in southwestern India. Despite their antiquity, the paintings remain remarkably well preserved, in part because of the protection afforded by the stone ledge.

A group of visitors admiring the impressive frescoes, Sigiriya Rock

The paintings of the damsels are naturalistic in style, with each of the figures possessing a distinct character. The girls are mostly bare chested and adorned with jewellery. Guides are able to point out the errors made by the painter, such as the girl with three hands, or the one with three nipples.

The touches of green are thought to be later additions to the frescoes, as other colours have been found underneath the coating.

Some of the frescoes were defaced by a vandal in 1967. Italian restoration expert Luciano Maranzi was then brought in to help restore the damaged paintings. In recent years, there has been much discussion over their fading colours and how to counter this; as well as accusations of neglect. However, the frescoes have also been damaged by the insects that have nested beneath the plaster, and exposure to the sun.

Situated at an elevation of about 100 m (330 ft), the viewing platform for the frescoes is reached via a metal spiral staircase. The frescoes are largely protected by the stone ledge, but are still susceptible to damage by wind and abrasive dust as well as the afternoon sun.

The principal colours used to paint these frescoes were red, yellow and brown; green was used occasionally. The colours were derived from natural materials, which were dried and crushed into pigment. The frescoes were then painted on wet plaster. As the paintings dried, the colours became permanently incorporated into the plaster.

Apsara and Attendant

An *apsara* is a celestial or water spirit in Hindu and Buddhist mythology. Painted on the ceilings of caves and temples as well as carved on pillars and in bas-reliefs, these voluptuous mythical beings are often pictured dancing, attending to the gods or even hovering above the Buddha. The Sigiriya damsels are believed to be *apsaras*, and the figures carrying platters of flowers and fruit are thought to be their attendants. This is attributed to their slightly darker skin tone and covered torsos.

All the Sigiriya damsels are shown only from the waist up, rising out of clouds.

The Ajanta Caves in Maharashtra, in India, are home to dry frescoes that date back to between the 2nd century BC and the 5th century AD. Painted in ochre, black, white and blue, these works of art depict scenes from the Buddha's life as well as his teachings.

⓫ Polonnaruwa

The well-preserved ruins of Polonnaruwa are often considered the highlight of the Cultural Triangle. The city was the centrepiece of the Sinhalese kingdom established by King Vijayabahu I, who ousted the invading Cholas in AD 1077. His successor, King Parakramabahu I, steered Polonnaruwa into its golden age during the 12th century. He developed the city on a massive scale and commissioned the construction of monasteries, temples and the enormous Parakrama Samudra, or the "Sea of Parakrama" tank. Nissankamalla was the third of the famous Polonnaruwa kings, and after his death the kingdom descended into chaos, primarily because of weak rulers and constant invasions. The city, finally abandoned in 1293, was quickly consumed by the jungle. Excavation and restoration work began in the 20th century, and in 1982 it was declared a UNESCO World Heritage Site.

Area illustrated

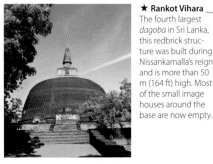

★ Rankot Vihara
The fourth largest *dagoba* in Sri Lanka, this redbrick structure was built during Nissankamalla's reign, and is more than 50 m (164 ft) high. Most of the small image houses around the base are now empty.

Rankot Vihara

Menik Vihara

Northern Gate

The Quadrangle
This enclosure *(see p173)* on a raised terrace is the highlight of a visit to Polonnaruwa. It is home to a number of important monuments, including the famous Vatadage that housed the Tooth Relic.

Bendiwewa

Quadrangle

Shiva Devale No 1

Entrance

Audience Hall

Council Chamber

Royal Baths

ISLAND GARDEN

Polonnaruwa Museum

Royal Palace

Council Chamber

Royal Baths

Royal Palace Gro

1ST CANAL ROAD

BATTICALOA ROAD

Southern Ruins 2 km (1 mile)

POLONNARUWA

Polonnaruwa Museum
The museum exhibits artifacts recovered from the site, including beautiful bronze statues. It also has scale models of how the city's buildings would have looked in their heyday.

★ Gal Vihara
This shrine comprises a group of four beautiful Buddha statues, carved out of a single slab of granite. The reclining Buddha is the main attraction, but there are also two seated Buddhas and one in the standing pose.

Lankatilaka
This image house was built by Parakramabahu I. The towering walls of the shrine enclose a huge, albeit headless, standing Buddha statue. Do not miss the bas-relief on the exterior walls.

0 metres		500
0 yards		500

Shiva Devale No 2
Dating from the Chola period, the well-preserved ruins of this temple are thought to be the oldest in Polonnaruwa. There are Tamil inscriptions on the walls.

Key

▬ Major road
═ Other road
═ Minor road

Polonnaruwa Railway Station 3 km (2 miles)

Exploring Polonnaruwa

Polonnaruwa's ruins are clustered together in various groups. The Royal Palace Group to the south of the entrance is where the remains of Parakramabahu's palace and the Audience Hall can be seen, and the spectacular Quadrangle north of the entrance is home to the splendid Vatadage that enshrined the Tooth Relic. There is a large concentration of religious structures in the northern part of the site, outside the original city walls. The Island Garden is situated close to the Polonnaruwa Museum, while the Southern Ruins are found a short distance further south along the lake. The well-preserved ruins of Polonnaruwa are too extensive to be explored on foot; cycling is recommended and bicycles are available for rent from guesthouses.

Visitors exploring the extensive ruins of the Royal Palace Group

🏠 Royal Palace Group

At the centre of the ancient city is the Royal Palace Group, where King Parakramabahu's palace, also known as Vejayanta Prasada, and other buildings were once protected by heavy fortifications. The palace is believed to have originally stood seven storeys high with a thousand rooms, although all that remains today is a three-storey building made of brick. The palace's great hall had a roof supported by 30 columns, and visitors can still see the holes in the walls that held the beams in place.

To the east of the palace is the Council Chamber, or Audience Hall, where the king would have met with his advisors and various officials. The roof of the chamber is long gone, but the base still remains, decorated with friezes depicting dwarves, lions and elephants. The staircase leading up to the landing has a fine moonstone at its base, ornamented balustrades, and two lions flanking the top step.

Towards the east of the Council Chamber are the geometric-shaped Royal Baths. It is thought that this area may have been a pleasure garden with trees and flowers surrounding the baths. Nearby are the remains of what was probably a bathhouse.

🏛 Shiva Devale No 1

Located north of the Royal Palace Group, this shrine, dedicated to Lord Shiva, is thought to have been built during a period of south Indian occupation of Polonnaruwa in the 13th century. No mortar has been used in the construction of the shrine; the stones fit together perfectly. The inner sanctum houses a *lingam* (see p93), and some very fine bronze statues that were found here are now on display in the Colombo National Museum (see pp78–9).

🏠 Buddha Seema Pasada

Situated near Lankatilaka, Buddha Seema Pasada was a large chapter house within a monastery complex. It is said that the original structure that stood here was as tall as 12 storeys. Monks' cells surround a pillared hall with a raised platform at its centre, which is thought to have been reserved for the highest-ranking member of the monastery. The hall is connected to the inner courtyard by four entrances, each decorated by a moonstone.

🏠 Kiri Vihara

Towards the north of Lankatilaka lies the Kiri Vihara, a *dagoba* very similar in style to the Rankot Vihara (see p170). It is believed to have been dedicated to Parakramabahu's wife, Subhadra. *Kiri* means milk in Sinhala, and the *dagoba* was named after the bright white plaster covering it, which was found in perfect condition when the building was discovered.

🏠 Menik Vihara

Close to the northern gate of the city is a path that leads to the remains of the Menik Vihara. The site has nothing more than the restored foundations of many monastery buildings as well as a small *dagoba*. The shrine's fragmented top has revealed the relic chamber within, which can be viewed from a platform.

The stark, milky white *dagoba* of the Kiri Vihara

The Quadrangle

North of Shiva Devale No 1 is the Quadrangle, one of Polonnaruwa's premier attractions. This complex is home to a number of fascinating buildings. Built on an elevated terrace, this rectangular enclosure houses the Vatadage, one of the most beautiful architectural structures in Polonnaruwa. A relic house built by Parakramabahu, the Vatadage comprises a central *dagoba* set on a raised terrace, surrounded by a brick wall. Entrances at the four cardinal points lead to the terrace, from which another four sets of steps climb up to the *dagoba*. Buddha statues greet visitors at the top step of the landing.

The exceptionally large and well-preserved Thuparama shrine

A moonstone embellishing the steps leading up to the central *dagoba* of the Vatadage

Located opposite the Vatadage, the Hatadage is a Tooth Relic temple built by Nissankamalla, and was originally a two-storey building. A beautiful moonstone adorns the entrance, and inside the shrine are three Buddha statues. Adjacent lies the Atadage that was built by Vijayabahu I to house the Tooth Relic when Polonnaruwa was made the capital of the kingdom. A few decorated pillars and the base are all that remains of the ancient building.

On the other side of the Hatadage is Gal Pota, a large granite slab that weighs over 25 tons (28 tonnes) and is over 8 m (26 ft) long. The inscriptions on it relate the works of King Nissankamalla. Beside Gal Pota is the Satmahal Prasada, which resembles a Khmer (Cambodian) temple in its stepped design.

Close to the gate west of the Vadatage is Nissankalata, also known as the Lotus Mandapa. Here lies a small *dagoba* set on a platform, encircled by stone pillars that are shaped like thrice-bent lotus buds on stalks. It is believed that Nissankamalla used this platform to listen to the chanting of religious texts.

The last of the Quadrangle's shrines is the Thuparama, located in the southwest corner of the enclosure. An image house that dates to the time of Vijayabahu, this ancient structure houses eight Buddha statues, some of which date from the Anuradhapura period. The thick walls of the shrine have loopholes that allow sunlight to penetrate inside, causing the limestone crystals in the Buddha statues to sparkle.

The Quadrangle

Sights list

① Vataḍage
② Hatadage
③ Gal Pota
④ Satmahal Prasada
⑤ Atadage
⑥ Nissankalata
⑦ Thuparama

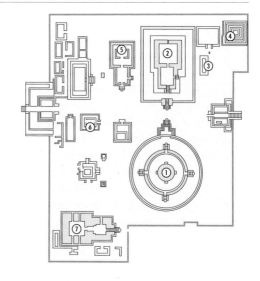

0 metres 500
0 yards 500

The ruins of the Council Chamber with its large granite lion, Island Garden

🄝 Island Garden

Just behind the Polonnaruwa Museum lie what are believed to be the ruins of Nissankamalla's royal palace. Built on the site of Parakramabahu's pleasure gardens, the complex comprises the remains of several buildings. The most interesting structure, however, is the Council Chamber. Although the roof has now gone, the plinth, and four rows of columns that presumably balanced the roof, survive. At the southern end of the plinth is a large granite lion, most likely marking the position of Nissankamalla's throne. The columns nearest to the lion have inscriptions identifying dignitaries, such as the prime minister, the record keeper and members of the chamber of commerce, who sat next to them during meetings with the king.

Large bearded statue carved out of a boulder, near Potgul Vihara

Towards the south of the Council Chamber is a stone mausoleum, possibly the site of Nissankamalla's cremation. The remains of the Royal Baths, fed by underground pipes from the Parakrama Samudra, are nearby. Also close to the Council Chamber is a mound where the remains of King Parakramabahu's Summer House can be found.

🄝 Southern Ruins

A short distance away from the rest of the ruins is Polonnaruwa's southern site. Visitors can either take a pleasant walk or cycle along the bank of the Parakrama Samudra to reach these ruins. Here lies the well-preserved Potgul Vihara, a monastery complex comprising, among other ruins, four *dagobas* that surround a circular brick building. The central structure, with its thick walls, is thought to have housed a library of sacred books. Some believe that it was built by Parakramabahu as a place where he could listen to a great Brahmanical sage named Pulasti.

To the north of Potgul Vihara is a large 4-m (12-ft) high statue of a bearded figure carved from a rock. It is notable for being less stylized than the other sculptures in Polonnaruwa. It is said by some that the statue is that of King Parakramabahu I himself. Others believe that it is a representation of a sage, possibly Kapila or Pulasti.

🄬 Habarana

Road map C3. 11 km (7 miles) NW of Sigiriya. 🄰 3,400. 🄰 🄰 🄰

A small, laid-back village, Habarana sits on an important route that connects the cities of Anuradhapura and Polonnaruwa. It is a major transport junction, with roads leading north towards Trincomalee and Jaffna as well as south towards Kandy and Colombo.

Habarana does not boast of many attractions. However, it is a convenient base to explore the Cultural Triangle as it offers easy access to almost all important sights, such as Anuradhapura, Polonnaruwa, Sigiriya and Dambulla. A safari to Minneriya or Kaudulla national parks, or Hurulu Eco Park to observe elephants and other wildlife can also be easily arranged from Habarana. There is a decent choice of relatively upmarket accommodation for tourists.

The village is home to the Habarana Lake, around which tour operators organize elephant rides. The footpath around the placid lake is great for a leisurely evening stroll. For those looking to relax after a day of sightseeing, there are a number of establishments in and around the village that offer personalized Ayurvedic treatments.

Tourists enjoying an elephant ride near the Habarana Lake

An elephant herd near the tank during the dry season, Minneriya National Park

⑬ Minneriya National Park

Road map C3. 32 km (20 miles) E of Habarana. **Tel** (060) 227 9243. **Open** 2–6pm daily. 🚌 🚹 🐾 Note: best visited between June and October. Hotels and guesthouses can arrange safaris to the park.

Along with the Kaudulla National Park towards the north and Wasgomuwa National Park in the south, Minneriya forms part of the elephant corridor that connects the protected areas located within the Cultural Triangle and facilitates elephant migration.

The large Minneriya Wewa, which is the focal point of the park, was built by King Mahasena in the 4th century and covers an area of 30 sq km (11 sq miles). Between the months of August and October, at the height of the dry season, elephants congregate at the tank. Their numbers peak during September; as many as 300 elephants have been recorded here at this time. This annual event is popularly known as "the Gathering" when the pachyderms come to the park for water and fresh shoots of grass that grow on the lake bed as the waters recede, as well as to look for mates.

Minneriya boasts a wide variety of habitats, ranging from wetland to tropical forest, and aquatic and forest birds can both be sighted here. There are also macaques, sambar deer, wild buffaloes, land monitors, and even some elusive leopard and sloth bears to be observed.

Visitors should note that at the time of the Gathering the park can get very busy and some concerns have been raised about the number of tourist jeeps and their effect on elephant movement.

⑭ Kaudulla National Park

Road map C3. 22 km (14 miles) NE of Habarana. **Tel** (027) 327 9735. **Open** 2–6pm daily. 🚌 🚹 🐾 Note: best visited between August and December. Hotels and guesthouses can arrange trips to the park.

Established in 2002, Kaudulla is also part of the elephant corridor. Like Minneriya, it has a tank as its centrepiece, which attracts a large number of elephants during the dry season. The park has a varied

habitat and supports wildlife that is very similar to Minneriya's; however, rusty spotted cats are also found here. Outside the dry season, much of the park is underwater, and the elephants migrate to the surrounding jungles. The park is home to a wide variety of bird species, which include spot-billed pelicans, lesser adjutant and cormorants. Boat rides on the lake can also be arranged.

When on a safari, be aware that jeeps do not get too close to the animals. It is always best to maintain a safe distance from elephants, as they may charge.

⑮ Hurulu Eco Park

Road map C3. 10 km (6 miles) NE of Habarana. **Open** 2–6:30pm daily. 🚌 🚹 🐾 Note: hotels and guesthouses can arrange trips to the park.

Part of the Hurulu Biosphere Reserve, Hurulu Eco Park opened to visitors in 2008. Hurulu is often suggested as an alternative when Minneriya and Kaudulla are too wet for any wildlife-spotting. Although the park does not have a large tank – it has small waterways that intersect – it attracts a good number of elephants and birds as well as other mammals such as deer, water buffaloes and monkeys. There are plans underway to merge the smaller abandoned tanks within the park to create one large tank, and to convert the jeep tracks running through the park into walking trails for visitors.

A colony of painted storks wading in Kaudulla Tank, Kaudulla National Park

⑯ Ritigala

Road map C3. 21 km (13 miles) NW of Habarana. ⓣ **Open** 7am–6pm daily.

A forest monastery complex now protected within the Ritigala Strict Nature Reserve, Ritigala is an enigmatic archaeological site. In the 9th century, the jungle-covered, monastic caves were inhabited by monks of the Pansakulika Order, who were sworn to a life of extreme austerity and were attracted to the area's remote location.

It may be possible to hire a guide at the reserve's visitor centre, which also has some information panels about the area. Beyond the entrance of the ruins is a path running around the periphery of the Banda Pokuna bathing tank, which has been partially restored. In the far corner are steps leading up to a walkway that links all of the complex's major buildings. Up ahead in the first clearing is one of the double platform structures Ritigala is known for, linked by a stone bridge. It is believed that the structures were used by the monks for meditation purposes and that the area underneath was flooded with water to keep the place cool. To the right of the platforms is another clearing, which is popularly described as the monastery hospital.

Further along the paved walkway, towards the left, lies what is believed to be the library. The next clearing has another, larger, raised platform and a smaller structure with a patterned urinal stone. The final clearing is home to another raised platform, which is not as well preserved.

⑰ Aukana

Road map C3. 37 km (23 miles) W of Habarana. ⓣ **Open** 7am–7pm daily.

The village of Aukana is best known as the site of a 12-m (40-ft) high standing Buddha statue carved from solid rock. It is an elegant, imposing sculpture, with some intricately

Beautifully carved staircase leading up to the terrace, Yapahuwa

carved details, such as the folds of the Buddha's robes. The Buddha stands in the *asisa mudra*, which is a variation of the *abhaya mudra*. Traditionally, this stance was rarely seen in Sri Lankan Buddhist statuary, although statues imitating the *mudra* can now be found throughout the island.

⑱ Sasseruwa

Road map C3. 12 km (8 miles) W of Aukana. ⓣ **Open** daily.

The Buddha statue at Sasseruwa is similar to the one at Aukana in height and posture, albeit rather clunky in appearance. A favourite legend surrounding the statues is that the one at Aukana was carved by a master and the one at Sasseruwa by his student. Aukana was completed first and to a higher standard so the student abandoned his sculpture in dismay.

Along with the Buddha statue – accessed via a flight of about 50 steps – there is also a bo tree

Buddhist frescoes adorning the walls of the cave temples, Sasseruwa

and a couple of cave temples, which are thought to be the remains of a monastic complex that once stood on the site.

⑲ Yapahuwa

Road map C4. 45 km (28 miles) SW of Aukana. ⓣ **Open** 8am–6pm daily.

This rock fortress, rising 90 m (295 ft) above the surrounding plains, was the centre of a short-lived Sinhalese capital established by King Bhuvanekabahu I during the 13th century. The king brought the Tooth Relic here to protect it against invasions from south India. However, after Yapahuwa fell to the Pandyan army in 1284, it was abandoned and taken over by monks.

Although there are remnants of the palace and the ancient city around the base, the real attraction here is a steep staircase that leads up to a natural rock terrace. The initial section of the staircase is plain but the top part is beautifully decorated with intricate carvings and impressive statues. There are large sculptures of lions and elephants flanking the stairs, as well as an imposing porch with pillars and window frames on either side. Panels around the base and sides of the stairs depict dancers and musicians. These carvings have a very distinctive south Indian influence.

A path at the rear left side of the terrace leads up to the summit, and there are panoramic views to be enjoyed from here.

Buddhist Mudras

In Buddhism, a *mudra* is defined as a gesture or a posture that has symbolic significance. Most *mudras* are performed using only the hands and fingers; however, there are some that involve the entire body. In Sri Lankan art, the Buddha is depicted in three main postures, namely the standing, the seated and the reclining. The seated and standing statues are characterized by gestures of the hand, which represent key events in the life of the Buddha, such as the moment of enlightenment and his first sermon at Sarnath. The Buddha's *parinirvana,* or final release, is represented by the reclining pose. The Buddha is most frequently portrayed either in the *dhyana mudra*, which is the meditation pose, or in the reclining *mudra*. The *mudras* most commonly seen in Sri Lanka are outlined below.

The reclining Buddha traditionally represents the Buddha at the time of his death. This pose is symbolic of his *parinirvana*. However, there are two types of reclining poses, the sleeping pose and the actual *parinirvana* pose. In the former, the toes of the Buddha are in a straight line.

The abhaya mudra or the "fearlessness" gesture shows the Buddha with his right hand raised to shoulder height, arm bent and the palm facing outwards. It is understood to mean "have no fear".

The bhumisparsha mudra depicts the Buddha touching the ground with the fingertips of his right hand, while his left hand rests in his lap. This gesture commemorates the Buddha's resolve in the face of the demon Mara's temptations and distractions.

The dhyana mudra is the meditation pose in which the Buddha sits in the lotus or half-lotus position with both hands in his lap; the right hand rests on the left.

The vitarka and dharmachakra mudras are the "explanation" and the "turning of the wheel" poses respectively. In both positions, the Buddha's index finger touches his thumb to form a circle, symbolic of the wheel of *dharma*. This is said to convince listeners of the truth of *dharma*.

❷ Anuradhapura

Founded in the 4th century BC, Anuradhapura was one of Sri Lanka's greatest centres of political and religious power. The ancient city is home to temples, immense *dagobas*, pools and ruined palaces, all of which hint at the splendour of the place at the height of its power during the 9th century AD. Anuradhapura suffered repeated incursions from south India, but it was only after the Cholas occupied the city in the 10th century that it fell into decline. It was reclaimed by the jungle and lay largely forgotten until the area was cleared in the 19th century. The ruins are spread out over a large area, but the main points of interest lie in the centre close to the Sri Maha Bodhi Tree, east around the Jetavanarama Dagoba and north around the Abhayagiri Dagoba.

Area illustrated

Thuparama Dagoba
The first *dagoba* to be built in Sri Lanka, Thuparama was constructed by King Devanampiya Tissa in the 3rd century BC and is said to house the right collarbone of the Buddha. Originally in the "heap of paddy" shape, the *dagoba* was restored to a bell shape when it was renovated in 1862. It is surrounded by the pillars of a *vatadage*, which was added in the 7th century.

★ **Ruwanwelisiya Dagoba**
Begun by King Dutugemunu in 2nd century BC, the 55-m (180-ft) high *dagoba* is enclosed by a striking wall with a frieze of elephants. Restorations over the years have changed the *dagoba*'s appearance, which was originally said to be bubble shaped.

★ **Isurumuniya Monastery**
Dating from the reign of Devanampiya Tissa, this rock temple houses a shrine with a reclining Buddha. The museum on site has some of the best sculptures in the city, including *The Lovers* from the 5th century.

For hotels and restaurants in this region see pp220–21 and p232

Jetavanarama Dagoba

This brick *dagoba* originally stood over 100 m (328 ft) high when it was constructed in the 3rd century. At the time of its construction, the *dagoba* was the third-tallest structure in the world after the pyramids in Egypt. The nearby Jetavanarama Museum has artifacts, such as jewellery, Buddha statues and carvings, from the site.

VISITORS' CHECKLIST

Practical information
Road map C3.
70 km (45 miles) NE of Yapahuwa.
Open 7am–10pm daily.
🚲 📷 ♿ Note: it is possible to hire a bicycle or three-wheeler to visit the ruins.

Transport
🚌 🚐 🚕

Key

▪▪▪ Main road
═══ Other road
─── Minor road

JETAVANARAMA MONASTERY

THUPARAMA MAWATHA

NANADANA RD

Halpan Ela

Jetavanarama Dagoba

TRINCOMALEE RD

Malwatu Oya

Buddhist University

SRI BARATHINDRA MW

INCOMALEE RD

Anuradhapura Railway Station 790 m (865 yards)

...ha ...Tree

SRI MAHA BODHI MW

Nuwara Wewa 1.5 km (1 mile)

★ Sri Maha Bodhi Tree
The largest and oldest of the many bo trees in the enclosure, the Sri Maha Bodhi is said to have grown from a cutting brought over from India by Princess Sanghamitta, sister of Mahinda, in the 3rd century BC.

0 metres   400
0 yards   400

KEY

① **Mirisavatiya Dagoba** was the first monument built by Dutugemunu after he captured Anuradhapura in the 3rd century BC.

② **The Archaeological Museum** houses the ticket office as well as a collection of carvings and statues from the site.

③ **The Folk Museum** has displays related to rural life in the province.

④ **The Brazen Palace** is originally said to have been a nine-storey building. Built by Dutugemunu, the palace was eventually burnt down and was rebuilt a number of times. All that remains today are the pillars from the reconstruction carried out by King Parakramabahu in the 12th century.

Anuradhapura's Tanks

Anuradhapura is surrounded by three tanks that were built to store water for the irrigation of fields surrounding the city. The largest of these tanks is Nuwara Wewa that lies to the east and is spread over an area of 120 sq km (46 sq miles). Built around 20 BC, it was expanded by later kings. To the south lies the 160-ha (395-acre) Tissa Wewa, which was built by Devanampiya Tissa, and to the north is the city's oldest tank, the 120-ha (296-acre) Basawakkulama, which is said to date back to the 4th century BC.

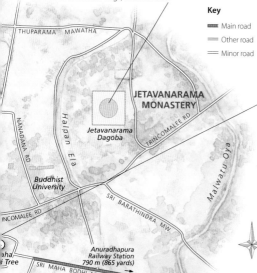

View of the Tissa Wewa, one of the three tanks surrounding Anuradhapura

Exploring Anuradhapura

The northern area of Anuradhapura is home to a cluster of interesting sights that provide more insight into the history of the city. Visitors should first stop at the Royal Palace complex, where the Mahapali Refectory and the Dalada Maligawa can be found, before heading further north to see the ruins of Abhayagiri, the third of Anuradhapura's monastic complexes; the other two are the Mahavihara and the Jetavanarama Monastery. Established by King Vattagamini Abhaya in 88 BC, it went on to become the largest and most influential monastery in the country, and by the 5th century, it was home to 5,000 monks. East of the monastery are the Samadhi Buddha statue and the Kuttan Pokuna, both of which are worth a visit.

Area illustrated

Mahasena's Palace

Ratna Prasada

WATAWANDANA RD.

Eth Pokuna

ABHAYAGIRI MONASTERY

LANKARAMA ROAD

Ratna Prasada
Founded in the outskirts of the city, this monastery dates from the 8th century. The monks of the monastery gave sanctuary to those in need. The guardstone at the entrance is the finest in Anuradhapura; it depicts a *nagaraja* (cobra king) sheltered under a seven-headed cobra.

Mahasena's Palace
Although not much remains of the original monastic complex, the moonstone here is one of the most beautiful on the island. It dates from around the 8th century, and features five circles representing the journey to attain nirvana.

KEY

① **The Abhayagiri Museum** houses an impressive collection of artifacts recovered during the excavation at Abhayagiri Monastery. Displays include jewellery, pottery and coins.

② **The Dalada Maligawa** is thought to be the original "Temple of the Tooth", where the Tooth Relic was kept when it arrived in Sri Lanka in AD 313.

Abhayagiri Dagoba
Built in 88 BC by Vattagamini Abhaya, the *dagoba* formerly stood 115 m (377 ft) tall. When the structure lost its pinnacle, it was reduced to a height of 70 m (230 ft).

Key
— Other road
— Minor road

Kuttan Pokuna
Although known as the "twin ponds", these two pools differ significantly in size. While the northern pond measures 40 m (131 ft) in length, the one to the south is 28 m (92 ft) long. They were built in the 8th century, and were probably used as ritual baths, as there are steps from each side leading into the water.

Samadhi Buddha
A fine example of Sinhalese sculpture, this statue dates back to the 4th century and depicts the Buddha in the *samadhi* (meditation) pose.

Mahapali Refectory
Once part of the Royal Palace, the refectory has a large stone trough that used to be filled with rice to feed the monks.

Royal Palace
This palace was built by King Vijayabahu I after he defeated the Cholas in AD 1077, although the capital had already moved to Polonnaruwa by then. While it is newer than a lot of other structures in the ancient city, little remains today apart from the terrace and the guardstones.

㉑ Mihintale

The sacred hill of Mihintale is where Mahinda, son of the Indian king Asoka, converted King Devanampiya Tissa to Buddhism in the 3rd century BC. It is said that King Tissa was chasing a stag during a hunting trip in the hills of Mihintale when he was approached by Mahinda, who wished to test the intelligence of the king with a riddle. King Tissa passed the test and was converted there and then along with his retinue of 40,000 courtiers. An important religious site, Mihintale attracts a large number of Buddhist pilgrims, particularly on Poson Poya Day in June. Exploring the site involves long climbs, so it is a good idea to visit it early in the morning or late in the afternoon.

Chetiya *dagoba*, the oldest at Mihintale. Originally higher than 30 m (98 ft), the *dagoba* stands at a height of only 12 m (39 ft). It has four *vahalkadas* (frontispieces) in the four cardinal directions and each of these is adorned with carvings of geese, dwarves and elephants. Some of the *vahalkadas* are flanked by stone columns that are ornamented with sculpted flowers and birds, and topped with figurines of animals. South of the *dagoba* is an enormous boulder bearing an ancient inscription in early proto-Brahmi script. There are caves and meditation ledges to explore nearby.

Frangipani trees sheltering a flight of stone steps

🛈 Hospital Ruins
The ruins of a 9th-century hospital built during the reign of King Sena II can be seen near the car park along a side road. Upon entering the ruins, visitors will come across a stone trough with its interior carved in the shape of a human form. The trough is thought to have been used as a medical bath where patients were immersed in healing oils. There are also the remains of treatment rooms leading off from the central courtyard.

A short walk east of the hospital is the museum, where archaeological finds from the site are displayed.

Stairway
Shaded by frangipani trees, the stairway leading to the summit comprises 1,840 rock-cut steps interspersed with terraces that allow visitors to catch their breath. While the first flight of

stairs is broad and shallow, the ones higher up are narrower and steeper. However, visitors who have difficulty climbing stairs can drive up Old Road and park near the Refectory Terrace to avoid the first set of steps.

🛈 Kantaka Chetiya
At the first small landing, steps lead off on the right to the remains of the Kantaka

🛈 Refectory Terrace
Situated on the left side of the second landing, the refectory has big stone troughs that would have been filled with food such as rice or porridge for the monks.

On the terrace right above is the image house, the entrance to which is flanked by two large stone slabs inscribed in Sinhala. Erected during the reign of King Mahinda IV (r.975–991), these tablets detail the rules and responsibilities for monks and other staff in the monastery. A short distance to the south lie the ruins of the stone pillars of the Conversation Hall where the monastery's community would have met.

To the right of the terrace is the small Singha Pokuna (Lion Pool), which is named after the weathered sculpture of a lion whose mouth served as the waterspout. The frieze above the lion sculpture is decorated with fine carvings of dancers and

Ruins of the stone troughs on the Refectory Terrace

View of the huge Mahaseya Dagoba from a distance

VISITORS' CHECKLIST

Practical information
Road map C3.
15 km (10 miles) E of
Anuradhapura. **Open** 6am–6pm
daily. 🔲 for the second terrace.

Transport
🚌 from Anuradhapura. 🚖

elephants. The other remains around here are said to be those of bathhouses for the monks.

🏛 Aradhana Gala

A set of steep stairs leads up to the upper terrace, where visitors have to buy a ticket and remove their shoes and hats. At the centre of the terrace is the Ambasthala Dagoba, which is believed to mark the spot where Mahinda met King Devanampiya Tissa. Next to it is a stone carving of the Buddha's footprint surrounded by railings and with coins offered by pilgrims scattered all over it. The ancient headless statue nearby is said to be of King Tissa. On the opposite side of the terrace are steps leading up to the big white seated Buddha statue.

East of the Ambasthala Dagoba, a flight of rock-cut steps leads to Aradhana Gala (Meditation Rock) from where there are great views of the surrounding countryside and the grand Mahaseya Dagoba.

A path from the upper terrace, leads down to Mahinda's Cave, a space beneath a huge boulder with a large flat stone believed to have been his bed.

🏛 Mahaseya Dagoba

From the southwest corner of the terrace, steps lead up to the summit where stands the 14-m (45-ft) high Mahaseya Dagoba. The *dagoba* is clearly visible from a distance and is where Mahinda's relics are said to be interred. There are

wonderful views stretching southwest to the *dagobas* of Anuradhapura from here. A Buddhist temple on the south side and a small Hindu *devale* on the west side adjoin the *dagoba*.

🏛 Naga Pokuna

After seeing the Mahaseya Dagoba, visitors retrace their steps to pick up their shoes and head down the stairs from the Ambasthala Dagoba. A path leads off to the left to Naga Pokuna (Snake Pool). This peaceful spot was named after the five-headed cobra carved on the rock face of the pool. The water stored here was supplied to the monastery below.

🏛 Et Vihara

A flight of around 600 steps leads to the ruins of the Et Vihara *dagoba*, located at the highest point in Mihintale.

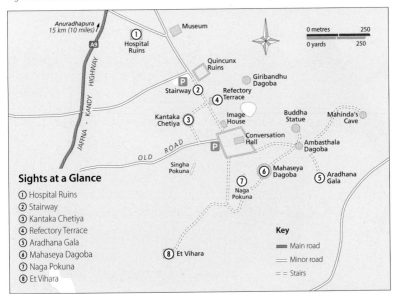

Sights at a Glance
① Hospital Ruins
② Stairway
③ Kantaka Chetiya
④ Refectory Terrace
⑤ Aradhana Gala
⑥ Mahaseya Dagoba
⑦ Naga Pokuna
⑧ Et Vihara

Key
▬▬ Main road
── Minor road
= = Stairs

For map symbols *see back flap*

THE EAST

After being isolated for long periods during the Civil War and battered by the 2004 tsunami, the East Coast is welcoming visitors once again. Although the scars of both still remain, the area is now in the midst of a revival. The tourism potential of its beautiful coastline has been recognized, and major plans are underway to improve the infrastructure. Along with exploring unspoiled beaches and jungle-covered ruins, visitors can enjoy whale-watching, wreck-diving and surfing.

Located in the dry zone, the East Coast is one of Sri Lanka's most ethnically diverse areas, with a mix of Sinhalese, Tamil and Muslim communities. Most of the area's population resides in towns and small fishing villages along the coastline, while places inland remain less developed and sparsely populated. The principal town on the East Coast is Trincomalee, which shaped much of the area's early history. Famous for its deep-water natural harbour, the town was the island's trading hub during the Anuradhapura and Polonnaruwa eras until the Colonial times.

The East began to decline when trade was diverted to the new ports at Galle and then at Colombo. The area's fortunes further diminished when it found itself enmeshed in the violent struggles between the LTTE and the Sri Lankan Army during the Civil War. The war ended in 2009, and since then much of the East Coast has opened up to tourists. The area is now peaceful, although there is still a military presence in many of its towns and villages.

Most visitors come here for the idyllic stretches of sand, such as the beaches of Uppuveli and Nilaveli as well as those of Passekudah and Kalkudah. However, surfing enthusiasts head for Arugam Bay, which offers the best surf in the country. Inland, the countryside is largely wild and home to several national parks, of which Kumana is a particular draw for birdwatchers. The area around Maduru Oya National Park is where the original inhabitants of the island, the Veddahs, still try to maintain their traditional way of life.

A cluster of shrines with brightly painted *gopurams* within Koneswaram Kovil, Trincomalee

◄ Coils of colourful fishing nets lying on the beach, Trincomalee

Exploring The East

The East Coast is home to beautiful beaches and is also considered to be one of the best places in Sri Lanka for surfing. Trincomalee, the capital of the province, is famed for its impressive natural harbour, but the majority of visitors base themselves at the peaceful beaches of Uppuveli and Nilaveli, north of the town. Both beaches afford superb opportunities for snorkelling, sport fishing and whale-watching. Further down the coast, Batticaloa offers one of the island's best wreck-dives to the HMS *Hermes* that lies off its shores. A short distance north stretch the formerly war-torn beaches of Passekudah and Kalkudah, which are now experiencing a resurgence in popularity among tourists. The surfing hotspot of Arugam Bay, at the southern end of the coastline, offers the best waves and also serves as a good base for trips to the Lahugala and Kumana national parks as well as the Kudumbigala Hermitage.

Surfing a wave at Arugam Bay

```
0 km          30
0 miles          30
```

Sights at a Glance

Herd of elephants near a watering hole, Lahugala National Park

7 PASSEKUDAH AND KALKUDAH

Vandalous Bay

Kalkudah Bay

Eravur

enkaladi

6 BATTICALOA

Batticaloa Lagoon

EASTERN

Navakiri Aru Tank

Koddaikallar

Kalmunai

Karativu

Ampara

iyagala

Hingurana   Akkaraipattu

Periya Kalappu Oya

Thambiluvil

Vinayagapuram

OYA NATIONAL ARK

LAHUGALA NATIONAL PARK

12

Karanda Oya

mbalanduwa

Pottuvil   *Mudu Maha Vihara*

ock Rock m (3,645 ft) *Heda Oya*

Magul Maha Vihara

11 ARUGAM BAY

Wila Oya

GAWILA

13 PANAMA

KUDUMBIGALA HERMITAGE **14**

15 OKANDA

KUMANA NATIONAL PARK **16**

Kiragaila Bay

Kumbukkan Oya   *Kumana Wewa*

Thatched umbrellas shading deck chairs on the beach, Nilaveli

Getting Around

Although public transport is easily available in the East, visitors looking for a quicker means of transportation are advised to hire a car and a driver to get around. Road conditions are slowly improving across the area and there are plans to build new routes to cut journey times. Buses travel regularly to, as well as along, the coast. Train services run to both Trincomalee and Batticaloa, but visitors will have to change at Gal Oya, if travelling between the two towns. Note that travelling south of Panama can still be difficult, as the road here is in a poor condition. The towns of Trincomalee, Batticaloa and Arugam Bay are all compact enough to walk around. However, visitors will need to rent a three-wheeler to explore further afield.

Key
- Major road
- Minor road
- Railway
- Provincial border
- △ Summit

For additional map symbols *see back flap*

❶ Trincomalee

The capital of Sri Lanka's Eastern Province, Trincomalee is famous for its deep-water natural harbour. Said to be one of the finest in the world, the harbour was bitterly fought over for its strategic importance during the Colonial era. The town suffered greatly during the Civil War and also sustained damage when the tsunami hit the coast in 2004. Despite all this, "Trinco" is now firmly back on the tourist trail, with building and renovation work underway in most parts of the town. Although most tourists come to visit the beaches that lie to its north, the town has a charm of its own, with faded Colonial buildings, a picturesque seafront and vibrant *kovils* that come alive in the evening with the beating of drums for the *puja* ceremony.

Scenic view of the town from Fort Frederick

🏛 Fort Frederick
Open daily.

The main attraction in Trinco is Fort Frederick, which sits on a strip of land that juts out into the Indian Ocean. Built by the Portuguese in 1623, the fort passed through Dutch and French hands before being finally taken over by the British in 1795. It remained under their control until Sri Lanka's independence in 1948. During this period, its name was changed from Fort of Triquillimale to Fort Frederick, after the Duke of York, the second son of King George III.

The fort is still in military use, but can be visited. The entrance is through the main gate, which dates from 1675. Inside, there are several Colonial buildings interspersed with old, wide-canopied trees. Among these buildings is **Wellesley Lodge**, where Arthur Wellesley, who went on to become the Duke of Wellington, is said to have stayed in 1800. Two cannons, a howitzer and a mortar can be spotted near the lodge.

A left fork off the main road leads to the Gokana Temple with a beautiful standing Buddha and good views of the town. The main road continues north to Swami Rock, a steep cliff that drops about 130 m (426 ft) to the sea and affords breathtaking views along the coast and out to the sea. At the highest point of the rock is **Koneswaram Kovil**, one of the five most sacred *Shaivite*

(dedicated to Lord Shiva) sites in Sri Lanka. A shrine is thought to have stood at this spot for about 2,500 years until it was destroyed by the Portuguese, and the remains pitched into the sea, in the 17th century. Today, a huge golden statue of Shiva, outside, dwarfs the brightly coloured temple and *gopuram*, which was built on the site of the original shrine in 1952.

While most people walk up to the temple, it is possible to hire a three-wheeler to reach the place. The best time to visit the temple is on Friday in the late afternoon when the evening prayers are held. Note that shoes must be taken off and left at the entrance of the temple complex.

A stroll around the side and back of the Koneswaram Kovil makes for a pleasant experience, with great views of the Indian Ocean. A number of modern statues of Hindu deities, as well as that of Rawana standing on a platform overlooking the ocean can be seen around the temple. The bits of coconut scattered about are from the Hindu ritual of breaking the coconut against the rock – it is considered inauspicious if the coconut does not break.

To the right of the temple is a tree with wooden cradles hanging from its branches, left by families praying for children. Nearby is another tree that clings precariously

The Recovery of the Lingam

The *lingam* enshrined in Koneswaram Kovil today, was pitched into the sea with the rest of the temple in 1624. The ruins of the temple

The Shiva *lingam*, Koneswaram Kovil

were discovered in the late 1950s by a dive team that included photographer Mike Wilson and author Arthur C Clarke. The priests were anxious to find the *lingam*, but it was not until 1962 when Mike Wilson was filming *Ranmuthu Duwa* that he spotted the sacred object while diving during a break from underwater shooting. The discovery affected him so deeply that he gave up his career and family and became Swami Siva Kalki. He remained in Sri Lanka living the life of an ascetic until his death in 1995.

Golden statue of the Hindu god Shiva at the entrance to Koneswaram Kovil

VISITORS' CHECKLIST

Practical information
Road map D3.
269 km (167 miles) NE of
Colombo.
🏠 57,000.

Transport
🚉 🚌 🛺 from Mutur.
🚕

to the cliff, its branches covered with prayer flags. This spot is known as **Lover's Leap**. It marks a spot where a Dutch woman, Francina van Rhede, supposedly jumped off the cliff in 1687 when her lover abandoned her and sailed away. That government archives suggest she was alive and well when the memorial commemorating the legend was erected lends little credence to the tale.

🏠 **Koneswaram Kovil**
Open daily. 📷 inner sanctum.
Note: donation is expected for keeping shoes.

Commercial Centre
West of Fort Frederick lies the town's commercial centre, which comprises three parallel streets: Main Street, Central Road and North Coast (NC) Road. At the confluence of NC Road and Central Road stands the clock tower, next to which is the busy fish market. The market is worth a quick visit, as is the fruit and vegetable market nearby.

A short distance south of the clock tower is the large Kali Kovil on Dockyard Road with a colourful *gopuram*. The late-afternoon *puja* (around 4–5pm) here is a lively affair with drums and ringing of bells. Nearby is an abandoned Christian cemetery where Colonial-era tombstones from the 1820s, dedicated to those who died mainly from malaria and other tropical diseases, can be seen beneath the undergrowth. The cemetery is also said to be the final resting place of the soldiers who succumbed to their wounds during the various battles fought in the town. Jane Austen's brother, Admiral Charles John Austen, who died of cholera, is thought to be buried here.

Dutch Bay
An atmospheric spot, the half moon-shaped Dutch Bay is a popular place at dusk when locals come to walk along the breezy seafront and relax in the sand. It is wise to seek local advice before going for a swim, as currents can be very dangerous at certain times of the year.

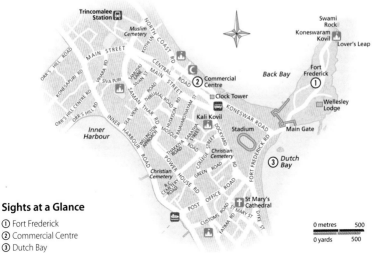

Sights at a Glance
① Fort Frederick
② Commercial Centre
③ Dutch Bay

For map symbols *see back flap*

Rows of gravestones at the well-kept Commonwealth War Cemetery

❷ Uppuveli and Nilaveli

Road map D2. Uppuveli: 4 km (2 miles) NW of Trincomalee; Nilaveli: 15 km (9 miles) NW of Trincomalee. 🏛 Uppuveli: 1,700; Nilaveli: 900. 🚌 from Trincomalee. 🛈

North of Trincomalee lie the villages of Uppuveli and Nilaveli that are known for their tranquil beaches. Among the island's most popular beaches before the Civil War, Uppuveli and Nilaveli received few tourists during the hostilities. In addition, the tsunami in 2004 hit the area with great force and destroyed many homes and businesses.

Over the last few years, efforts have been made to improve the tourist infrastructure. Today, the beaches are once again attracting tourists who come here to lounge on the vast stretches of white sand backed by palm trees and to swim in the clear blue ocean. Despite the continued military presence, the beaches make for a serene getaway with a number of hotels and guesthouses on offer. Several day-trip options are available from both the beaches. Besides boat tours to Pigeon Island, diving or sport fishing trips can also be easily arranged. It is also possible to go on whale- and dolphin-watching excursions in season, which lasts from March to April and August to September.

❸ Commonwealth War Cemetery

Road map D2. 200 m (219 yards) N of Uppuveli. Nilaveli Road. 🛈 **Open** dawn–dusk daily. ♿ Note: donation is appreciated.

Located within walking distance of Uppuveli, the impeccably kept Commonwealth War Cemetery makes for a sombre visit. The 362 graves at the cemetery are mainly of servicemen who died in Sri Lanka during World War II, when Trincomalee was an important base. In April 1942, the town suffered Japanese air raids that also sank several British and Australian ships in the Indian Ocean.

Organized in rows, each of the headstones bears symbols that identify the deceased as seamen or part of the air crew. The symbols also denote the nationality: gravestones of those from New Zealand, for example, are engraved with the silver fern. The moving epitaphs here are a grim reminder of the horrors of World War II. One such epitaph is that of a nurse called Joan Barker, which reads "A short but tremendously useful life".

Those who wish to have a look at the register of the graves can contact the warden who is usually on site.

Visitors snorkelling off the rocky coast, Pigeon Island

❹ Pigeon Island

Road map D2. 1 km (0.6 miles) NE of Nilaveli. 🏞 🚤 Note: the island can only be reached by boat. Additional fee for the boat.

About 1 km (0.6 miles) offshore from Nilaveli is the marine national park of Pigeon Island, named after the blue rock pigeons that nest here. This rocky island has two small beaches and is a major draw among tourists for the excellent snorkelling opportunities in the shallow waters of the bay. Although

Brightly painted boats lining the shore of the peaceful Nilaveli Beach

For hotels and restaurants in this region see p221 and p233

the area was affected by coral bleaching in 2011, live coral can still be seen here in addition to a number of tropical fish species and other marine life. Visitors are advised to be careful while walking barefoot on the beach as dead coral sometimes washes up onto the sand.

Pigeon Island is particularly popular at weekends and during public holidays. It is a good idea to arrive early as the island gets crowded by lunch time in high season, which extends from May to September.

Pilgrims dousing themselves with the warm waters, Kanniyai Hot Wells

❺ Kanniyai Hot Wells

Road map D2. 20 km (12 miles) W of Uppuveli. 🚍 **Open** 7am–7pm daily. 🅿

The Kanniyai Hot Wells comprise seven warm natural springs enclosed in seven square-shaped wells. The spring water is thought to have therapeutic properties; those with skin problems or ailments such as arthritis and rheumatism come here looking for relief. Since the wells are too small to bathe in, locals and pilgrims use buckets to pour water over themselves – tourists are encouraged to join in, too. The temperature of water varies in each of the wells.

Standing Buddha, Velgam Vihara

There are two legends associated with the wells. One of these claims that Lord Vishnu created the wells when he appeared to Rawana, the king of Lankapura, on this spot. It is believed that when Lord Vishnu struck the ground with his sword, water poured forth. The other maintains that King Rawana created the wells so he could conduct the funeral rites for his mother.

A trip to the Kanniyai Hot Wells can be combined with a visit to the atmospheric remains of **Velgam Vihara**, which lie 6 km (4 miles) north of here. Known to Hindus as Natanar Kovil, this Buddhist monastery is thought to have been built by King Devanampiya Tissa in the 2nd century. It escaped destruction in the 10th century when the Cholas from south India invaded Sri Lanka. Instead of destroying it as they did many other Buddhist shrines and temples, the Cholas renovated the building and also used it as a place of worship.

The extensive ruins here include an image house, a well-preserved standing Buddha and a *dagoba*. Tamil inscriptions dating from the 10th century can still be seen around the site.

Nearby stands a small museum devoted to an LTTE bombing in 2000 that massacred around 26 civilians and Sinhalese soldiers. Filled with disturbing images of the bombing, this museum is not for the faint-hearted.

🏛 Velgam Vihara
Open dawn–dusk daily. 🅿 Note: donation is appreciated.

HMS Hermes

An air raid by Japanese bombers in April 1942 led to the sinking of Royal Navy aircraft carrier HMS *Hermes* along with the escort Australian destroyer HMAS *Vampire* off the East Coast of Sri Lanka. Around 307 men lost their lives in the sinking. The Japanese also attacked a number of other ships further north that morning and sank another four of them.

The wreck of HMS *Hermes* lies off the coast of Batticaloa (*see p194*) and is well known as a dive site for experienced technical divers. Relatively inaccessible during the Civil War, the site today offers good visibility and opportunities to explore the abundant marine life. The wreck is reached at a depth of 44 m (145 ft) and moderate to strong currents run over it. Note that diving is only possible from March to October. There are a number of other wrecks on the ocean floor, some of which can be visited along with the HMS *Hermes*.

The wreck of HMS *Hermes* covered in colourful soft corals

Breathtaking view of one of the two beaches of Pigeon Island hemmed in by rocks ▶

Fisherman casting a net in the Batticaloa Lagoon, Batticaloa

❻ Batticaloa

Road map E4. 138 km (86 miles) SE of Trincomalee. 🏠 579,000. 🚉 🚌 🚕

Popularly known as "Batti", the town of Batticaloa was out of bounds to visitors during the Civil War, when it was the site of violent strife as the Sri Lankan Army and the LTTE fought each other. These skirmishes resulted in widespread destruction and loss of life, and Batticaloa was left a shell. It is only since 2007 that the town has started attracting visitors once again with its beaches and Colonial relics.

A walk around the old part of Batticaloa is a good way to see the town's attractions, with side streets leading to Colonial buildings, busy shops and local eateries, or quiet corners of green. Surrounded on three sides by the large Batticaloa Lagoon, the old town is accessed by a bridge running south from the town centre. Watching the fishermen cast

Boy scout statue

nets in the lagoon here is one of the most picturesque sights visitors will see in Sri Lanka.

The **Old Dutch Fort** is the town's main attraction. The fort is entered via Court House Road and it is possible to explore most of the area within on foot. Originally built by the Portuguese in 1628, the fort was captured by the Dutch 10 years later and was subsequently rebuilt. Inside, the central courtyard contains government and NGO offices as well as a museum with Colonial-era artifacts. Flanked by two old cannons, the gate on the eastern side of the fort overlooks the lagoon.

A few minutes northwest of the fort is the clock tower where stands the statue of a boy scout, commemorating 80 years of the Scout Movement that was founded by Lord Robert Baden-Powell. Nearby is the market, which is best visited in the morning or evening when the catch of the day can be seen.

South of the clock tower are some attractive Colonial buildings. Among these is **St Michael's College**, which is one of the largest schools in the Eastern Province. It was founded in 1873 by Reverend Ferdinand Bonnel and was privately run until the 1970s. Directly opposite stands **St Mary's Cathedral**, with a powder-blue Neo-Classical exterior. The building was damaged by a cyclone in the 1970s, after which it was repaired, but underwent further restoration work in the late 1980s and 90s. It was also where Tamil politician Joseph Pararajasingham was assassinated during Midnight Mass in 2005.

Environs
Separated from Batticaloa by the lagoon and reached by the Kallady Bridge, the laid-back suburb of **Kallady** offers a strip of golden sand. Note that the water here is rough and not suitable for swimming.

Striking blue-and-white façade of St Mary's Cathedral, Batticaloa

The Singing Fish of Batticaloa

View of the Kallady Bridge

The stretch of the Batticaloa Lagoon under the Kallady Bridge is believed to be home to Batticaloa's singing fish. Between April and September, around the time of the full moon, the fish are said to make noises that are described as the twanging of a violin string or a "multitude of tiny sounds". It is possible to hire a fisherman for a boat trip at night to listen to the sounds. Some people claim that if an oar is dipped into the water and the other end is held to the ear it makes the sound clearer, although it is said the noises have grown fainter over the years. There have been a number of theories to explain the strange sounds, ranging from courting mussels to the movement of water at the bottom of the lagoon.

Splashing around in the shallow waters at the palm-fringed Passekudah Beach

❼ Passekudah and Kalkudah

Road map D3. Passekudah: 28 km (17 miles) NW of Batticaloa; Kalkudah: 27 km (16 miles) NW of Batticaloa. 🚌 from Batticaloa. ⓣ

Before the Civil War, the beaches of Passekudah and Kalkudah along the East Coast of Sri Lanka were a huge draw for tourists. But the devastation during the war and the tsunami in 2004 scarred the landscape and visitors all but stopped coming here. However, the beaches are still considered to be attractive spots with white sand, clear blue water and fishing boats in the bay.

The shallow waters of the Passekudah Bay are popular with families. In recent years, efforts have been made to develop the infrastructure at the beaches, especially at Passekudah, which is now home to the superb Maalu Maalu beach resort *(see p221)*. Due to the developmental work in progress, visitors may be confronted with building activity here instead of peace and quiet.

Kalkudah Beach, by contrast, is a relatively unspoiled stretch of golden sand backed by palms. Be aware that the sea at Kalkudah is deeper and can be rough at times.

❽ Gal Oya National Park

Road map D5. 80 km (50 miles) SW of Batticaloa. 🚌 from Batticaloa to Ampara, then taxi to Inginiyagala. ⓣ **Open** 6am–6pm daily. 🗐 🗒

Covering an area of 540 sq km (208 sq miles), the picturesque dry-zone reserve of Gal Oya is

situated in a part of Sri Lanka little visited by tourists. At the centre of the park is the Senanayake Samudra, a vast reservoir that was created in 1948. The park itself was established in 1954 to protect the catchment area around this body of water. Dotted with many small islands, the reservoir is one of the largest lakes in Sri Lanka.

A number of water birds can be spotted around the reservoir, including the white-bellied fish eagle, the rare painted francolin, Layard's parakeet and Indian nightjars, and it is also possible to catch sight of elephants on the islands. In addition, grey langurs, wild boar, water buffaloes and deer can also be seen in the park. It is possible to tour the park in a jeep but travellers are recommended to take a boat trip to see the islands on the reservoir. Among the highlights is the appropriately named Bird Island, a nesting site where the

dense forest cover and rocky outcrops are home to a huge diversity of birds.

❾ Monaragala

Road map D5. 151 km (94 miles) SW of Batticaloa. 🏔 448,000. 🚌 ⓣ

Monaragala, meaning "the rock of peacock landing", derives its name from the imposing and densely forested Peacock Rock that it nestles beneath. A typical Sri Lankan town, Monaragala offers some good nature walks through the surrounding countryside, which is surprisingly lush. A diverse variety of wildlife, including elephants, buffaloes, peacocks and deer can also be seen along these walks.

Monaragala makes a good base for exploring the stunning Buddhist statues in Maligawila *(see p196)* and also serves as a gateway to Arugam Bay *(see p196)*, one of Sri Lanka's best surfing spots.

A road passing through the lush countryside, Monaragala

❿ Maligawila

Road map D5. 17 km (10 miles) S of Monaragala. 🚌 from Monaragala. ⓣ **Open** dawn–dusk daily.

The village of Maligawila is home to two enormous Buddhist statues that stand hidden among the trees of the unspoiled lowland jungle. Carved out of limestone, the impressive figures date from the 7th century and are thought to have been part of a monastery. The statues, which had toppled over and lain in pieces for centuries, were raised to a standing position in the late 1980s and reassembled over the following years.

The site is reached by a path that begins at the car park and winds through the woods to a point where it splits to lead to each of the statues. The left fork leads to the first of the two statues – an 11-m (36-ft) high standing Buddha. The image is supported by a brick arch at the back, which makes it possible to walk all the way around to admire the craftsmanship and marvel at its size.

The right fork takes visitors to the stairs that lead up to the *bodhisattva* statue, which is covered by a large canopy. To the left of the steps, under a protective covering, is a 10th-century pillar that bears an inscription from the reign of Mahinda IV. It details the work undertaken by the king to support the Buddhist order and some rules about the administration of Buddhist sites.

Evocative remains of an image house enclosing the statues, Mudu Maha Vihara

⓫ Arugam Bay

Road map E5. 76 km (47 miles) E of Monaragala. 🏠 3,500. 🚌 ⓣ

Famous for its surfing, Arugam Bay offers much to tempt even those who are not keen to ride the waves. With its laid-back atmosphere and rustic beachside huts, the village is a haven for holidaymakers on the East Coast.

Arugam Bay village is largely made up of one main street that runs parallel to the beach and is lined with restaurants, guesthouses and surf shops. The ideal time to surf here is between May to October. In the low season, which extends from November to April, many businesses remain closed and it can get very quiet around the village. The south end of the beach is usually strewn with blue fishing boats and colourful nets, marking the tiny fishing settlement of Ulla. Note that this end of the beach is the safest for swimming in season.

The 2004 tsunami brought a lot of damage to Arugam Bay. There has been extensive renovation work since then with an aim to promote Arugam Bay as a mainstream tourist destination, while also improving the infrastructure required to reach here. However, the locals fear that such tourism developments might alter the atmosphere and the unique character of the village.

A three-wheeler carrying surfboards

Environs
A short distance to the north of Arugam Bay lies **Pottuvil**, which is separated from the village by the Arugam Lagoon. This small town is where most of the buses for Arugam Bay arrive and depart from. Take a trip on Pottuvil Lagoon to see the rich aquatic life of the mangrove swamp. In addition to water birds, it is possible to catch sight of monkeys and even crocodiles. Guesthouses in Arugam Bay can arrange boat trips on the lagoon.

Nearby on the coast are the ruins of **Mudu Maha Vihara**. Standing amid the sand are the remains of the walls of an image house and a striking standing Buddha sculpture as well as images of two *bodhisattvas*.

Children praying at the feet of the standing Buddha statue, Maligawila

For hotels and restaurants in this region see p221 and p233

Surfing in Sri Lanka

Good waves and the possibility of surfing year-round bring surfing enthusiasts to Sri Lanka. The island boasts a number of superb places with breaks to suit every level of expertise. Hikkaduwa *(see pp102–103)* remains the favourite spot on the West Coast owing to its relaxed atmosphere, the choice of accommodation near the surfing breaks and the nightlife. Further along the coast to the south, Midigama *(see p117)* and Ahangama are better suited for the more serious surfer, with long walling lefts and a lot of coral and rock. Other surf hotspots along the South Coast include Mirissa *(see p118)* and Weligama *(see p117)*. The best-known destination on the East Coast is Arugam Bay, and the area around the village boasts a number of good surf spots. Some of the popular breaks that surfers flock to include the Point, Pottuvil Point, Peanut Farm, Crocodile Rock and Okanda Point. The season on the West Coast extends from November to April, and then the East Coast takes over from May to October.

Surf schools in prime surfing destinations across Sri Lanka offer board hire and repair, surf tours to major surfing spots and professional lessons as well.

Group or private surf lessons can be arranged at most beaches. Sri Lanka has some ideal surf spots for beginners, where the waves are smaller.

Surfers of varying levels of expertise are drawn to Sri Lanka's surf destinations. The waves here are fairly consistent and are usually around 1 m (3 ft) to 2 m (6 ft).

International surfing competitions bring surfers from all over the world to Sri Lanka. Arugam Bay and Hikkaduwa are the venues for many such important events, and have hosted competitions such as the Sri Lanka Champion of Champions Surf Contest in the past.

View of a temple nestled under a drip ledge, Kudumbigala Hermitage

⑫ Lahugala National Park

Road map D5. 19 km (10 miles) NW of Arugam Bay. Monaragala Road. ⓣ **Open** 6am–6pm daily. 🌿

Located within easy reach of Arugam Bay, this small national park offers the chance to see a wide range of aquatic birds as well as elephants. Of the three reservoirs here, the Lahugala Tank is a good place to spot storks and pelicans. During the dry season (July and August), herds of elephants congregate at the tank to eat the *beru* grass, which grows in profusion around the water.

Environs
The evocative ruins of **Magul Maha Vihara** are situated 6 km (4 miles) southwest of the park. Inscriptions found at the site confirm that the monastery complex was built by King Dhatusena in the 5th century and restored in the 14th century. Only a small section of the complex has been excavated while the rest is still covered in thick jungle; look out for the *dagoba*, the image house and the well-preserved moonstone ringed with elephants and their *mahouts*.

🏛 **Magul Maha Vihara**
Open dawn–dusk daily.
Note: donation is appreciated.

⑬ Panama

Road map E5. 12 km (7 miles) S of Arugam Bay. 🚍 4,000. 🚌 ⓣ

A tiny, isolated village, Panama offers a wide unspoiled beach that stretches east of the settlement. The sand dunes and rock boulders lend the beach a desert island feel. Note that the sea here is rough and not suitable for swimming. The only other attraction is a white *dagoba* at the entrance to the village, which is hard to miss.

⑭ Kudumbigala Hermitage

Road map E5. 14 km (9 miles) SW of Panama. ⓣ **Open** dawn–dusk daily.

Hidden away among thick jungle, the beautiful forest hermitage ' of Kudumbigala is a tranquil and atmospheric spot. Spread over an expanse of 47 sq km (18 sq miles), the hermitage consists of hundreds of shrines set in rock caves, some of which contain inscriptions in Brahmi. The site is said to date back to the 2nd century and was originally established as a refuge for Buddhist monks seeking isolation and a life of meditation. It is still visited by monks who come here to meditate.

The summit of the highest rock, crowned by a cylindrical *dagoba*, offers breathtaking views across the lush landscape. The summit is reached by a flight of rock-cut steps.

⑮ Okanda

Road map E5. 18 km (11 miles) SW of Panama. 🚍 900. 🚌 from Panama. ⓣ

Located just east of the entrance to Kumana National Park, Okanda is an important stop for those undertaking the Pad Yatra pilgrimage from Jaffna *(see p205)* to Kataragama *(see p128)*. The town is home to the ancient **Velayudha Swami Temple**, which lies at the base of a rocky outcrop. Legend has it that this is the spot where Skanda and his consort Valli arrived in Sri Lanka in stone boats. Pilgrims stop at the shrine for a 15-day festival in July. The peak of the rock is crested by the **Valli Amman Kovil**; a simple shrine of sticks and leaves built by the Veddahs formerly stood here.

A few minutes' walk east of the Velayudha Swami Temple is a beach that was a popular surfing spot before the Civil War made Okanda hard to access. However, intrepid enthusiasts are now returning here to ride the waves and also to escape the high season at Arugam Bay.

The intricately carved Velayudha Swami Temple, Okanda

⓰ Kumana National Park

Road map D5. 120 m (131 yards) E of Okanda. 🚹 **Open** 6am–6pm daily. 🅿 🚫 Note: hire a jeep at Arugam Bay to enter the park.

Formerly known as the Yala East National Park, the Kumana National Park was closed for a large part of the Civil War before reopening in 2010. Located on the pilgrimage route to Kataragama, the park is one of the five blocks of the Yala National Park.

The 357-sq km (138-sq mile) park is noted for its impressive range of resident and migratory birds, which include painted storks, cormorants and Eurasian spoonbills – there have also been occasional sightings of the endangered black-necked stork. The park's most significant feature is the Kumana Villu, a huge mangrove swamp lake fed by the Kumbukkan Oya river by way of a long narrow channel. A range of water birds

Elephants and spotted deer at the Kumana Villu swamp area, Kumana National Park

Eurasian spoonbill

nest in these mangroves during May and June. Besides the wetlands, the park's thriving bird population is also supported by an array of lagoons and salt marshes. A number of mammals, including elephants, wild boar, fishing cats and golden jackals, are known to inhabit the park. The place is a nesting ground for several species of turtles as well.

Kumana National Park is also home to some archaeological ruins. Among the highlights is the sacred site of Bambaragasthalawa that comprises rock caves with inscriptions and a badly damaged 11-m (36-ft) tall Buddha statue dating from the 9th century. At Bowattegala lie the remains of a rock temple dating from the 3rd century BC.

⓱ Maduru Oya National Park

Road map D4. 91 km (56 miles) N of Monaragala. 🚹 🚫 Note: hire jeep at Dambana to visit the park.

Maduru Oya was designated a national park in 1983. The entrance to the park lies in the village of Dambana, located 25 km (15 miles) northeast

of Mahiyangana (*see p144*). The park was created to protect the catchment areas of nearby reservoirs and attracts abundant birdlife. In addition, there is the usual fauna to look out for, such as elephants, sambar deer and monkeys.

The indigenous people of the island, the Veddahs, live in an area known as Henanigala on the edge of the park. Visitors can browse through some of their crafts for sale at the main entrance. The Veddahs were turfed out when Maduru Oya became a national park, and are only allowed to enter during the day if they have a permit. In March 2012, a Veddah man was shot and killed for hunting with the wrong permit; their hunting rights have since been withdrawn.

The Veddahs

The Veddahs or *Wanniyala-Aetto* (forest people) are the original forest-dwelling inhabitants of Sri Lanka and are thought to have lived on the island for millennia. Over the years, many Veddahs have been assimilated into the local Sinhalese and Tamil communities, although there are some who have resisted government resettlement schemes and have tried to carve out a life that retains their traditional beliefs and customs – including ancestor worship and coexisting in harmony with nature – and the hunter-gatherer lifestyle of their forefathers. Colonization, land development, implementation of reserves and national parks as well as the Civil War have all affected the Veddah way of life and their traditional land is fast disappearing. Today, Veddah settlements can be found around Dambana to the east of Manampitiya – they have been living here since being moved from their home in Maduru Oya.

Veddah men out on a hunt

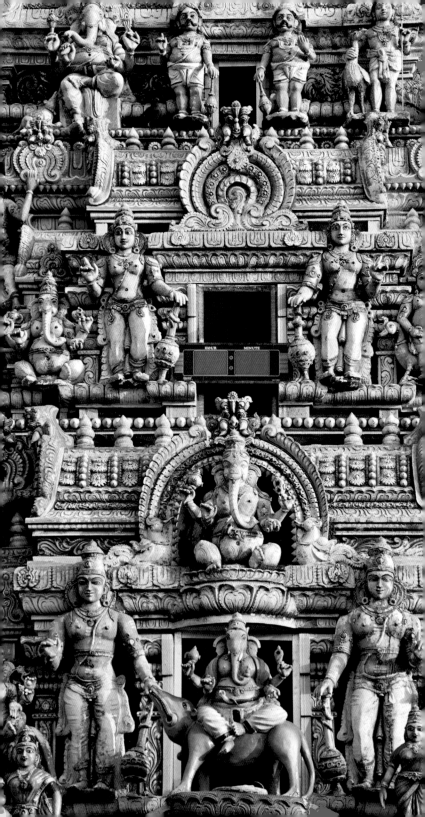

HOUR   MINUTE

JAFFNA AND THE NORTH

The northernmost district of Sri Lanka is only a few miles from India and similarities to the Indian Tamil culture are obvious in this part of the island. The province is a de facto Tamil heartland where Hinduism replaces Buddhism and Tamil is spoken in place of Sinhala. The sparsely populated region even looks different from the rest of the island, with its red earth and palmyra trees.

Inhabited since antiquity by Tamils from southern India, the north is visibly different from the rest of Sri Lanka. There is a strong Indian influence in this part of the country, but the Sinhalese, the Arab traders, as well as the Dutch, Portuguese and British colonialists have all left their mark.

The Sri Lankan Civil War has had a tremendous impact on the region. Cut off from the rest of the country for years during the war, the north still bears stark reminders of the conflict in the form of bullet-ridden buildings and a strong military presence. It is gradually recovering from its traumatic past and tourists, both Sri Lankan and foreign, are flocking to the Northern Province now that it is open for business again. The infrastructure is still a little fragile in

this part of Sri Lanka, but visitors are drawn to the area just the same to experience its natural, eerie beauty.

The journey north to Jaffna can be broken at various key points along A9 highway, including at Kilinochhi, where many war memorials can be seen. Mannar Island and Jaffna have atmospheric ruins of Colonial fortifications, with the latter boasting an impressive Dutch fort. Jaffna also has many vibrant *kovils* as well as an abundance of churches. The Jaffna Peninsula is a quiet region with sun-drenched coasts and vast tracts of palmyra trees, excellent for birdwatching. However, the remote islands, situated southwest of the peninsula, are the true jewels in Jaffna's crown, with their gorgeous beaches possessing an unmistakable charm.

A pristine beach backed by tropical trees at Delft, Jaffna Islands

◀ Hindu deities depicted on the *gopuram* of a temple, Vavuniya

Exploring Jaffna and the North

After decades of isolation due to the Civil War, the Northern Province is gradually resurfacing as an important centre of Tamil culture. Jaffna is the most popular destination and this is where most visitors choose to base themselves. Colourful *kovils* reveal the strong presence of Hindu Tamils in this town, although Christianity is also a dominant religion. The town is a great base for day trips around the peninsula – some tourists also venture out to the Jaffna Islands, particularly Karaitivu or Kayts, to relax on the beach. Towards the southwest of the province, Mannar Island is connected to the mainland by a causeway. Visitors to the island often take the ferry to the famous Adam's Bridge, a series of sandbanks stretching all the way to India.

Colourful boats at the beach, Point Pedro, Jaffna Peninsula

Striking exterior of the Nallur Kandaswamy Temple, Jaffna

For hotels and restaurants in this region see p221 and p233

Key

━━━ Major road

┅┅┅ Minor road

╌╌╌ Railway

▪▪▪ Provincial border

Sights at a Glance

❶ Vavuniya

❷ Mannar Island

❸ Highway A9

❹ Jaffna

❺ Jaffna Peninsula

❻ *Jaffna Islands pp208–209*

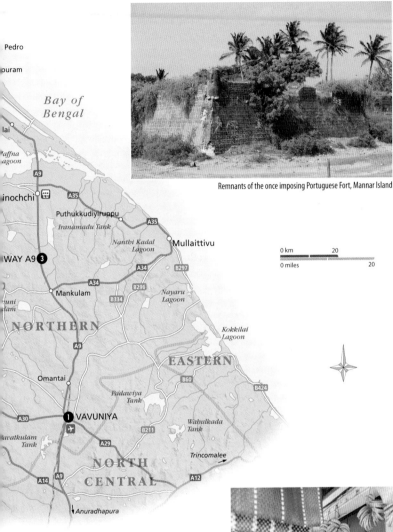

Remnants of the once imposing Portuguese Fort, Mannar Island

Pedro
puram

Bay of
Bengal

lai

affna
agoon

A9

inochchi

A35

Puthukkudiyiruppu

Iranamadu Tank

A35

Nanthi Kadal Lagoon

Mullaittivu

WAY A9 **3**

A34

B297

Mankulam

A34

B296

Nayaru Lagoon

B334

NORTHERN

A9

Kokkilai Lagoon

EASTERN

Omantai

B60

Padawiya Tank

B424

A30

1 VAVUNIYA

Wahalkada Tank

avatkulam Tank

B211

A29

Trincomalee

NORTH CENTRAL

A14 **A9**

A12

Anuradhapura

0 km — 20
0 miles — 20

Getting Around

The roads in the Northern Province are improving and work is underway to reopen the railway line between Vavuniya and Jaffna. Many people choose to take the train from Colombo to Vavuniya and then the bus to get to the town. However, there are direct buses from Colombo as well. Visitors can also fly to Jaffna from Colombo Airport *(see p266)*. Mannar can be reached by car or bus. The local buses are a good way to get around or a car and driver can be hired. To cover short distances in Jaffna, a three-wheeler can be hired. Bikes are another good option and can be rented at some guesthouses. Ferries run to Jaffna's outlying islands.

Variety of palmyra goods for sale, Jaffna

For map symbols *see back flap*

Enormous baobab tree dating from the 15th century, Talaimannar

❶ Vavuniya

Road map C2. 63 km (39 miles) N of Anuradhapura. ☒ 75,000. 🚌 🚆 🛈

For years Vavuniya has been the terminus of the Northern Line, cementing its reputation as a transit town for the journey towards the northern part of Sri Lanka. However, the line is being reconstructed and it is hoped trains will soon be running all the way up to Jaffna.

The town does not have many attractions, but there are some interesting *kovils* as well as the golden-domed **Grand Jummah Mosque**, an architectural gem.

☪ Grand Jummah Mosque
Horowapatana Road. **Open** 7am–7pm Sat–Thu, noon–2pm Fri.

Environs
About 4 km (2 miles) north-west of the town centre lies **Madukanda Vihara**. The temple is said to be built on the spot where the Tooth Relic rested on

Ornately carved *gopuram* with detailed statuary, Vavuniya

its journey to Anuradhapura. The complex has an image house and some ancient ruins with the guardstones still intact.

🏛 Madukanda Vihara
Open 9am–7pm daily

❷ Mannar Island

Road map B2. 63 km (39 miles) N of Vavuniya. ☒ 11,100. 🚌 🚆 🛈

Linked to the mainland by a causeway, Mannar feels fairly remote, perhaps because the original bridge was blown up in a bomb attack in the 1990s and it took until 2010 for a permanent replacement structure to be completed.

Mannar town, located in the southeast corner of the island, is the main settlement. Its principal attraction is a Portuguese **Fort**, near the town's entrance, which was later reinforced by the Dutch. Catholicism is prevalent in this area and the **St Sebastian Church**, with a slightly Moorish appearance, is especially revered by the community. Mannar is also famous for its baobab trees, believed to have been brought to Sri Lanka by the Arabs. There are some huge specimens, including one located to the north of town. It is said to have been planted in the 15th century.

At the island's western end is **Talaimannar**, from where ferries formerly shuttled between Sri Lanka and India. Towards the west of Talaimannar is **Adam's Bridge**, a series of sandbanks that extend all the way to India. According to the Indian epic

Ramayana, this makeshift bridge was constructed by the monkey god Hanuman in order to cross the sea between India and Sri Lanka. These days, the army runs boat trips out to these sand islands.

⛪ St Sebastian Church
7th Cross Street, Sinnakadai. **Open** 6am–8pm daily.

❸ Highway A9

Road map C2. N of Vavuniya. 🚌 🛈

The area north of Vavuniya stretching to Jaffna is abuzz with construction projects and de-mining activities now that the Civil War has ended. The A9, once bitterly fought over by both sides and dubbed "The Highway of Death" because of the number of people killed, has become a war-tourism hotspot.

The town of **Kilinochchi**, about 80 km (50 miles) north of Vavuniya, was the headquarters of the LTTE until it was captured by the army in 2009. The rebels had established law courts, administrative offices and even a bank here, but very little was left standing after they fled.

There is a large damaged water tank lying on the side of the main road – it was destroyed by the LTTE as they retreated. Down the road, lies the first of the many war memorials along the A9 – an enormous wall pierced by a shell. It was erected in 2010 in memory of the Sri Lankan

Wall pierced by an artillery shell, a famous war memorial along the A9

army's fallen soldiers. Further up the highway is the **Elephant Pass**, a narrow causeway that separates Jaffna Peninsula from the mainland. This was the site of two fierce battles during the war, and a number of war memorials stand here. The charred remains of a bulldozer is among the most revered. Used by the LTTE in 1991 in an attack against the army, the bulldozer was stopped by an army man who jumped aboard it to detonate a grenade, thereby sacrificing his life. There is a plaque erected in his memory.

❹ Jaffna

Road map B1. 169 km (105 miles) NE of Mannar Island. 🚗 169,000. 🚌 🛈

The Jaffna Peninsula has seen the number of visitors soar since the end of the Civil War, and some residents who had moved away on account of the violence have started to return. The area's main town, Jaffna, is very different from the rest of Sri Lanka, primarily because of the scars it bears from the long conflict. Although there are very few tourist sights, it is still a fascinating place to visit.

Built by the Dutch between 1680 and 1792 on the site of an earlier Portuguese construction, the enormous **Jaffna Fort** suffered during the fighting; renovation efforts are ongoing. It is possible to walk around the ramparts and see some of the original coralline bricks used in the construction of the edifice. Other important sights in town include the **Jaffna Public Library**, which was torched by Sinhalese mobs in 1981, and the **Clock Tower**, which was erected in 1875 to a design by British architect JG Smither.

All the main religions have their representative houses of worship in Jaffna, but the large Christian churches are hardest to miss. The Main Street is lined with atmospheric church buildings, including St James Church and the enormous **St Mary's Cathedral**, built by the Dutch. The latter has a pleasing

Gopuram of the Nallur Kandaswamy Temple, near Jaffna

interior and shady grounds where visitors can rest awhile and take in the peace and quiet.

Jaffna's modest **Archaeological Museum** is situated west of the town centre. It contains 15th-century artifacts excavated from Kantharodai (*see p206*) along with Hindu and Buddhist antiquities. Jaffna also boasts a vibrant market towards the west of the bus station. Although it is stocked with many day-to-day items, palmyra bags and mats

are among the most popular products for sale. There is also a covered produce market where vendors sell a wealth of fresh fruit and vegetables.

🏛 **Archaeological Museum**
Navaly Road. **Open** 8am–5pm Wed–Mon.

⛪ **St Mary's Cathedral**
Press Road. **Open** 6am–8pm. ⛪ 6am Mon–Sat, 6am, 7:15am & 4:30pm Sun.

Environs
Located about 2 km (1 mile) northeast of Jaffna is the beautiful **Nallur Kandaswamy Temple**. Dedicated to Skanda or Murugan, the original temple was destroyed by the Portuguese in the 17th century and the current building dates to the 19th century. The temple features a richly decorated interior, with an ornate ceiling. The temple is the centre of the 25-day long Nallur Chariot Festival, which reaches its peak on the 24th day when a large carved wooden cart is paraded through the streets.

🛕 **Nallur Kandaswamy Temple**
Open 5am–5pm daily. 🎉 Jul/Aug: Nallur Chariot Festival. 🖥 **nallurtemple.com**

Jaffna Public Library

The Public Library at Jaffna was set on fire by an anti-Tamil mob for over two days in 1981. Thousands of books and artifacts were destroyed, including priceless *ola*-leaf manuscripts. After having weathered further assaults over the coming years, it was finally restored in 2001 and opened to the public in 2003; books were donated from all over the world to help re-stock the shelves. Today, the imposing, Mughal-style building boasts an extensive collection of Tamil and English works. The statue in its grounds is that of goddess Saraswati, the Hindu deity of knowledge.

Reconstructed Jaffna Public Library building

❺ Jaffna Peninsula

Located at the northernmost tip of Sri Lanka, the fertile Jaffna Peninsula is still fairly isolated from the rest of the country. Some evidence of the Civil War still remains in the form of roofless buildings and heavily militarized areas, but temples are being repainted and renovated, and houses are being rebuilt. Travelling around this primarily rural peninsula is an excellent way to catch glimpses of a world that remains untouched by modernity. Attractions include multiple *kovils* with their extravagantly decorated interiors and colourful *gopurams*, and ancient *dagobas* steeped in history. Visitors may even come across Hindu religious processions making their way through the villages.

A sign welcoming visitors to the fishing settlement of Valvedditturai

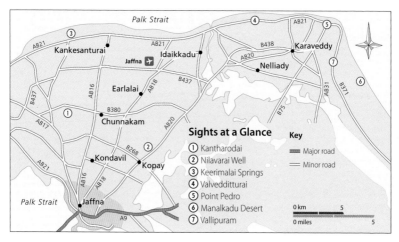

Sights at a Glance

① Kantharodai
② Nilavarai Well
③ Keerimalai Springs
④ Valvedditturai
⑤ Point Pedro
⑥ Manalkadu Desert
⑦ Vallipuram

Key

▬▬ Major road
══ Minor road

0 km 5
0 miles 5

🏛 Kantharodai

10 km (6 miles) N of Jaffna. **Open** daily. Note: Armed guards present at site. Shoes should be removed before entering.

An unusual and atmospheric spot, Kantharodai is an archaeological site comprising a cluster of squat miniature *dagobas*.

Buddhist *dagobas* at the Kantharodai archaeological site

They are thought to be around 2,000 years old, although their exact purpose or significance remains a mystery. According to some, the *dagobas* enshrine remains of monks. Another theory indicates that they were constructed and consecrated in fulfillment of prayers. Other finds from excavations of the site are on display in the Archaeological Museum (*see p205*) in Jaffna.

Nilavarai Well

Near Puttur, 10 km (6 miles) NE of Jaffna. **Open** daily. ♿

According to legend, the Hindu god Rama shot an arrow into the ground and created the Nilavarai Well to quench his thirst. Although not much to look at, the well is an interesting natural phenomenon and is thought to be directly connected to the sea. While the water at the top is fresh, it becomes more saline deeper in the well.

🏛 Keerimalai Springs

20 km (12 miles) N of Jaffna. **Open** daily.

Located at the peninsula's northern edge are the Keerimalai hot springs, one for men and one for women. The latter is walled but the men's pool has a good view of the sea.

According to local folklore, a 7th-century Chola princess had such a disfigured face that she resembled a horse, until she bathed in these waters and was cured of her affliction. In gratitude, she ordered the construction of the **Maviddapuram Kandaswamy Temple**, found south of the area.

The springs attract many visitors who come to immerse themselves in the therapeutic waters. There is another temple, the **Naguleswaram Siva Kovil**, nearby. The damage it sustained in the late 1990s is no longer apparent and the interior has been repainted in a riot of colours.

🏛 **Maviddapuram Kandaswamy Temple**
Open 6am–6pm daily.

🏛 **Naguleswaram Siva Kovil**
Open 6am–6pm daily.

Valvedditturai

30 km (19 miles) NE of Jaffna. 📷 former site of Prabhakaran's house
A fishing town, Valvedditturai is most famous as the birthplace of the founder of the LTTE, Velupillai Prabhakaran. However, the elusive guerilla leader's childhood home was destroyed in 2010.

Valvedditturai has a couple of interesting temples, including the **Amman Temple** towards the east of the village. Behind this shrine is a temple dedicated to Shiva, formerly owned by Prabhakaran's family.

🏛 **Amman Temple**
Open 6am–6pm daily.

Point Pedro

33 km (21 miles) NE of Jaffna. Note: Photography is generally not permitted but it is worth asking the sentry for permission. The lighthouse cannot be visited.

Point Pedro is the peninsula's second largest town and its lighthouse marks Sri Lanka's northernmost point. The lighthouse, unfortunately, is still considered a High Security Zone (HSZ) and cannot be

Fishing boats moored at the busy fisherman's beach, Point Pedro

visited. However, the road in front can be accessed and visitors may be able to photograph the lighthouse with the permission of the sentry stationed nearby. Fisherman's beach, loacted just 2 km (a mile) beyond the military zone, is attractive and worth a stroll.

🏜 Manalkadu Desert

11 km (7 miles) S of Point Pedro.
Towards the south of Point Pedro is a stretch of white-sand coastal dunes, somewhat grandly called the Manalkadu Desert. The remains of **St Anthony's Church**, dating from the early 20th century, can be

VISITORS' CHECKLIST

Practical information
Road map C1. Point Pedro is 33 km (21 miles) NE of Jaffna.

Transport
🚌 are available all around the peninsula. 🚕 can be hired from Jaffna.

seen here, half-buried in the sand. Nearby is a group of grave markers, mostly dating to the 2004 tsunami. There is also a beach lapped by bright blue water. However, the remains of houses destroyed by the tsunami have not yet been cleared, and getting to the beach would involve navigating through them.

Vallipuram

4 km (2.5 miles) S of Point Pedro.
Vishnu *kovil*: **Open** 5am–5pm. 📷 Inner sanctum.
Once considered to be one of Jaffna's main towns, Vallipuram still attracts visitors who come to see the *kovil* dedicated to the Hindu god Vishnu. The temple is second only in size to the Nallur Kandaswamy Temple (*see p205*). It underwent extensive renovation in 2012, during which a new roof was installed and the building repainted.

Magnificent *gopuram* of the Vishnu *kovil* in Vallipuram

❻ Jaffna Islands

Stretching out into the waters of the Palk Strait, the Jaffna Islands lie to the west of the Jaffna Peninsula. A trip to this string of small islands can feel like journeying to the end of the earth – they are sparsely populated, with white sand, blue sea and palmyra trees. Kayts, Karaitivu and Punkudutivu are connected to the mainland by causeways, whereas Nainativu and Delft can only be accessed by boat. For a relaxing day on the beach, Karaitivu or Kayts are the best options, while the more isolated Delft is the place for those seeking to get away from it all. Besides providing a welcome relief from the hustle and bustle of the cities, these islands also offer some superb birdwatching.

The striking cobra fountain, Nainativu

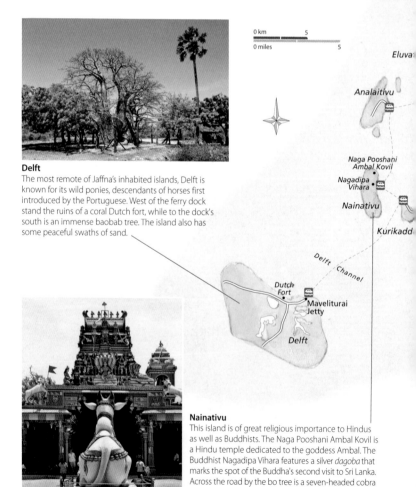

Delft

The most remote of Jaffna's inhabited islands, Delft is known for its wild ponies, descendants of horses first introduced by the Portuguese. West of the ferry dock stand the ruins of a coral Dutch fort, while to the dock's south is an immense baobab tree. The island also has some peaceful swaths of sand.

0 km — 5
0 miles — 5

Eluva

Analaitivu

Naga Pooshani
Ambal Kovil

Nagadipa
Vihara

Nainativu

Kurikadd

Delft Channel

Dutch
Fort

Maveliturai
Jetty

Delft

Nainativu

This island is of great religious importance to Hindus as well as Buddhists. The Naga Pooshani Ambal Kovil is a Hindu temple dedicated to the goddess Ambal. The Buddhist Nagadipa Vihara features a silver *dagoba* that marks the spot of the Buddha's second visit to Sri Lanka. Across the road by the bo tree is a seven-headed cobra fountain, where pilgrims often pose for photographs.

Punkudutivu

The main reason to visit Punkudutivu is to catch a ferry to either Nainativu or Delft from the jetty west of the island. Visitors can watch fishermen at work while travelling along the causeway.

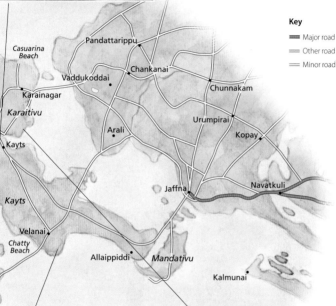

Key

▭▭ Major road
══ Other road
═ Minor road

Map locations: Pandattarippu, Casuarina Beach, Chankanai, Vaddukoddai, Chunnakam, Karainagar, Karaitivu, Urumpirai, Arali, Kopay, Kayts, Kayts, Jaffna, Navatkuli, Velanai, Chatty Beach, Allaippiddi, Mandativu, Kalmunai, Punkudutivu, Palk Strait, enhiel rt

Kayts

The largest of these islands, Kayts is the nearest to Jaffna. South of the island is the Chatty (Velanai) Beach, a popular stretch of sand. To the northwest is Kayts town, from where there are ferries to Karaitivu. The town also affords excellent views of the off-shore Hammenhiel Fort, which dates from the 17th century.

Karaitivu

The highlight here is Casuarina Beach, which lies on the north end of the island. Popular with locals and foreign tourists, this beach is safe for swimming. Basic facilities such as changing rooms and toilets are available on the beach.

For map symbols see back flap

MINISTRY OF CRAB

Crab Tribune

ost Sought After Seafood Restaurant

cate that Singapore
i and no pepper.

MINISTRY OF CRAB
ri lankan lagoon crab

TRAVELLERS' NEEDS

The Crab Island

Whole cones of locally grown
Black Pepper, ground on a
traditional
Sri Lankan
Miris gala (mira gala)

Why our Pepper Crab is so good

WHERE TO STAY

There is a diverse range of accommodation on offer in Sri Lanka, from extravagant five-star hotels to basic guesthouses. Luxury and boutique hotels abound in Colombo and other main tourist cities such as Kandy, Bentota and Nuwara Eliya. There are also a number of characterful places to choose from, including tea plantation bungalows, ecolodges and hotels designed by celebrated architect Geoffrey Bawa. Budget travellers will find ample hotels and guesthouses, some serving excellent home-cooked meals, in most parts of the country. Homestays are another popular option and present an opportunity to experience life in rural Sri Lanka and sample authentic local cuisine. As prices for all accommodation rise during high season, it is advisable to make reservations in advance.

Prices and Taxes

The price of accommodation in Sri Lanka fluctuates depending upon the season. Hotels hike their rates during high season, which lasts from December to March on the West and South coasts as well as the Hill Country, and from April through September on the East Coast. Rates also tend to rise in towns and cities in the hinterland when an important local festival, such as the Esala Perahera *(see p139)* in Kandy, is taking place, or during important national holidays as well as Christmas and New Year. In low season, it may be possible to negotiate a lower price at some establishments.

Most high-end places impose additional taxes on accommodation charges, including service charge, a 15 per cent government tax and, occasionally, a development tax. As this can add as much as 27 per cent to the bill, it is always best to check if the price quoted by a hotel is inclusive of taxes.

Booking

It is a good idea to book accommodation for at least the first couple of nights before arriving in Sri Lanka. However, if prior arrangements have not been made, visitors are likely to find a guesthouse with a spare room when travelling around the island, especially during low season. Tourists planning to visit during high season or an important local event are advised to book a hotel well in advance as places can get very busy.

Quiet poolside during off season at Palace Mirissa Hotel, Mirissa

Many mid-range and top-end hotels in Sri Lanka now offer online booking services. It is also possible to make reservations over the telephone. Be warned, however, that there have been instances when bookings made in advance, usually those arranged over the phone, have not been honoured. To avoid this, carry a print out of the email confirmation of your booking as proof.

The more upmarket hotels will sometimes ask for an advance deposit at the time of booking. Ensure that this has been deducted from the total bill at the time of check out.

Be aware that accommodation touts are rife in Sri Lanka and often operate as three-wheeler drivers near bus or railway stations. They offer incredible, albeit rather dubious discounts to tourists, and can be quite persistent. Touts are best avoided by booking a hotel in advance.

Travelling with a Driver

Visitors who choose to arrange their car and driver independently of a tour operator must make sure that the establishments they stay at have facilities for the driver. Most top-range and mid-range hotels offer quarters for drivers. However, basic guesthouses might not, and visitors are expected to cover costs of accommodating the driver.

Tipping

In upmarket hotels, it is expected that guests tip the hotel porters who carry their

The Trevene in Nuwara Eliya, a decent budget option during peak season

luggage. If you are pleased with the service you may want to tip the housekeeping staff. If a service charge has not already been added to the bill, you might want to consider leaving a little extra. It is worth remembering that hotel staff wages in the country are often quite low.

Facilities for Children

Some establishments have designated play areas as well as children's pools, and even provide baby-sitting services. Others organize activities such as arts and crafts. Family rooms are available in most hotels or else an extra bed can be requested. Staff at hotels and guesthouses will always make children feel welcome.

Facilities for Disabled Travellers

A number of the newer and more upmarket hotels have facilities for disabled travellers. These include ramps for lobby access, wheelchair accessible elevators and rooms, emergency alarms as well as handrails. Although lower-end establishments may not provide such amenities, the staff in most places will be attentive to the needs of visitors with disabilities. Reputable tour operators will be able to recommend places that cater to travellers with special requirements, or the hotels can be contacted directly.

The Colombo Hilton hotel rising above the cityscape

Chain and Luxury Hotels

High-end hotels abound on the Sri Lankan tourist circuit. The **Hilton**, **Aitken Spence**, **John Keells** and **Jetwing Hotels** are among notable hotel groups with representation in the country. These chains feature a number of establishments that offer spacious suites, excellent service and modern amenities in cities such as Colombo, Habarana, Kandy, Negombo as well as other major tourist destinations.

Apart from chain hotels, Sri Lanka also has a range of independent luxury hotels, with prices and standards comparable with the West. Most of these are housed in buildings dating from the Colonial era. These buildings were either purpose-built during Colonial times or have been recently restored, modernized and converted into plush hotels, exuding old-world charm and excellent standards of service.

Rooms at these upmarket establishments are stylish and equipped with all mod cons such as air conditioning, satellite TV and Internet access. Other facilities include swimming pools, indulgent spas, gyms, gift shops and a range of dining options. Business travellers are well catered for at these hotels that often have exclusive business centres with printing services, meeting rooms and video conferencing facilities. These hotels are mainly found in Colombo, Galle and Kandy.

Boutique Hotels and Villas

The island country offers a range of boutique hotels and villas that are usually small, distinctive and set in picturesque, private locations, such as Lunuganga (see p100). Many of these hotels are also in restored Colonial buildings – their interiors are often tastefully and creatively decorated and the service is excellent. As a result, prices are often high. These properties, particularly those in the Hill Country, arrange activities for guests, offer spa treatments and organize excursions.

Sri Lanka also has a number of stunning hotels designed by Geoffrey Bawa. These modern hotels stand out from the crowd because of their outstanding architecture or exceptional location. An example is the Kandalama hotel (see p220), which is nestled within a cover of jungle and blends well with its surrounding landscape.

Lively evening atmosphere outside Galle Face Hotel, Colombo

Vil Uyana ecolodge perched above a lake surrounded by lush trees, Sigiriya

Tea Plantation Bungalows

One of Sri Lanka's most rewarding experiences is staying in a bungalow on a tea planta-tion. These properties, once owned by tea estate managers, have been converted into guesthouses or hotels and are surrounded by lush tea gardens. Boasting breathtaking views, the bungalows usually come with a caretaker and a cook, although some are self-catering. **Tea Trails** *(see p219)* rents out four Colonial-era villas in the area around Dickoya – it is possible to rent the whole property or a room for the night.

Resort Hotels

Beach resort hotels are mainly aimed at visitors arriving in Sri Lanka on a package holiday, and offer a range of prices and services. These resorts usually include easy access to the beach, great swimming pools as well as buffet meals, and are ideal for those who want to just sit back and relax. The West Coast is home to a number of Ayurvedic resorts, where visitors can stay for a couple of weeks to undergo a personalized treatment plan. Prior reservation at these hotels is recommended.

Ecolodges

Nature lovers may want to stay in one of the numerous eco-friendly lodges in the country, which are located in forested or jungle areas and blend well with their natural surroundings. These usually offer a range of outdoor activities, including birdwatching, guided hikes, boat trips and cycle rides.

Close proximity to nature is the primary attraction of the ecolodges: they are not the best choice for visitors expecting five-star luxury. Accommodation ranges from basic to reasonably upmarket, although the lodges remain rustic and unique; some even boast quirky features, such as open-air bathrooms.

Government Rest Houses

These rest houses were originally built to house travelling officials during the Colonial era. Despite no longer being government-run, many of them have now been revamped for the use of tourists. The **Ceylon Hotels Corporation (CHC)**, part of the Galle Face Hotel Group, manages a number of these rest houses in popular tourist areas. These mid-range establishments are mostly set in renovated buildings in great locations, and offer good-value rice and curry lunches.

Guesthouses and Budget Hotels

Guesthouses and budget hotels can be easily found all over the island, but are somewhat scarce in Colombo where low-end accommodation is harder to come by. Guesthouses come in all sizes – some are family homes that rent out a few rooms, while others are like small hotels. The range and quality of services goes up with the price. It is likely that the more modestly priced options would not have hot water. Visitors are recommended to view the rooms before committing themselves.

Homestays

The popularity of homestays in Sri Lanka is steadily increasing and they can be found all around the country. Homestays offer a great opportunity to interact with locals and occasionally sample excellent home-cooked meals. The **Sri Lankan Homestay** website is good for booking homestays, or they can be arranged via tour

Colonial-style bedroom at Khalid's Guesthouse, Galle

The swanky Safari Hotel overlooking the Tissa Wewa, Tissamaharama

operators. One of the best ways to choose a homestay, however, is to speak to other travellers and go by their recommendations.

National Parks and Camping

There are bungalows to rent in some of the Sri Lankan national parks. However, staying in these is hard to arrange, especially for the independent traveller, as they have to be reserved in person at the **Department of Wildlife Conservation** in Colombo, usually months in advance. National park bungalows can also be quite expensive once the park fee and service charges have been added. Some tour operators may be able to arrange for permission to camp overnight in a national park.

Rental Apartments

Visitors planning to stay in a particular area of Sri Lanka for a prolonged period of time could consider renting an apartment. This practice is becoming increasingly popular and there are a number of agencies offering flats to rent in and around Colombo. The **Hilton Colombo Residences** offers serviced apartments with excellent facilities, but something more basic can be arranged through websites such as **Roomorama**. It is also possible to rent villas and bungalows, which are usually set in idyllic surroundings.

Recommended Hotels

The hotels in this book have been carefully selected and are among the best in Sri Lanka in their respective categories: Luxury, Boutique, Heritage, Ecolodge, Ayurvedic resort, Beach resort, Budget and Guesthouse. They underline the diverse range of accommodation available on the island, which caters to all tastes and pockets, however, the range and standards of hotels in Jaffna and the North may not match those found elsewhere on the island. Many of the interesting and remarkable places in the country are not necessarily the most expensive ones, so look out for the hotels marked as DK Choice. These establishments have been highlighted in recognition of an extraordinary feature – a stunning location, inviting atmosphere, notable history or quite often outstanding value for money.

Impressive exterior of the Hill Club Hotel, Nuwara Eliya

DIRECTORY

Chain and Luxury Hotels

Aitken Spence
Level 5, Aitken Spence Tower II, 315 Vauxhall Street, Col 2. **City map** 3 C1. **Tel** (011) 230 8408.
W aitkenspencehotels.com

Hilton
Tel 0870 5 90 90 90 (UK), 1 800 445 8667 (US).
W hilton.com

Jetwing Hotels
Jetwing House, 46/26 Navam Mawatha, Col 2. **City map** 3 B1. **Tel** (011) 234 5700.
W jetwinghotels.com

John Keells
130 Glennie Street, Col 2. **City map** 3 A1. **Tel** (011) 230 6600.
W johnkeellshotels.com

Tea Plantation Bungalows

Tea Trails
46/38 Nawam Mawatha, Col 2. **City map** 3 B2. **Tel** (011) 230 3888.
W teatrails.com

Government Rest Houses

Ceylon Hotels Corporation (CHC)
Galle Face Hotel, 2 Galle Road, Col 3. **City map** 3 A1. **Tel** (011) 558 5858. W ceylonhotels.lk

Homestays

Sri Lankan Homestay
Sri Lanka Tourism Development Authority, 80 Galle Road, Col 3. **City map** 3 A2. **Tel** (011) 476 6330.
W srilankanhomestay.com

National Parks and Camping

Department of Wildlife Conservation
Tel (011) 288 8585.

Rental Apartments

Hilton Colombo Residences
200 Union Place, Col 2. **City map** 3 A2. **Tel** (011) 534 4644.
W colomboresidence. hilton.com

Roomorama
W roomorama.com

Where to Stay

Colombo

Mount Lodge $
Guesthouse
69A Hotel Rd, Mount Lavinia
Tel *(077) 773 3313*
w nisalaarana.com
Set amid tropical gardens. Rooms have private outdoor space. Serves great *hoppers* for breakfast.

Tropic Inn $
Guesthouse
30 College Ave, Mount Lavinia
Tel *(011) 273 8653*
w tropicinn.com
Small place with rooms of varying sizes. The beach is a 2-minute walk away. Friendly staff. Free Wi-Fi.

YWCA National Headquarters $
Budget **Map** 3 B2
7 Rotunda Garden, Col 3
Tel *(011) 232 8589*
Basic accommodation in a central location.

Havelock Place Bungalow $$
Boutique
6/8 Havelock Place, Col 5
Tel *(011) 258 5191*
w havelockbungalow.com
Characterful and peaceful rooms in a pair of converted bungalows.

Lake Lodge $$
Guesthouse **Map** 3 B2
20 Alvis Terrace, Col 3
Tel *(011) 232 6443*
w taruhotels.com
Situated near Beira Lake, this place has simple yet comfortable rooms.

Renuka & Renuka City $$
Luxury **Map** 3 B3
328 Galle Rd, Col 3
Tel *(011) 257 3598*
w renukahotel.com
Popular with business travellers, this well-located hotel offers rooms in two adjoining buildings.

Bawa's House $$$
Boutique **Map** 3 C4
No 11, 33 Lane, off Bagatelle Rd, Col 3
Tel *(011) 433 7335*
w geoffreybawa.com
Stay at Bawa's town house, in a two-room suite that includes a tastefully decorated living room.

CASA Colombo $$$
Boutique **Map** 3 B5
231 Galle Rd, Bambalapitiya, Col 4
Tel *(011) 452 0130*
w casacolombo.com
Small, chic hotel in a renovated mansion, with individually decorated rooms. Attentive service.

Cinnamon Grand $$$
Luxury **Map** 3 B2
77 Galle Rd, Col 3
Tel *(011) 243 7437*
w cinnamonhotels.com
Five-star hotel with swimming pools, a gym and a kids' playroom. Excellent restaurants.

Cinnamon Lakeside $$$
Luxury **Map** 1 C5
115 Sir Chittampalam A Gardiner Mawatha, Col 2
Tel *(011) 249 1000*
w cinnamonhotels.com
Smart rooms and good restaurants, including a sushi bar. Overlooks Beira Lake.

DK Choice

Galle Face Hotel $$$
Heritage **Map** 3 A1
2 Galle Rd, Col 3
Tel *(011) 558 5858*
w gallefacehotel.com
This seafront hotel overlooks Galle Face Green. Opened in 1864, its interior retains a Colonial feel. The hotel comprises two wings: Classic and the more contemporary Regency. Rooms and suites are well-appointed with all mod cons. The hotel boasts numerous bars and restaurants. Enjoy high tea or watch the sunset while soaking in the sea views.

Hilton Colombo $$$
Luxury **Map** 1 B4
2 Sir Chittampalam A Gardiner Mawatha, Col 2
Tel *(011) 249 2492*
w hilton.com
Modern hotel with great views, especially from the upper floors. Facilities include speciality restaurants and a shopping arcade.

Simple room at Neela's Guesthouse in Narigama, near Hikkaduwa

Tintagel $$$
Boutique **Map** 3 E2
65 Rosemead Place, Col 7
Tel *(011) 460 2121*
w tintagelcolombo.com
Former home of the Bandaranaike family, the stylish Tintagel has a spa, a steam room and a library.

Mount Lavinia Hotel $$$
Heritage
100 Hotel Rd, Mount Lavinia
Tel *(011) 271 1711*
w mountlaviniahotel.com
Situated on a headland with a private beach. Although the hotel has been modernized, it retains an old-world charm.

The West Coast

DK Choice

BENTOTA: The Villa $$$
Boutique **Map** B6
138/22 Galle Rd
Tel *(034) 227 5311*
w paradiseroadhotels.com
Located a short distance from Bentota, this 19th-century villa was converted into a luxury hotel by Geoffrey Bawa in the 1970s. The 15 rooms and suites are individually decorated. There are two pools, an open-air bar and board games available. The café serves good-quality food. Guests can get a 10 per cent discount at the Paradise Road lifestyle shop on site.

BENTOTA: Saman Villas $$$
Boutique **Map** B6
Aturuwella
Tel *(034) 227 5435*
w samanvilla.com
Beautiful suites, some with their own lap pool, in a hotel built on a rocky outcrop. Stunning views of the Indian Ocean.

HIKKADUWA: Neela's $
Guesthouse **Map** B6
634 Galle Rd, Narigama
Tel *(091) 438 3166*
Friendly, popular beachside establishment. Some of the rooms offer fine sea views.

HIKKADUWA: Surf Villa $
Guesthouse   **Map** B6
Milla Rd
Tel *(077) 760 4620*
w srilankasurftour.com
Popular with surfers, this villa offers spacious rooms and free breakfasts.

HIKKADUWA: Chaaya Tranz $$$
Beach Resort   **Map** B6
Galle Rd
Tel *(091) 227 8000*
w chaayahotels.com
Rooms and suites overlook the sea. There is a rooftop spa, a pool and a range of dining options.

KALPITIYA PENINSULA:
Palagama Beach $$
Beach Resort   **Map** B3
Alankuda Beach
Tel *(077) 735 2200*
w palagamabeach.com
Romantic beach cabanas and large villas. Infinity pool and spa as well.

KALPITIYA PENINSULA:
Bar Reef $$$
Beach Resort   **Map** B3
Palmyrah Ave, Alankuda Beach
Tel *(077) 106 0020*
w barreefresort.com
Simple cabanas and villas with outdoor showers. Saltwater pool.

KALPITIYA PENINSULA:
Udekki $$$
Beach Resort   **Map** B3
Alankuda Beach
Tel *(077) 744 6135*
w udekki.com
Most rooms here are in a shared villa, but families can rent individual villas and even self-cater.

NEGOMBO: Star Beach $
Guesthouse   **Map** B4
83/3 Lewis Pl
Tel *(031) 222 2606*
w starbeachnegombo.com
Most rooms have fans rather than air conditioning. Rooms upstairs are better; some have ocean views.

NEGOMBO: The Icebear
Beach Guesthouse $
Guesthouse   **Map** B4
103-2 Lewis Pl
Tel *(071) 423 7755*
w icebearhotel.com
Characterful Swiss-owned guesthouse with rooms in buildings set around a lovely tropical garden.

NEGOMBO: Jetwing Beach $$$
Beach Resort   **Map** B4
Porutota Rd, Ethukala
Tel *(031) 227 7140*
w jetwinghotels.com
Stylish hotel with several dining options and a swimming pool. Spa and gift shop on site.

Deck chairs next to the infinity pool, Palagama Beach

The South

GALLE: Rampart View $
Guesthouse   **Map** B6
37 Rampart St
Tel *(091) 222 6767*
w gallefortrampartview.com
Spotless rooms and spectacular ocean views from the rooftop terrace. Free Wi-Fi.

GALLE: Khalid's Guesthouse $$
Guesthouse   **Map** B6
102 Pedlar St
Tel *(077) 317 7676*
Quiet and welcoming hotel with Colonial-style rooms. Meals on request. Alcohol not allowed.

GALLE: Amangalla $$$
Boutique   **Map** B6
10 Church St
Tel *(091) 223 3388*
w amanresorts.com
This luxurious hotel, within the ramparts of the Galle Fort, offers rooms and suites furnished with antiques. Lovely pool and gardens.

GALLE: Galle Fort Hotel $$$
Boutique   **Map** B6
28 Church St
Tel *(091) 223 2870*
w galleforthotel.com
Recipient of a UNESCO Heritage Award, this beautiful Colonial mansion offers elegant rooms and suites.

GALLE: Jetwing Lighthouse $$$
Luxury   **Map** B6
Dadella
Tel *(091) 222 3744*
w jetwinghotels.com
Designed by Bawa, Jetwing Lighthouse has minimalistic rooms and suites, some with ocean views. Spa, pools and squash as well as tennis courts.

GALLE: The Fort Printers $$$
Boutique   **Map** B6
39 Pedlar St
Tel *(091) 224 7977*
w thefortprinters.com
A mix of the Colonial and the contemporary. Well-lit rooms with wooden furniture.

GALLE: The Sun House $$$
Boutique   **Map** B6
18 Upper Dickson Rd
Tel *(091) 438 0275*
w thesunhouse.com
A former spice merchant's villa with elegantly decorated rooms. Excellent food. The Cinnamon Suite is recommended.

KOGGALA: The Fortress $$$
Luxury   **Map** C6
Matara Rd
Tel *(091) 438 9400*
w fortressresortandspa.com
Breathtaking rooms and suites at this opulent beachside hotel. There is also a spa and a pool.

MIRISSA: Rose Blossom
Guest House $
Guesthouse   **Map** C6
Opposite Giragala Village, Bandara Mulla
Tel *(077) 713 3096*
Small, friendly guesthouse with clean but basic rooms.

MIRISSA: Sun 'n' Sea $
Guesthouse   **Map** C6
1 Banadara Mulla
Tel *(077) 833 9958*
Rooms right on the beach. Good food. Helpful management.

MIRISSA: Hotel Silan Mo $$
Mid-range Hotel   **Map** C6
Main Rd
Tel *(041) 2254974*
w silanmo.com
Located across the road from the beach. Rooftop pool.

For more information on types of hotels *see page 215*

MIRISSA: Palace Mirissa $$
Beach Resort   Map C6
Copparamulla
Tel *(041) 322 5130*
W **palacemirissa.com**
Bungalows dotted around lush grounds. Spectacular views. Half-board or full-board only.

POLHENA: Sunil
Rest Guesthouse $
Guesthouse   Map C6
Off Beach Rd
Tel *(077) 943 4193*
Rooms are spread between two neighbouring properties. Home cooking and bike hire. No hot water.

TANGALLA: Goyambokka
Guesthouse $
Guesthouse   Map C6
Goyambokka
Tel *(047) 224 0838*
W **goyambokkaguesthouse.**
page.tl
This little house offers four rooms, one with a private balcony. Large garden and superb food.

TANGALLA: Green Garden
Cabanas $
Guesthouse   Map C6
Goyambokka
Tel *(047) 224 2478*
W **greengardencabanas.com**
Welcoming guesthouse with a range of rooms around a garden.

TANGALLA: Nugasewana Eden $
Guesthouse   Map C6
Mahawela Rd
Tel *(047) 224 0389*
W **nugasewana.com**
Popular place, with some rooms opening onto wide balconies with sea views. Serves delicious food.

TANGALLA: Sandy's
Beach Resort   Map C6
Marakolliya
Tel *(047) 720 0289*
W **sandycabana.com**
Basic beachfront resort in a quiet location with cabanas and home-cooked meals.

TANGALLA: Mangrove Beach
Cabanas $$
Ecolodge   Map C6
Marakolliya
Tel *(077) 790 6018*
W **beachcabana.lk**
Cabanas and mud houses on a secluded palm-fringed beach. Bathrooms are reached via a ladder.

TANGALLA: Amanwella $$$
Luxury   Map C6
Godellawella
Tel *(047) 224 1333*
W **amanresorts.com**
Contemporary suites with plunge pools that are tucked among the trees. Beachfront infinity pool.

TISSAMAHARAMA: Elephant
Camp Guesthouse $
Guesthouse   Map D6
Kataragama Rd
Tel *(072) 493 4992*
Set in a small garden, this family-run guesthouse has clean but simple rooms.

TISSAMAHARAMA: Refresh $
Guesthouse   Map D6
Kataragama Rd
Tel *(047) 223 7357*
Attractive and comfortable rooms arranged around a small courtyard. Popular restaurant.

TISSAMAHARAMA: Priyankara $$
Mid-range Hotel   Map D6
Kataragama Rd
Tel *(047) 223 7206*
W **priyankarahotel.com**
Large and immaculate rooms with balconies overlooking paddy fields. Traditional Sri Lankan cuisine is served at the on-site restaurant.

TISSAMAHARAMA: The Safari $$$
Luxury   Map D6
Kataragama Rd
Tel *(047) 567 7620*
W **the-safari-tissamaharama-**
sri-lanka.ww.lk
Lakeside hotel with tasteful rooms. Pool overlooks the Tissa Wewa. Tennis courts on site.

UDA WALAWE: Kalu's
Hideaway $$
Boutique   Map C5
Walawegama
Tel *(047) 492 9930*
W **kalushideaway.com**
Small hotel with modern rooms. Restaurant and pool on site.

UNAWATUNA: Brink House $
Guesthouse   Map C6
Welledevala Rd
Tel *(091) 224 2245*
W **brinkhouseunawatuna.**
site11.com
Peaceful, family-run guesthouse. Rooms upstairs have balconies.

UNAWATUNA: Strand $
Guesthouse   Map C6
218 Yaddehimulla Rd
Tel *(091) 222 4358*
W **homestay-strand.net**
Located away from the beach in expansive grounds, this family villa offers a variety of rooms and an apartment. Weekly stays preferred.

UNAWATUNA: Sun-n-Sea $
Guesthouse   Map C6
324 Matara Rd, Ganahena
Tel *(091) 228 3200*
W **sunnsea.net**
Simple rooms in this friendly beachfront establishment.

UNAWATUNA: Banana
Garden $$
Guesthouse   Map C6
Beachfront
Tel *(091) 438 1089*
W **unawatunahotel.com**
Very close to the beach. Rooms are spotless but vary in size.

UNAWATUNA: Secret
Garden Villa $$
Guesthouse   Map C6
Beach Rd
Tel *(091) 761 4119*
Colonial villa and a modern bungalow snugly set amid a tropical garden.

UNAWATUNA: Unawatuna
Beach Resort $$
Beach Resort   Map C6
Beachfront
Tel *(091) 438 4545*
W **unawatunabeachresort.com**
Brightly decorated rooms, some with sea views. The resort organizes whale-watching trips.

WELIGAMA: Samaru Beach
House $
Guesthouse   Map C6
544 New Bypass Rd, Pelana
Tel *(041) 225 1417*
W **guesthouse-weligama**
samaru.com
Popular with surfers. Clean rooms and great food. Surfboards for rent.

Sitting area overlooking the beautiful garden at Secret Garden Villa, Unawatuna

Key to Price Guide *see page 216*

WELIGAMA: The Green Rooms $$
Guesthouse   Map C6
Main Rd
Tel *(077) 111 9896*
🅦 **thegreenroomssrilanka.com**
Surf lodge set on the beach.
Accommodation is in wooden
cabanas or air-conditioned rooms.
Surf lessons are offered.

DK Choice

**WELIGAMA: Barberyn Beach
Ayurveda Resort $$$**
Ayurvedic   Map C6
Near Abimanagama Rd
Tel *(041) 225 2994*
🅦 **barberynresorts.com**
A tranquil seafront resort set
in beautiful grounds, Barberyn
is recommended for those who
want to follow an Ayurvedic
treatment plan. Meditation
and yoga, as well as Ayurvedic
cookery demonstrations are
also on offer. Rooms are spacious
and come with en suite bathrooms. There is a pool and
beach access. Full-board only.

WELIGAMA: Mandara Resort $$$
Beach Resort   Map C6
416/A Pelena
Tel *(041) 225 3993*
🅦 **mandararesort.com**
Quiet beachfront hotel with
stylish modern rooms, some with
plunge pools or Jacuzzi.

WELIGAMA: Taprobane Island $$$
Luxury   Map C6
Tel *(091) 4380275*
🅦 **taprobaneisland.com**
Five elegant rooms with en suite
bathrooms. Lovely tropical garden
and infinity pool. Resident staff.

**YALA NATIONAL PARK: Chaaya
Wild $$$**
Luxury   Map D5
Kirinda Palatupana
Tel *(047) 223 9450*
🅦 **chaayahotels.com**
Well-equipped "Beach" and
"Jungle" bungalows with mini-bar
and flat-screen TV. Near the park
and good for wildlife-spotting.

Kandy and
the Hill Country

**DALHOUSIE: Slightly
Chilled Guest House $$**
Guesthouse   Map C5
Main Rd
Tel *(051) 351 9430*
🅦 **slightlychilled.tv**
Friendly place with varied rooms,
some with great views of Adam's
Peak. Bicycles available for rent.

Typical room at the Sevana Guest House,
Kandy

**DICKOYA: Tea Trails
Bungalows $$$**
Heritage   Map C5
Tel *(011) 230 2888*
🅦 **teatrails.com**
Choose from four Colonial
bungalows that were once the
homes of tea estate managers.
Full-board stays.

ELLA: Ella Holiday Inn $
Guesthouse   Map D5
Main St
Tel *(057) 222 8615, 072 4656292*
🅦 **ellaholidayinn.com**
Clean, comfortable rooms, some
with balconies. Tasty food.

ELLA: Waterfalls Homestay $
Guesthouse   Map D5
Watagodawaththa
Tel *(057) 567 6933*
🅦 **waterfalls-guesthouse-ella.com**
Excellent location, rooms and
food. Friendly owners. Great value.

ELLA: Zion View $$
Guesthouse   Map D5
Wemulla hena
Tel *(057) 222 8799*
🅦 **ella-guesthouse-srilanka.com**
Family-owned place at a scenic
location with rooms opening onto
wide, shared balconies. Delicious
home-cooked Sri Lankan food.

**HAPUTALE: Amarasinghe Guest
House $**
Guesthouse   Map C5
Thambapillai Ave
Tel *(057) 226 8175*
Homely establishment with
comfortable rooms; some on the
first floor have great views.

**HAPUTALE: Kelburne Mountain
View Cottages $$**
Heritage   Map C5
Dambetenne Rd
Tel *(011) 257 3382*
🅦 **kelburnemountainview.com**
Intimate cottages set amid a
tea plantation. Spectacular views
and lots of peace and quiet.

**HAPUTALE: Olympus Plaza
Hotel $$**
Mid-range Hotel   Map C5
75 Welimada Rd
Tel *(057) 226 8544*
🅦 **olympusplazahotel.com**
Comfortable rooms, if a bit bland.
Good location.

KANDY: McLeod Inn $
Guesthouse   Map C4
65a Rajapihilla Mawatha
Tel *(081) 222 2832*
Good-size, clean rooms. Pay a
little extra for the rooms with a
view over Kandy. Friendly owners.

KANDY: Sevana Guest House $
Guesthouse   Map C4
84 Peradeniya Rd
Tel *(081) 567 4443*
🅦 **sevanakandy.com**
Welcoming family guesthouse.
Extra charge for air conditioning,
hot water and balcony.

KANDY: Hotel Suisse $$
Mid-range Hotel   Map C4
30 Sangarajah Mawatha
Tel *(081) 223 3024/5*
🅦 **hotelsuisse.lk**
Strikes a good balance between
Colonial and modern decor. The
Kandy Lake is nearby.

KANDY: Amaya Hills $$$
Luxury   Map C4
Heerassagala
Tel *(081) 447 4022/8*
🅦 **amayaresorts.com**
Nestled in the hills west of Kandy.
Wide range of rooms, including
split-level suites.

KANDY: Chaaya Citadel $$$
Luxury   Map C4
*124 Srimanth Kuda, Rawatte
Mawatha*
Tel *(081) 223 4365*
🅦 **chaayahotels.com**
Located outside Kandy on the
Mahaweli river. Offers comfortable
and attractive rooms with balconies.

KANDY: Theva Residency $$$
Boutique   Map C4
*10-1, 6th Lane, off Upper Tank Rd, off
Circular 2 Rd, Hantanna*
Tel *(081) 738 8296*
🅦 **theva.lk**
Attractive hotel with a range
of rooms and lovely views.
Superb food.

**KARAMBAKETIYA: Corbert's
Rest $**
Ecolodge
In the Knuckles Range
Tel *(081) 286 8025*
🅦 **corbertsrest.com**
Cottages and camp sites. Limited
hot water and electricity. Popular
with trekkers and birdwatchers.

For more information on types of hotels *see page 215*

KITULGALA: Borderlands $$$
Camping   Map C5
Hatton Rd
Tel *(077) 789 9836*
w discoverborderlands.com
Riverside camp with tents on
stilted platforms and shared bath-
rooms. Organizes rafting trips.

DK Choice

MAKULDENIYA: Rangala
House $$
Boutique   Map C4
92b Bobebila
Tel *(081) 240 0292*
w rangalahouse.com
A converted tea planter's
bungalow set in lush grounds,
Rangalla is a great place to get
away from it all. There are four
en suite rooms and a spacious
sitting area. The verandah
offers splendid views over the
gardens and beyond to the tea
plantations. Amenities include
a solar-heated swimming pool
and a tennis court. The chef
conjures up fantastic food.
Great for birdwatchers.

NUWARA ELIYA: The Trevene $
Heritage   Map C5
17 Park Rd
Tel *(052) 222 2767*
w hoteltrevenenuwaraeliya.com
Rooms in this Colonial bungalow
have fireplaces and period furniture. Those overlooking the
garden are more expensive.

NUWARA ELIYA: Hill Club $$
Heritage   Map C5
Up the path from Grand Hotel,
29 Grand Hotel Rd
Tel *(052) 222 2653*
w hillclubsrilanka.net
Enjoy the British Colonial
atmosphere at this private resort.

DK Choice

NUWARA ELIYA: Heritance
Tea Factory $$$
Heritage   Map C5
Kandapola
Tel *(052) 222 9600*
w heritancehotels.com
Nestled among tea estates, this
characterful hotel is a converted
19th-century tea factory that has
kept its original exterior intact.
Inside, there are reminders of
the building's history; the
former engine room is now the
kitchen and the tea-packing
room has been converted into
a bar. Rooms are comfortable
and traditionally furnished.
One of the restaurants is in a
converted old railway carriage.

Colonial-era building of the Hill Club fronted by a well-manicured lawn, Nuwara Eliya

SINHARAJA: Rainforest Edge $$
Ecolodge   Map C6
Balawatukanda, Weddagala
Tel *(045) 225 5912*
w rainforestsedge.com
Secluded hotel with stylish rooms
and outdoor bathrooms. Full board.

The Cultural Triangle

ANURADHAPURA: Milano
Tourist Rest
Guesthouse   Map C3 $
596/40 JR Jaya Mawatha
Tel *(025) 222 2364*
w milanotouristrest.com
Good budget option with
well-furnished rooms. Alfresco
dining and bike hire.

ANURADHAPURA: Randiya $$
Mid-range Hotel   Map C3
394/19A Mudhitha Mawatha
Tel *(025) 222 2868*
w hotelrandiya.com
Large and clean rooms in a
modern house. Offers bike hire.

ANURADHAPURA: Ulagalla
Resort $$$
Luxury   Map C3
Thirapanne
Tel *(011) 567 1000*
w ulagallaresorts.com
All modern conveniences but in
a lovely rural setting. Chalets have
living areas and plunge pools.

DAMBULLA: J.C.'s Village $
Guesthouse   Map C3
175 Kapuwaththa
Tel *(066) 228 4411*
w jcsvillage.com
Quiet and relaxing spot with
bungalows dotted around the
forested grounds. Delicious food.

DAMBULLA: Amaya Lake $$$
Luxury   Map C3
Kap Ela, Kandalama
Tel *(065) 446 1500*
w amayaresorts.com
Tastefully decorated bungalows
situated in beautiful grounds

on the banks of Kandalama
Lake. Open-sided restaurant
and bar.

DK Choice

DAMBULLA: Kandalama $$$
Luxury   Map C3
Along Kandalama Rd
Tel *(066) 555 5000*
w heritancehotels.com
Designed by Geoffrey Bawa,
this hotel is set on the banks
of the Kandalama tank and
blends with its natural jungle
surroundings. There are
splendid views of Sigiriya
Rock and the location is ideal
for watching wildlife. Rooms
and suites are split between
two wings and are comfortably
furnished. There are three pools,
a spa and a range of activities
on offer.

HABARANA: Chaaya Village $$$
Luxury   Map C3
Main Rd, next to Cinnamon Lodge
Tel *(066) 227 0047*
w chaayahotels.com
Serene lakeside hotel that lies
sprawled across several acres of
verdant land. Rooms have garden
or lake views. A couple of suites
are also available.

HABARANA: Cinnamon
Lodge $$$
Luxury   Map C3
Next to Chaaya Village on Main Rd
Tel *(066) 227 0011*
w cinnamonhotels.com
Two-storey chalets with
verandahs or balconies dotted
around large grounds. The hotel
is popular with groups.

POLONNARUWA: Devi Tourist
Home $
Guesthouse   Map D3
Lake View Garden Rd
Tel *(027) 222 3181, 077 908 1250*
Homely guesthouse with
functional rooms and clean
bathrooms. Excellent dinners.

POLONNARUWA: Siyanco $$
Mid-range Hotel **Map** D3
1st Canal Rd, behind Habarana Rd
Tel *(027) 222 6868*
W **siyancoholidayresort.com**
Siyanco is a well-located hotel
offering comfortable rooms.
Some rooms are newer and
larger than others.

SIGIRIYA: Flower Inn $
Guesthouse **Map** C3
Near Sigiriya Rock
Tel *(066) 567 2197*
Basic rooms in two neighbouring
buildings. Decor is kitsch but
hosts are friendly.

SIGIRIYA: Hotel Sigiriya $$
Mid-range Hotel **Map** C3
2 km (1 mile) from Sigiriya Rock
Tel *(066) 493 0500*
W **serendibleisure.com**
Comfortable air-conditioned
rooms. There is an open-air
restaurant and Ayurvedic spa.

SIGIRIYA: Vil Uyana $$$
Luxury **Map** C3
Inamaluwa
Tel *(066) 492 3584*
W **jetwinghotels.com**
Secluded spot with bungalows on
stilts in a variety of settings, rang-
ing from paddy fields to gardens.

The East

ARUGAM BAY: Geckos $
Guesthouse **Map** E5
Beachside, Main St
Tel *(077) 159 1265*
W **geckoarugambay.com**
Provides cabanas, rooms and an
apartment. Some are equipped
with air conditioning.

DK Choice

**ARUGAM BAY: Samantha's
Folly** $
Guesthouse **Map** E5
Beachside, Main Rd
Tel *(077) 338 7808*
Samantha's Folly offers a choice
of beachfront cabanas or "follies".
These follies resemble thatched
beach huts with tented sides,
and are fairly open with shared
bathrooms. Decent food.

ARUGAM BAY: Hideaway $$
Guesthouse **Map** E5
Roadside, Main Rd
Tel *(063) 224 8259*
W **hideawayarugambay.com**
Accommodation is in the main
villa that has four bedrooms and
a cozy lounge. There are also
bungalows set amid the garden.

BATTICALOA: Deep Sea Resort $
Guesthouse **Map** E4
New Fisheries St, Nawalady
Tel *(031) 371 7451*
W **deepsearesort.webs.com**
Basic, spotless rooms catering
mainly to those diving the
HMS *Hermes*.

DK Choice

**KUCHCHAVELI: Jungle
Beach** $$$
Beach Resort **Map** D2
North of Nilaveli
Tel *(011) 233 1322*
W **junglebeach.lk**
A beautiful jungle hideaway
on a secluded bay, Jungle
Beach offers large, stylishly
decorated rooms with a rain
shower. iPod dock in a range
of cabins nestled amid the
mangroves. Beach cabins have
easy access to the sea. Dine
in the restaurant or on the
verandah. The place is great
for wildlife-watching.

NILAVELI: Seaway Hotel $
Guesthouse **Map** D2
Beachfront
Tel *(077) 724 5329*
Clean, good-size rooms and great
food. Views over the sea can be
enjoyed from the verandah.

**NILAVELI: Pigeon Island Beach
Resort** $$$
Beach Resort **Map** D2
Nilaveli Beach
Tel *(026) 492 0633*
W **pigeonislandresort.com**
Whitewashed, beachfront hotel
with a variety of activities such
as diving and snorkelling trips.
Some rooms and suites boast
sea views.

Basic room with twin beds at the Fits
Pavilion, Jaffna

PASSEKUDAH: Maalu Maalu $$$
Beach Resort **Map** D3
Passekudah Bay
Tel *(065) 738 8388*
W **maalumaalu.com**
This peaceful and relaxing resort
offers two-storey chalets and
suites, most with sea views.
Ground floor units have a terrace
while rooms on the upper floor
have a balcony. Spa on site.

TRINCOMALEE: Welcombe $
Budget **Map** D3
66 Lower Rd, Orr's Hill
Tel *(026) 222 3885*
W **welcombehotel.com**
Perched on the headland, this
boat-shaped hotel overlooks
the harbour. Colourful and
stylish rooms.

UPPUVELI: Palm Beach Resort $
Guesthouse **Map** D2
12 Alles Garden, Nilaveli Rd
Tel *(026) 222 1250*
Located away from the beach, this
guesthouse offers simple rooms.
Most people come for the food.

UPPUVELI: Chaaya Blu $$$
Beach Resort **Map** D2
Half a kilometre off the road
Tel *(026) 222 2307*
W **chaayahotels.com**
Attractive hotel with rooms,
suites and beachfront chalets.
Good restaurant. Organizes
excursions to Trincomalee
and Pigeon Island.

Jaffna and the North

**JAFFNA: Cosy Restaurant
Hotel** $
Guesthouse **Map** B1
15 Sirampiradi Lane
Tel *(021) 222 5899*
Centrally situated. Rooms are
basic and located above a restau-
rant. Bring a mosquito net.

JAFFNA: Green Grass Hotel $
Budget **Map** B1
Off Hospital Rd
Tel *(021) 222 4385*
W **jaffnagreengrass.com**
Green Grass Hotel is close to
town. Comfortable rooms and
friendly service. Swimming pool.

JAFFNA: Fits Pavilion $$
Mid-range Hotel **Map** B1
40 Kandy Rd
Tel *(021) 222 3790*
W **fitsair.com**
Seven air-conditioned bedrooms
with attached baths in a restored
Colonial villa and adjoining
building. The rustic interior is
tastefully decorated.

For more information on types of hotels *see page 215*

WHERE TO EAT AND DRINK

Sri Lanka boasts a unique culinary heritage – a fusion of traditional dishes with recipes and cooking techniques brought to the island by traders and colonialists. However, dining out has not really taken off outside Colombo and other tourist hotspots such as Kandy, Galle and the beach resorts. Eating establishments vary from air-conditioned fine-dining restaurants and beach cafés offering platters of fresh seafood to bakeries serving delectable short eats. Restaurants and upmarket hotels in Colombo are the best places to try out fusion cooking. Eateries catering to tourists across the island will usually offer Continental dishes, some Sri Lankan staples and Chinese options such as fried rice or noodles. Traditional Sri Lankan food is best sampled at a small family-run guesthouse.

Vendor preparing *vadai*, a typical Sri Lankan snack, Dutch Bay, Kalpitiya Peninsula

Restaurants

Visitors to Colombo have the option of choosing from fine-dining and mid-range restaurants to roadside eateries and food courts in shopping malls. Restaurants in the capital offer a diverse range of international cuisines such as Italian, Japanese and Swiss. However, there is no shortage of establishments specializing in traditional Sri Lankan fare. Some high-end hotels house a number of restaurants offering a choice of cuisines. Others simply serve buffets or à la carte meals with moderately spiced Sri Lankan dishes to suit the tourist palate. The capital also has a selection of good south Indian restaurants. Additionally, Western-style coffee shops and fast food chains such as Pizza Hut and KFC can be found here. Restaurants usually stay open until about 10pm or later in Colombo.

Elsewhere on the island, most tourists eat in their own hotels or guesthouses owing to a lack of independent restaurants. However, the growing number of visitors has led to more establishments cropping up. Seafood lovers will be spoilt for choice on the coast, where a number of restaurants and beach shacks offer fresh and delicious seafood dishes. In addition, there are *kades* (local eateries) serving staple Sri Lankan dishes such as *hoppers* (see pp224–5).

Street Food

Street vendors, usually preparing snacks such as *vadai* (a spicy, deep-fried lentil doughnut), can be commonly seen in Sri Lanka. There are also many roadside restaurants, mostly frequented by locals, where patrons can watch the food being prepared. The *kottu roti* is a speciality of such eateries. This doughy pancake is fried with meat and vegetables on a large hotplate while simultaneously being chopped up with a cleaver.

Lunch packets containing rice, curry and a boiled egg or a piece of meat make for a good, inexpensive and simple meal. Packed in polystyrene boxes, these are piled on street counters or on tables arranged along the roadside from morning to early afternoon.

Vegetarian Options

Although a lot of meat dishes are served in Sri Lanka, it is relatively easy to find vegetarian options in hotels, guesthouses and high-end restaurants. Alternatively, visitors can seek out the many strictly vegetarian south Indian restaurants scattered across the country.

Rice and curry meal, Elephant Camp Guesthouse, Tissamaharama

Blackboard menu showing the day's special, Green Room

Sri Lankan cuisine offers a number of delicious vegetarian curries, along with *dhal* (a curry made from lentils and other pulses), *rotis* and *hoppers*. Vegans and strict vegetarians should note, however, that Maldive fish is a staple in Sri Lankan cooking. It is dried and grated and used as an ingredient in several dishes, including *pol sambol* (see pp224–5) – a common accompaniment to rice, *hoppers* and other vegetarian meals.

What to Drink

The usual international soft drinks are ubiquitous in Sri Lanka but many local brands, such as the popular Elephant House ginger beer, can be found in stores. Fresh juice is another great option as Sri Lanka boasts a staggering variety of fruit. Try the wood apple juice when it is in season or enjoy lime juice with soda. The sweet *thambili* (coconut water) is a refreshing alternative to water. Vendors selling tender yellow coconuts can be found all over the island.

Lager is one of the main alcoholic drinks in Sri Lanka. Local lager brands include Lion and Three Coins; note that Lion Stout has high alcohol content. Toddy, the fermented sap from the coconut palm, is usually drunk in shacks in toddy-producing areas. Refined toddy is called arrack, which is a national drink. It is either

taken neat or topped with Coke or lemonade, and often used as a base for cocktails. Imported spirits and wine are available but both are expensive. Alcohol is not sold on *poya* days. However, some tourist restaurants and hotels may occasionally serve it discreetly in a teapot.

Etiquette

It is customary for Sri Lankans to eat with their fingers. Tourists are usually provided with cutlery; if there is none at the table, do not hesitate to request it. In many places there will be a washbasin for washing hands before and after a meal, while some restaurants provide finger bowls for this purpose.

Lion beer bottle

Prices and Payment

Eating out in Sri Lanka is very reasonable. However, many restaurants add a service charge to the bill, and more upmarket places will apply additional charges including government tax. If the service has been particularly good, and a charge has not already been added to the bill, diners may leave a little extra for the servers.

Credit cards are usually accepted in upmarket restaurants in Colombo and in the main tourist cities such as Kandy and Galle, especially if they are housed in high-end hotels. Smaller restaurants and roadside eateries will only accept payment in cash.

Alfresco seating at the Barefoot Café, a popular lunch time spot in Colombo

Recommended Restaurants

The restaurants in this guide have been selected across a wide price range to give a cross-section of options available. Establishments have been chosen for the quality of food, atmosphere and location. There are all sorts of speciality restaurants offering cuisines ranging from authentic Sri Lankan to Chinese, German and even international fusion. Seafood is an important part of the Sri Lankan diet, and many restaurants dish out excellent fare. A large proportion of the listings have been dedicated to Colombo, owing to the varied culinary options available in the capital. Note that the establishments marked DK Choice have been highlighted in recognition of a distinctive feature – exceptional cuisine or lovely surroundings.

Selection of fresh seafood at the Refresh Hotel, Tissamaharama

The Flavours of Sri Lanka

Sri Lankan cooking takes delicious advantage of the wide variety of native fruit and vegetables, as well as the many spices that grow on the island. Coconut and coconut milk are also major ingredients, and are used in sweets, curries and relishes. Rice is a staple, with its flour forming the basis of many popular dishes such as *dosas*, which are pancakes often filled with spiced potatoes. Chicken, beef and pork are the main meats, although goat and mutton are also used. Fresh and dried seafood is, of course, plentiful.

Curry leaves

Several types of dried seafood on sale at a Colombo fish market

and served with coconut milk. *Kola kanda* is a herbal porridge made with rice and coconut. In hotels, breakfast is often a buffet at which visitors can sample a range of Sri Lankan specialities, although normally tailored to the tourist palate. At guesthouses, it is more usual to be served fried eggs and toast plus a fruit plate, unless a Sri Lankan breakfast has been requested in advance.

Breakfast

String *hoppers* are messy balls of steamed rice noodles often eaten for breakfast in Sri Lanka along with a thin *dhal* or curry. Rice-flour pancake *hoppers* may also be served. Another popular breakfast dish is *pittu* – rice flour steamed in a cylinder with layers of grated coconut

Rice and Curry

The dish of "rice and curry" in Sri Lanka is rarely, if ever, as simple as its name might suggest. On the contrary it can be, and frequently is, a veritable banquet comprising a large platter of rice surrounded by a number of smaller dishes made from vegetables, meat or fish and accompanied by chutneys, a *sambol* (relish) and poppadums.

Coriander seeds · Fenugreek · Cardamom pods · Dried red chillies · Black peppercorns · Goraka · Pandan leaves · Cinnamon sticks · Cloves · Cumin seeds

Selection of typical Sri Lankan spices and flavourings

Regional Dishes and Specialities

Regional variations in Sri Lankan cuisine mainly reflect the availability of particular produce, the location and religious customs. However, the influence of Arab traders, the Dutch, the Portuguese and the Malays can also be seen in the use of certain ingredients and names.

Sri Lankan dishes are quite distinct from those of neighbouring India, but Indian food is widely served on the island and there are numerous good south Indian restaurants.

Coconuts

Biryani, a popular dish of rice cooked in stock, with meat and a boiled egg, is spicier than its Indian counterpart. Rice and curry is served mainly at lunchtimes; in the evenings local eateries are more likely to feature *hoppers* and *roti* on the menu. The latter, a rice-flour flatbread, is folded into a small parcel around a spicy filling. *Kottu roti* is the same bread, but finely chopped and sizzled, along with meat, vegetables and spices, on a hotplate.

Hoppers are bowl-shaped pancakes eaten at breakfast or dinner. Fillings may include eggs, yogurt or honey.

A variety of vegetables for sale at a stall in Galle

Desserts

Sri Lankan desserts are very sweet. Jaggery – boiled and set palm syrup *(kitul)* – is the main sweetener. Buffalo-milk yogurt is usually served in clay pots with a jug of palm honey or *kitul* to be poured over. Stalls selling it can be seen at the side of the road. Jaffna is famous for its cream houses, the ice cream at which is almost fluorescent in colour. *Kiribath*, a national dish served on special occasions, is rice boiled in milk to form a sticky cake, eaten with jaggery.

SHORT EATS

"Short eats" are snacks served in local eateries and from street stalls all over the island. They range from deep-fried lentil *vadai* (fritters) to meat patties, Chinese spring rolls and *rotis*. They are usually served on one large plate and diners are then charged for whatever they eat. Visitors should be aware, however, that any snacks not eaten will be served again later, and so it is possible that many hands may have been in contact with the food by the time it reaches the table. The best and safest way to try short eats – and they can be very delicious – is to drop by very early in the morning or just after lunch, when a visit can be timed to coincide with a steaming hot batch fresh from the oven or fryer.

At lunchtime in local eateries and at some tourist restaurants there will often be a rice and curry buffet, sometimes served in clay pots. The smaller rice and curry dishes showcase the island's spices, and will usually comprise such items as fish curry, *dhal*, curried okra or chilli potatoes. Pumpkin curry is frequently served too, as is aubergine, but visitors may also come across such treats as curried mango or jackfruit. A popular relish is *pol sambol*, made from grated coconut, chilli and salty shredded Maldive fish (cured and dried tuna), which has quite a kick to it. *Seeni sambol* is gentler and uses onion and tamarind for a sweet-sour taste. The rice used is predominantly of the boiled white variety, but red rice is also served in some places.

No Sri Lankan curry is considered complete without fenugreek seeds, which add a slight note of bitterness to the dish. Sri Lanka also has its own version of curry powder, which can include coriander, cumin, fennel seeds, fenugreek and cardamom.

Street vendor making *konda keum*, a deep-fried, sweetened dough cake

Lamprais is a Burgher delicacy of rice, dry curries and *frikkadels* (Dutch meatballs) wrapped in a banana leaf and baked slowly.

Ambul Thiyal, a dry and sour fish curry, is flavoured with many spices, but the key one is *goraka* (dried segments of a bitter fruit).

Wattalappam is a dessert similar to crème caramel, but made from coconut milk and sweetened with palm syrup.

Where to Eat and Drink

Colombo

Coco Veranda
Café $
Map 3 E2
32 Ward Place, Col 7
Tel *(011) 763 5635*
Trendy coffee bar serving hot and cold teas and coffee, as well as a range of cakes, burgers and Italian dishes. Free Wi-Fi.

Coffee Stop
Café $
Map 3 B2
Cinnamon Grand, 77 Galle Rd, Col 3
Tel *(011) 249 7382*
A piazza-style café in the hotel lobby. Offers sweet and savoury treats, including waffles, crepes, sandwiches and cakes, along with coffee and milkshakes.

Crescat Food Court
Sri Lankan/International Map 3 A2
89 Galle Rd, Col 3
Tel *(077) 342 713*
A food court with counters serving Thai, Malaysian and Sri Lankan fare. Western chains such as Pizza Hut are also present.

Green Cabin
Sri Lankan $
Map 3 B5
453 Galle Rd, Col 3
Tel *(011) 258 8811*
Delectable food, such as *hoppers* and devilled dishes. The lunchtime buffet is good value. The pastry counter next to the restaurant offers takeaway cakes and short eats.

Odel Food Court
International $
Map 3 D2
5 Alexandra Place, Lipton Place, Col 7
Tel *(011) 268 2712*
The open-air food court at the entrance to Odel *(see p237)* has counters serving ice cream and juices, Indian short eats and fast food.

Perera & Sons
Café $
Map 3 B3
17 Galle Rd, Col 3
Tel *(011) 232 3295*
Café famous for its made-to-order cakes, snacks and breads. Has branches all over Sri Lanka, including several in Colombo.

Shakthi
Sri Lankan $
Map 1 B4
YMCA, 39 Bristol St, Col 1
Tel *(011) 232 5252*
Simple Sri Lankan fare is served in the somewhat noisy YMCA café. No cutlery is provided, and food is served until it runs out. Self service.

The Tea Cup
Café $
Map 3 B4
339 RA de Mel Mawatha, Col 3
Tel *(011) 258 4980*
Variety of hot and iced teas, cakes, delicious brownies and snacks served on the lawn. Surprisingly quiet despite proximity to the road. Free Wi-Fi.

Yaal
Sri Lankan $
56 Vaverset Place, Col 6
Tel *(077) 222 2022*
Spicy fare from Jaffna served on a banana leaf. Dishes include a range of curries, string *hoppers*, *pittu* and *biryani*. The *rasam* (south Indian lentil soup) is delicious, but very spicy.

Barefoot Café
Café $$
Map 3 B5
706 Galle Rd, Col 3
Tel *(011) 258 9305*
Tucked away in a courtyard behind the Barefoot store *(see p237)*, this café offers light meals and snacks as well as desserts and smoothies. Jazz on Sunday. Free Wi-Fi.

Chutneys
Indian $$
Map 3 B2
Cinnamon Grand, 77 Galle Rd, Col 3
Tel *(011) 243 7372*
Tasty south Indian dishes on offer. Lots of vegetarian options and a variety of *dosa*. Dishes in the comprehensive menu are arranged according to the four south Indian states. Helpful staff.

Great Wall
Chinese $$
Map 3 B5
491 Galle Rd, Col 3
Tel *(011) 250 8555*
Good-value set menus as well as à la carte dishes at this restaurant, which has a number of branches around Colombo. Food is predominantly non-vegetarian.

HVN
International $$
Map 3 B5
231 Galle Rd, Col 4
Tel *(011) 452 0130*
HVN is located within the Casa Colombo hotel. Decor is a little kitsch, but both the Sri Lankan and international food is tasty. There is a tapas menu as well.

Loon Tao
Chinese $$
43/12 College Ave, Mount Lavinia
Tel *(011) 272 2723*
Beachfront restaurant specializing in Chinese seafood. The menu has something for everyone, with dishes such as lamb ribs in garlic and mixed vegetable curry.

Palmyrah
Sri Lankan/Indian $$
Map 3 B3
328 Galle Rd, Col 3
Tel *(011) 257 3598*
Quiet restaurant in the basement of the Renuka Hotel. Come here to try traditional dishes, particularly the *hoppers* and specialities from Jaffna such as whole crab curry. Friendly staff.

Paradise Road Café
Café $$
Map 4 D2
213 Dharamapala Mawatha, Col 7
Tel *(011) 268 6043*
Located in a beautiful Colonial mansion, upstairs from its namesake store, this café serves light meals, sandwiches and snacks. The café provides a welcome respite from the clamour of the city.

A serving of chicken curry and rice at the Barefoot Café, Colombo

Raja Bojun $$
Sri Lankan   **Map** 3 A2
Seylan Towers, Galle Rd, Col 3
Tel *(011) 471 6171*
Raja Bojun serves traditional food. Try the lunch or dinner buffet – a good way to taste lots of dishes. Enter via the Seylan Bank complex.

Shanmugas $$
Indian
53/3 Ramakrishna Rd, Col 6
Tel *(011) 236 1384*
Vegatarian restaurant serving a choice of south Indian dishes and some north Indian ones. *Thalis* (meal made up of a selection of dishes) available at lunchtime. There is a lunch buffet on Sunday.

WIP (Work in Progress) $$
International   **Map** 1 B4
Old Dutch Hospital, Echelon Square, Col 1
Tel *(011) 244 1275*
Managed by the Hilton, WIP serves food with a German influence. Specialities include schnitzel, sausages and many pork dishes.

7° North $$$
Mediterranean   **Map** 1 C5
Cinnamon Lakeside, 115 Sir Chittampalam A Gardiner Mawatha, Col 2
Tel *(011) 249 1948*
Enjoy tapas, cocktails and mock-tails at a table overlooking the Beira Lake, or tuck into à la carte Mediterranean dishes while seated by the pool. Busy at weekends.

California Grill $$$
International   **Map** 1 B4
Galadri Hotel, 64 Lotus Rd, Col 1
Tel *(011) 254 4544*
Diners come to California Grill for tasty steaks and seafood served in comfortable and romantic surrounds. Breathtaking views of the sea and the city skyline.

DK Choice

Chesa Swiss $$$
Swiss   **Map** 3 B3
3 Deal Place, Col 3
Tel *(011) 257 3433*
Chic Swiss restaurant housed in a Colonial villa. The lunch menu features salads, soups and a large variety of crepes, while Swiss favourites, such as raclette and fondue, as well as grilled meats and risottos make up the dinner menu. There is also a degustation menu. Dine in the main room or alfresco in the garden. Impressive wine list.

Cricket Club Café $$$
International   **Map** 3 C4
34 Queen's Rd, Col 3
Tel *(011) 250 1384*
Pub grub – burgers, bangers and mash and huge salads – is the speciality at the Cricket Club Café. Dishes are named after cricket legends and quirky memorabilia adorns the walls. The TV screens sports channels.

Curry Leaf $$$
Sri Lankan   **Map** 1 B4
Hilton Hotel, 2 Sir Chittampalam A Gardiner Mawatha, Col 2
Tel *(011) 249 2492*
Open-air all-you-can-eat buffet restaurant. Offers seafood cooked to order and a range of Sri Lankan curries as well as *hoppers* and *kottu roti*.

Emperor's Wok $$$
Chinese   **Map** 1 B4
Hilton Hotel, 2 Sir Chittampalam A Gardiner Mawatha, Col 2
Tel *(011) 249 2492*
The large à la carte menu features Cantonese and Szechuan dishes (meat, fish and vegetarian). Dim sum available at weekends. Choose a table overlooking the landscaped gardens.

DK Choice

Gallery Café $$$
International   **Map** 3 C5
2 Alfred House Rd, Col 3
Tel *(011) 258 2162*
A beautiful café and restaurant housed in Geoffrey Bawa's former office. Come for tea and cake, sip a cocktail or enjoy a romantic meal. Specialities include baked crab, spinach crepes and black pork curry. Their desserts are legendary. Book in advance for dinner. The café hosts temporary exhibitions.

Golden Dragon $$$
Chinese   **Map** 3 A1
Taj Samudra Hotel, 25 Galle Face Centre Rd, Col 3
Tel *(011) 244 6622*
A spacious restaurant serving Szechuan cuisine. In addition to meat and seafood dishes, a number of vegetarian options are on offer. Spicy dishes are clearly marked on the menu.

Governor's Restaurant $$$
International/Sri Lankan
Mount Lavinia Hotel, 100 Hotel Rd
Tel *(011) 271 1711*
The main restaurant in the Mount Lavinia hotel, Governor's offers an enormous buffet as well as theme nights and jazz and

Elegantly decorated interior of the Governor's Restaurant, Mount Lavinia

blues on Sundays. A cocktail on the terrace is reason enough to head here.

Il Ponte $$$
Italian   **Map** 1 B5
2 Sir Chittampalam A Gardiner Mawatha, Col 2
Tel *(011) 249 2492*
Located beside the pool in the Hilton, Il Ponte serves thin-crust pizza, a range of pasta options, and meat and fish dishes. Excellent fresh-baked breads, convivial atmosphere and attentive staff.

Lagoon $$$
Seafood   **Map** 3 B2
Cinnamon Grand, 77 Galle Rd, Col 3
Tel *(011) 234 7371*
Contemporary restaurant with an open kitchen. Patrons can opt for the seafood platter or pick a fish of their choice from the counter and have it cooked to order. There is also a Sunday buffet.

La Rambla $$$
International
69 Hotel Rd, Mount Lavinia
Tel *(011) 272 5403*
Close to the Mount Lavinia Hotel, this restaurant has a good atmosphere. It serves seafood and Mediterranean dishes, as well as a selection of cakes and desserts.

La Voile Blanche $$$
International   **Map** 1 C2
43/10 Beach Rd, Mount Lavinia
Tel *(011) 456 1111*
Beachfront restaurant offering a range of seafood as well as grilled meats and pasta dishes. Rice and curry and snacks are also served, along with seasonal specials.

For more information on types of restaurants *see p223*

Patrons enjoying dinner at the Ministry of Crab, Colombo

London Grill $$$
International   **Map** 3 B2
Cinnamon Grand, 77 Galle Rd, Col 3
Tel (011) 249 7379
Atmospheric fine-dining restaurant
known for its steaks. Also offers
dishes such as Gorgonzola rabbit
and braised pork belly. Limited
menu for vegetarians.

Ministry of Crab $$$
Seafood   **Map** 1 B4
*Old Dutch Hospital, Echelon Square,
Col 1*
Tel (011) 234 2722
Lively restaurant that specializes
in crab dishes. Highlights include
traditional chilli crab and pepper
crab. Also serves prawn and
chicken dishes as well as the
catch of the day. Open kitchen.

Nihonbashi $$$
Japanese   **Map** 3 A1
11 Galle Face Terrace, Col 3
Tel (011) 232 3847
Stylish restaurant serving good
Japanese food. Set menus at
lunchtime. Dinner includes yakitori
or teriyaki dishes, katsu chicken
curry and even sushi and sashimi.
Set dinner menu.

Royal Thai $$$
Thai   **Map** 1 C5
*Cinnamon Lakeside, 115 Sir
Chittampalam A Gardiner
Mawatha, Col 2*
Tel (011) 249 1000-1945
Savour Thai food in comfortable
surroundings. Menu includes
dishes such as Pad Thai, lagoon
prawns in chilli sauce and
vegetable green curry. Outdoor
tables overlook the Beira Lake.

Seafood Cove $$$
Seafood
Mount Lavinia Hotel, 100 Hotel Rd
Tel (011) 271 1711
Tuck into fresh lobsters, crabs,
cuttlefish, squid, oysters, prawns
or seer fish curry while sitting at a
table set right on the beach.

Sea Spray $$$
Seafood   **Map** 3 A1
Galle Face Hotel, 2 Galle Rd, Col 3
Tel (011) 254 1010
Enjoy a buffet and seafood
BBQ on a terrace overlooking
the ocean. Tables closest to
the water need to be booked
in advance.

Spoons $$$
International   **Map** 1 C5
*Hilton Hotel, 2 Sir Chittampalam A
Gardiner Mawatha, Col 2*
Tel (011) 249 2492
Dishes such as steak, and olive
and pesto crusted salmon are
favourites here, although there
is also a good degustation menu.
Lunch menu changes weekly.
Modern decor.

Sugar 41 $$$
International   **Map** 4 D3
41, Maitland Crescent, Col 7
Tel (011) 268 2122
Nestled in the heart of Colombo,
Sugar 41 offers patrons a variety
of creative cocktails and a full
menu featuring tapas, soups
and mains.

**The Bavarian
Restaurant & Bar** $$$
International   **Map** 3 A1
Galle Face Court, Col 3
Tel (011) 242 1577
This popular restaurant boasts a
large menu, with meaty dishes
such as bratwurst, white sausage
and steaks as well as seafood
and vegetarian options. Portions
are generous.

The Mango Tree $$$
Indian   **Map** 3 B2
82 Dharmapala Mawatha, Col 7
Tel (011) 587 9790
Choose from a variety of *naan*
to accompany the north Indian
dishes. Wash everything down
with *lassi*. Alternatively, patrons
can choose their own fish and
cooking style.

The West Coast

DK Choice

BENTOTA: Diya Sisila $$
Seafood   **Map** B6
Elpitiya Rd
Tel (077) 740 2138
A small and serene place, away
from the main Bentota drag.
The restaurant is known for its
seafood, but rice and curry can
also be arranged. Diners can
sit either in the garden or on
a platform over the water. It is
a good idea to book a table in
advance and pre-order so that
fresh catch from the river can
be brought in.

BENTOTA: Golden Grill $$
International   **Map** B6
National Holiday Resort
Tel (034) 227 5455
Serves good food at reasonable
prices in pleasant surroundings.
The diverse menu offers a lot
of options, and encompasses
both Western and local cuisine.
The grilled seafood dishes here
are particularly famous.

BENTOTA: Lunuganga $$
Sri Lankan/
International   **Map** B6
South of Bentota
Tel (034) 428 7056
Combine lunch or afternoon
tea with a tour of the enchanting
landscaped gardens designed
by Geoffrey Bawa. Savour a Sri
Lankan or Western-style meal
made with seasonal produce,
or tuck into tea and scones on
the terrace. Book garden tour
in advance.

BENTOTA: Susantha's $$
International   **Map** B6
*Hotel Susantha Garden, National
Holiday Resort Rd*
Tel (034) 227 5324
Friendly restaurant with plenty
of choice. There is grilled seafood,
pizza, snacks as well as rice and
curry on offer. Food is fresh
and reasonably priced. The
place is a little hard to find, but
worth a visit.

HIKKADUWA: Brother's Spot $
International   **Map** B6
Galle Rd, Narigama
Tel 912 2777973
Small, basic roadside spot
serving simple dishes made with
fresh ingredients. Great option
for breakfast; try the delicious
pancakes. Also offers Chinese
fare, some Italian options
and seafood.

HIKKADUWA: Cool Spot $
Seafood   Map B6
327 Galle Rd, opposite Chaaya Tranz
Long-established roadside
restaurant with a small terrace
downstairs; there is also seating
upstairs. Diners come for the
curry and the fresh seafood.
Platters are ideal for sharing.

**HIKKADUWA: Drunken
Monkey** $
International   Map B6
*International Beach Hotel, Galle Rd,
Narigama*
Tel *(091) 227 7202*
Situated on the beach, this
place serves a range of tourist
staples and fresh devilled
seafood. Quite popular.

HIKKADUWA: The Coffee Shop $
Café   Map B6
Galle Rd, Wewala
Tel *(071) 089 3976)*
This café, situated on the main
road, serves excellent coffee
and scrumptious home-made
cakes. Diners can sit outdoors
and people-watch or curl up
indoors with a good book from
the library.

HIKKADUWA: Refresh $$$
International   Map B6
384 Galle Rd
Tel *(091) 505 8108*
Open-sided restaurant with beach
views. Although the menu is
extensive, the seafood is a must-
try. Vegetarian dishes are also
available. Good atmosphere.

NEGOMBO: Dolce Vita $
International   Map B4
27 Portutota Rd
Tel *(077) 743 6318*
An Italian-Sri Lankan beachfront
venture. Offers pancakes for
breakfast, soups and sandwiches
for lunch, and pizza and pasta in
the evening. Coffee, tea as
well as milkshakes and home-
made ice cream available.

**NEGOMBO: Icebear
Century Café** $
Café   Map B4
25 Main St
Tel *(031) 223 8097*
This café occupies a tastefully
decorated Colonial house in
town. Serves good coffee, a range
of cakes and soups as well as
sandwiches. Ideal lunch stop.

NEGOMBO: Coconut Primitive $$
Sri Lankan/International   Map B4
108 Lewis Place
Tel *(031) 222 5300*
Popular eatery with an extensive
menu serving pizza, pasta,
meat dishes, a few Sri Lankan

specialities and fresh seafood.
Delicious banana fritters
for dessert.

NEGOMBO: Edwin's $$
Sri Lankan   Map B4
204 Lewis Place
Tel *(031) 223 9164*
Feast on large portions of tasty
Sri Lankan fare such as *rotis*, rice
and curry as well as devilled
dishes. Note that some dinner
dishes need to be ordered 30
minutes in advance. Good value.

NEGOMBO: Bijou $$$
International   Map B4
Portutota Rd
Tel *(031) 227 4710*
Swiss-owned restaurant. Large
menu with grilled seafood, fillet
steaks and specialities such as
goulash, wiener schnitzel and
stroganoff. Vegetarian options
and noodle dishes also available.
Fondue needs to be ordered
in advance.

NEGOMBO: Lord's $$$
International   Map B4
80B Portutota Rd
Tel *(077) 723 4721*
Chic eatery with art gallery
and complimentary fish foot
spa. Food ranges from Sri Lankan
to Asian fusion and even some
British dishes. There is regular live
music, as well as a cultural show
every Wednesday evening.

The South

GALLE: Mama's Roof Café $
Sri Lankan   Map B6
76 Leyn Baan St
Tel *(091) 222 6415*
Busy rooftop restaurant with views
over the Galle Fort to the sea. Sri
Lankan and Western meals and

snacks on offer; the rice and
curry is recommended. There
is usually a long wait for both
table and food.

DK Choice

**GALLE: Serendipity
Arts Café** $
Café   Map B6
65 Leyn Baan St
Tel *(077) 952 5602*
Friendly café with a relaxed air
offering Sri Lankan staples as
well as sandwiches, burgers,
short eats and cake. The walls
are crammed with art, and
there are magazines and books
for visitors to browse through.
The café frequently organizes
exhibitions and evening events.
The place is approached via
Hospital Street and walking
tours of the Fort start from here.

GALLE: Amangalla $$$
Sri Lankan/International
Fusion   Map B6
10 Church St
Tel *(091) 223 3388*
Fine dining in a Colonial atmosphere. Come for lunch or dinner
in the dining room with its
crisp white linen and antique
silverware. Alternatively, enjoy a
spot of afternoon tea in the cool
verandah that faces the tree-
lined street. Attentive staff.

GALLE: Cinnamon Room $$$
Sri Lankan   Map B6
Jetwing Lighthouse, Dadella
Tel *(091) 222 3744*
Sri Lankan and Indian specialities
are served with a modern twist
at this romantic and atmospheric
restaurant. Fine dining, with
fantastic views of the ocean and
great food. Good wine list.
Saturday is BBQ night.

Sri Lankan art adorning a wall panel at Dolce Vita, Negombo

For more information on types of restaurants *see p223*

GALLE: Fort Printers $$$
Sri Lankan/International
Fusion **Map** B6
39 Pedlar St
Tel *(091) 224 7977*
This eatery serves light lunches
of soups, salads and sandwiches.
Dinner menu comprises mostly
seafood, but meat eaters and
vegetarians are also catered for.
Eat in the dining room or at a
table overlooking the pool.

GALLE: Galle Fort Hotel $$$
Asian Fusion **Map** B6
28 Church St
Tel *(091) 223 2870*
Have a light lunch, sip a cocktail
or enjoy a four-course dinner
sitting on the verandah overlooking the pool. Relaxing
ambience. Make reservations
in advance for dinner.

GALLE: Sun House $$$
Sri Lankan/International
Fusion **Map** B6
18 Upper Dickson Rd
Tel *(091) 438 0275*
Guests can feast on an English or
Sri Lankan breakfast, relish a
delicious light lunch or choose
from a gourmet dinner menu of
fusion food that changes daily –
with a choice of three desserts.
Non-guests can walk-in at
lunchtime. There is also an
alfresco grill restaurant. Good
wine list. Book in advance.

DK Choice

**MIRISSA: Dewmini Roti
Shop** $
Café **Map** C6
*Inland, take the side road
opposite Ocean Moon and
follow the signs*
Tel *(071) 516 2604*
Dewmini started out as a
modest *roti* cart on the main
road but has expanded and
moved to a more permanent
location in the last couple
of years. It serves delectable
kottu roti as well as its varia-
tions such as banana and
chocolate *roti*. Breakfast options
are also available and rice and
curry can be preordered. The
owners offer cookery lessons.

MIRISSA: Mirissa Eye $$
Seafood **Map** C6
Mirissa Beach
An atmospheric beachfront
café, Mirissa Eye serves delicious
seafood. It also offers some
noodle dishes and a few
international choices but the
real reason to come is for
the fish dishes.

TANGALLA: Cactus Lounge $$
Seafood **Map** C6
Pallikaduwa
Tel *(077) 622 1139*
Situated on a sheltered beach,
Cactus Lounge is the place
to sample fresh seafood and
snacks. Serves lunch and
dinner. The banana fritters are
recommended for dessert.

TANGALLA: Rest House $$
Sri Lankan **Map** C6
Overlooking the harbour
Tel *(047) 224 0299*
Head here for a no-frills rice
and curry lunch in airy surrounds.
Enjoy a drink on the verandah
that overlooks the harbour while
waiting for the food.

**TANGALLA: Sha Sha
Seafood** $$
Seafood **Map** C6
Marakolliya
Tel *(077) 624 8608* **Closed** *Apr–Jul*
Simple, delicious seafood
cooked to perfection. Romantic,
candlelit, beachside dining. Call
in advance to find out the day's
special and to book a table.
Friendly staff.

**TANGALLA: Starfish Beach
Café** $$
Seafood **Map** C6
Madilla Beach
Tel *(047) 224 1005*
A relaxing and friendly
spot with hammocks strung
between the trees. Serves
local dishes and fresh seafood.
BBQs on Saturdays.

TANGALLA: Turtle Landing $$
Seafood **Map** C6
Pallikaduwa
Tel *(071) 684 0283*
A shack on the beach that offers
fresh seafood. Opt for the lobster
or calamari. Friendly owner.

**TANGALLA: Buckingham
Place** $$$
Sri Lankan/International **Map** C6
Rekawa beach
Tel *(047) 348 9447*
The restaurant at the elegant and
upmarket Buckingham Place
hotel has a menu that changes
regularly. Non-guests should
book in advance.

**TISSAMAHARAMA: New
Cabana** $$
Sri Lankan **Map** D6
Kataragama Rd
Fresh seafood and rice and
curry. Diners are encouraged
to bring their own alcohol.
Service can be slow, but the
food is worth the wait.

TISSAMAHARAMA: Refresh $$$
International **Map** D6
Kataragama Rd
Tel *(047) 223 7357*
The varied menu at this
restaurant includes Western
dishes as well as a few Chinese
and Sri Lankan options. Excellent
food and generous portions.

UNAWATUNA: Hot Rock $
Seafood/Sri Lankan/
International **Map** C6
Beach Rd
Tel *(091) 224 2685*
Comfortable and colourful
place that serves rice and
curry, seafood and Western
fare including burgers.

**UNAWATUNA: One Love
Restaurant** $
Sri Lankan **Map** C6
Beach Rd
This joint has a ramshackle
appearance but serves amazing
curries; their pumpkin curry is a
must-try. However, service can
be slow and space is limited.
No alcohol.

A typical *kottu roti* with toppings at the Dewmini Roti Shop, Mirissa

Modest exterior of the Ella Curd Shop, Ella

UNAWATUNA: Blowhole $$
Sri Lankan/International **Map** C6
Temple Rd, turn right by the temple and cross the footbridge
Set back from the beach, this open restaurant offers delightful, fresh Sri Lankan and Western food. Try the curries, pancakes and pizza. Blowhole also serves beer on the rocks as the sun sets. Rooms are available for rent.

UNAWATUNA: Kingfisher $$
Seafood/International **Map** C6
Dewala Rd
Tel *(077) 340 8404/5*
Dine to the sound of the waves at this beachfront restaurant. Serves fresh seafood as well as snacks such as wraps and a range of Western and Asian dishes. Good atmosphere. Book in advance.

UNAWATUNA: Pink Elephant $$
Sri Lankan/International **Map** C6
Yakdehimulla Rd
Tel *(077) 077 9793*
A peaceful place away from the sand, Pink Elephant serves excellent food. Most people come for the rice and curry, but the menu also offers great salads. The restaurant is usually busy so book in advance or arrive early.

UNAWATUNA: South Ceylon $$
Vegetarian **Map** C6
Beach Access Rd
Tel *(077) 698 6492*
Breezy, two-storey wooden building on the main road offering delicious vegetarian food, ranging from curry to enchiladas. Homemade bread. Those with a sweet tooth can indulge in scrumptious cakes and pancakes. Vegans are also catered for.

UNAWATUNA: Sunil's Garden Coffee Bar $$
Café **Map** C6
Beach Rd
Tel *(091) 222 6654*
A garden café, nestled amid the foliage. Limited menu includes pizza and snacks. Excellent coffee and homemade cake. Free Wi-Fi.

Kandy and the Hill Country

ELLA: Ella Curd Shop $
Sri Lankan **Map** D5
Main St, opposite the bus stop
Tel *(057) 222 8655*
Come to this simple eatery for rice and curry or *kottu roti*. Try the curd and honey, from which the place gets its name.

ELLA: Rawana Holiday Resort $
Sri Lankan **Map** D5
On hill above village
Tel *(057) 222 8794*
This eatery serves excellent Sri Lankan rice and curry. Specialities include the garlic clove curry and sweet and sour aubergine. Step in during the day to book a table.

ELLA: Café Chill (Nescoffee Shop) $$
Sri Lankan/International **Map** D5
Main St
Tel *(077) 180 4020*
Feast on rice and curry as well as Western fare such as pizza and burgers. Smoothies, juices and cocktails are also on the menu.

ELLA: Dream Café $$
Sri Lankan/International **Map** D5
Main St
Tel *(057) 222 8950*
A firm favourite in Ella, this restaurant is known for its great curries as well as pizza and Western meals. Seating is in a garden courtyard, which is set just below road level. Free Wi-Fi.

ELLA: Grand Ella Motel $$
Sri Lankan **Map** D5
Main St
Tel *(057) 222 8655*
The restaurant opens onto a garden terrace that affords expansive views of Ella Gap. Enjoy a meal or a cup of tea while admiring the breathtaking scenery.

DK Choice

ELLA: Zion View $$
Sri Lankan **Map** D5
Wemulla hena
Tel *(057) 222 8799*
Zion View serves a delectable three-course dinner on the terrace overlooking Ella Gap. The tomato, ginger and garlic soup is delightful, but is available only in high season or when the hotel is busy. Tables need to be booked in advance.

KANDY: Devon Restaurant $
Sri Lankan/International **Map** C4
11 Dalada Veediya
Tel *(081) 222 4537*
Family-friendly restaurant with an extensive menu and good food. There is also a self-service restaurant on site, in addition to a bakery for short eats and cakes.

KANDY: Foodlands $
Sri Lankan **Map** C4
59 Yatinuwara Veediya
Tel *(081) 222 3221*
A favourite with locals, Foodlands serves stir-fried noodles and local dishes, including great *biryani*. Service is quick.

KANDY: Slightly Chilled Bamboo Garden Lounge $
Chinese/International **Map** C4
29A Anagarika
Tel *(081) 223 8267*
Vibrant and friendly, this restaurant offers a good range of international and Chinese dishes. Their sizzling plates are famous; the chilli cuttlefish sizzler is a must-try. Happy hour is from 5pm to 6pm.

KANDY: Sri Ram $
Indian **Map** C4
87 Colombo St
Tel *(081) 567 7287*
A small restaurant, Sri Ram serves south Indian food. *Thalis* and *biryanis* are available during lunchtime. The dinner menu is more varied. There are also packed lunches to take away.

For more information on types of restaurants *see p223*

KANDY: Captain's Table $$
Chinese   **Map** C4
Dalada Veediya, near the clock tower
Tel *(081) 222 4527*
Captain's Table, a sister
establishment of the Devon
Restaurant *(see p231)*, serves generous portions of good Indian and
Chinese fare. Cool, quiet ambience; no alcohol allowed.

KANDY: Flower Song $$
Chinese   **Map** C4
137 Kotugodella Veediya
Tel *(081) 222 9191*
Good Chinese food with a
Sri Lankan twist is served at this
friendly and welcoming spot. In
addition to excellent starters, the
extensive menu boasts chicken,
beef and pork mains as well as
fresh seafood. Vegetarian options
are available as well. There are
some delectable desserts to
choose from. Large portions.

KANDY: Sharon Inn $$
Sri Lankan   **Map** C4
59 Saranankara Rd
Tel *(081) 220 1400*
This restaurant's speciality is
an elaborate and tasty rice and
curry meal. The lightly spiced
curry is cooked to cater to the
tourist palate. Arrive early to
secure a table outdoors or book
in advance.

KANDY: White House $$
Sri Lankan/International   **Map** C4
21 Dalada Veediya
Tel *(081) 223 2765*
The ground-floor bakery sells
short eats and scrumptious
cakes, while the restaurant on
the first floor serves a range of
Chinese, Indian, Sri Lankan and
Western dishes.

**NUWARA ELIYA: De Silva
Food Centre** $
Sri Lankan/International   **Map** C5
New Bazaar St, next door to Milano
Tel *(052) 222 3833*
De Silva Food Centre offers short
eats and snacks to take away.
There is also rice and curry
in addition to a range of
Chinese and Sri Lankan dishes.
Vegetarian items as well.

NUWARA ELIYA: Milano $
Sri Lankan/International   **Map** C5
24 New Bazaar St
Tel *(052) 222 2763*
A friendly place, Milano is
popular with locals and visitors
alike. The restaurant offers large
portions of good Sri Lankan,
Chinese and European food.
Snacks and short eats are sold
throughout the day. They do not
serve alcohol.

NUWARA ELIYA: Pastry Shop $
Café   **Map** C5
Grand Hotel, Grand Hotel Rd
Tel *(052) 222 2881*
Counter next door to the Grand
Indian serving tasty short eats
and cakes, and cardamom tea.
There is also a small seating area.

NUWARA ELIYA: Grand Indian $$
Indian   **Map** C5
Grand Hotel, Grand Hotel Rd
Tel *(052) 222 2881*
Indian restaurant in the Grand
Hotel that resembles an orangery.
Offers lunch and dinner. *Thalis*
and a range of curries – meat, fish
and vegetarian – are served.

NUWARA ELIYA: Hill Club $$$
International   **Map** C5
29 Grand Hotel Rd
Tel *(052) 222 2653*
The place for Colonial nostalgia.
Become a temporary member to
eat in the formal dining room
where waiters wear white gloves
and tables are candlelit. Set menu
or à la carte. Dress for dinner.

NUWARA ELIYA: King Prawn $$$
Chinese   **Map** C5
Glendower Hotel, 5 Grand Hotel Rd
Tel *(052) 222 2501*
The menu here offers a variety
of tasty dishes. Staff is attentive
and the dining room pleasant.
Popular among tourists.

DK Choice

NUWARA ELIYA: TCK 6685 $$$
International   **Map** C5
Kandapola
Tel *(052) 222 9600*
Part of the Heritance Tea Factory
hotel, TCK 6685 is a train carriage
from the 1930s. Formerly used
to transport tea, the carriage
has now been converted into
a fine dining restaurant. An
elaborate six-course set menu
of international dishes, with
a variety of options, ensures
a unique dining experience.
Seating is limited. Book in
advance, particularly if not
a guest at the hotel.

The Cultural Triangle

ANURADHAPURA: Casserole $$
Chinese   **Map** C3
279 Main St
Tel *(025) 222 4443*
Casserole lacks character but the
air conditioning is very welcome.
The menu is vast and fairly standard but food is tasty. Set menus
are good value.

The De Silva Food Centre bustling with
diners at lunch, Nuwara Eliya

DK Choice

ANURADHAPURA: Shalini $$
Sri Lankan   **Map** C3
41/388 Harischandra Mawatha
Tel *(025) 222 2425*
The rice and curry menus at
Shalini are varied and the fare is
more authentic than the usual
tourist places. The cucumber
curry is delicious as is the *dhal*.
There are also a few non-curry
alternatives available. Quiet and
homely, Shalini is popular with
small groups. Eat on the terrace
amid the treetops.

POLONNARUWA: Rest House $$
Sri Lankan/International   **Map** D3
By the tank and museum
Tel *(027) 222 2299*
Come here for the rice and curry
and the beautiful views over
the Parakrama Samudra in
Polonnaruwa.

POLONNARUWA: Siyanco $$
Sri Lankan/International   **Map** D3
1st Canal Rd, behind Habarana Rd
Tel *(027) 222 6868*
Large, pleasant restaurant with
a wide range of dishes on offer.
Opt for the à la carte menu or
a three-course special. The Sri
Lankan meals are particularly
good. Service can be slow.

SIGIRIYA: Hotel Sigiriya $$$
Sri Lankan/International   **Map** C3
2 km (1 mile) from Sigiriya Rock
Tel *(066) 493 0500*
Most people eat at their hotel or
guesthouse in Sigiriya, but if you
venture out, consider coming
here. Sri Lankan and Western
dishes buffet or à la carte. Hotel
is popular among groups.

The East

ARUGAM BAY: Geckos $$
International Map E5
Panama Rd
Tel *(063) 224 8212*
Feast on burgers or a full English breakfast at this beachfront place. Alternatively, there are lighter options and seafood specials. Service is quite slow.

ARUGAM BAY: Mambos $$
Seafood/International Map E5
Main Point Rd
Tel *(077) 352 8181*
Serves decent seafood and international meals. BBQ once a week. The place is very lively on Saturday, which is beach party day.

ARUGAM BAY: Samantha's Folly $$
Sri Lankan/International Map E5
Beachside, Main Rd
Tel *(077) 338 7808*
Good choice of tasty Sri Lankan and Western food. Think varied breakfast options, curries, burgers, snacks and sandwiches. Also serves the best coffee around.

ARUGAM BAY: The Green Room $$
Seafood/Sri Lankan Map E5
Main Rd
A popular place to eat, which can result in a long wait for food. Offers a varied menu and serves good curries and seafood.

ARUGAM BAY: Stardust Beach Hotel $$$
Seafood/International Map E5
Beachside, by Pottuvil Lagoon
Tel *(063) 224 8191*
Relaxing guesthouse that serves fresh and crispy salads, great soups, as well as Western and seafood dishes. Occasional seafood BBQ; be sure to preorder.

BATTICALOA: Sunshine Bakery $
Café Map E4
136 Trincomalee Rd
Tel *(065) 222 5159*
Bakery with a small seating area, selling short eats, *samosas* (fried pastry with a savoury vegetarian or non-vegetarian filling) and cakes. Also has an outlet opposite that sells fresh *dosa*.

TRINCOMALEE: Kumar's Cream House $
Café Map D3
102 Post Office Rd
Look out for Kumar's bright yellow sign. The place is great for ice cream; try the famous banana split. Short eats and snacks are also served.

TRINCOMALEE: Welcombe $$$
Sri Lankan/International Map D3
66 Lower Rd, Orr's Hill
Tel *(026) 222 3885*
The glass-fronted restaurant offers an à la carte seafood menu as well as an array of Sri Lankan dishes. Great views of the harbour. The staff is helpful and attentive.

DK Choice

UPPUVELI: Palm Beach Resort $$
Italian Map D2
12 Alles Garden, Nilaveli Rd
Tel *(026) 222 1250*   **Closed** *Nov–mid-Jan*
Beautiful, simple, home-cooked Italian food is prepared with fresh ingredients at Palm Beach Resort. The menu changes daily depending on what is available. The pasta here is fantastic. This is also the place to come for a good cup of coffee. Very popular, so book in advance. The charming owners are very friendly.

UPPUVELI: The Crab $$$
Seafood Map D2
Chaaya Blu Hotel, half a kilometre off road
Tel *(026) 222 2307*
Beach restaurant specializing in crab dishes, such as Thai-style crab salad, baked crab or the Blu Supreme of Crab, which is the house special. Serves delicious seafood such as prawns, lobster and fish dishes as well. Round off the meal with an indulgent dessert.

Jaffna and the North

JAFFNA: Malayan $
Sri Lankan Map B1
36–38 Grand Bazaar, New Kasthuriyar Rd
Come prepared to eat local fare off a banana leaf with your fingers. The vegetarian food here is good, and the *vadais* are exceptionally tasty.

JAFFNA: Rio Cream House $
Café Map B1
448A Point Pedro Rd, near Nallur Kandaswamy Temple
Tel *(021) 222 7224*
A well-liked ice cream parlour, with a menu of tempting sweet delights. The ice cream is fluorescent in colour, but is a welcome relief in the heat. Selected short eats are also on the menu.

JAFFNA: Green Grass Hotel $$
Sri Lankan Map B1
Off Hospital Rd
Tel *(021) 222 4385*
Green Grass is a good place to try Jaffna-style curries. The menu is varied and includes some Indian and Chinese dishes. Friendly and accommodating service.

Visitors enjoying a quiet evening at the Geckos restaurant, Arugam Bay

For more information on types of restaurants *see p223*

SHOPPING IN SRI LANKA

Sri Lanka offers shoppers a unique selection of items, such as traditional handicrafts, precious gemstones and fresh spices as well as collectable antiquities. Colombo has the best shopping on the island: its malls and boutiques stock designer clothes, artwork, books and popular souvenirs. Other large towns also have shops dedicated to tourists, and it is worth spending time in the local markets, which feature heaps of colourful fresh produce. Those with a penchant for indigenous crafts can browse the many small-town workshops that sell an array of hand-carved masks, impressive metal and lacquerwork, and elaborate batik. Additionally, a wide variety of gems can be found in jewellery stores all over Sri Lanka, and in nearly every high-end hotel. The coveted Ceylon tea and spices are ubiquitous as well, and make for excellent presents to take home.

Variety of hand-woven merchandise at a street shop in a Sri Lankan town

When bargaining, it is best to check out the price and quality of goods at a number of outlets before beginning negotiations. Buyers are advised to haggle in a friendly manner and retain a sense of proportion; being aggressive will definitely not help secure the best price. Bargaining is about settling on a sum that is agreeable to both parties, so it is important not to quote unrealistically low prices and lose out on a good deal in the process.

Opening Hours

Most shops in Sri Lanka are open from 10am to between 7 and 10pm on weekdays. On Saturdays, some stores close at lunch, which lasts from noon to 3pm. A number of businesses, especially in Colombo, open on Sundays as well, although the opening hours are shorter, from 10am to 5pm. In contrast, supermarkets and department stores keep longer hours and are usually open through the week and also on weekends. Opening times on *poya* days are usually the same as on Sundays.

Prices and How to Pay

Most big stores, particularly those in cities, have fixed prices. However, it may be worth asking for a discount when buying from a smaller shop or making a major purchase, such as jewellery. Note that prices in upmarket hotel shops are likely to be higher than elsewhere. Major credit cards such as Visa and MasterCard are accepted in all big stores. If paying by credit card, buyers must be careful that the card never leaves their sight and ensure that the voucher is filled out in front of them, to avoid fraud. It is a good idea to carry cash for purchases in street markets.

Bargaining

Bargaining is common at street stalls and markets where prices are not marked on the goods.

Touts

In Sri Lanka, many drivers and guides have arrangements with certain shops and spice gardens, which give them a commission when they bring customers to these shops. Visitors in turn end up paying inflated prices for products to cover the touts' commission. Therefore, it is advisable for visitors to let the driver know that they are not interested in shopping and to politely but firmly refuse any offers of fantastic bargains.

Fragrant spices on display at a spice garden, Colombo

Expansive interior of the fashionable Odel department store, Colombo

Shipping

A number of international courier companies, such as DHL, TNT Express and FedEx, have representation in Colombo, and will ship items purchased in Sri Lanka. Visitors must ensure that they have the necessary documentation before flying home.

Antiques and Export Restrictions

Antique lovers can look forward to procuring palm-leaf manuscripts, Colonial-era furniture and ornaments, as well as Moorish porcelain in Sri Lanka. Shops selling these items can be found in Colombo, Galle and Ambalangoda. However, it is illegal to take antiques out of the country without a licence. Defined as any object that is more than 50 years old, an antique can only be exported with the permission of either the Director of the **National Archives** or the Director General of the **Department of Archaeology**.

Hand-painted Ganesha souvenir

Departmental Stores and Malls

Plush, Western-style shopping malls are springing up in most large cities in Sri Lanka, such as Colombo, Kandy and Galle. They stock a variety of products, ranging from clothes and homeware to electronics. The larger ones even have supermarkets as well as food courts with several service counters.

Colombo has a number of these shopping centres, notable among which are **Majestic City**, boasting a cinema and many garment stores, and **Liberty Plaza**, which has the distinction of being the capital's first mall. **Crescat Boulevard** is the most upmarket option with tea shops, book stores, boutiques selling shoes and clothes as well as a supermarket in the basement. The city is also home to the **Odel** department stores that offer customers a fine selection of designer apparel, fashion accessories and souvenirs. Their flagship store is housed in a Colonial building and serves as a tourist destination in its own right. It has food outlets serving sushi and sandwiches, as well as range of dining options at the entrance.

A sub-brand of Odel, known as **Luv SL**, has outlets in Colombo and Kandy where shoppers can buy sarongs, T-shirts, mugs, cloth bags, notebooks, picture frames and also miniature elephant statues.

Markets and Bazaars

The main reason to browse the markets in Sri Lanka is to marvel at the mounds of fruit and vegetables, fresh catch of the day as well as sacks of chillies and fragrant spices. Some of the most vibrant markets can be found in Jaffna, Beruwela, Nuwara Eliya and Kandy. Smaller villages often host a weekly market where a variety of merchandise can be found. When in Colombo, be sure to explore the narrow streets of the Pettah *(see p68)*, where vendors sell everything from stationery and mobile phones to jewellery.

Responsible Tourism

Sri Lanka adheres to the Convention on International Trade in Endangered Species of Wild Fauna and Flora (CITES), whose aim is to ensure that international trade does not threaten the survival of wild animals and plants. In accordance, possession and export of products made from animal fur, skin or ivory is illegal; offenders are liable to a fine. It is also unlawful to export coral, shells and turtle eggs since the purchase of these encourages mercenaries to damage the delicate marine environment to cater to demand.

Turtle eggs – an endangered commodity

Pavement stall in Colombo selling an assortment of merchandise

Handicrafts

The diversity of traditional crafts is one of the main delights of shopping in Sri Lanka, with every region of the country specializing in a particular skill.

Ambalangoda, on the West Coast, is famous for the brightly painted hand-carved masks originally worn by low-country dancers. In addition to several shops, the town has many workshops, such as the one attached to the Ariyapala & Sons Mask Museum *(see p102)* where it is possible to observe artisans at work and buy from them directly.

In the south, Galle is famous for its shops selling beautiful lace and crochet work. Good-quality leather goods can be bought in markets and street stalls in Colombo and Negombo. Leather bags can be a particularly good bargain if shoppers are willing to haggle. Popular with tourists and locals alike, the elegant palmyra leaf bags can be found for sale in the markets in Jaffna. Kandy and its surrounds excel in lacquerware and brass, wood and silver work. The markets here teem with objects such as tea sets, candlesticks and bowls adorned with fine carvings and inlay.

Sri Lanka is also known for high-quality batik – an Indonesian art brought to the country by the Dutch. Sarongs, table runners and wall hangings decorated with patterns ranging from Kandyan dancers to more abstract designs are specialities.

The government-run chain of craft outlets called **Laksala** has fixed prices and several branches across Sri Lanka. The **Kandyan Art Assocation** is another government sales outlet that boasts a variety of goods and demonstrations of various crafts.

Contemporary Design

Over the years, a number of "lifestyle" shops have cropped up in Sri Lankan cities. They offer high-end goods, some of which are created by local artists and designers by blending traditional crafts and patterns with contemporary styles. **Barefoot**, which has a couple of branches in Colombo as well as a shop in Galle, is probably the best-known brand. It has a variety of products, ranging from vibrantly-coloured fabrics, soft toys and napkin rings to sarongs. **Paradise Road**, also in Colombo, stocks leather-bound diaries and address

Low-country dance mask

books, candles and tableware. The store has a number of branches in the city, including one dedicated to furniture.

Art

Colombo is home to a number of art galleries such as the Barefoot Gallery, **Hempel Galleries** and the **Saskia Fernando Gallery**. Works by well-known local artists are displayed and are sometimes available for purchase. The Green Path opposite the Colombo National Museum often functions as a space where amateur artists showcase their artworks. Once a year, it hosts the Kala Pola art market, where regional artists exhibit their work for sale. During the **Colombo Art Biennale**, paintings and other works by artists are showcased at various venues throughout the city for a week.

Clothing

Sri Lanka is a major garment manufacturing centre and good-quality, reasonably priced clothes can be purchased throughout the country. **Odel** is a favourite with tourists but other nationwide stores such as **Cotton Collection**, **NoLimit**, **House of Fashions** and **Fashion Bug** are also great for modern designs. However, traditional wear is best bought from the smaller shops, particularly in Colombo, which stock saris and *salwar kameez* in a wide range of materials, designs and colours.

Brightly coloured interior of Barefoot, with clothes, fabrics and knick-knacks on display

Dazzling selection of gemstones at a jewellery shop, Ratnapura

Gems

The country is famous for its precious and semi-precious stones, and shops selling gemstones and jewellery can be found all over. It is also possible to have a piece of jewellery made to specifications. Colombo has a number of jewellery shops on Sea Street in the Pettah and two floors of the World Trade Center in Fort are dedicated to gems.

In the gem capital of Ratnapura visitors are likely to come across people trading gems on the streets, who often attempt to sell fake items. Do not succumb to any offers made by streetside vendors, and purchase stones or jewellery only from a reputable dealer who has a proper licence. Gemstones can also be verified for authenticity at a branch of the **National Gem and Jewellery Authority**, but customers are expected to buy the stone before the shop agrees to verification.

Tea

Tea is for sale everywhere in Sri Lanka. Dilmah and Mlesna are the main brands on offer, and they can be easily found in tea boutiques in most shopping malls. All supermarkets have a wide selection of both loose tea and tea bags. Visitors can also purchase tea at the airport terminal.

Alternatively, aficionados can buy directly from the many tea factories in the Hill Country, such as the Mackwoods Labookellie Tea Estate (see p145). For the best-tasting beverage, look out for unblended, single estate high-grown teas.

Books

A large selection of inexpensive novels are available at the bookshops in Colombo. **Vijitha Yapa** bookshop has branches nationwide and stocks everything from children's books to travel guides. Barefoot also has an excellent collection of books including works by Sri Lankan authors. Those interested in books on Buddhism can buy them at the **Buddhist Centre** in Colombo or the **Buddhism Publication Centre** in Kandy.

Coffee table books on various subjects, displayed in a book store, Colombo

DIRECTORY

Antiques

Department of Archaeology
Sir Marcus Fernando Mawatha, Col 7.
Tel (011) 269 2840.

National Archives
7 Reid Avenue, Col 7.
Tel (011) 269 4523.

Departmental Stores and Malls

Crescat Boulevard
89 Galle Road, Col 3.
Tel (011) 554 0402.

Liberty Plaza
Corner of RA de Mel Mawatha and Ananda Kumaraswamy Mawatha, Col 3.

Luv SL
Old Dutch Hospital, Bank of Ceylon Mawatha, Fort, Col 1. **Tel** (011) 244 8873.
W odel.lk

Majestic City
Galle Road, Col 4.

Odel
5 Alexandra Place, Col 7.
Tel (011) 462 5800.
W odel.lk

Handicrafts

Kandyan Art Association
72 Sangaraja Mawatha, Kandy.
Tel (081) 222 3100.

Laksala
W laksala.lk

Contemporary Design

Barefoot
706 Galle Road, Col 3.
Tel (011) 258 9305.
W barefoot ceylon.com

Paradise Road
213 Dharmapala Mawatha, Col 7.

Tel (011) 268 6043.
W paradise road.lk

Art

Colombo Art Biennale
W colomboart biennale.com

Hempel Galleries
30/3 Barnes Place, Col 7.
Tel (077) 790 7321.
W hempel.galleries.com

Saskia Fernando Gallery
61 Dharmapala Mawatha, Col 3. **Tel** (011) 742 9010.
W saskiafernando gallery.com

Clothing

Cotton Collection
W cottoncollection.lk

Fashion Bug
W fashionbug.lk

House of Fashions
W houseoffashions.lk

NoLimit
W nolimit.lk

Gems

National Gem and Jewellery Authority
25 Galle Face Terrace, Col 3. **Tel** (011) 239 0657.
W srilankagem autho.com

Books

Buddhist Centre
380 Bauddhaloka Mawatha, Col 7.
Tel (011) 268 9786.

Buddhist Publication Centre
54 Sangaraja Mawatha, Kandy.
Tel (081) 223 7283.

Vijitha Yapa
32 Thurstan Road, Col 7.
Tel (011) 257 7624.
W vijathayapa.com

What to Buy in Sri Lanka

Shopping in Sri Lanka is very different from other Asian destinations such as Vietnam or Thailand, where markets are crammed with goods. However, the island offers shoppers some beautiful examples of traditional craftsmanship, such as decorative masks, lacquerware and batik. These can either be purchased from government-run outlets or directly from artisans. Sri Lanka also has an enormous choice of discount clothing and visitors can explore the garment shops for excellent bargains. Paintings by local Sri Lankan artists are great souvenirs and tea and spices are also popular purchases. Visitors buying jewellery or gems are advised to do so from a reputable trader.

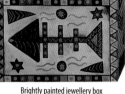

Brightly painted jewellery box

Lacquerwork

Objects such as bookends, boxes and door handles are coated with lacquer and make for excellent gifts. However, bear in mind that an inferior and quicker method of painting the wood and covering it with varnish is sometimes passed off as lacquerwork.

Handicrafts

A number of traditional crafts in Sri Lanka rely on the tourist trade to survive. Hand-carved masks and batik are found for sale in handicraft outlets all over the island, whereas lacework and metalware are available only in specific areas. Sri Lanka is also a great place to find stylish craftwork with a contemporary twist, particularly in Colombo's upmarket boutiques.

Fish-shaped table mat

Kolam Masks

These masks, traditionally worn during devil dances, are painted in vivid colours and have distinctive features. They depict different characters, including demons.

Vibrant kolam mask

Crocheted table mat

Lacework

Lacemaking was introduced to Sri Lanka by the Portuguese in the 16th century. Today, lace and crochet products such as curtains and table linens can be found on the south coast near Galle.

Palmyra Products

Jaffna is a great place to buy baskets, wallets and bags woven from palmyra leaves. The markets have a wide selection of products – remember to bargain.

Sturdy bag made of palmyra leaves

Silverware and Brassware

A wide variety of statues, embellished trays, tea sets and candlesticks are produced in Kandy and its adjoining areas. Trays that have been made using the repoussé technique, wherein objects are hammered into relief from the reverse side, are common.

Brass statue of a seated Buddha

Gems and Jewellery

Sri Lanka is famous for its moonstones, blue sapphires, rubies, cat's eyes and zircons. It is possible to buy gemstones, or gold and silver jewellery set with gems. Kandyan jewellery has more intricate filigree and is usually available in silver. In addition, traditional south Indian gold jewellery can be purchased.

Zircons

Beaded necklace with coin pendants

Blue sapphire

Textiles

Western-style clothing at reasonable prices is widely available in Colombo. Smaller shops found in markets throughout the country are the best places for purchasing traditional attire such as saris.

A turquoise silk sari draped on a mannequin

Ceramics

Sri Lanka produces attractive porcelain decorated with exquisite designs, some of which are hand-painted or engraved. Ranging from tableware and tea sets to decorative ceramic elephants, these items make good souvenirs.

Ceramic souvenir

Spices

All traditional spices such as cinnamon, turmeric, cumin and chilli powder are available at spice gardens. However, supermarkets offer these at more reasonable prices. Visitors purchasing from town markets and bazaars may have to haggle over the price.

Assortment of spices

Ayurvedic cosmetics

Ayurvedic Products

Ayurvedic products can be found for sale all over Sri Lanka. One of the most popular items is Siddhalepa Balm, which can be picked up in supermarkets and is used for headaches as well as general aches. Visitors can try Spa Ceylon *(see p242)* for scented candles, essential oils, beauty products and gift sets.

Tea

Tea is sold in specialist tea shops, at tea factories and in supermarkets across the island. Loose tea and tea bags are both available, as is tea paraphernalia like pots and strainers. Often packaged in attractive wooden boxes, woven baskets, elephant-shaped receptacles and silver-plated teapots, tea is an excellent gift item.

Tea picked from different regions of Sri Lanka

ENTERTAINMENT IN SRI LANKA

The entertainment scene in Sri Lanka is more or less confined to Colombo, with events outside the city revolving around the larger hotels for the most part. The capital offers myriad options for visitors, ranging from contemporary theatre and the latest cinematic blockbusters to traditional dance recitals. There are also many excellent galleries and cultural centres where patrons can admire, and sometimes purchase, local Sri Lankan art. In addition, the bars and nightclubs found across the city often organize live music performances. On the southwest coast, Hikkaduwa is known for its spirited nightlife, while resort towns across the island have bars catering to tourists. Sri Lanka also hosts international sports events, such as cricket matches, and its colourful religious festivals held annually offer a fascinating insight into the country's religious and cultural diversity.

Practical Information

Venue listings for Colombo can be found in English-language publications such as the *Life Times* and *Living Colombo Guide*. However, it is advisable to check the venue's website for specific information on events since they are often not adequately advertised. Websites such as **What's up Colombo** and **YAMU** provide detailed event listings, ranging from cinema shows and pub quizzes to chamber orchestra concerts.

Dramatic exterior of the Nelum Pokuna Theatre, Colombo

Traditional Dance

Sri Lanka's long and rich dance tradition is a unique reflection of the country's cultural heritage. The Tourism Ministry organizes a dance performance known as "Feel Sri Lanka" every Friday evening at the **Hotel School Auditorium** in Colombo. The programme showcases a new dance troupe every week. The **Nelum Pokuna Theatre**, also in Colombo, is another popular venue that stages occasional performances. It is also possible to catch a show at some hotels in the capital as well as in Negombo and along the coast.

The Esala Perahera *(see p139)* in Kandy offers a superb opportunity to experience Kandyan dance and music. Visitors who can't make it to the festival can enjoy nightly dance performances at a handful of venues around the city, such as the Kandyan Art Association *(see p236)*. Aimed at tourists, these shows are highly entertaining but are not particularly authentic, encompassing snippets taken from various dances. To watch a performance of original *kolam* dancing, visitors can contact the **Bandu Wijesooriya School of Dancing** in Ambalangoda, which puts on shows on Fridays.

Contemporary Theatre

Opportunities to catch good-quality performances in most Sri Lankan cities are few and far between. However, there are both amateur stage groups and troupes with professional local and Western actors in Colombo. For English-language productions as well as musical theatre and music festivals, try the **Lionel Wendt Centre**. The Nelum Pokuna Theatre hosts operas as well as concerts.

Music

Baila is a popular form of music in Sri Lanka. It originated among African slaves who were brought to the island in the 16th century. It entered the mainstream in the 1960s and is still a popular form of entertainment. Concerts are regularly held in towns such as Chillaw and Negombo.

Kandyan dance performance at the Hotel School Auditorium, Colombo

Rock music, hip hop, electronic and house all have quite a following on the island among the younger generation, while fans of soul and blues will also find the occasional gig or concert. The **Ceylonese Rugby & Football Club** organizes HSBC Sunday Jazz in the afternoon, and Barefoot Café *(see p226)* hosts live jazz most Sunday lunchtimes. **Rhythm & Blues** has regular live music performances across a range of genres, and the Big Ears Music Series, which takes place at the **Musicmatters** institute every other Friday, is known for eclectic performances by students.

Colombo also has a thriving Western classical music scene, with performances mainly by Sri Lankan artists. The **Symphony Orchestra of Sri Lanka** and the **Chamber Music Society of Colombo** are among the prominent music companies. Detailed schedules are listed on their websites.

Cinema

Cinemas in Sri Lanka exist only in the main towns and cities, with the largest number being in Colombo. Some show the latest Hollywood blockbusters while others only screen local productions as well as Bollywood films. **Liberty Lite** in Colombo boasts all the latest releases and **Majestic Cinema** is one of the only two theatres in the country that can screen movies in 3D.

Promotional poster outside a cinema in the Fort area, Colombo

Cultural Centres

There are a number of cultural centres in Sri Lanka, which organize exhibitions, talks, music recitals and film screenings. **Alliance Française** and the **British Council** both have offices in Colombo and Kandy. The former often shows French films with English subtitles, while both host cultural events and film festivals. The **Goethe Institute** and **The American Center** in Colombo are other organizations that organize similar events such as film forums, art workshop for kids and monthly film screenings. Details of these events are either posted on their website or on noticeboards.

Bars, Nightclubs and Casinos

Nightlife is virtually nonexistent outside the major hotels in most Sri Lankan towns. However, local bars and drinking dens can be found in some places.

The nightlife in the capital is definitely getting livelier. New bars and clubs are opening all over the city, and things are buzzing during weekends.

Visitors can head to the **Echelon Pub** at the Hilton or the **Inn on the Green** at the Galle Face Hotel to enjoy a traditional English pub experience. The chic **Gallery Café Bar** has excellent cocktails to be sampled, while **7° North** at the Cinnamon Lakeside Hotel boasts a pleasant location as well as a decent wine list. Rhythm & Blues hosts regular live music, and **Stella** at the Hilton is a great karaoke bar.

Popular nightclubs in the capital include **Club Mojo** at the Taj Samudra, **Amuseum** next to Galle Face Hotel, **Club Fuga** and **Kama Lounge**. Colombo is also home to a number of casinos, including the **MGM**, **Bellagio** and **Bally's** casino, where drinks and food are free for gamblers.

The nightlife on the West Coast mainly revolves around the resort towns. The **Drunken Monkey** bar in Hikkaduwa and the **Kingfisher** in Unawatuna are especially popular with tourists. However, guesthouses and hotels may be able to direct guests to other lesser-known establishments. Kandy also has some chic spots to hang out, such as **The Pub**, which serves good food and beer and has a balcony overlooking the main street. **Le Garage** nightclub at Amaya Hills near Kandy is crowded during weekends.

Alfresco seating at the crowded Gallery Café Bar, Colombo

Galle International Stadium, one of the most famous stadia in Sri Lanka, rebuilt after the tsunami

Ayurvedic and Spa Treatments

Many hotels in Sri Lanka have in-house Ayurvedic wellness centres or spas, which have relaxing treatments for guests. These include massages as well as herbal baths, hot-oil treatments, beauty treatments and aromatherapy. Among the most well-known hotels boasting this facility is the **Jetwing Lighthouse** in Galle. The hotel has an award-winning spa, which offers treatment programmes lasting up to five days. The **Sahana Spa** at Saman Villas in Bentota is also very well regarded. In addition, there are many Ayurvedic resorts dedicated to providing a holistic experience to visitors. Prime examples are the Barberyn Beach Ayurvedic Resort *(see p219)* in Weligama offering yoga and meditation lessons, and **Jetwing Ayurveda Pavilions** in Negombo.

The capital also boasts a number of choices for visitors, such as the **Angsana City Club and Spa**, and **Spa Ceylon**, which has a handful of branches in the city. For Ayurvedic treatments, consider visiting the **Siddhalepa Ayurveda Spa**.

Cookery Classes

Although culinary holidays are not yet the norm in Sri Lanka, some tour operators will be able to arrange a relevant itinerary for interested visitors. One of the best is the "My Sri Lanka with Peter Kuruvita" tour that is run by **World Expeditions**. Acclaimed Sydney chef Peter Kuruvita, who has presented a TV programme on the Food Network about Sri Lankan food, leads visitors on a journey to discover the cultural and culinary diversity of his homeland. En route, he helps them prepare some delicious staples of Sri Lankan cuisine.

For visitors who wish to organize something independently, there are plenty of guesthouses and hotels on the West Coast, and in Kandy and Ella, that offer cookery classes. **Sonja's Health Food Restaurant** in Unawatuna runs a popular day course. Most classes include a trip to the market for ingredients and then a sit-down meal to eat what has been prepared.

Spectator Sports

Cricket is the main spectator sport in Sri Lanka and a national passion. The country has not won a cricket World Cup since 1996 but came close in 2011, when it co-hosted the event. International matches in formats such as Test and Twenty20 (T20) are held here, while domestic cricket tournaments are also organized; an opportunity to watch a live game at a stadium is not to be missed. In addition, cricket-crazy locals playing a match are a common sight in parks and open spaces.

There are many stadiums on the island, including **Galle International Stadium**, the **Sinhalese Sports Club Ground** in Colombo and the **Rangiri Dambulla**, as well as the newer venues at Pallekele and near Hambantota. Tickets may be purchased directly from the venues or from the **Sri Lanka Cricket** website. Tour operators may also be able to arrange these for fans of the sport, who visit Sri Lanka especially to support their touring cricket team. Special cricket itineraries are available from operators such as **Red Dot**.

Body steam bath with fresh Ayurvedic herbs in the Siddhalepa Ayurveda Spa, Colombo

DIRECTORY

Practical Information

What's up Colombo
w whatupcolombo.lk

YAMU
w yamu.lk

Traditional Dance

Bandu Wijesooriya School of Dancing
417 Main St, Ambalangoda.
Tel (091) 225 8948.

Hotel School Auditorium
78 Galle Road, Col 3.
Map 3 B3.

Nelum Pokuna Theatre
Nelum Pokuna Mawatha, Col 7. Map 4 D3.
Tel (011) 266 9024.
w lotuspond.lk

Contemporary Theatre

Lionel Wendt Centre
18 Guildford Crescent, Col 7. Map 4 D3.
Tel (011) 269 5794.
w lionelwendt.org

Music

Ceylonese Rugby & Football Club
28, Malalasekara Mawatha, Col 8. Map 4 E4. Tel (011) 258 2162. w crandfc.lk

Chamber Music Society of Colombo
w colombochamber music.org

Musicmatters
92/1A D S Senanayaka Mawatha, Borella, Col 8.
Map 4 F3.
Tel (011) 268 6615.
w musicmatters srilanka.com

Rhythm & Blues
19/1 Daisy Villa Avenue, Col 4. Map 3 C5. Tel (011) 536 3859.

Symphony Orchestra of Sri Lanka
w sosl.org

Cinema

Liberty Lite
37/A Dharmapala Mawatha, Col 3.
Map 3 B3.
Tel (011) 232 5533.
w libertylite.lk

Majestic Cinema
Level 4, Majestic City, Col 4. Map 3 B5.
Tel (011) 258 1759.

Cultural Centres

Alliance Française
18 Coniston Place, Col 7.
Map 4 D4. Tel (011) 258 9814. w alliancefr kotte.lk

British Council
49 Alfred House Gardens, Col 3. Map 3 B5.
Tel (011) 752 1521.
w british council.org

Goethe Institute
39 Gregory's Road, Col 7.
Map 4 E3. Tel (011) 269 4562. w goethe.de

The American Center
44 Galle Road, Col 3.
Map 3 B3. Tel (011) 249 8100. w srilanka.us embassy.gov

Bars, Nightclubs and Casinos

7° North
Cinnamon Lakeside, 115 Sir Chittampalam A Gardiner Mawatha, Col 2.
Map 1 C5. Tel (011) 249 1000. w cinnamon hotels.com

Amuseum
Galle Face Hotel, 2 Galle Road, Col 3. Map 3 A1.
Tel (800) 548 7895.
w amuseum.lk

Bally's
34 D R Wijewardana Mawatha, Col 10. Map 2 D4. Tel (011) 233 1150.
w ballyscolombo.com

Bellagio
430 RA De Mel Mawatha, Col 3. Map 3 B4.
Tel (075) 588 6688.
w bellagio colombo.com

Club Fuga
1st Floor, 418 Metropolitan Building, Galle Road, Col 3. Map 3 B3. Tel (011) 555 0640.

Club Mojo
Taj Samudra, 25 Galle Face Centre Road, Col 3.
Map 3 A1. Tel (077) 753 7502. w tajhotels.com

Drunken Monkey
Narigama, Hikkaduwa.
Tel (091) 227 7202.

Echelon Pub
Echelon Square, Col 1.
Map 1 B4. Tel (011) 254 4644. w colombo1.com

Gallery Café Bar
2 Alfred House Road, Col 3.
Map 3 B5. Tel (011) 258 2162. w paradiseroad.lk

Inn on the Green
2 Galle Road, Col 3. Map 3 B3. Tel (011) 254 1010.
w gallefacehotel.com

Kama Lounge
32B Sir Mohamed Macan Markar Mawatha, Col 3.
Map 3 A1. Tel (011) 233 9118. w kama colombo.com

Kingfisher
Unawatuna. w king fisherunawatuna.com

Le Garage
Amaya Hills, Heerassagala, near Kandy. Tel (081) 447 4022.

MGM
772 Galle Road, Col 4.
Map 3 A5. Tel (011) 250 2268.

Stella
Echelon Square, Col 1.
Map 1 B4. Tel (011) 249 2492. w colombo1.com

The Pub
Dalada Vidiya, Kandy.

Ayurvedic and Spa Treatments

Angsana City Club and Spa
Crescat City, 75B Galle Road, Col 3.
Map 3 A2.
Tel (011) 242 4245.
w angsana spa.com

Jetwing Ayurveda Pavilions
Ethukale, Negombo.
Tel (031) 227 6719.
w jetwing hotels.com

Jetwing Lighthouse
Dadella, Galle. Tel (091) 222 3744. w jetwing hotels.com

Sahana Spa
Saman Villas, Aturuwella, Bentota. Tel (034) 227 5435. w samanvilla.com

Spa Ceylon
46 Park St, Col 2. Map 3 C2. Tel (011) 534 0011.
w spaceylon.com

Siddhalepa Ayurveda Spa
33 Wijerama Mawatha, Col 7. Map 4 E3.
Tel (011) 269 8161.
w siddhalepa.com

Cookery Classes

Sonja's Health Food Restaurant
Unawatuna Beach Road, Unawatuna. Tel (077) 961 5310.

World Expeditions
w worldexpeditions. com

Spectator Sports

Galle International Stadium
Sea St, Galle.

Rangiri Dambulla
Ambepussa-Kurunegala-Trincomalee Highway, Dambulla Map C3.
Tel (011) 268 1601.
w srilankacricket.lk

Red Dot Tours
Tel 0870 231 7892 (from UK), (011) 789 5810.
w reddottours.com

Sinhalese Sports Club Ground
Maitland Crescent, Col 7.
Map 4 E3. Tel (011) 269 5362.

Sri Lanka Cricket
w srilankacricket.lk

OUTDOOR ACTIVITIES AND SPECIAL INTERESTS

Sri Lanka's diverse terrain means that visitors can enjoy an impressive range of outdoor activities here. The spectacular scenery found throughout the island can be explored on foot or by bike. The more adventurous can also discover Sri Lanka's natural heritage on boat tours, hot-air balloon rides and whitewater rafting excursions. While the coastal regions are great for a wide variety of watersports, including surfing, diving and snorkelling, the mountainous interior provides the perfect terrain for adventure activities such as trekking and mountain biking. The island's many national parks are a delight for birders and wildlife-watchers. Those looking for a more relaxed holiday can opt for spa treatments at Ayurvedic resorts as well as sessions at yoga and meditation retreats.

Jeep safari in Uda Walawe National Park, the best place in the country to see elephants

Tour Operators

A number of companies, both in Sri Lanka and abroad, offer a range of tours focusing on various outdoor activities and special interests. **Aitken Spence** is a reliable Sri Lankan tour company. While the US-based **Absolute Travel** offers itineraries to suit every budget and interest, **Audley Travel** in the UK organizes tailor-made trips to the island. In Australia, **Exotic Lanka Holidays** specializes in the region. Red Dot (*see p242*) and **Walkers Tours** also arrange trips across the country.

Wildlife-watching

Home to over 20 national parks encompassing a variety of terrains, from the tropical rain-forests in Sinharaja Forest Reserve to the high-altitude grasslands in Horton Plains, Sri Lanka offers great opportunities for wildlife-viewing. Trips to these national parks generally yield sightings of a diverse range of mammals and birds. While elephants and water buffaloes can be spotted in Uda Walawe (*see pp122–3*), Yala West (*see pp126–7*) is the place to see leopards and black-necked storks. There is also superb whale- and dolphin-watching at Mirissa (*see p118*) on the South Coast and Kalpitiya (*see p92*) on the West Coast.

Most national parks remain open from 6:30am to 6:30pm daily. It is essential to hire a jeep to get around all national parks, with the exception of Horton Plains where walking is allowed. Jeeps can easily be arranged either at the hotel or through a tour operator. All vehicles are assigned a tracker who accompanies visitors to the park. The best time to visit national parks is either early in the morning or late afternoon when the animals are most active.

Jetwing Eco Holidays is a Sri Lankan ecotourism tour operator that runs excellent wildlife tours as well as specialist trips dedicated to whale-watching, wildlife photography and natural history. Visitors can also check out the specialist tour agencies **Bird and Wildlife Team** and **Naturetrek**, which provide a wider variety of excursions focusing on birds, butterflies, botanical gardens and blue whales. For camping safaris in Wilpattu, Yala West and Uda Walawe national parks, **Leopard Safaris** is a good option.

Spoonbills wading in a lagoon, Bundala National Park

Birdwatching

Sri Lanka is a well-known birdwatching destination. The island's diverse ecosystems harbour as many as 400 bird species, over 30 of which are endemic. A visit to one of the many national parks will almost always be rewarded with sightings; Bundala National Park *(see p124)* is especially noted for good birding. However, those hoping for some serious birdwatching can take a trip with a tour operator who can put together birding itineraries for a variety of habitats such as coastal wetlands and rainforests. Bird and Wildlife Team and Jetwing Eco Holidays also offer specialist tours centred on seabirds and even owls.

The best time to spot migrant birds is between October and April. It is advisable to bring binoculars and a field guide to help with identification.

Golf

Sri Lanka has three beautiful golf courses at Colombo, Kandy and Nuwara Eliya. The **Victoria Golf and Country Resort** near Kandy is an 18-hole course overlooking the Victoria Reservoir. Laid out by British golf course designer Donald Steel in 1999, it is considered to be one of the most beautiful courses in the world. It also offers horseriding, tennis, swimming and Ayurvedic massages.

Established in the 19th century by the British, the **Nuwara Eliya Golf Club** and the **Royal Colombo Golf Club** still retain a Colonial air. The Nuwara Eliya

Trekkers negotiating a path through the wilderness in Horton Plains National Park

course is particularly tight and challenging and is best played in dry season. Red Dot Tours offers a variety of golf holiday packages.

Swimming

The beaches of Passekudah *(see p195)*, Unawatuna *(see p116)* and Uppuveli *(see p190)* offer great swimming opportunities. Swimmers are advised to exercise caution during the wet season, extending from April to October, when the sea is rough. Watch out for undertows and riptides, particularly during the monsoon. These currents can be strong enough to drag you out to sea. It is best to ask local advice before venturing into the water. Be sure to heed the red flags erected on the beaches outside big hotels and resorts that warn of hazardous swimming conditions.

The sea may not be very inviting in places such as Negombo and Colombo, but visitors can always take a dip

in their hotel pool. Most large hotels will allow non-residents to use the swimming pool or tennis courts for a small fee.

Hiking

With picturesque scenery and a temperate climate, the Hill Country offers excellent opportunities for hiking. In Nuwara Eliya *(see pp144–5)*, it is possible to go for short treks to Single Tree Hill or for a day-long hike to the village of Shantipura. Knuckles Range *(see p144)* is also popular among hikers for its diverse terrain of grasslands, mountain peaks and streams. In addition, the town of Ella *(see p149)* makes a superb base for scenic walks.

Horton Plains National Park *(see pp146–7)*, with trails looping through forests and past waterfalls, is a paradise for hikers. There is plenty of good hiking in the ridges and valleys of Sinharaja Forest Reserve *(see p153)* as well – visitors can hire knowledgeable guides at the **Sinharaja Rest**. Those seeking a more challenging hike can attempt Adam's Peak *(see pp148–9)*.

Red Dot Tours organizes treks in the Hill Country and provides route descriptions to those interested in independent walking trips. Visitors can sign up with **Sri Lanka Trekking** for short or multi-day treks from Nuwara Eliya, Haputale or Ella. **Eco Team** arranges treks in Horton Plains, Knuckles Range and Belihul Oya. These expeditions can be as long as 14 days and are graded from easy through to tough.

Enjoying a game of golf at Nuwara Eliya Golf Club, Nuwara Eliya

Cycling

Cycling is fast gaining popularity in Sri Lanka, owing to the island's compact size and the diversity of its terrain. The main highways, with speeding cars and maniacal bus drivers, can be dangerous and very busy, but elsewhere on the island there are canal paths, back roads and tracks to explore. In addition, travelling at a more leisurely pace will enable you to meet the locals and experience everyday life in Sri Lanka.

Cycling through the tea estates in the Hill Country is particularly enjoyable, not just for the spectacular scenery but also because it is cooler than the hot and humid lowlands. Those keen to attempt shorter rides can hire cycles in Negombo (see p94), and ride along the city's canals. Cycling is also a great way to explore the historical ruins at Polonnaruwa (see pp170–74).

A number of tour operators such as **Adventure Asia**, **Exodus**, Eco Team and World Expeditions run organized cycling tours in the country. The tours usually combine cycling or mountain-biking with sightseeing or adventure activities such as rafting. They often have back-up vehicles with spares and first-aid equipment. Operators can usually customize tours to suit your ability and fitness, although some may require you to have off-road experience. Those planning to cycle independently should bring their own gear as good-quality cycles for longer trips are

Hot-air balloons floating above the picturesque countryside

not always available, and once outside the major towns spares will be hard to come by.

Hot-air Ballooning

Balloon flights are a great way to explore the landscape of the Cultural Triangle. Balloons usually leave early in the morning from near the Kandalama Lake and take in the Dambulla Cave Temples (see pp162–3) and Sigiriya Rock (see pp166–9). The season runs from October/November through to April, and flights usually end with a champagne breakfast at the landing site. Trips are run by several tour companies, including Adventure Asia, Eco Team and **Sun Rise in Lanka Ballooning**.

Walking Tours

The **Sri Serendipity Publishing House** in Galle organizes interesting guided walking tours of the Galle Fort and Colombo.

The Galle Fort walks explore the area's history, architecture, wildlife, gardens and food. The "Meet the Artisans, Artistes and Antique Dealers" walk offers visitors the chance to observe craftsmen making masks, casting jewellery and painting temples. Walks in Colombo mostly explore Slave Island, Borella Cemetery and Galle Face Green. Art lovers can go for the "Art Walk", which focuses on the city's well-known art galleries.

Whitewater Rafting

The stretch of Kelaniya river in Kitulgala (see p148) offers the best whitewater rafting on the island. The Grade 3 rapids here are suitable for beginners and intermediate rafters. Experienced rafters can arrange for trips on the Sitawaka river at Avissawella, where rapids are Grade 4. It is also possible to raft on the Mahaweli and Kalu rivers.

Rafting itineraries vary from half-day to multi-day trips. Adventure Asia and Eco Team organize tours of varying duration on the Kelaniya; be sure to book in advance. Visitors can also arrange trips with **Rafter's Retreat** in Kitulgala. Jetwing Eco Holidays offers a two-week excursion that includes rafting, kayaking and canoeing.

Surfing

Visitors from across the world head to Sri Lanka every year to ride the waves that wash ashore on the East and the West coasts. The surfing season extends from November to April at Hikkaduwa

A group of cyclists exploring the back roads

(see p102) on the West Coast, and from May to October at Arugam Bay (see p196) on the East Coast.

The main surfing destinations on the island offer surf lessons as well as boards hire and repair services. Tour operators such as **Mambo's** arrange surf tours on both coasts as well as trips that include camping on the beach. There are also surf villas on the island, such as The Green Rooms (see p219) in Welligama. Here, beginners can take the "learn to surf" package or join a surf camp. The guesthouse also offers tailor-made trips for experienced board riders.

Windsurfing and Kitesurfing

Bentota (see p98) and Negombo are popular places for windsurfing on the West Coast. The windsurfing season lasts from November to April on this coastal belt, after which the East Coast takes over from April to September. Uppuveli and Nilaveli beaches (see p190) offer ample opportunities for windsurfing with their great surf. **Sunshine Watersports Center** in Bentota is a VDWS- (Verband Deutcher Windsurfing Schule, Germany) certified company that provides internationally recognized windsurfing courses.

Kitesurfing is a relatively new sport in the country. The best time for kitesurfing on the West Coast is from May to October, when the wind conditions are suitable for the sport. While most kitesurfers head for the

Windsurfing, one of the most popular watersports in Sri Lanka

Kalpitiya Peninsula, it is also possible to enjoy the sport in Negombo, Hikkaduwa and Bentota. **Kitesurfing Lanka** is a reputed operator that runs lessons for kitesurfers of varying levels of expertise, hires out equipment and arranges kiteboarding trips. The instructors here are IKO (International Kiteboarding Organization) certified.

Diving and Snorkelling

Schools of tropical fish, colourful coral reefs and fascinating shipwrecks make diving a rewarding experience in Sri Lanka. The island is also a good and an inexpensive place to learn to dive. There are a number of dive centres on the West and South coasts – Hikkaduwa being one the most popular. A number of dive centres are now springing up along the East Coast as well.

Of the numerous wreck-dives in Sri Lanka, the dive to HMS *Hermes* (see p189) off the coast of Batticaloa is considered to be the best. It is a very deep dive, however, and is suitable for experienced divers. **Sri Lanka Diving Tours** organizes diving trips to the site and also provides the necessary equipment. Other recommended wreck-dives are the SS *Worcestershire* and *Pecheur Breton* near Colombo, SS *Rangoon* off Unawatuna and SS *Conch* off Hikkaduwa. Those who enjoy reef dives will not be disappointed either. Third Reef off Negombo and Black Tip Rock at Pigeon Island offer the chance to see many species of fish, marine turtles and stingrays. Another option is the Great Basses Reef southeast of Kirinda, where divers can explore caves, sandstone reefs and ravines. **Colombo Divers** offer dive trips and training in Mount Lavinia and Negombo.

The best months to dive on the West Coast extend from January to March, and from June to August on the East Coast. Avoid diving during the monsoon when the sea is rough. Visitors are advised to ensure the instructors are PADI or SSI certified.

Hikkaduwa and Pigeon Island draw crowds of snorkellers for their abundant tropical fish and coral reefs. Other snorkelling hotspots include Weligama and Tangalle. Most places along the coast hire out snorkel equipment or organize trips, but if you plan to snorkel extensively consider bringing your own gear.

A diver exploring the wreckage of SS *Conch* off the island's West Coast

A yoga teacher demonstrating a basic yoga pose in the Secret Garden Villa, Unawatuna

Boat Trips and Fishing

There are several places in Sri Lanka that people can explore by boat. Besides enjoying boat rides across Lake Gregory in Nuwara Eliya and Kandy Lake, visitors can also take boat tours of the country's numerous lagoons. These fascinating excursions offer the chance to see the diverse aquatic life of mangrove swamps. In Negombo, hotels and guesthouses can organize a trip on the lagoon (see p94) with a local fisherman. It is also possible to arrange boat trips on Pottuvil Lagoon (see p196) near Arugam Bay as well as on the Bentota Ganga Lagoon.

Sri Lanka's extensive coastline and numerous lakes offer plenty of opportunities for fishing. While inland fishing is possible year-round, deep-sea fishing is seasonal and depends on the monsoon. Fishing trips can range from a full-day to a multiple-day itinerary. Tour operators such as Eco Team offer tailor-made fishing trips.

Yoga

A number of guesthouses and hotels across the island offer yoga sessions. However, those seeking private yoga teachers can check out Amangalla Resort (see p217) within the Galle Fort, or **Maya Villa** in Tangalle. In Unawatuna, the **Secret Garden Villa** offers daily lessons to groups of 14 in a beautiful setting; visitors can also organize a private session. Set amid paddy fields, **Ulpotha**, near Anuradhapura, has yoga programmes that are presided over by international yoga teachers and complemented by a largely vegan and wheat-free menu. Another option is the tranquil **Talalla Retreat**, which organizes lessons year-round and also provides two intensive yoga retreats every month; personalized retreats can be arranged as well.

There are also a number of resorts on the island that provide Ayurvedic cures for various ailments, and many of these centres offer yoga and guided meditation as part of their treatment plan. Visitors can stay at these places for two weeks or more and can take up a treatment plan based on the various therapies available.

Buddhism and Meditation

Several Ayurvedic resorts on the island hold meditation sessions as part of a treatment plan. These sessions are usually conducted by a Buddhist monk and are often followed by discussions about Buddhist philosophy. Barberyn Beach Ayurveda Resort and Secret Garden Villa offer meditation sessions of varying duration.

Those interested in gaining a greater understanding of Buddhist philosophy and meditation can enrol with specialized meditation and Buddhist centres that offer programmes of up to two weeks. Note that these are serious meditation retreats where the accommodation is generally very basic. The majority of meditation courses are centred around Kandy, of which the **Nilambe Buddhist Meditation Centre** is a good option.

Visitors enjoying a guided river safari on the Pottuvil Lagoon

DIRECTORY

Tour Operators

Aitken Spence
315, Vauxhall Street,
Col 02.
City map 3 C1.
Tel (011) 249 9601.
w aitkenspence
travels.com

Absolute Travel
15 Watts Street,
5th Floor, New York,
NY 10013.
Tel 212 627 1950.
w absolutetravel.com

Audley Travel
New Mill, New Mill Lane,
Witney, Oxon, UK.
Tel 01993 838 000.
w audleytravel.com

**Exotic Lanka
Holidays**
Australia.
Tel 1300 374 734.
w exoticlanka
holidays.com.au

Walkers Tours
130 Glennie Street, Col 2.
City map 3 B1.
Tel (011) 230 6306.
w walkerstours.com

Wildlife-watching

**Bird and
Wildlife Team**
71 CP De Silva Mawatha,
Kaldemulla, Moratuwa.
Tel (011) 318 1519.
w birdandwildlife
team.com

**Jetwing Eco
Holidays**
Jetwing House,
46/26 Navam Mawatha,
Col 2.
City map 3 B2.
Tel (011) 238 1201.
w jetwingeco.com

Leopard Safaris
Tel (071) 331 4004 or
(077) 731 4004.
w leopard
safaris.com

Naturetrek
Naturetrek, Cheriton
Mill, Hants SO24 0NG,
UK.
Tel 01962 73 30 51.
w naturetrek.co.uk

Golf

**Nuwara Eliya
Golf Club**
Near Victoria Park,
Nuwara Eliya.
Tel (052) 222 2835.
w negc.lk

**Royal Colombo
Golf Club**
22 Model Farm Road,
Col 8.
Tel (011) 269 5431.
w rcgcsl.com

**Victoria Golf and
Country Resort**
Tel (081) 237 6376.
w golfsrilanka.com

Hiking

Eco Team
20/63, Fairfield Gardens,
Col 8.
Tel (011) 583 0833.
w srilankaeco
tourism.com

Sinharaja Rest
Koswatta, near Kuduwa
entrance.
Tel (045) 225 5201.

Sri Lanka Trekking
9 Bingathana,
Diyatalawa.
Tel (057) 223 1903.
w srilankatrekking
club.com

Cycling

Adventure Asia
1112/7 Pannipitiya Road,
Thalangama South,
Battaramulla.
Tel (011) 586 8468.
w ad-asia.com

Exodus
Grange Mills,
Weir Road, London,
SW12 0NE.
Tel 0845 564 48 59.
w exodus.co.uk

World Expeditions
81 Craven Gardens,
Wimbledon, London
SW19 8LU.
Tel 020 8545 90 30.
w worldexpeditions.
co.uk

Hot-air Ballooning

**Sun Rise in Lanka
Ballooning**
Tel (077) 352 2013.
w srilanka
ballooning.com

Walking Tours

**Sri Serendipity
Publishing House**
65 Leyn Baan Street,
Galle Fort, Galle.
Tel (077) 683 8659.
w sriserendipity.com

Whitewater Rafting

Rafter's Retreat
Kitulgala.
Tel (036) 228 7598.
w raftersretreat.com

Surfing

Mambo's
434/3 Galle Road,
Wewala, Hikkaduwa.
Tel (077) 782 2524 or
(077) 352 8181.
w mambos.lk

Kitesurfing and Windsurfing

Kitesurfing Lanka
Thandayal Thottam,
Kandakuliya.
Tel (077) 368 6235.
w kitesurfing
lanka.com

**Sunshine
Watersports Center**
River Avenue,
Aluthgama
Tel (034) 428 9379.
w sunshine
watersports.net

Diving and Snorkelling

Colombo Divers
43/17, Beach Road,
Mount Lavinia.
Tel (077) 366 8679.
w colombo
divers.com

Sri Lanka Diving Tours
93/1 C, Poruthota Road,
Palagathure, Kochchikade
11540.
Tel (071) 827 4470.
w srilanka-diving
tours.com

Yoga

Maya Villa
Old House, Temple Road,
Aranwella, Tangalle.
Tel (047) 567 9025.
w mayatangalle
srilanka.com

Secret Garden Villa
Beach Access Road,
Unawatuna.
Tel (091) 224 1857.
w secretgarden
unawatuna.com

Talalla Retreat
Sampaya House, Talalla
South, Gandara.
Tel (041) 225 9171.
w talallaretreat.com

Ulpotha
Galgiriyawa.
Tel 020 8123 3603 (UK).
w ulpotha.com

Buddhism and Meditation

**Nilambe Buddhist
Meditation Centre**
Nilambe.
w nilambe.net

SURVIVAL GUIDE

PRACTICAL INFORMATION

Tourism in Sri Lanka has witnessed a boom since the end of the Civil War in 2009, and hotels, guesthouses and resorts have opened up all over the island. However, infrastructure is still developing away from the main tourist sights in the North and the East Coast. Mid-range and high-end accommodation is plentiful, but good budget rooms are rare in some places, particularly Colombo.

The capital offers a wide range of restaurants catering to all tastes and budgets, but this is not the case for the rest of the island. Sri Lanka has a widespread public transport network of buses and trains, and roads are currently being upgraded and train lines extended across the island. Be prepared for the steep fee for sights in the Cultural Triangle and the entry to the national parks.

When to Go

Sri Lanka has two monsoon seasons, each affecting different parts of the island. While this complicates the climate patterns of this small country, it also means that there is always good weather somewhere. In general the southwest monsoon, which affects the West and southwest coasts as well as the Hill Country, brings rain between April or May and September, and the less severe northeast monsoon lasts from October to February or March. Although it is still possible to visit these areas during this season, note that guesthouses and restaurants in some places stay closed and the sea is rough.

The Hill Country has rainfall year-round, but the lower temperatures here can be a welcome relief from the heat of the lowlands. The north is particularly hot and humid from April until September.

The best time to visit is from December to April, but this is also when most tourists come, and prices rise significantly over the Christmas and New Year period.

Boats and paddles for kayaking laid out on the beach, Unawatuna

What to Pack

Visitors should be able to find almost all essentials they need in the cities and large towns. Sunscreen can be expensive and of lower SPF, so it might be a good idea to bring your own supply. A wide-brimmed hat will be a very useful protection from the sun, and consider packing a small umbrella and a light raincoat. The best fabric for Sri Lanka's climate is lightweight, pale-coloured cotton or linen. However, a jumper for the Hill Country is useful as it can be chilly. If you are staying in high-end hotels or plan on hitting the town in Colombo you may want to pack a smart outfit. Choose shoes that can be easily slipped on and off for when you are visiting temples and sacred sites – sandals and flip-flops can be bought locally. If you plan to hike, pack a pair of comfortable walking shoes.

A torch and spare batteries are always useful. Do remember to take chargers or leads for phones or cameras as well. Birdwatchers must not forget

to pack a pair of binoculars. It is a good idea to e-mail copies of important documents to yourself, such as the main page of your passport and insurance details.

Advance Booking

If you want to watch the Esala Perahera (see p139) in Kandy in July or August, make sure you book accommodation well in advance, and be prepared for high prices. The same applies if visiting Nuwara Eliya during the Sinhalese-Tamil New Year celebrations in April.

Visas and Passports

Visitors to Sri Lanka must have a passport valid for at least six months from their date of entry. All visitors require a visa to travel to Sri Lanka. The **Electronic Travel Authority** (ETA) is an online visa application process, but those who have difficulty accessing it can apply for a visa at the Sri Lankan High Commission

Locals carrying umbrellas as protection from the strong sun

◀ A colourful array of the ubiquitous three-wheelers, Colombo

in person or by post before they travel. Visas are valid for 30 days but can be extended for between three and six months by applying to the **Department of Immigration and Emigration** in Colombo. Business visas can no longer be obtained online and should be arranged through the embassy in your home country before travel. Transit visas of up to 48 hours are issued free of charge, and children under 12 years are exempt from visa charges (as are nationals of Singapore and the Maldives).

Immunization

Visit your general physician or travel clinic well before leaving for Sri Lanka to discuss any vaccinations that may be needed. For trips of any length, travellers should be up to date with polio, diphtheria, tetanus and hepatitis A vaccinations. Others worth considering are typhoid, rabies and hepatitis B, depending on the length of stay and what activities will be undertaken. A yellow fever vaccination certificate is only required if coming from an area with a risk of yellow fever transmission. Malaria *(see pp258–9)* is present in some rural parts of Sri Lanka and necessary precautions should be taken if travelling to these areas. Avoiding mosquito bites island-wide will lessen the chances of contracting mosquito-borne diseases such as dengue.

Customs Information

It is permissible to bring in 1.5 l (50 fl oz) of spirits, two bottles of wine, 250 ml (8.5 fl oz) of eau de toilette and a small quantity of perfume as well as souvenirs up to a value of US$250. When leaving Sri Lanka, you can export up to 10 kg (22 lb) of tea duty-free. You are not allowed to take more than 250 LKR in cash out of the country; remaining funds should be changed into foreign currency before leaving. Be sure to do this before entering the departure lounge, where there are no currency exchange

Passport with a Sri Lankan visa stamped by immigration

facilities. Those who want to export antiques or old books will need authorization from the Director of the National Archives and the Archaeological Commissioner. Items covered under the Convention on International Trade in Endangered Species are prohibited, including coral or shells, and any animals or birds (dead or alive). Check the **Sri Lanka Customs** website for more information.

Pornography and any material ridiculing religious beliefs are not permitted to be imported or exported. Penalties for drug trafficking and possession are severe and include the death penalty.

Opening Hours

In general, government offices are open Monday to Friday from 9 or 9:30am to 4:30 or 5pm. On *poya* days *(see p43)*, most businesses will be closed, as will government offices and banks. Over Sinhalese and Tamil New Year most places, apart from businesses run by Muslims, shut down for a few days. Visitors may find some

of the latter, however, closed for a couple of hours on Friday afternoons.

Tourist Information

There are a handful of Sri Lankan tourism offices in Europe, Asia, the Middle East and the US. On the island itself, the main tourist information centre can be found in Colombo, opposite the Cinnamon Grand *(see p216)*. There is an information kiosk at the Bandaranaike International Airport as well as in Kandy and Sigiriya. In addition, independent tour operators and staff in hotels and guesthouses can offer information. A number of travel websites on the Internet provide up-to-date information, and while in Sri Lanka you will come across publications that outline various events and sights. Maps are easy to come by too.

Admission Charges

Most museums, botanical gardens, archaeological sites and national parks will charge an entrance fee. A two-tiered pricing system is in force in Sri Lanka, whereby foreigners pay significantly more than locals. Entry charges for national parks and attractions in the Cultural Triangle are markedly higher than some other sights. There are often additional charges for cameras and video cameras, particularly in museums.

Temples frequented by tourists usually charge an entry fee; other places of worship further off the tourist trail usually have a donation box.

A wide selection of teas available for purchase in a souvenir shop

Shoe rack for foreigners outside the Temple of the Tooth, Kandy

Etiquette

Sri Lankans are used to visitors and most breaches of etiquette will usually be immediately forgiven. Remember, however, to always use your right hand when giving or receiving, as the left hand is considered unclean. Try and dress conservatively; nudity or topless sunbathing is not allowed on Sri Lankan beaches.

A Sri Lankan greeting you are bound to hear is *Ayubowen* (may you have long life). The person will utter it with their palms pressed together. If you are greeted in this manner, respond in kind. Overt displays of affection are frowned upon, and homosexuality is illegal so couples should be discreet.

When visiting temples and mosques, it is important to dress modestly. Do not wear skimpy or revealing outfits and make sure legs and shoulders are covered; to do otherwise will cause offence. Buddhist and Hindu temples require you to remove your shoes and head-gear before entering; socks are useful because the ground can get very hot, and umbrellas will protect against the sun. Some Hindu temples, particularly in the North, may also request that men remove their shirts before entering. There are also those that do not allow non-Hindus into the inner sanctum or ban women from entering altogether. Note that there can be serious repercussions if it is felt you have been disrespectful to the Buddha.

Beggars and Scamsters

Visitors will encounter beggars in Sri Lanka, but instead of handing out money or sweets

consider donating to a school or a charity in the area. You are also advised to be wary of people on the beach or in tourist towns who might approach you for money claiming to be collecting for a good cause. They will usually have documentation to show and a piece of paper where they will ask you to sign your name and mark down the amount you are willing to donate. These people are not legitimate.

Language

The official languages of Sri Lanka are Sinhala and Tamil. Sinhala is spoken by about three quarters of the population; Tamil is more prevalent in the north and east of the island, as well as on the tea plantations in the Hill Country. English is widely spoken and understood, particularly in the larger cities and tourist areas.

A typical street sign in multiple languages

Photography

Sri Lanka is a very photogenic country. Some people, such as the stilt fishermen and the tea pluckers, might expect a fee for posing for photographs, but it is polite to ask for permission before taking anybody's picture.

Photography is sometimes prohibited in temples; note that using flash can damage murals. Never pose for photographs in front of a Buddha statue or painting. You can, however, stand to the side of the Buddha as long as your back is not to the image.

You will also see signs indicating where photography is not allowed, for example at airports, ports, near military bases or dams. Heed these signs to avoid getting into trouble with army personnel. Photography permits are required for some archaeological sites and museums. The fee are displayed at the ticket booth.

Memory cards are easy to come by in cities and most large towns. There are also places where you can burn your images onto a CD. Remember to insure your camera before setting off for Sri Lanka.

Tipping

A majority of hotels and restaurants – except for the most inexpensive options – include a service charge of 10 per cent on any bill. Wages in Sri Lanka remain very low in the hospitality sector, and so if you are particularly pleased with the service you might want to leave a little extra in cash – 10 per cent of the bill before service charge and government tax are added should suffice.

Visitors are also expected to tip drivers, guides in national parks and hotel porters – unless, of course, they do an

A group of visitors taking photographs of a performer at the Kandyan Art Association, Kandy

Children snorkelling in the shallow waters, Hikkaduwa

unsatisfactory job. Remember to give a small amount to the person taking care of shoes and hats outside temples.

Travellers with Disabilities

Facilities for disabled travellers are still relatively basic in Sri Lanka, and government buildings and places of interest seldom have ramps or rails. Public transport does not cater to people with limited mobility, but it may be possible to rent a vehicle and driver to get around. Pavements are difficult to negotiate as they are often narrow, uneven and pot-holed.

Although the majority of hotels or guesthouses are not equipped to accommodate travellers with disabilities, high-end options in the coastal tourist resorts to the south of the country do offer the relevant facilities. There are also a number of one-storey hotels or guest-houses, and those where you can request ground floor rooms.

Travelling with Children

Children will be welcomed and indulged at most restaurants and hotels. Many hotels and guest-houses have triple or family rooms and it is easy to request an extra bed. Restaurants usually offer some Continental options, and tourist hotels are used to catering to Western palates, so it is possible to find food that is not spicy and will suit children. Nappies and baby food should be available in supermarkets in the big towns and cities.

Although there are not many child-specific sights, the beaches and the array of wildlife on the island are usually a big hit with little visitors.

Time and Calendar

Sri Lanka is 5.5 hours ahead of Greenwich Mean Time (GMT) and 10.5 hours ahead of US Eastern Standard Time (EST). The Western Gregorian Calendar is used for official and commercial purposes, but the lunar calendar dictates religious events such as festivals.

Electricity

The electrical current in Sri Lanka is 230–240 volts. Round, three-pin sockets are the most common and adaptors are widely available. Power cuts do happen, and while top-line hotels usually have generators, guests will have to make do with a torch or candle in most guesthouses; so it is a good idea to carry a torch.

Responsible Tourism

When in Sri Lanka, try to ensure that your money goes to the local population – for instance, choose local brands rather than imported goods and eat in local restaurants rather than at international chains. Ecolodges are also becoming increasingly popular. These are usually situated in very scenic locations and make for a great stay.

Browsing through local crafts and textiles at Barefoot, Colombo

DIRECTORY

Embassies and High Commissions

Australia
21 Gregory's Road, Col 7.
Tel (011) 246 3200.
W srilanka.embassy.gov.au

Canada
33A, 5th Lane, Colpetty, Col 3.
Tel (011) 522 6232.
W canadainternational.gc.ca

France
89 Rosmead Place, Col 7.
Tel (011) 263 9400.
W ambafrance-lk.org

Germany
40 Alfred House Avenue, Col 3.
Tel (011) 258 0431.
W colombo.diplo.de

India
36–38 Galle Road, Col 03.
Tel (011) 232 7587.
W hcicolombo.org

United Kingdom
389 Bauddhaloka Mawatha,
Col 7. **Tel** (011) 539 0639.
W ukinsrilanka.fco.gov.uk

United States
210 Galle Road, Col 3.
Tel (011) 249 8500.
W srilanka.usembassy.gov

Visas and Passports

Department of Immigration and Emigration
41 Ananda Rajakaruna Mawatha, Col 10.
Tel (011) 532 9000.
W immigration.gov.lk

Electronic Travel Authority
W eta.gov.lk

Customs Information

Sri Lanka Customs
W customs.gov.lk

Tourist Information

Colombo
Sri Lanka Tourism Promotion Bureau, 80 Galle Road, Col 3.
Tel (011) 243 7059.
W srilanka.travel

Kandy
Kandy City Centre, Level 2.
Tel (081) 222 2661.

Personal Security and Health

Sri Lanka is generally a safe destination, although visitors can often be an easy target for scammers and pickpockets. Violent crime is rare but it is essential to take basic security precautions and avoid risky situations where possible. Healthcare in Colombo and Kandy is good, but elsewhere it may be lacking, and for anything serious it is a good idea to head back to the capital. Visitors should get travel insurance before setting off. Remember to stick to bottled water and ensure that you are well protected from the sun's strong rays.

A crowded street in the Pettah, Colombo

General Precautions

Travelling in Sri Lanka is by and large relatively safe, but there are still some basic safety precautions that you should take. Avoid carrying large sums of money with you; instead, use the hotel safe (don't forget to ask for a receipt). Consider buying a money belt that fits under your clothes, and keep money for small purchases in an easily accessible purse. Avoid leaving valuable items such as jewellery, mobile phones and cameras lying around in your room, as there have been occasional reports of thefts from hotels and guesthouses.

Pickpocketing does happen in crowded areas, so be especially vigilant on buses, on the beach or while attending festivals. Secure your camera and do not wear a lot of jewellery when out and about.

Avoid isolated areas at night, especially if alone.

It is also a good idea to keep copies of important documents such as your passport in a safe, accessible place, or e-mail copies to yourself for backup.

One of the main problems tourists face in Sri Lanka is credit card fraud *(see p260)*. Keep a close eye on your card when using it to make payments. Also inform your bank back home about your travel plans in advance so that it does not freeze your account.

Driving in Sri Lanka is difficult and is not advisable for the uninitiated. Road accidents are frequent so consider hiring a car and driver to get around the country, or take advantage of the scenic train routes; hitchhiking is not advisable. Be careful when walking on busy roads as traffic can be chaotic.

After road accidents, drowning is the second most common cause of death among tourists in Sri Lanka. When swimming, be wary of dangerous currents and riptides; swim between the flags at resorts, and elsewhere, ask the locals before jumping in.

There is still unexploded ordnance in Sri Lanka, but only off the beaten track where it is unlikely that visitors will stray. If you do visit an area that is known to be mined – there are signs alerting you to the fact – keep to the marked paths.

Scams

Tourists in Sri Lanka are sometimes seen as easy prey with an unlimited supply of money by con artists. In popular tourist areas, and particularly in Colombo around the Fort or along Galle Road, you may be approached by a person claiming to work at your hotel or posing as a fellow tourist or a port worker. These seemingly friendly people will usually offer to show you around or suggest going to a bar for a drink. Others may offer to escort you to a temple, elephant festival or a gem fair. If you decide to take them up on their offer, you might find yourself settling large bar tabs, paying excessive three-wheeler prices or even buying fake gems.

If you are taken to a shop, restaurant, guesthouse or hotel by a three-wheeler driver, chances are the prices will be inflated to pay the driver's

Three-wheeler are best hired after negotiating a fee, to avoid being swindled

Women travellers are advised to dress modestly to avoid unwanted attention

commission for bringing you to the establishment. Beware of taxi and three-wheeler drivers who claim that the guesthouse or hotel you have chosen is closed – this is usually untrue. It is advisable to negotiate a price before taking a three-wheeler ride.

Police

If you are robbed, report it to the police and get a copy of the report for your insurance claim. There are now police posts at tourist resorts as well as near major tourist sights, and officers here should speak English.

Military Presence

There continues to be a strong military presence in some areas of Sri Lanka, particularly in the north of the country, around Colombo Fort and at the Bandaranaike International Airport. Be sure to carry identification with you and remember that taking photographs of military installations or around other sensitive areas such as the port in Colombo is not allowed.

Women Travellers

Women travelling in Sri Lanka may find that they attract considerable unwanted male attention, whether travelling solo or not. The most common problem is staring and sometimes verbal harassment – although the sucking teeth sound you may hear is used to get anyone's attention and

is not only directed at women. Disregard and ignore any comments. If travelling alone, you may want to consider inventing a fictitious husband back home and wearing a fake wedding ring. Sri Lanka is still a conservative country and women travellers are advised to dress modestly and take a cue from local women.

Do not walk around on your own at night, or on isolated beaches and around large and seemingly empty archaeological sites – there have been reports of attacks on women around Sigiriya Rock. It is also best not to take taxis or three-wheelers on your own late at night, and definitely do not ride in a three-wheeler or taxi if the driver is accompanied by other men.

Public transport can be very busy and travellers are often tightly packed, particularly on inner-city buses. If you feel someone is pressing against you, jam your bag in the way, or if you feel uncomfortable get off the bus and catch the next one. On buses and trains, try and sit with a family or another woman – in some rural areas you will find older women patting the seat next to them inviting you to sit down – or move to another train carriage if you feel isolated. However, travelling in Sri Lanka is not a struggle, and such unpleasant incidents are not the norm.

Local bars are hardly visited by local women and you might feel quite out of place and uncomfortable at one. Instead, head to a hotel bar or one that caters to tourists.

Hospitals and Medical Facilities

Standards of medical care in Sri Lanka are good. There are several private hospitals and clinics in Colombo and its suburbs. If you are seriously ill or need emergency dental work, consider trying to reach the capital or Kandy for medical attention. For more minor ailments there is usually a hospital in all large towns. Before being admitted, check that your medical insurance will cover the bill.

Your hotel, resort or guesthouse should be able to put you in touch with an English-speaking doctor. There are plenty of well-stocked pharmacies on the island and many have pharmacists who can speak English. Ayurvedic medicine (see pp38–9) is also widely practised in Sri Lanka.

White police car displaying emergency numbers

Wear loose-fitting clothes in the hot, humid Sri Lankan weather

Travel Insurance

Before travelling to Sri Lanka, it is a good idea to invest in a travel insurance policy that will cover you for medical emergencies as well as theft. If you plan to try any adventure activities such as whitewater rafting or diving while on the island, ensure that these are covered by your policy. Keep the documents at hand in case you need to contact the insurance company.

Heat and Humidity

The sun in Sri Lanka is fairly strong and it is possible to get sunburnt even in the relatively cool climes of the Hill Country. Protect yourself from the sun by using a high SPF sunscreen, and wearing a hat, sunglasses and loose-fitting clothes. Ideally, you should also keep out of the sun during the middle of the day. Do not forget to drink plenty of water to avoid dehydration and give yourself a few days to acclimatize to the heat. Prolonged exposure to the sun can cause heatstroke; symptoms include a high body temperature, severe headaches and disorientation.

Prickly heat is an uncomfortable rash formed when the sweat pores become blocked and tiny blisters appear. Cool showers (remember to pat yourself dry to avoid further irritation), talcum powder or calamine lotion, and loose, cotton clothes will help. Air conditioning will also offer some relief.

First-aid Kit

It is easy to find most medicines in Sri Lanka, although do check the expiry date beforehand. It is a good idea, however, to travel with a basic first-aid kit, as there is always the risk of counterfeit medication. Remember to pack any specific, personal medicines, as well as aspirin or painkillers, motion sickness tablets if required, an antiseptic cream or iodine tincture. Carry anti-fungal lotion, plasters, insect repellent and tweezers too. It may also be a good idea to include some antihistamines.

Bottled water

A typical stall with a wide selection of fresh fruit for sale, Colombo

Food and Water-borne Diseases

Many visitors to Sri Lanka suffer from a bout of diarrhoea, caused by a change in diet or bad sanitation. Remember to wash your hands before eating and avoid any fruit you haven't washed and peeled yourself. Cold cooked foods, salads and buffets that seem to have been standing for a long time should be avoided, as should any unpasteurized dairy products. Buy hot snacks from the stalls immediately after they have been deep-fried; those displayed in cafés have often been handled by numerous people throughout the day. Power cuts are quite common in Sri Lanka, so do not eat anything that you think may have been defrosted and then re-frozen; or eat at a place that has a generator.

To avoid diseases like typhoid and cholera, stick to bottled mineral water or boil or filter your drinking water. It is also best to stay away from ice unless it has been made with purified water. Bottled mineral water is easily available; make sure the seal has not been broken. If diarrhoea does strike, make sure you drink plenty of fluids to avoid dehydration or use oral rehydration sachets from the nearest pharmacy. If the diarrhoea persists, or there is an accompanying fever or blood or pus in your stool then consult a doctor. If you need to travel, medication such as Imodium will temporarily suppress the symptoms.

Insect-borne Diseases

While malaria in Sri Lanka has been greatly controlled, a risk exists year-round, mainly in the area north of Vavuniya and the northeastern coastal districts; the danger is greater around the time of the monsoon. If you are planning to travel to these parts of the island, carry anti-malarial tablets and take proper precautions

Bed with a mosquito net in a hotel room, Kalpitiya Peninsula

against being bitten. Use a mosquito repellent containing DEET on exposed skin, and wear trousers and long-sleeved tops in the evenings. Make sure where you are sleeping is mosquito proof; if sleeping under a mosquito net check it for holes. A combination of chloroquine and proguanil prophylaxis is usually recommended, but if you're only going to be in a malarial area for a few days Malarone might be a better option. If you experience flu-like symptoms or have a high fever for an extended period of time after returning from your trip, consult your doctor.

Even if you are not travelling to the malarial zones of Sri Lanka it is a good idea to protect yourself from mosquito bites at all times to avoid other diseases such as dengue and chikungunya. Remember these can be transmitted by mosquitoes during the day as well.

Sexually Transmitted Diseases

HIV and other sexually transmitted diseases are not rare in Sri Lanka, and visitors must take adequate precautions including practising safe sex. While infected syringes are not a common problem, ask for the syringe packets to be opened in your presence. Contaminated blood poses a bigger risk – do not accept a blood transfusion unless absolutely necessary.

Rabies

Rabies is often associated with dogs but it can be carried by other mammals. If you are bitten, scratched or licked by an animal on an open wound seek medical attention immediately. Scrub the wound with soap under running water and then pour a strong iodine-based solution or strong alcohol on it. If you have already been vaccinated you will need two more doses of the vaccine three days apart. If you have not been vaccinated you will need five doses of the rabies immunoglobulin (RIG) vaccination. Bear in mind that RIG is rare and expensive in Asia.

Although rabies does not pose a huge risk as such, pre-exposure vaccines should be considered by those who will be in close contact with animals or are staying in Sri Lanka for a long period of time. The vaccine is given in three doses over a minimum period of 21 days.

Cuts, Bites and Stings

If you are cut, ensure the wound is cleaned properly and apply an antiseptic – this is particularly important as wounds can easily become infected in warm climates. Coral cuts are notorious for getting infected and require extra care.

Leeches are commonly found in places such as the Sinharaja Forest Reserve, Adam's Peak and the Knuckles Range. Apply repellent to your skin and also to your shoelaces, and tuck your trousers into your socks. Leeches are persistent, however, and you will probably see them edging their way up your leg. They can be flicked off at this stage but if you find one that has latched on, do not pull it off. Instead, use some salt, drops of iodine or a squirt of Dettol solution to make it let go. Clean the bite and apply an antiseptic.

There are poisonous snakes in Sri Lanka but chances of being bitten by one are very slim. Still, take precautions and do not wander through the undergrowth barefoot or in flip-flops. If you are bitten by a snake, seek immediate medical help.

Public Toilets

Unfortunately, public toilets in Sri Lanka are rare and not very clean. Tourist accommodation and sights will have sit-down flush toilets, but elsewhere you may find they are of the squatting variety. Ensure you have toilet paper or tissues at hand.

Path leading up to Adam's Peak, notorious for being infested with leeches in the wet season

Banking and Currency

The official currency of Sri Lanka is the Sri Lankan Rupee (LKR). It is possible to import and export Sri Lankan Rupees up to Rs 5,000, but it is illegal to bring Indian or Pakistani rupees into the country. Money can be exchanged for a decent rate at the Bandaranaike International Airport on arrival. In Colombo, around tourist resorts and in larger towns, traveller's cheques can be exchanged at banks, bureaux de change and larger hotels. ATMs are also widespread on the island. Credit cards are widely accepted in high-end establishments and larger shops, but cash is more useful in smaller towns. Keep small denomination bills and coins handy to pay for purchases in small shops, tipping and for three-wheelers.

Entrance to an ATM of the Bank of Ceylon, a major Sri Lankan bank

Banks and Exchange Bureaux

There are a large number of banks in Sri Lanka including the **Bank of Ceylon**, **People's Bank**, **Hatton National Bank**, **Sampath Bank**, **Commercial Bank** and **Seylan Bank**. Most banks open from 9am until 1pm or till 2:30 or 3pm on weekdays. Some branches are open on Saturday mornings, but this is rare and more often only the case in Colombo.

Changing Money

Bandaranaike International Airport has exchange counters that offer the same rates as banks in Colombo, making them a good option for those not carrying any local currency.

Other than banks, most top-range hotels can change cash, but the rates are not usually very competitive. When changing money try and get small denomination notes, which are the most useful, and do not accept any that are torn or in poor condition. Keep your transaction receipts, as you may need at least one if you want to change rupees before leaving the country.

ATMs

ATMs can be found across Sri Lanka and many now accept foreign debit cards; if in doubt, check the sign above the machine for your card type. Many travellers now opt to use ATMs instead of traveller's cheques or changing money. ATMs are accessible 24 hours a day and the money is dispensed in rupees. Your bank back home will charge a transaction fee, so you may wish to find out how much this is before leaving for Sri Lanka. It is also recommended that you tell your bank you are travelling to the island. Keep receipts from your ATM transactions.

Credit Cards

Card fraud is a problem in Sri Lanka so keep an eye on your card when making payments and check your statements when you get home. Most major credit cards can be used at big hotels, upmarket restaurants and big stores; the most widely accepted cards are Visa and MasterCard. Some places also accept American Express. If necessary, you can also get a cash advance from a bank against your credit card but charges apply. Make a note of your credit and debit card details along with the number to call in case of loss or theft.

Traveller's Cheques

Traveller's cheques are often seen as a secure way to carry large amounts of money but they are declining in popularity

One of the many authorized money exchange shops on Lotus Road, Fort, Colombo

and it is better to use credit and debit cards or exchange cash. If you do wish to take traveller's cheques, those issued by recognized companies such as Thomas Cook, Visa and American Express in pound sterling, US dollars or euros are accepted by banks in Sri Lanka. Top-line hotels will also cash traveller's cheques but the rates won't be as good. Keep a record of the serial numbers on the cheques, as well as proof of purchase in case of theft. Note that changing traveller's cheques is easiest in Colombo and main resort areas.

Banknotes

Sri Lankan banknotes come in denominations of Rs 20, Rs 50, Rs 100, Rs 500, Rs 1,000, Rs 2,000 and Rs 5,000. When changing money, check that the notes correspond to those pictured here.

20 rupees

50 rupees

100 rupees

500 rupees

1,000 rupees

2,000 rupees

5,000 rupees

Coins

Sri Lankan coins come in denominations of Rs 1, Rs 2, Rs 5 and Rs 10. All are embossed with the Armorial Ensign of Sri Lanka on one side, and the coin's value, year of issue and the name of the country written in Sinhala on the other side.

1 rupee

2 rupees

5 rupees

10 rupees

Communications

Internet access is widespread in Sri Lanka, post offices can be found all over the island and making international phone calls should pose no problems for visitors. A range of English-language periodicals are available, although international publications are harder to find, and those in languages other than Sinhala, Tamil or English are rare. Satellite TV is popular, and offers a wide range of viewing options. If travelling with your mobile phone, check roaming charges before setting off; and if planning on buying a Sri Lankan SIM card, ensure that your phone supports it before paying out.

Dialog and M3 counters at the Bandaranaike International Airport

International and Local Telephone Calls

International calls can be easily made from Sri Lanka. However, making international or domestic calls from your hotel will be very expensive. Sri Lanka has a number of communication centres, usually identified by red signs, which offer more reasonable charges that are calculated by the minute; prices vary from centre to centre so it is worth looking around. It is also possible to make international and local

A typical coin-operated pay phone on a street in Colombo

calls from phone booths, for which you will need to purchase a phone card from a nearby shop.

Telephone numbers are usually 10 digits long; those with only seven digits are probably old numbers and those beginning with 07 are mobile numbers. When calling a number in Sri Lanka you must include the area code if dialling from one town to another.

Mobile Phones

Mobile phones are often referred to as hand phones in Sri Lanka and are very common. Most foreign mobile phone networks should be able to operate on roaming in Sri Lanka, but a US phone that is not a tri-band may not work. If you have a smartphone, consider turning the data roaming function off to avoid large bills.

The main mobile phone providers in Sri Lanka are **Etisalat**, **Mobitel**, **Dialog**, **Airtel** and **Hutch**. If you are staying in Sri Lanka for a few weeks or more, consider investing in a pay-as-you-go SIM card, which is an inexpensive option; note that you will have to supply a copy of your passport when purchasing one. Remember to check that your phone accepts SIM cards from other networks before buying one, or arrange to have it unlocked.

Credit to top-up your phone can be bought from a number of shops and supermarkets. Sometimes, however, the top-up is done directly by the shopkeeper and you are not given a voucher. In this case hang around until you have received the confirmation text, just in case the transaction has not gone through properly.

It is possible to rent mobile phones while in Sri Lanka, but since the cost of an unlocked handset is very reasonable you are probably better off just buying a new one if you can't or don't want to use your own. Make sure your travel insurance covers your mobile. Bring your network's contact number so that you can have your phone locked immediately in case of theft.

Internet

Internet access is widespread across Sri Lanka. In Colombo, you will find cafés offering free

Useful Dialling Codes

- For international calls, dial 00, followed by the country code, the area code and then the phone number.
- Country codes: Australia 61; France 33; New Zealand 64; UK 44; USA and Canada 1.
- To call Sri Lanka from abroad, dial 00 (or whatever you need to dial internationally), then 94, which is the Sri Lanka country code. Then dial the area code, but take off the zero, and then the number.
- Some useful area codes are Colombo: 011; Kandy: 081; Hikkaduwa, Unawatuna and Galle: 091; and Bentota: 034.

Wi-Fi, as well as hotels and shopping malls with Dialog Wi-Fi hotspots – for these you will usually have to purchase a prepaid card with an access code. An increasing number of hotels and guesthouses offer Internet access or Wi-Fi, often for a fee. Prices for Internet in some upmarket hotels can be astonishingly high, whereas some of the guesthouses will offer it for free. There are Internet terminals in most towns, usually in Internet cafés or communications centres where Skype is also normally available.

Postal and Courier Services

Chances are that you will never be that far away from a post office in Sri Lanka. Domestic post has a reputation for being slow and unreliable, but anything you send internationally should take about a week to reach Europe or the US. You can also opt for EMS-Speed Post, which costs more but takes about half the time. For valuable items, use a courier such as **DHL** or **FedEx**.

If you do decide to post something from Sri Lanka, either leave it at your hotel reception or take it to the post office, as post boxes are not always emptied on a regular basis. It is recommended that you stand at the post office counter and watch the stamps

A wide selection of local newspapers including the *Daily News* and *Daily Mirror*

One of the many red post boxes found across Sri Lanka

being affixed to your letter or postcard after you have paid for them, as this should ensure they are not re-used on something else. A package will be checked before it is posted, so remember to take it in unsealed.

Opening hours for post offices vary but most start business early in the morning and the larger branches do not close until well into the evening; some stay open as late as 9pm. Post offices are closed on Sundays and public holidays. Poste restante is available in larger towns and cities.

Newspapers and Magazines

The main English-language newspapers published in Sri Lanka are the *Daily News*, *The Island* and the *Daily Mirror*. The latter is considered the most independent of the three, while the *Daily News* is government owned. There are also some English-language Sunday papers. International newspapers can be harder to find, although publications such as *The Guardian* and *The New York Times* are available at their respective embassies. *Travel Lanka* is a free monthly guide for tourists and is available in major hotels and from the tourist offices, but *Explore Sri Lanka* is probably more useful and interesting. It has feature articles about the island and useful advice

for visitors, and can sometimes be found in hotels and cafés popular with tourists.

The media is largely censored by the government, and although online news sources are very popular on the island, any that are considered critical of the government are often blocked. There have been reports of Sri Lankan journalists being threatened and attacked, and some have even disappeared.

Television and Radio

State TV channels include the Independent Television Network (ITV) and Rupavahini, but most Sri Lankans watch satellite TV, which is usually available in hotels and guesthouses. On satellite, visitors will be able to watch CNN and BBC World, plus a range of entertainment programmes and US TV series.

The government-owned Sri Lanka Broadcasting Corporation (SLBC) transmits programmes in English, Tamil and Sinhala, and dominates the airwaves. There are also a number of independent radio stations and the BBC World Service in Sinhala and Tamil is popular.

TRAVEL INFORMATION

Most visitors fly to Sri Lanka; the only other way to arrive is on a cruise ship into Colombo or Galle. Visitors from Europe and Australasia will find it relatively straightforward to reach the island; those from the Americas will have a longer journey. While on the island, many people choose to hire a car and driver to travel around, but Sri Lanka is also well served by public transport. Road users, including bus drivers, often drive recklessly so not many travellers rent their own transport, although some do hire motorbikes to explore the island. A train ride through the Hill Country is one of the highlights of a visit. There are also a couple of airlines that operate domestic flights to some of the main tourist destinations and Jaffna. Three-wheelers are found everywhere and are good for short journeys.

Aircraft of SriLankan Airlines, the island's national carrier

Arriving by Air

Bandaranaike International Airport, located 30 km (19 miles) north of Colombo, is the main international airport in Sri Lanka. The nascent **Mattala Rajapaksa International Airport**, located near Hambantota in southern Sri Lanka, operates flights to Dubai and Beijing.

SriLankan Airlines is the country's national carrier and it operates direct flights to many European, Asian and Middle Eastern destinations. It is also possible to fly to Sri Lanka on one-stop flights with a number of other prominent airlines including **American Airlines**, **British Airways**, **Cathay Pacific**, **Emirates**, **Jet Airways**, **Malaysian Airlines**, **Singapore Airlines**, **Thai Airways** and **United Airlines**. Visitors from Europe and North America transit through either Asian or Middle Eastern hubs, often on partner airlines including **Etihad Airways**, **Qatar Airways**, **Kuwait Airways**, **Oman Air** and **Royal Jordanian Airlines**. Australasia flights stop over in Asia, for example, in India or Singapore, before continuing on to Sri Lanka. Stopover times vary considerably so look out for these when booking.

Air Fares

The cost of flying to Sri Lanka varies depending on the airline you choose and when you plan to travel; prices are highest around Christmas and New Year. Try and arrange to travel midweek if you can as the prices are often lower than those available on weekends. Remember the earlier you book your flights, the better the chance of finding a good deal. Package tours sometimes boast the best deals and custom-made trips and are worth considering. Special packages and discounted fares may also be available on websites such as **Expedia**. Visitors in Germany can try **Fluege** and those in the UK may find good deals on **Sri Lanka Tours**.

Arriving in Sri Lanka

Visitors should arrange a visa (*see pp252–3*) before travelling to Sri Lanka. While still on the plane, passengers will be handed an immigration card to fill in. If you cannot find yours on landing or have made a mistake, replacements are available near the immigration desks. Your card will need to be submitted along with your passport at the airport's immigration counter; bring along proof of your ETA entry visa (*see p253*) as well. In the arrivals hall are a number of currency exchange counters offering competitive rates,

Interior of the Bandaranaike International Airport

Tourists waiting for taxis outside Bandaranaike International Airport

as well as ATMs. There is a Sri Lankan Tourist Board office as well.

Airport Transfers

Many people arrange to be picked up from the airport by their hotel or tour operator. It is also possible to arrange a prepaid taxi from the counter in the arrivals hall. The taxi ride to Negombo will take about 20 minutes and cost around Rs 1,400; getting to Colombo Fort will take about an hour and cost around Rs 3,000; a taxi to Kandy will take about three hours and cost Rs 8,000. There is also a shuttle service from outside arrivals that takes passengers to the nearby bus station.

Arriving by Sea

Unless you arrive on a cruise ship it is not possible to travel to Sri Lanka by sea. The ferry service

between Colombo and Tuticorin in India resumed in June 2011 after many years but was later suspended. There have been talks of running the ferry again or replacing it with a smaller vessel.

Cruise liners generally stop in Colombo for the day, such as the 116-Day World Sojourn, run by **Seabourn**, which departs from Los Angeles in January and reaches Sri Lanka in early April. **Holland American Line** offers a number of cruises that stop in Colombo, including the 51-day Spice Route to Singapore which starts in Rotterdam in January and reaches Sri Lanka about a month later. Many liners offer excursions that can be booked in advance and take visitors to sights including Kandy, tea plantations and the Pinnawela Elephant Orphanage *(see p143)*. For those wanting to spend more time in Colombo, **Voyages**

of Discovery offers the Grand Voyage around Shores of the Indian Ocean, which includes three days in Colombo and one at Hambantota. Other cruise operators include **Silversea** and **Cunard Line**.

Green Travel

As flying is the main way to reach the island, travellers to Sri Lanka may wish to offset their carbon footprint. Once on the island, you can travel by train or bus to reach some of the main tourist sights. Work is currently underway to extend the rail network. Hiring a bicycle is a also good way to explore places such as the ruins of Polonnaruwa *(see pp170–74)*. There are a number of ecotourism tour operators *(see p244)* on the island, who are passionate about protecting Sri Lanka's rich biodiversity.

Check-in counter at the Bandaranaike International Airport

DIRECTORY

Arriving by Air

American Airlines
w aa.com

Bandaranaike International Airport
Katunayake.
Tel (011) 225 2666.
w airport.lk

British Airways
w britishairways.com

Cathay Pacific
w cathaypacific.com

Emirates
w emirates.com

Etihad Airways
w etihadairways.com

Jet Airways
w jetairways.com

Kuwait Airways
w kuwait-airways.com

Malaysian Airlines
w malaysiaairlines.com

Mattala Rajapaksa International Airport
w airport.lk

Oman Air
w omanair.com

Qatar Airways
w qatarairways.com

Royal Jordanian Airlines
w rj.com

Singapore Airlines
w singaporeair.com

SriLankan Airlines
w srilankan.lk

Thai Airways
w thaiair.com

United Airlines
w united.com

Air Fares

Expedia
w expedia.com

Fluege
w fluege.de

Sri Lanka Tours
w srilankatours.co.uk

Arriving by Sea

Cunard Line
w cunardline.com

Holland American Line
w hollandamerica.com

Seabourn
w seabourn.com

Silversea
w silversea.com

Voyages of Discovery
w voyagesofdiscovery.co.uk

Getting around Sri Lanka

There are several means of travelling within Sri Lanka. The Colonial-era train network is a popular draw and is a great way to enjoy the scenery. Buses reach nearly all corners of the island and those operating outside the main centres are a great way to meet local people. In tourist areas, taxis and three-wheelers are easily available, and it is possible to rent a car with a driver or a bicycle to get around. Roads are currently being improved and motorways built, and work to rebuild and extend the railway line is ongoing. For those who are pressed for time, there are domestic flights to some tourist destinations in addition to regular flights between Jaffna and Colombo.

A FitsAir passenger craft on the tarmac, Colombo Airport

Domestic Flights

If you are short on time, consider taking a domestic flight. SriLankan Airlines *(see p264)* operates the SriLankan Air Taxi flights between Colombo and places such as Kandy, Koggala, Trincomalee or Batticaloa; planes can also be chartered. **Cinnamon Air** flies to the same destinations, as well as to Sigiriya. **Helitours**, which is the commercial branch of the Sri Lankan Air Force, offers flights to Batticaloa, Trincomalee and Jaffna, but these are less frequent; they too have planes that can be chartered. A popular option for those visiting Jaffna is **FitsAir**, which flies to the north of the island from **Colombo Airport** once or twice daily.

Railway Network

The Sri Lankan rail network was built by the British during the 19th century and it still retains a Colonial-era charm. The scenic Colombo to Kandy trip is a favourite among visitors, and travelling through the tea plantations and past misty peaks to Nanu Oya (Nuwara Eliya), Haputale, Ella and Badulla is also highly recommended. Efforts to reopen the rail link between Vavuniya and Jaffna, and the branch line between Vavuniya and Mannar are underway. There are also plans to extend the railway line to Kataragama, Habarana and Hambantota. Although travelling by rail remains a popular option, remember that trains are slow and that there are frequent delays.

Sri Lanka Railways operates three main train lines that branch out from Colombo: the Hill Country line runs from Colombo to Kandy and then on to Badulla; the northern line runs from Colombo to Vavuniya and is set to go as far as Jaffna in the future; and the south coast line currently reaches as far as Matara. There are also branch lines to Trincomalee and to Batticaloa via Polonnaruwa. The line between Galle and Matara was badly damaged by the tsunami in 2004, but the repair work has now been completed. This is a commuter service through the Colombo suburbs, and can be slow and crowded. There are also slow trains that run via Negombo and Chilaw and a line that goes as far as Avissawella. Slow trains are sometimes the only choice but if possible it is obviously better to book a seat on an express train. Approximate journey times range between two to four hours between Colombo Fort and Galle; two-and-a-half to three hours between Colombo Fort and Kandy; around three-and-a-half hours from Kandy to Nanu Oya; and four to five hours from Colombo Fort to Vavuniya.

Train Travel

Depending on your destination and when you choose to travel, there are a number of different options available with varying price tags. On all services you will find second- and third-class carriages – the former are slightly more comfortable with some padding on the seats and are occasionally less crowded. On selected services and the faster intercity trains, there are first-class carriages. These can range from observation cars, with seats facing large windows at one end of the carriage, on the Hill Country route to air-conditioned carriages and sleeper berths on longer, overnight journeys.

Train winding through the picturesque Hill Country

Train schedules on display at the Fort Railway Station, Colombo

Luxury coaches, run by private companies, are available on some services. The **Blue Line Company** operates the Rajadhani Express on some trains to Kandy, Badulla and Batticaloa. **ExpoRail** services are available on some trains going to Kandy, Vavuniya, Badulla and Trincomalee. Both offer air conditioning, food and drink, Wi-Fi, sockets and comfortable seats with ample leg room.

A railway crossing sign along a train route, Haputale

Train Tickets

Advance bookings for luxury services are recommended and can be made on the Blue Line and ExpoRail websites. If you are looking to travel in a first-class carriage, particularly in one with an observation car, note that these can be booked in advance. There is an office at the far end of **Fort Railway Station**, in Colombo, where tickets for these can be bought, and there is a board detailing the class of seats available on the different trains. If you are travelling with tour operators, they will arrange all train tickets. It is possible to reserve second-class seats on intercity and sleeper services at the station. All other tickets can be bought on the day of travel; try to be at the station at least 30 minutes before the train is due to leave to buy your ticket.

If you wish to buy your train ticket before leaving for Sri Lanka, an agency like Red Dot Tours (see p242) can help, but their prices will be higher.

Train timetables can be accessed via the Sri Lankan Railways website, but it is always better to check at the station for changes and cancellations before travelling. There will usually be a board at the station with all the departure information available.

Getting around Colombo

Colombo is quite spread out, and heat and car fumes make covering it on foot a less appealing option. Many visitors choose to travel in three-wheelers; fares are more expensive in Colombo than elsewhere and can sometimes be higher than taxis. Three-wheelers around hotels, restaurants and department stores are usually the most expensive so consider walking a short distance to find a cheaper ride. Many three-wheelers are now metered and they have a sign on the roof advertising the fact. If you choose an unmetered three-wheeler, agree on a price before getting in. Radio taxi firms in Colombo, such as **Kangaroo Cabs**, are easier to book. Some hotels and tour operators offer city tours in air-conditioned cars and there is a **Colombo City Tour** open-topped double decker bus that runs on weekends. If you find a three-wheeler

driver you like and feel is genuine, you can always employ him to take you around the city sights.

(see p242)

DIRECTORY

Domestic Flights

Cinnamon Air
Tel (011) 247 5451.
cinnamonair.com

Colombo Airport
airport.lk

FitsAir
Tel (011) 255 5156.
expoavi.com

Helitours
Tel (011) 314 4944.
helitours.lk

Railway Network

Sri Lankan Railways
railway.gov.lk

Train Travel

Blue Line Company
Tel (071) 035 5355. blueline.lk

ExpoRail
Tel (077) 799 7711.
exporail.lk
railway.gov.lk

Train Tickets

Fort Railway Station
Pettah, Col 1. Tel (011) 243 42 15,
reservations (011) 243 2908.

Getting around Colombo

Colombo City Tours
Tel (077) 759 9963.
colombocitytours.com

Kangaroo Cabs
Tel (011) 258 8588.
2588588.com

One of the many radio taxis serving Colombo

Travelling by Road

The road network in Sri Lanka is extensive, varying from newly laid highways to pothole-ridden tracks. There is currently a lot of work underway to improve some of the main road networks, and the new expressway between Colombo and Galle has significantly reduced journey time to the south coast. Driving is on the left, with right-hand drive cars. It is best to hire a car and driver to get around the island. Bus journeys are an interesting way to see the country, but can be uncomfortable and are best suited for short trips. Three-wheelers are every-where and can be very useful for getting between towns or visiting nearby sights. Hitchhiking is not recommended.

Colourful three-wheelers lined up at one of the stands, Colombo

Buses

Buses travel to almost everywhere on the island. While not the most comfortable option, they are a convenient and cheap means of transport; tourists, however, may be asked to pay more than the locals. Bus drivers can be reckless, travellers often have to stand for all or most of the way and the journey might be accompanied by blaring Sinhalese pop music or Bollywood hits.

There are two types of buses: the CTB (Ceylon Transport Board) buses run by the government and those run by private companies. The CTB buses are the slowest and cheapest, they stop frequently and if you don't get on at the beginning of the journey you may find it near impossible to squeeze in. Private buses can be coaches, minibuses or white versions of CTB buses; some also have air con-ditioning. Note that these stop less frequently – some even travel non-stop to

destinations – and it is often possible to buy a separate seat for your luggage.

Most towns have one or more bus stations, and larger stations should have an information booth where visitors can ask about times and destinations. Most buses will have the final destination marked on the front, but if you are unsure check with the driver before boarding. If you arrive at the bus station

A fleet of buses near the railway station in Colombo

in a three-wheeler, the driver will often be able to take you straight to the right bus.

Three-wheelers

Three-wheelers are motorized rickshaws or *tuk tuks*, often personalized by their driver, and are found all over Sri Lanka. Many of the three-wheelers in Colombo are now metered (look for the sign on the roof), but elsewhere you may have to agree to a price before setting off. Make sure you have small denomination notes or ask the driver if he has change before embarking on the journey. Three-wheelers can be a very practical option for short dis-tances, for example within towns or for visiting nearby sights. They can accommodate up to three people, or two with backpacks.

Car Rentals and Licences

Unless you are used to driving in Asia you may want to avoid hiring your own car. For anyone who does decide to hire a car, there are a number of self-drive car hire firms in Sri Lanka, including **Avis**.

To be able to drive in Sri Lanka you will need to obtain an International Driving Licence before leaving for your trip. You will then need to take it to the **Automobile Association of Ceylon** (AA) office in Colombo to get it endorsed. Some car rental agencies can take care of this for you.

Hiring a Car and Driver

Many visitors choose to hire a car and driver to explore Sri Lanka. This can be parti-cularly useful in the Cultural Triangle as there are several interesting, smaller sights that are difficult to reach by public transport. A car and driver offers great flexibility and can be arranged through tour operators such as **Lion Royal**, **Malkey** and Red Dot Tours (see p242), as well as car rental companies. If you just want a car and driver for the day,

Cycling, a popular means of exploring Sri Lanka among tourists

hotels can often organize this. If you know someone who has visited Sri Lanka before, it is worth asking if they can recommend a driver.

Prices vary depending on the make of the vehicle, the distance travelled and features included in the price. Shorter trips are usually calculated on mileage, for example, if you just want a car and driver for the day, others have a fixed daily rate. Organize your car and driver through a reputable company and ensure that your driver speaks some English.

A typical road sign

If you are not interested in shopping or visiting spice gardens let the driver know, and if you have specific accommodation options in mind tell him and make sure he agrees, as there are many drivers who will want to take you to restaurants, hotels and shops where they receive a commission. Most large hotels will have free accommodation available for drivers and will provide meals for them. Smaller guesthouses may charge extra, so agree in advance who will cover this amount. It is also worth checking before setting off if fuel is included in the rental price or if you will need to budget for it.

Do not forget to tip your driver at the end of your trip – this is often the main source of income for them.

Cycling

At certain times of the year, especially around the Sinhalese-Tamil New Year, bicycle races take place all over the island. In Jaffna, cycles are still the main mode of transport for most people. Many operators organize cycle tours around Sri Lanka and some visitors bring their own bicycles over for the duration of their stay. Many tourist areas, such as Polonnaruwa , offer cycles for hire.

Before taking a bicycle out for a spin, check its condition, especially that the brakes work. Watch out for pedestrians, vehicles and animals when out on the roads.

Motorbikes

Hiring motorbikes is becoming a popular way to explore the island, but it is only recom-

Motorbikes and bicycles available for rent in Narigama, near Hikkaduwa

mended for experienced riders who have ridden on Asian roads before. Colombo and Negombo are the main bases for hiring motorbikes, but you may find them in other tourist spots as well. If you do hire a motorbike, do so through an operator such as **Casons Car Rental** rather than informally so that you are covered in case of accident or theft. Ensure that you secure the motorbike overnight and never leave your bags unattended. Check its condition before renting and also know who will be covering the cost of any repairs needed. By law, riders and passengers must wear crash helmets. Even though it is hot, wear long trousers and full sleeves while riding to avoid severe sunburn.

General Index

Page numbers in **bold** refer to main entries

Acknowledgments

Dorling Kindersley would like to thank the following people whose help and assistance contributed to the preparation of this book.

Main Contributor
Rachael Heston

Additional Photography
Ian O'Leary; Rough Guides / Gavin Thomas.

Fact Checkers
Shafni Awam, Adam Bray

Proofreaders
Aruna Ghose, Divya Chowfin

Indexer
Helen Peters

Sinhala and Tamil Translations
Andiamo! Language Services Ltd

Editorial Consultant
Scarlett O'Hara

Design Assistance
Amisha Gupta

Design and Editorial
Publishing Director Georgina Dee

Publisher Vivien Antwi

List Manager Kate Berens

Executive Editor Michelle Crane

Senior Editor Sadie Smith

Project Editor Greg Dickinson

Senior Executive Cartographic Editor Casper Morris

Senior DTP Designer Jason Little

Production Controller Linda Dare

Additional Design and Editorial Assistance
Fay Franklin
Janis Utton

Special Assistance
Dorling Kindersley would like to thank the following for their assistance:

Aruna Warushahhennadige at Bandaranayake International Airport Katunayake; Mr H D Ratnayake and Ms Nayana Kulathunga at the Department of Wildlife Conservation; Jayathunga Herath at Elephant Camp Guesthouse Tissaharama; Priyanka Tisseverasinghe at Geoffrey Bawa Trust; Jayathunga Herath at Elephant Camp Guesthouse Tissaharama; Sarangi Thilakasena at Sri Lanka Tourism Promotion Bureau; Dominic Sansoni at Three Blind Men.

Photography Permissions
Dorling Kindersley would like to thank all the museums, galleries, churches and other sights that allowed us to photograph at their establishments:

Colombo National Museum; Department of Wildlife Conservation for permission to photograph inside the national parks; Dehiwala Zoo; Galle National Museum; Geoffrey Bawa Trust for the Geoffrey Bawa buildings; Kandy National Museum; Maritime Archaeology Museum; Maritime Museum; Martin Wickramasinghe Museum; National Railway Museum.

Works of art have been reproduced with the kind permission of the following copyright holders:

Sinhalese Warrior Sculptures 34tr, *Erotic Dance* 35tr © Laki Senanayake.

Picture Credits
a = above; b = below/bottom; c = centre; f = far; l = left; r = right; t = top

The publisher would like to thank the following for their kind permission to reproduce their photographs:

123RF.com: Manganganath 225c; Iryna Rasko 114–115.

4Corners: Aldo Pavan 2–3; Reinhard Schmid 40br.

Alamy Images: Mohammed Abidally 123tl, 242t, Asia Images Group Pte Ltd 38–39c, Robert Bannister 25cb, Sabena Jane Blackbird 235br, Tibor Bognar 124bl, Koen Broker 54bc, Michele Burgess 47tl, 122clb, 181cr, Andrew Cawley 31bc, Michal Cerny 24bl, City Image 73br, Craft Images 31tr, Mark Daffey 122cl, 122bl, Dbimages 30bl, DK India Collection 99cr, Dmitry Rukhlenko - Travel Photos 19b, 164–165, Ephotocorp 180br, FLPA 24cb, 125bl, 153br, Alexey Gnilenkov 24clb, Hemis 28tr, 166tr, Neil Hepworth 121br, Heritage Image Partnership Ltd 259br, Horizons WWP 35bc, 92b, Peter Horree 46clb, Ernie Janes 24tr, Marcin Kosciolek 48clb, H Lansdown 125clb, Emmanuel Lattes 131b, Frans Lemmens 46cl, Yadid Levy 36bl, 241b, Look Die Bildagentur Der Fotografen Gmbh 155b, 179br, Lookinglost 101bl, Mediacolor's 88, Dorota Nowańska 38tr, Papilio 15tr, 125cl, 147bl, Premaphotos 24crb, RGB Ventures LLC dba SuperStock 127cb, Robert Harding Picture Library Ltd 169br, Pep Roig 89b, Nick Servian 125cr, Philip Sharp 37c, Nandana De Silva 250–251, Kumar Sriskandan 36tr, 99cl, 99clb, Jochen Tack 39crb, 242bl, The Natural History Museum 239tr, Ian Trower 240bl, Clive Tully 148bl, Dieter Wanke 99bl, Finnbarr Webster 37crb, 126cl, 185b, Maximilian Wein 25br, Wiskerke 34tr, Jan Wlodarczyk 58clb, 108cla.

Anton Photography: 194bl.

AWL Images: Nigel Pavitt 8–9; Travel Pix Collection 140–41.

Bandaranaike Internatonal Airport: 265crb.

Bharatiya Kala Prakashan: Ashwin Raju Adimari 120bl.

The Bridgeman Art Library: Elephant hunt in the region of Logalla, from 'Travels of Prince Emanual Andrasy in Eastindian Ceylon, Java, China and Bengal', engraved by Ciceri and Adams, published 1859 (colour litho), Andrasy, Graf Emanuel (Mano) (fl.1859) (after) / Private Collection / The Stapleton Collection / 26cl.

Corbis: 28c, Bettmann 52tl, 52bl; Demotix / Angelo Samarawickrema 113bc,/ Sanka Vidanagama 197br; Lindsay Hebberd 129cr; JAI / Ian Trower 94bl; National Geographic Society / Gilbert H. Grosvenor 50crb; Ocean 25cl; Nigel Pavitt 215tl; Reuters / Anuruddha Lokuhapuarachchi 40cl, 54tl, 54cb; Reuters / Anuruddha Lokuhapuarachchi / X00167 129crb; Reuters / Dinuka Liyanawatte 42tl; Reuters / Ho 55tl; Reuters / X01095 54crb; Reuters / STR / SRI LANKA / X01315 264cl; Robert Harding World Imagery / Godong 35bl,/ Ian Trower 48tr, 181br.

CPA Media: 46crb, 46–47c, 47c, 47bc, 50tl, 50bc, 51tc, 51bl.

Digant Desai: 103tr.

Dreamstime.com: Bigjo5 239cra; David Edbury 247b; Dmitrii Fadeev 167bl; Filip Fuxa 56–57; Inavanhateren 171cr; Iuliia Kryzhevska 166cl; Zuzana Randlova 148tl; Simonwehner 167cr, 169tl; Toxawww 62bl.

Fits Aviation: 266cl.

FLPA: David Hosking 24fcrb; Minden Pictures / Flip Nicklin 119clb,/ Pete Oxford 127br.

Geoffrey Bawa Trust: 77cl, 77bl, 100tr.

Getty Images: AFP / Stringer / Ishara S.kodikara 21tr, 21bl, 31cb, 41br, 42cr, 43tl, 52cb, 53tr, 55br, 67br; Tomas Del Amo 39tr, 39bl; Peter Barritt 37tr, 44, 137tc; Bloomberg 235t; Cultura Travel / Philip Lee Harvey 18, 46tr; Agron Dragaj 184; Jason Edwards 175tl; Rob Francis 199tr; Bartosz Hadyniak 199br; Lonely Planet Images / Antony Giblin 225tl; Diana Mayfield 206bl; Kevin Miller 36–37c; Flip Nicklin 119br; Thilanka Perera 105b; Wolfgang Poelzer 119bl; Popperfoto 151bl; Jerry Redfern 175br; Andy Rouse 59bc; Oliver Strewe 126clb, 129clb, 222cl; Time & Life Pictures 53bc; Hande Guleryuz Yuce 38br.

Hilton Colombo Residences: 213tr.

Jathika Namal Uyana: 161br.

Kelly Florence Jeffs: 101crb.

Mary Evans Picture Library: Grenville Collins Postcard Collection 45bc, Illustrated London News Ltd 51crb.

Masterfile: R. Ian Lloyd 60.

Ministry of Crab: 210–211, 228tl.

Mount Lavinia Hotel: 227tr.

naturepl.com: Elio Della Ferrera 24cl.

Photoshot: ANT Photo Library 24bc, 25cra.

V.K Rajamani: 47tr.

Secret Garden Villa: 248t.

Laki Senanayake: 35tr.

Spa Ceylon: 239clb.

Sun Rise Ballooning: 246tr.

SuperStock: Age Fotostock 130.

Three Blind Men: Dominic Sansoni 35cr, 129cl, 129br, 177cl, 192-193.

Dilan Walgampaya: 166br.

www.DiveSriLanka.com: Ajith Fernando 191br.

Front Endpaper

Alamy Images: Mediacolor's c; Getty Images: Agron Dragaj tr; Masterfile: R. Ian Lloyd bl; SuperStock: Age Fotostock cr.

Jacket

Front: 4Corners: Fridmar Damm c; Dorling Kindersley: Idris Ahmed bl; Spine: 4Corners: Fridmar Damm.

All other images © Dorling Kindersley
For further information see: www.dkimages.com

Phrase Book

Sinhala, also known as Sinhalese, is the native language of the Sinhalese people, the largest ethnic group in Sri Lanka, totalling about 16 million. It is also the second language of other minority ethnic groups in the country. Tamil, a Dravidian language, is predominantly spoken by the Tamil people of northeastern Sri Lanka. Of the various dialects used by Sri Lankan Tamils, the two major ones are Indian

Tamil and Jaffna Tamil, with the latter spoken in the Jaffna Peninsula in the northern part of the island. The two dialects differ in styles of speech and accent, although both are mutually comprehensible. Other regionally distinct dialects are Negombo Tamil and Batticaloa Tamil, which are spoken in the coastal regions, and Hill Country Tamil, used by the tea plantation workers.

Guidelines for Pronunciation

The Sinhala alphabet is referred to as an "abugida" or "alphasyllabary", meaning that consonants are written with letters while vowels are indicated with *pilla* (diacritics) on those consonants. The complete alphabet consists of 54 letters: 18 vowels and 36 consonants. However, only 36 of these letters (12 vowels and 24 consonants) are required for writing colloquial Sinhala.

The current Tamil script consists of 12 vowels, 18 consonants and one special character, the *āytam*. The vowels and consonants combine to form 216 compound characters, giving a total of 247 characters. All consonants have an inherent vowel "a", as with other Indic scripts. This inherency is removed by adding a title called a *pulli*, to the consonantal sign.

When reading the phonetics, pronounce syllables as if they form English words. Note that double consonants highlight the need to stress the sound, such as a "pp" instead of a single "p" or 'dhdh' rather than a single "dh".

Vowels

u	as in **u**p (short)
aa	as in f**a**r (long)
a	as in **a**pple
e	as in **e**ver (short)
ay	as in pl**a**y (long)
i	as in p**i**n (short)
ee	as in fl**ee** (long)
o	as in **o**ver (short)
oa	as in **o**ver (but longer)
oo	as in p**u**ll (short)
ou	as in c**oo**l (long)
er	as in b**ur**n (don't pronounce the 'r')
ai	as in f**l**y
ei	as in w**ai**t
ouw	as in h**ow**
ull	as in g**u**ll

Consonants

dh	as in wea**th**er
d	as in **d**ay
th	as in **th**irty
ng	as in si**ng**
gn	as in Ke**ny**a
g	as in **g**un
j	as in **j**ug

ENGLISH	SINHALA	SINHALA PHONETIC	TAMIL	TAMIL PHONETIC
In an Emergency				
Help!	**Udhaw karanne!**	*Udh-ouw ker-ru-n-ner!*	**Udhavungal!**	*oo-dher-voo-ng-ull!*
Fire!	**Gindhara!**	*gin-dhe-rer!*	**Neruppu!**	*ne-roop-poo!*
Where is the nearest hospital?	**Langama ispirithaalaya kohedhe!**	*Lung-er-mer-is-pi-ri-thaa-ler-yer ko-hay-dhe!*	**Arughil ulla aaspaththiri engay?**	*a-roo-hil ul-ler aas-puth-thi-ri eng-gay?*
Call an ambulance!	**Ambulance ekakata kathaa karanne!**	*ambulance e-ker-ker-ta ka-thaa ker-run-ner!*	**Ambulansai koopudungal!**	*ambulans-ai koo-poo-doong-ull!*
Call the police!	**Polisiyata kathaa karanne!**	*Poli-si-yer-ter ka-thaa ker-run-ner!*	**Polissai koopudungal!**	*Po-lis-sai koo-poo-doong-ull!*
Call a doctor!	**Dhostere kenekuta kathaa karanne!**	*Dho-sther-er-ke-ne-koo-ter ka-thaa ker-run-ner!*	**Doctorai koopudungal!**	*doctor-ai koo-poo-doong-ull!*
Communication Essentials				
Yes	**Ow**	*Ouw*	**Aamaam**	*aam-aam*
No	**Nay**	*Ney*	**Illai**	*Ill-ai*
Hello	**Ayubowan**	*aa-you-bo-wu**nn***	**Vanakkam**	*va-nerk-kum*
Goodbye	**Mung yunnung (I am going)**	*mung yun-**nung***	**Naan porane (I am going)**	*Naan poa-ray-n*
Please	**Karunakara**	*ku-roo-naaker-rer*	**Thayavu seithu**	*thu-yer-voo sei-dhoo*
Thank you	**sthuthi**	*s-thoo-thee*	**Nandri**	*nun-dree*
I don't understand	**Mata theruney nay**	*mu-ter they-roo-nay ney*	**Enakku puriyavillai**	*en-uk-koo poo-ri-yer-vill-ai*
I don't know	**Mama dhanney nay**	*Ma-mer dhun-nay ney*	**Enakku theriyaadhu**	*en-uk-koo they-ri-yaa-dhoo*
Sorry	**Kanagaatui**	*kun-er-gaa-too-yi*	**Mannikkavum**	*mun-nik-ker-voom*
Excuse me	**Mata Sama venna**	*Mu-ter-sa-maa ven-**ner***	**Vali vidungal (Please give way)**	*va-li vi-doong-gal*
			Manniyungal (Pardon me)	*mu**n**-ni-yoong-gull*
What?	**Mokaddhe?**	*mo-ku**dh-dhe**?*	**Enna?**	*en-ner?*
Why?	**Ei?**	*e-yi?*	**Yen?**	*yay-n?*
Where?	**Kohedhe?**	*ko-hay-dher?*	**Engey?**	*eng-gay?*
When?	**Kavadhadhe?**	*ku-ver-dhaa-dher?*	**Eppa?**	*ep-per?*
How?	**Kohomadhe?**	*ko-ho-mer-dher?*	**Eppudi?**	*ep-**poo**-dee?*
Useful Phrases				
How are you?	**Oya kohomadhe?**	*o-yaa ko-ho-mer-dher?*	**Eppudi irukureengal?**	*ep-**poo**-dee i-roo-koo-reeng-**gull**?*
Very well, thank you	**Mama hondhing, sthuthi**	*mu-mer hon-dheeng, s-thoo-thee*	**Naan nalla irukiren, nandri**	*naan nal-laa i-roo-ki-ray-n, nun-dree*
Not very well	**Vadi hondhing nemey**	*va-dee hon-dheeng nay-may*	**Romba nalla illai**	*rom-ber nal-laa il-lai*
What is this?	**Mey mokadhdhe?**	*may mok-a**dh-dh**er?*	**Idhu enna?**	*i-dhoo en-ner?*
How do I get to…?	**…ekata yanney kohomadhe?**	*…e-ker-ter yu**nn**-ay ko-ho-mer-dher?*	**…iku povadhu eppudi?**	*…ikoo po-ver-dhoo ep-**poo**-dee?*
Where is the restroom/toilet?	**…eka kohedhe?**	*…eka ko-hay-dher?*	**…engulladhu toilet?**	*…eng-**gul**-ler-dhoo? Taai-let?*
	Viveka kaamaraya/vesikilya?	*vi-ve-ker kaa-mer-rer-yer/ va-si-ki-li-yer?*		
Do you speak English?	**Oya ingireesi kathaa karanavaadhe?**	*oh-yaa i-**g**i-ree-si ku-thaa ker-er-ner-vaa-dher?*	**Neengal aangilam pesuveerghala?**	*neeng-gal aang-gil-am pay-soo-veer-hala?*
I can't speak Sinhala/Tamil	**Mata singhala/dhamila kathaa karanne behey**	*mu-ter sing-her-ler/dhu-mi-ler ka-thaa ker-run-ner bey-hey*	**Enakku singhalam/thamil pesa mudiyaadhu**	*e-nuk-**koo** sing-herl-lum/ tha-mil pay-ser moo-di-yaa-dhu*
Useful Words				
I	**Mama**	*mu-mer*	**Naan**	*Naa-n*
woman/women	**geheniya/gehenu**	*gey-hey-ni-yer/ gey-hey-noo*	**pen/penghal**	*pe**nn**/pe**nn**-ghull*
man/men	**pirimiya/pirimi**	*pi-ri-mi-yaa/pi-ri-mi*	**aan/aanghal**	*aan/aan-ghull*
child/children	**lamaya/lamai**	*lu-mer-yaa/lu-mai*	**pillai/pillaighal**	*pill-ai/pill-ai-hull*
family	**pawula**	*pu-woo-ler*	**kudumbam**	*koo-doom-bum*
good	**hondhai**	*hon-dhai*	**nallam**	*nul-lam*
bad	**narakai**	*nu-rer-kai*	**koodaadhu**	*koo-daa-dhoo*

English	Sinhala	Pronunciation	Tamil	Pronunciation
open	erilaa	*a-ree-laa*	thirandhulladhu	*thi-run-dhul-ler-dhoo*
closed	vahala	*vu-hu-laa*	moodiyulladhu	*moo-di-yool-ler-dhoo*
left	vama	*vu-mer*	idathu	*i-der-dhoo*
right	dhakuna	*dhu-koo-ner*	valathu	*vu-ler-dhoo*
straight ahead	keling issaraha	*ke-ling is-ser-rer-haa*	neraagha munnaal	*nay-raa-her moon-naal*
near	langai	*lung-gai*	arughil	*a-roo-ghil*
far	dhurai	*dhoo-rai*	dhooram	*dhoo-rum*
entrance	dhoratuwa	*dho-rer-too-ver*	vaasal	*vaa-sull*
exit	pitavena dhora	*pi-ter-ve-ner dho-rer*	veliyerum vali	*ve-li-yay-room vu-li*
toilet	vesikiliya	*va-si-ki-li-yer*	toilet	*taal-let*
area code	praadheshaya kethaya	*praa-dhey-sher-yer kay-ther-yer*	paghudi kuriyeedu	*pa-hoo-dhee koo-ri-yee-doo*
post office	thepel kanthoruwa	*tha-pal kun-tho-roo-ver*	thabaal aluvalagham	*thu-baal u-loo-vu-ler-herm*
letter	liyuma	*li-yoo-mer*	kadidham	*ku-dee-dherm*
address	yomuwa	*yo-moo-ver*	mughavari	*moo-her-vu-ree*
street	veedhiya	*vee-dhee-yer*	theru	*they-roo*
town	nagharaya	*nu-gher-rer-yer*	nagharam	*nu-gher-rerm*
village	gama	*guh-mer*	graamam	*graa-mum*
Internet café	antharjaala aapana shaalaava	*un-thur-jaa-ler aa-per-ner shaa-laa-ver*	inaiyakham	*in-ai-yer-herm*
e-mail	e-thepel	*ee-they-peyl*	minnanjal	*minn-unj-erl*

Money

I want to change £100 into Sri Lankan currency.	Mata, Engalanthayey salli powum seeyak, Lankavey salli valata maaru karanne oney	*mu-ter, eng-ger-lun-ther-yay sull-i pow-oom see-yuk, lung-kaa-vey sul-li ver-ler-ter maa-roo ker-run-ner oan-ay*	Enakku, Ingalandhin kaasu nooru powunghalai, Ilangaiyin kaasaaha maatra vendum	*ey-nak-koo, ing-er-lun-dhin kaa-soo noo-roo pow-oon-hul-ai, I-lung-gai-yin kaa-saa-her maa-trer vayn-doom*
exchange rate	vinimaya anupathikaya	*vi-ni-mer-yer a-noo-paa-thi-ker-yer*	maatru vighidham	*maa-troo vee-hee-dherm*
I'd like to cash these traveller's checks.	Mata mey sanchaaraka checkpath, salli valata maaru karanne oney	*mu-ter may sun-chaa-rer-ker check-puth, sul-lee ver-ler-ter maa-roo ker-run-ner oan-ay*	Enakku indha payanighalin kaasolaihalai kaasaagha maatra vendum	*e-nuk-koo in-dher pu-yer-nee-her-lin kaas-oal-ai-her-yil kaa-saa-her maa-trer vayn-doom*
bank	bankuwa	*bank-oo-ver*	vangi	*vung-gee*
money/cash	salli/mudhal	*sull-ee/moo-dhul*	kaasu/panam	*kaa-soo/pu-num*
credit card	naya kaadpatha	*nu-yer kaad-pu-ther*	kadan attai	*ku-den ut-tai*

Making a Telephone Call

I'd like to make a telephone call	Mata dhurakathana emathumak karanne oney	*mu-ter dhoo-rer ku-ther-ner amer-thoo-muk ker-run-ner oan-ay*	Enakku oru tholaipesi alaipai etpaduththa vendum	*e-nuk-koo o-roo tho-lai-pay-see a-lai-pai ayt-pa-doo-ther vayn-doom*
I'd like to make an international phone call	Mata anthar jaathika dhurakathana emathumak karanne oney	*mu-ter un-thur jaa-thee-ker dhoo-rer ku-ther-ner ema-thoo-muck ker-run-ner oan-ay*	Enakku oru sarvadhesa tholaipesi alaipai etpaduththa vendum	*e-nuk-koo o-roo surr-ver dhey-ser tho-lai-pay-see a-lai-pai ate-pa-dhu-ther vayn-doom*
mobile phone	Jangama dhurakathanaya	*jung-ger-mer dhoo-rer ka-ther-ner-yer*	Kai pesi	*kai pay-see*
telephone enquiries	Dhurakathana vimasum	*dhoo-rer ku-ther-ner vim-er-soom*	Tholaipesi visaaranaighal	*tho-lai-pay-see visaa-ra-nai-hal*
public phone box	Podhu dhurakathana pettiya	*po-dhoo dhoo-rer ku-ther-ner pet-ti-yer*	Podhu tholaipesi petti	*po-dhoo tho-lai-pay-see pet-ti*

Shopping

Where can I buy…?	…ganne puluwang kohendhe?	*…gun-ner poo-loo-wung ko-hen-dher?*	…engey vaangalaam?	*…eng-ay vaang-er-laam?*
How much does this cost?	Meykhe keeyadhe?	*May-ke yer-dher?*	Idhu evalavu?	*I-dhoo ev-ver-ler-voo?*
May I try this on?	Meykhe endhalaa balanne puluwangdhe?	*May-ker en-dher-laa ba-lan-ner poo-loo-wung-dher?*	Idhai uduthu paakalaama?	*I-dhai oo-doo-thoo paa-ker-laa-maa?*
I would like…	Mama kemathi…	*Ma-mer ka-mer-thee…*	Enakku viruppam…	*E-ner-koo vi-roop-pam…*
Do you have…?	… thiyanavaadhe?	*thi-yer-ner-vaa-dher?*	… iru kiradha?	*i-roo-ki-rer-dhaa?*
Do you take credit cards?	Oba naya kaadpath gannavaadhe?	*O-ber-nu-yer kaad-pa-th gun-ner-vaa-dher?*	Kadan attai eduppeerghala?	*Ku-den at-tai e-doo-peer-her-laa?*
What time do you open/close?	Oba keeyatadhe arinney/vahanney?	*O-ber-Kee-yer-ter-dher u-rin-ney/va-ha-ney?*	Ethanai manikku thirappeerghal/saathuveerghal?	*E-ther-nai mu-nik-koo thi-rer-peer-hal/saa-thoo-veer-hul?*
How much?	Keeyadhe?	*Kee-yer-dher?*	Evvalavu?	*Ev-ver-ler-voo?*
Expensive	Ganang vedi	*Gu-nung va-dee*	Kooda vilai	*Koo-der vi-lai*
cheap	Laabai	*Laa-bai*	Malivu	*Mu-lee-voo*
size	Pramaanaya	*Prer-maa-ner-yer*	Alavu	*U-ler-voo*
colour	Paata	*Paa-ter*	Niram	*Ni-rum*
bookstore	Poth saapuwa	*Poth saa-poo-wer*	Puththaha kadai	*Pooth-ther-her ku-dai*
department store	Departhamenthu Alevisala	*De-paa-r-ther-may-n-thoo A-le-vi-sa-ler*	Thurai kadai	*Thoo-rai ka-dai*
market	Velendha Pola	*Ve-le-n-dher-Po-ler*	Sandhai	*Sundh-dhai*
pharmacy	Farmasiya / Beheth saapuwa	*Faa-mer-si-yer / Bay-,heth saa-poo-wer*	Marunthu kadai	*Mu-roon-dhoo ku-dai*
supermarket	Supiri velendha sala	*Soo-pi-ri ve-len-dher sa-ler*	Supermarket	*Soo-per-maar-kayt*
souvenir shop	Sihivatana alevi sala	*Si-hi-vu-ter-ner u-lay-vee sa-ler*	Ninaivu porulkadai	*Ni-nai-voo po-rool-hull ka-dai*

Sightseeing

travel agent	Sanchaaraka niyojithaya	*Sun-chaa-rer-ker ni-yo-ji-ther-yer*	Prayana muhavar	*Prer-yaa-ner moo-her-verr*
tourist office	Sanchaaraka kaaryalaya	*Sun-chaa-rer-ker kaarr-yaa-ler-yer*	Suttrula aluvalaham	*Soot-troo-laa a-loo-vu-ler-hum*
beach	Vella / verala	*Va-ler / ve-rer-ler*	Kadatkarai	*Ku-dut-ku-rai*
bay	Bokka	*Bok-ker*	Virikuda	*Vi-ree-koo-daa*
festival	Utsavaya	*Oot-ser-ver-yer*	Thiruvila	*Thi-roo-vi-laa*
island	Dhupatha	*Dhou-per-ther*	Theevu	*Thee-voo*
lake	Veva	*Va-ver*	Eri	*Ay-ree*
forest	Keleva	*Ka-ley-ver*	Kaadu	*Kaa-doo*
mountain	Kandha	*Kundh-dher*	Malai	*Mu-lai*
river	Ganga	*Gung-er*	Aaru	*Aa-roo*
temple	Pansala	*Pun-ser-ler*	Kovil	*Koa-vil*
museum	Kouwthukagaraya	*Kouw-thoo-kaa-gaa-rer-yer*	Arungkaatchiyagam	*A-roong-kaat-chi-yer-herm*

Getting Around

When does the train for…leave?	…ter yana kochchiya, keeyatadhe pitath venney?	*…ter yu-ner koa-ch-ch-i-yer, kee-yer-ter-dher pit-uth ven-ney?*	…irku pohum rail vandi, ethanai manikku kilambum?	*…ir-koo poa-hoom ra-yil vun-dee, eth-th-un-ai mun-ik-koo ki-lum-boom?*

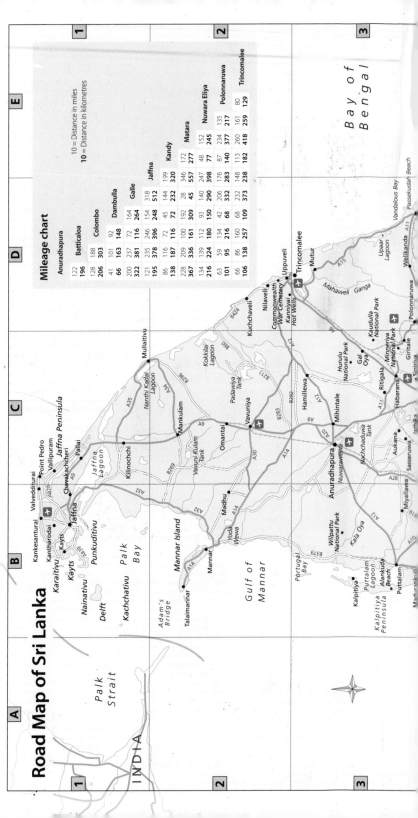

Road Map of Sri Lanka

Mileage chart

10 = Distance in miles
10 = Distance in kilometres

Anuradhapura										
122	Batticaloa									
196										
128	92	Colombo								
206	148									
41	101	164	Dambulla							
66	163	264								
200	72	154	Galle							
322	116	248								
121	246	318	144	Jaffna						
195	396	512	320							
86	235	199	28	346	Kandy					
138	378	309	45	557	277					
228	116	192	140	247	48	Matara				
367	187	161	290	398	77	245				
134	209	100	93	206	87	234	Nuwara Eliya			
216	336	72	332	283	140	377	217			
63	139	112	42	176	135	152	Polonnaruwa			
101	224	180	68	283	217	245				
66	59	134	68	148	260	80	Trincomalee			
106	95	216	109	238	418	129				

Labels on map:

India
Palk Strait
Palk Bay
Jaffna Peninsula
Jaffna Lagoon
Gulf of Mannar
Adam's Bridge
Mannar Island
Kalpitiya Peninsula
Puttalam Lagoon
Bay of Bengal

Kankesanturai, Valvedditurai, Point Pedro, Karaitivu, Kayts, Kantharodai, Kachcheri, Chavakachcheri, Pallai, Nainativu, Punkuditivu, Delft, Kachchativu, Jaffna, Kilinochchi, Mullaitivu, Mankulam, Vavuniya, Omantai, Madhu, Yoda Wewa, Talaimannar, Mannar, Kalpitiya, Alankuda Beach, Puttalam, Wilpattu National Park, Kala Oya, Portugal Bay, Anuradhapura, Nuwarawewa, Mihintale, Nachchaduwa Tank, Aukana, Sasseruwa, Miyallawa, Hamillewa, Padawiya Tank, Nanthi Kadal Lagoon, Kokkilai Lagoon, Kuchchaveli, Nilaveli, Commonwealth War Cemetery, Kanniyai Hot Wells, Trincomalee, Uppuveli, Mutur, Upaar Lagoon, Mahaweli Ganga, Wellikanda, Passekudah Beach, Vandalous Bay, Polonnaruwa, Girital, Minneriya National Park, Kaudulla National Park, Ritigala, Gal Oya, Hurulu National Park, Habarana, Sigiriya

A9, A14, A20, A28, A30, A32, A35, A6, A11, A12, A10, A15, A2, B383, B69, B80, B403, B296, B211, B283, B379, B28

milk	**Kiri**	*Ki-ri*	Paal	*Paa-l*
soft drinks	**Sisil beema**	*Si-si-l bee-mer*	Menpaanam	*Men-paa-num*
beer	**Beer**	*Beer*	Beer	*Beer*
wine	**Vine**	*Vine*	Vine	*Vine*
glass	**Vidhuruwa**	*Vee-dhoo-roo-wer*	Tumbler	*Tumbler*
bottle	**Bothalaya**	*Boa-ther-ler-yer*	Pottil	*Poa-till*

Health

I do not feel well.	**Magey engata hari ney**	*Mu-gay ang-er-ter hu-ri ney*	Ennudaya udambukku sari illai	*En-noo-der-yer oo-dum-boo-koo sa-ri **Ill**-ai*
I have a fever.	**Mata una vagey**	*Mu-ter oo-ner vu-gay*	Enakku kaichchal adikiradhu	*En-uk-koo kai**ch-ch**ul u-di-ki-rer-dhoo*
I'm allergic to	**Mata … ekata asaath-mikathvayak thiyanava**	*Mu-ter … e-ker-ter a-saath-mi-kuth-ver-yuk thi-yer-ner-vaa*	Enakku …ikku ovvamai ondru ulladhu	*En-ak-**k**oo …ik-**k**oo ov-vaa-mai on-droo u**ll**-er-dhoo*
accident (traffic)	**Hadhisi anathurak (thadabadaya)**	*Hu-dhi-si u-ner-thoo-ruk (thu-der-bu-der-yer)*	Vibaththu (pokkuvarathu)	*Vi-buth-thoo (poa-koo-vu-ruth-thoo)*
ambulance	**Gilan rathaya (ambulansaya)**	*Gi-lun ruth-er-yer (ambulan-set-yer)*	Noyaali vandi	*Noa-yaa-li vun-di*
antibiotics	**Prathijeevaka**	*Prer-thi-jee-ver-ker*	Nunnuyir ethirpi	*Noon-noo-yir e-dhir-pi (aanti-biotic)*
blood	**Ley**	*Lay*	Iraththam	*I-ruth-**thum***
blood pressure (high/low)	**Rudhirapeedanaya (adhi/adu)**	*Roo-dhi-rer-pee-der-ner-yer (a-dhi/ a-doo)*	(adhiha / kuraindha) Iraththa aluththam	*(a-dhi-**h**er / koo-rain-dher) I-ruth-**th**er a-loo**th-th**um*
diabetes	**Dhiyavediyaava**	*Dhi-yer-va-di-yaa-ver*	Neerilivu noi	*Nee-ri-li-voo noa-yi*
diarrhoea	**Bada burul veema**	*Bu-der boo-rool vee-mer*	Bedhi	*Bay-dhee*
dizzy	**Oluwa kerekkille**	*O-loo-wer ka-rer-ki**ll**-er*	Thalaisuttral	*Tha-lai-soot-**tr**ull*
doctor	**Dhostara**	*Dhos-ther-er*	Maruthuvar	*Mu-roo-thoo-ver*
flu	**Una**	*Oo-ner*	Salikaichchal	*Sa-lee-kaai**ch-ch**ul*
food poisoning	**Ahara vishaveema**	*Aa-haa-rer vi-sher-vee-mer*	Unavu nanjaaghudhal	*Oo-ner-voo nunj-aa-hoo-dhul*
heart	**Herdheya**	*Herr-dher-yer*	Irudhayam	*I-roo-dher-yum*
hospital	**Rohala**	*Roa-hu-ler*	Aspathri	*Aas-**puth-thi**-ree*
illness	**Asaneepaya**	*U-ser-nee-per-yer*	Noi	*Noa-yi*
injection	**Injection**	*Injection*	Injection / oosi	*Injection / ou-see*
malaria	**Maleriyaava**	*Ma-lay-ri-yaa-ver*	Maleria	*Mul-ay-riya*
medicine	**Beheth**	*Bay-hay-th*	Marundhu	*Mu-roon-dhoo*
prescription	**Beheth thunduwa**	*Bay-hay-th thoon-doo-ver*	Marundhu cheettu	*Mu-roon-dhoo cheet-too*

Time and Season

minute	**Vinaadiya**	*Vi-naa-di-yer*	Nimidum	*Ni-mi-dum*
hour	**Peya**	*Pa-yer*	Manithiyaalam	*Mu-ni-thi-yaa-lum*
day	**Davasa**	*Dhu-ver-ser*	Naal	*Naa-ll*
week	**Sumanaya**	*Soo-maa-ner-yer*	Vaaram	*Vaa-rum*
month	**Maasaya**	*Maa-ser-yer*	Maatham	*Maa-dhum*
year	**Avuruddha**	*Uv-oo-roodh-dher*	Varusham	*Vu-roo-shum*
Monday	**Sandhudha**	*Sun-dhoo-dhaa*	Thingal	*Thi-ng-gull*
Tuesday	**Angaharuwaadha**	*Ung-er-hu-roo-waa-dhaa*	Sevvai	*Sev-**v**aai*
Wednesday	**Badhadha**	*Bu-dhaa-dhaa*	Pudhan	*Poo-dhun*
Thursday	**Brahaspathindha**	*Bru-haas-pa-thin-dhaa*	Viyaalan	*Vi-yaa-lun*
Friday	**Sikuradha**	*Si-koo-raa-dhaa*	Vellikilamai	*Vel-li-ki-ler-mai*
Saturday	**Senasuraadha**	*Se-ner-soo-raa-dhaa*	Sanikilamai	*Su-ni-ki-ler-mai*
Sunday	**Iridha**	*I-ri-dhaa*	Gnaayiru	*Nyaa-yi-roo*
season	**Kaalaya**	*Kaa-ler-yer*	Paruvam	*Pu-roo-vum*
spring	**Vasanthakaalaya**	*Vu-sun-ther-kaa-ler-yer*	Vasandhakaalam	*Vu-sun-dher-kaa-lum*
summer	**Gimhaanakaalaya**	*Gim-haa-ner-kaa-ler-yer*	Kodaikaalam	*Koa-dai-kaa-lum*
autumn	**Sarathkaalaya**	*Su-ruth-kaa-ler-yer*	ilaiyudhirkaalam	*I-lai-oo-dhir-kaa-lum*
winter	**Seethakaalaya**	*Shee-ther-kaa-ler-yer*	Kulirkaalam	*Koo-leer-kaa-lum*
rain (it is raining)	**Vahinava**	*Vu-hi-ner-vaa*	Malai peyghiradhu	*Mu-lai payi-hi-rer-dhoo*
wind	**Hulanga**	*Hoo-lung-ger*	Kaattru	*Kaat-troo*
sunny	**Awwa**	*Ouw-er*	Veyil	*Ve-yill*
weather	**Kaalagunaya**	*Kaa-ler-goo-ner-yer*	Kaalanilai	*Kaa-ler-ni-lai*
warm/cold	**Rasne / seethalai**	*Russ-nay / see-ther-lai*	Veppam / kulir	*Vep-pum / koo-leer*
What time is it?	**Velaava keeyadhe?**	*Ve-laa-ver kee-yer-dher?*	Mani enna?	*Mu-nee en-ner?*
12:00:00 noon	**Dhaval dholaha**	*Dhu-vul dho-ler-haa*	Nanpahal	*Nun-pu-hul*
midnight	**Jaamaya**	*Jaa-mer-yer*	Nalliravu	*Nu**ll**-i-rer-voo*
morning	**Udhay**	*Oo-dhay*	Kaalai	*Kaa-lai*
midday	**Dhaval**	*Dhu-vul*	Paghal	*Pug-hal*
afternoon	**Pasvaruwa**	*Pus-vu-roo-ver*	Madhiyaanam	*Mudh-dhi-yaa-num*
evening	**Havasa**	*Hu-ver-ser*	Maalai	*Maa-lai*
night	**Reh**	*Rey*	Iravu	*I-rer-voo*

Numbers

1	**Ekai**	*E-kai*	Ondru	*On-droo*
2	**Dhekai**	*Dhe-kai*	Irandu	*I-rern-doo*
3	**Thunai**	*Thoo-nai*	Moondru	*Moon-droo*
4	**Hatharai**	*Hu-ther-ai*	Naalu	*Naa-loo*
5	**Pahai**	*Pu-hai*	Aindhu	*A-yin-dhoo*
6	**Hayai**	*Hu-yai*	Aaru	*Aa-roo*
7	**Hathai**	*Hu-thai*	Elu	*Ay-loo*
8	**Atai**	*U-tai*	Ettu	*Et-**t**oo*
9	**Namayai**	*Nu-mer-yai*	Onbadhu	*On-ber-dho*
10	**Dhahayai**	*Dhu-haa-yai*	Paththu	*Puth-**th**oo*
15	**Pahalavai**	*Pu-haa-ler-vai*	Padhinaindhu	*Pa-dhi-nain-dhoo*
20	**Vissai**	*Viss-ai*	Iruvadhu	*I-roo-ver-dhoo*
30	**Thihai**	*Thi-hai*	Muppadhu	*Moo**p-p**er-dhoo*
40	**Hathalihai**	*Huth-ther-li-hai*	Naapadhu	*Naa-per-dhoo*
50	**Panahai**	*Pun-er-hai*	Aimbadhu	*Aim-ber-dhoo*
60	**Hettai**	*Ha-tai*	Aruvadhu	*A-roo-ver-dhoo*
70	**Hethewai**	*Hath-**they**-wai*	Eluvadhu	*E-loo-ver-dhoo*
80	**Asuwai**	*A-soo-wai*	Embadhu	*Em-ber-dhoo*
90	**Anuwai**	*A-noo-wai*	Thonnooru	*Thon-**n**oo-roo*
100	**Seeyai**	*See-yai*	Nooru	*Nou-roo*
200	**Dheyseeyai**	*Dhay-see-yai*	Iranooru	*i-rer-nou-roo*
1000	**Dhaahai**	*Dhaa-hai*	Aayiram	*Aa-yi-rum*
10000	**Dhaha dhaahai**	*Dha-haa dhaa-hai*	Pathaayiram	*Pu-th-**thaa**-yi-rum*
100000	**Lakshayai**	*Luk-sher-yai*	Latcham	*Lut-chum*

English	Sinhala	Pronunciation	Tamil	Pronunciation
A ticket to…please.	Karun karala…ter Eka tikattuwak…	Ka-roo-naa-ker-rer-laa … ter e-ker ti-kut-oo-wak…	Thayavu seydhu, …ikku oru ticket tharavum.	Thu-yer-voo sei-dhoo, …ik-koo o-roo ticket thu-rer-voom.
How long does it take to get to…?	…ter yanna velaava kochcharak ganeedhe?	…ter yun-ner ve-laa-ver koch-cher-ruk gun-ee-dher?	…irku poha evvalavu neyram sellum?	…ir-koo po-her ev-ver-ler-voo ney-rum sell-oom?
I'd like to reserve a seat, please.	Karuna karala, Mang venuven eka aasayanak wen karanne	Ka-roo-naa-ker-rer-laa Mung ve-noo-veng eka aa-ser-ner-yuk veng ker-run-ner.	Enakkaaha oru seatai odhukavum.	E-nerk-kaa-her o-roo seat-tai o-dhook-ker-voom.
Which platform for the…train?	…. Kochchiya koi platform ekey dhe?	… koa-ch-chi-ya koi platform e-kay dher?	… rail vandiku endhe platform?	… ra-yil vun-dik-koo en-dher platform?
train station	Dhumriya pala	Dhoom-ri-yer per-ler	Rail nilayam	Ra-yil ni-ler-yum
airport	Guwan thotupala	Goo-wun tho-tooper-ler	Vimaana nilayam	Vi-maa-ner ni-ler-yum
bus station	Bus nevathumpala	Bus na-ver-thoom-per-ler	Bus nilayam	Bus ni-ler-yerm
a one-way ticket	Thani gaman ticket ekak	Thu-nee gu-mun ti-kat e-kuk	Oru vali ticket ondru	O-roo vu-li ti-ket on-droo
a return ticket	Prathyaagamana ticket ekak	Prer-thyaa-gu-mer-ner ti-kat e-kuk	Irandu vali ticket ondru	I-rern-doo va-li ti-ket on-droo
taxi	Kulee rathayak	Koo-lee ru-ther-yuk	Taaksi	Taak-si
car	Car eka	Car e-ker	Car	Car
bus	Bus eka	Bus e-ker	Bus	Bus
train	Kochchiya	Koa-ch-chi-yer	Rayil vandi	Ra-yil vun-di
plane	Plane eka	Plane e-ker	Vimaanam	Vi-maa-num
plane ticket	Plane ticket eka	Plane ti-kat e-ker	Vimaana ticket	Vi-maa-ner ti-ket
motorbike	Motor cycleye	Moa-ter cy-kel-er-yer	Motaar cykil	Mo-toarr cy-kill
bicycle	Bysikalaya	By-si-kerl-er-yer	Cykil	Cy-kill
ferry	Dhoney	Dhoa-nee	Padaghu	Pu-der-ghoo

Accommodation

English	Sinhala	Pronunciation	Tamil	Pronunciation
Do you have a vacant room?	Hiss kaamarayak thiyanavaadhe?	Hiss kaa-mer-rer-yuk thi-yer-ner-vaa-dher?	Kaaliyaana arai ondru irukkiradhaa?	Kaa-li-yaa-ner a-rai on-droo i-rook-ki-rer-dhaa?
Double/twin room	Dvithva kaamaraya	Dhvi-th-ver kaa-mer-rer-yer	Irattai arai	I-rut-tai a-rai
Single room	Thani kaamaraya	Tha-ni kaa-mer-rer-yer	Ottrai arai	Ott-rai u-rai
I have a reservation.	Mang venuveng, veng kara etha	Mung ve-noo-veng, veng ker-er-a-ther	Enakkaaha odhukka pattulladhu	En-uk-kaa-her o-dhoo-ker pat-tool-ler-dhoo
hotel	Hotelaya	Ho-tel-er-yer	Hotel	Hoa-tal
guesthouse	Guesthouse eka	Guesthouse e-ker	Virundhinar vidudhi	Vi-roon-dhi-narr vi-doo-dhee
room (single, double)	Kamaraya (thani, dvithva)	Kaa-mer-rer-yer (tha-ni, dhvi-th-ver)	Arai (ottrai, irattai)	A-rai (ott-rai, i-rut-tai)
air conditioning	AC ethi	AC e-thi	AC uliyal	AC ooll-er
bathroom	Naana kamaraya	Naa-ner kaa-mer-rer-yer	Kuliyal arai	Koo-li-yull a-rai

Eating Out

English	Sinhala	Pronunciation	Tamil	Pronunciation
A table for two please.	Dhennekuta meysayak	Dhen-nay-koo-ter may-ser-yuk	Irandu peyarukku oru meysai	I-rern-doo pay-er-roo-koo o-roo may-sai
May I see the menu?	Mata Menu eka balanne puluwangdhe?	Mu-ter me-noo e-ker bu-lun-ner poo-loo-wung-dher?	Menuvai paarka mudiyuma?	Me-noo-vai paar-ker moo-di-yoo-maa?
I am a vegetarian.	Mama elavalu vitharai kanney	Mu-mer e-ler-ver-loo vi-ther-ai kun-nay	Naan saivam mattum thaan saapiduven	Naan sai-vum mut-toom thaan saa-pi-doo-ven
Can I have the bill, please?	Karuna kara bila dhennewadha?	Ku-roo-naa ker-er bi-ler dhe-ner-wu-dher?	Billai tharavum	Bill-ai thu-rer-voom
spicy (hot)	Dhevillai / serai	Dha-vill-ai / sa-rai	Urappu	Oo-rerp-poo
sweet	Pani rasa	Pa-ni ru-ser	Inippu	I-nip-poo
knife	Pihiya	Pi-hi-yer	Kaththi	Kuth-thee
fork	Garappuwa	Gey-rerp-poo-wer	Mullkarandi	Mool-ka-run-dee
spoon	Handhe	Handh-dher	Karandi	Ku-run-dee
restaurant	Avanhala	A-vun-hul-er	Unavagham	oo-ner-vu-hum
western food	Batahira kema	Bu-ter-hi-rer ka-mer	Metrkaththiya unavu	Mayt-kuth-thi-yer oo-ner-voo
Sri Lankan specialities	Lankavey vishesha shuth-ver-yer	Lung-kaa-vay vi-shay-	Ilangaiyin sirappunavugal	I-leng-ger-yin si-rup-poo-navu-ghull

Menu decoder

English	Sinhala	Pronunciation	Tamil	Pronunciation
apple	Appel	A-perl	Aappil	Aap-pill
banana	Kesel	Ke-sel	Valaipalam	Vaa-lai-pa-lum
bamboo shoots	Una dhalu	Oo-ner dhu-loo	Moongil kuruthu	Moon-gill koo-rooth-thoo
beef	Harak mas	Hu-ruk muss	Maatterachchi	Maat-te-ruch-chi
bread	Paang	Paa-ng	Paan	Paan
chicken	Kukul mas	Koo-kool muss	Koli erachchi	Koa-li er-ruch-chi
chilly	Miris	Mi-riss	Kochchikai	Koch-chi-kai
coconut	Pol	Poll	Thengai	Thayng-gaai
crab	Kakuluvo	Ku-koo-loo-vo	Nandu	Nun-doo
dessert	Athurupasa	a-thoor-oo-pu-ser	Palavaghai unavu	Pu-ler-vu-hai oo-ner-voo
duck	Thara	Thaa-raa	Vaaththu	Vaath-thoo
egg	Biththara	Bith-ther-er	Muttai	Moot-tai
fish	Maalu	Maa-loo	Meen	Meen
fruit	Palathuru	Pu-ler-thoo-roo	Palam	Pu-lum
garlic	Sudhu loonu	Soo-dhoo lou-noo	Vellai poodu	Vell-ai pou-doo
ginger	Inguru	Ing-goo-roo	Inji	In-jee
lamb	Batalu mas	Ba-ter-loo muss	Aatterachchi	Aat-te-rerch-chi
lemongrass	Sera	Say-rer	Sera	Say-rer
lobster	Pokirissa	Po-ki-ri-ss-aa	Periya iraal	Pe-ri-yer i-raal
milk	Kiri	Ki-ri	Paal	Paa-l
mushrooms	Hathu	Ha-thoo	Kaalaan	Kaa-laan
meat	Mas	Muss	Eraichchi	E-raich-chi
onion	Lunu	Lou-nou	Vengayam	Veng-aa-yum
papaya	Gaslabu	Guss-lu-boo	Pappali	Pup-paa-li
pepper	Gummiris	Gum-mi-riss	Milaghu	Mi-ler-hoo
pork	Urumas	Ou-roo-muss	Pandri erachchi	Pun-dri er-aich-chi
potato (sweet potato)	Ala (bathala)	A-ler (buth-er-ler)	Kilangu (vattraalai kilangu)	Ki-lung-goo (vutt-raa-lai ki-lung-goo)
prawn	Isso	Iss-o	Iraal	I-raal
rice	Bath	Buth	Soaru	Soa-roo
salad	Saladhu	Sa-laa-dhoo	Salad	Sa-lud
salt	Lunu	Loo-noo	Uppu	Oop-poo
sugar	Seeni	See-ni	Seeni	See-ni
vegetables	Elavalu	E-ler-ver-loo	Marakari	Ma-rer-kur-ri
drinks	Beema	Bee-mer	Paanangal	Paa-nung-al
tea	They	Thay	Theyneer	Thay-neer
coffee	Kopi	Koa-pee	Kopi	Koa-pee
water	Vathura	Vu-thoo-rer	Thannir	Thun-neer
mineral water	Bothal kala vathura	Boa-thul ker-ler vu-thoo-rer	Pottilil adaikkapatta neer	Poa-till-il a-dai-ker-put-ter neer